Under Construction

Under Construction

Working at the Intersections of Composition Theory, Research, and Practice

edited by

CHRISTINE FARRIS

and

CHRIS M. ANSON

UTAH STATE UNIVERSITY PRESS
Logan, Utah
1998

Utah State University Press
Logan, Utah 84322-7800

Copyright © 1998 Utah State University Press
All rights reserved.

Typography by Wolfpack
Cover design by Stephen Adams

Manufactured in the United States of America.

02 01 00 99 98   5 4 3 2 1

Library of Congress Cataloging-in-Publication Data

Under construction : working at the intersections of composition
theory, research, and practice / Christine Farris and Chris Anson,
editors.
p. cm.
Includes bibliographical references and index.
ISBN 0-87421-257-X
ISBN 0-87421-256-1 (pbk.)
1. English language—Rhetoric—Study and teaching. 2. English
language—Rhetoric—Study and teaching—Theory, etc. 3. Report
writing—Study and teaching. 4. Report writing—Study and
teaching—Theory, etc. I. Farris, Christine, 1949- II. Anson,
Christopher M., 1954-
PE1404 .U53 1998
808'.042'07—ddc21
98-25490
CIP

CONTENTS

Complicating Composition

Christine Farris and Chris M. Anson

AS A FIELD OF PROFESSIONAL INQUIRY INTERTWINED WITH THE PRACTICE AND teaching of its own subject, composition studies has enjoyed the steady pace of its own recent evolution. Few composition scholars twenty years ago would have imagined the rate at which the field is now developing, exploding beyond its boundaries, creating new alliances, and locating new sites for inquiry and knowledge production. These current transformations owe in part to the inevitable burgeoning of a theoretically interdisciplinary field with a strong orientation toward self-reflection. They also owe to unprecedented changes underway in higher education, changes pressured by shifts in the politics and economics of university administration, the advent of new technologies, population changes that affect student demographics, and the creation of alternative structures and contexts for teaching and learning.

Composition, in seeking a disciplinary identity, is questioning the ways it creates and mediates knowledge and the ways in which that knowledge informs and is informed by various contexts for research and practice. This collection focuses on the ways in which composition reconsiders established dichotomies, examines new connections among areas of inquiry, and suggests avenues for inquiry that have transformative consequences for the sites of theory, research, and teaching.

When we first proposed this volume of essays, we sought submissions that reconsidered the relationship among theory, research and practice, expecting that our focus would primarily be on the changing face of composition research. Our open call and invitation to individual scholars, however, resulted in very few reports of research studies, but rather in contributions that reflect the extent to which the theory/research/practice relationship now occupies our disciplinary thinking.

Since the publication of Stephen North's *The Making of Knowledge in Composition: Portrait of an Emerging Field* (1987), the past decade has seen attention to research methodology largely displaced by conflict between theory and practice. This conflict, still rooted, one might argue, in the desire for a unified theory, often centers on the extent to which any theory employed by compositionists must grow, if not from research, then from practice, or at least have direct pedagogical implications. While North sought to recuperate the contributions of practitioners, his characterization of their knowledge as "lore" and their relationship to scholars as a power struggle has contributed to an anxious debate among compositionists. Joseph Harris (1994, 1997), reflecting the view of many in the field, finds it necessary to declare that the composition classroom remains at the center of his concerns and that theory ("how knowledge gets made") only interests him insofar as it influences practice (x).

On the other hand, Sidney Dobrin argues in his recent book, *Constructing Knowledges*, that "theory can exist without practical applications" (152). Our authors' reconsiderations, located all along this continuum, have enabled us to put together a collection that questions disciplinary hierarchies and values new practices as scholarship at the same time that it questions their capacity for building disciplinary knowledge and identity. It is our aim that this collection not dichotomize, privilege, or balance the three terms in the composition theory/research/practice "equation."

The contributions to this volume reflect how much the field has changed since the two of us first entered it in the late 1970's, a time often characterized as a "paradigm shift" away from the analysis of well-written products toward interest and intervention in the writing process. It was a time when a number of compositionists, influenced by work in cognitive development psychology, sought a universal model of the writing process presumably shared by effective writers. Particularly those who sought disciplinary status for composition embraced the notion that knowledge about writing and the teaching of writing was made and validated through empirical studies. Suspicion of quantitative research and universal knowledge-making has since resulted in composition specialists' investigation of new venues and local conditions in which writing is practiced and taught as well as the reestablishment of links with historical, textual, and cultural inquiry in the rest of English studies.

Oversubscription to the "paradigm shift" narrative, however, presumes either a linear progression from current-traditionalism to social constructionism or a hierarchical tension among North's scholars, researchers and practitioners that has never been that simple—not *then*, when the two of us, in the span of less than a decade, could have been found theoretically embracing the ideas of Freire, Moffett, and Burke; teaching freewriting and journals alongside the cumulative sentence or the Toulmin scheme; or conducting research using everything from T-units to thick description. Nor is the identity secure or the struggle over *now*, when, in this volume, one author can make the case that our disciplinary authority is slipping away as empirical methodology loosens (MacDonald), while another argues for the absence of any safe house for knowledge-making outside of the vexed political gatekeeping position that composition occupies in English departments and institutions (Vandenberg).

Tied to its quest for disciplinary legitimacy, composition studies has sought but never achieved a coherence made possible by a unified theory. While hardly the empirical-privileging scrutinizers of composition research studies of earlier decades (e.g., Braddock, et al. 1963), compositionists such as James Berlin, Stephen North, and Louise Phelps have nevertheless decried the contradictory theories reflected in the practices of composition teachers. Despite North's characterization of composition as a battleground, no one brand of research, as Beth Daniell has pointed out, has managed to win out and unify all the knowledge of composition that we have accumulated using different theories (129).

Reluctant to assume a top-down, research-to-theory-to-practice relationship, compositionists increasingly claim to favor some sort of a dialectical relationship between theory and practice. Often drawn from hermeneutics or a Freirean notion of praxis, the assumption is that teachers' critical reflection on their actual practice enables them to construct an ever-changing theory while in the process of changing that practice (Ferry, this volume). Zebroski complicates the dialectical view by arguing in this volume that theory can be viewed as one of several practices which interact and are affected by related writing, teaching, curricular, and disciplinary practices. Grimm, Wysocki and Cooper also argue that research is not a product, but a set of practices, whose evaluation must include the effects on those studied. Nevertheless, like Wendy Bishop, they experiment with different written representations of their research and discuss the critical perspectives made possible by that experimentation. This notion that theory, research, and teaching are all *practices* providing a location from which to view and critique the others is one that appeals to us in constructing this volume and one which offers a way out of battling binaries.

The shift in theoretical perspective from author-as-subject to an acknowledgment of multiple subject positions and the resulting increase in context-specific literacy and pedagogy research have called into question the possibility of a coherent theory of composition. Compositionists' knowledge-making activity is increasingly bound up in context and self-reflexivity rather than in a quest for models that will tell us the best way to produce "good writing" or the most effective teachers of writing.

In resisting objective and neutral methodologies, more and more composition scholars are theorizing their own positions, questioning assumptions underlying traditional scholarship, and interrogating uses of research that would conceal problematic power relations between researchers and subjects (Bleich 179). As Kirsch and Ritchie encourage, the research itself increasingly includes investigation of what has shaped the researcher's perspectives and an acknowledgment of "what is contradictory, and perhaps unknowable" (9). Many of the authors in this volume (Rose and Lauer; Chiang; Grimm, et al.; Okawa) build into their essays acknowledgement of their positions as scholars and researchers and examine their "findings" as cultural and ideological products. At that same time, some of them are quick to point out the limits and consequences of new theories and methodologies for composition as a disciplinary community (Seitz; MacDonald; Neff; Ray and Barton).

Increasingly, compositionists have more confidence in the recognition that teaching makes knowledge, and that practice, overdetermined as it is, continually calls into question the traditional purpose of theory—to explain unaccounted-for phenomena and solve new problems. Lore, as North distinguishes it from traditional disciplinary knowledge production, can, Harkin argues, be thought of as postdisciplinary *theory*, because it allows for practitioners' often contradictory attempts to solve writing problems with more than one cause, rather than using theory in the traditional way to contain situations (134).

Beth Daniell has argued that while composition theories may lack the authority to dictate pedagogy, as rhetoric, they are what persuade us to teach writing in the ways that we do (130). At the same time that theories may contain the discipline by "serving the interests of . . . groups within that discipline" (131), they are what enable us, she says, to "create a community in which we can figure out what we, individually and collectively, believe about our work" (135). In that rhetorical and political sense, theory is practice. But, as several of the authors in this volume (Ferry; Vandenberg; Howard) ask, whose "work" and whose interests define us and remain at the center of composition as a discipline? Can theory, research, and practice in ever new relationships intersect and hold an expanding community together or drive it apart into separate communities whose power and authority may be in jeopardy?

Composition's calling into question its knowledge comes at a time when the authority of that expert knowledge may be at risk. In the wake of shrinking graduate programs and the responsibility-centered-management of academic departments in the new corporate universities, the literature components of some English departments are beginning to reclaim an expertise in the teaching of writing or, in some instances, to efface that expertise, deeming it no longer necessary, politically appropriate, or cost-effective.

Much composition scholarship in fact contributes to this withering away of the more public conception of composition. Our growing understanding of complex context-specific literacy practices runs counter to institutional conditions that assume composition is an essential set of transparent skills to be conveyed one-time-only to first year students by exploited instructors. If retooled writing courses do result from the disciplinary boundary crossing of compositionists into deconstruction, feminist, multicultural, and cultural studies, what in the experiences of teachers and students justifies or interrogates these theories in practice? How does interdisciplinary inquiry expand avenues and change how and what we research and teach? What locates theorists, courses, teachers, and programs that might grow from this research within "composition"? Several of the authors in this volume locate their concerns about composition's "identity crisis" in a disjuncture between theory and pedagogy, whether questioning composition's attempts to achieve more disciplinary status (Ferry; Vandenberg; Howard) or its failure to focus more attention on knowledge-building inside the field (MacDonald; Neff).

Composition research now includes not just historical, quantitative and qualitative "studies" of student writing but also local knowledge—teacher-talk, teacher-reflection, ethnographies of literacy practices in non-academic settings, and autoethnographies—which are viewed as politically empowering to both teachers and students (Mutnick; Yancey; Bishop). If lore is theory, then are all practitioners theorists? If engaged in reflective practice, is everyone a researcher? If there are composition "experts," what is it that they know, how do they know it, and to what new and better uses will the discipline put the generalizable knowledge it makes?

While the views explored in this collection vary, they reflect a common charge: on what basis will we defend an expertise that is increasingly interdisciplinary if not post-disciplinary? In grappling with this question, each of the four sections in this book is designed to reverberate with the others but also to offer a somewhat sharper focus on a set of issues relevant to the overall theory/research/practice theme of the collection.

Part One, "Complicating the Research/Theory/Practice Relationship," contains essays by Christopher Ferry, Peter Vandenberg, and James Zebroski. Each of these chapters, in its own way, examines the relationships between scholarship and teaching practices in the field. Christopher Ferry shows how "work" in composition, particularly what we call "practice," is often abstracted from its material conditions. To remedy a field that has become "an unbalanced praxis" that focuses on theory at the expense of work, his Freirean "discontinuous continuum" allows for the valorization of work beyond the simple elevation of lore. Instantiating Ferry's assumptions in the context of publication, Peter Vandenberg then examines the hierarchy of productivity in composition, one in which work is bifurcated into tangibles rewarded in the academic credit cycle (e.g., publication) and intangibles such as teaching. Reverberating with Vandenberg's critique of the binary nature of scholarship and teaching, James Zebroski then rejects the assumption that theory informs practice by proposing a model of theorizing in which theory becomes one of several historically situated practices which develops only in a complex connection with signifying, teaching, curricular, and other practices.

Part Two, "Critiquing Theories in Practice," extends the line of thought developed in Part One by examining in more detail the disjunctures between current theory and practice in particular educational contexts, calling into question new and old composition assumptions. In keeping with Vandenberg's observation of the split that results from composition's identification with postmodern scholarship, Rebecca Moore Howard, in an analysis of textbook representations of plagiarism, shows how even in the midst of new theorizing about the power of collaboration in writing, composition, struggling to deal with a "double consciousness," remains true to the hierarchical values of autonomous authorship and reveals how its theories are more lay theories than disciplinary ones. Taking as his domain another area of strong theoretical influence on composition, David Seitz describes an ethnographic study of how undergraduates, especially those of working class background, responded to a cultural studies agenda in a composition course. Seitz questions the extent to which composition studies, while claiming to privilege practice, actually allows practice to influence theoretical assumptions about identity and difference. The personal narrative, as one domain of practice, serves as the focal point for Deborah Mutnick's essay in which she reconsiders theoretical assumptions about the role of personal narrative, distinguishing between uncritical expressivism and the conceptual narrative of scholars, researchers and students that subjects both writer and reader to conscious critique and suggesting, along with Seitz, that deeper issues of class and race underly the theoretical schism between process and social-epistemic approaches. Rounding out this section, Brian Huot and Michael Williamson read the field's antipathy toward and distrust of assessment next to radical changes in assumptions about testing theory and practice. Instead of rejecting the practice of assessment, they believe compositionists need to realize that the present theoretical landscape allows the means for a shift in power from central to local stakeholders.

Part Three, "Refiguring and Relocating Research" examines research in the field by reconsidering assumptions and then by suggesting new relationships, sites for investigation, and connections with theory and practice. Susan Peck MacDonald begins this section by resuscitating empiricism from the stranglehold of postmodern indeterminacy. By comparing older, more positivistic assumptions about research with newer, more versatile conceptions, MacDonald argues for the importance of the concept of generalization in the field. One such extension in the realm of naturalistic inquiry is "grounded theory," the centerpiece of Joyce Magnotto Neff's contribution. Grounded theory extends the methodologies of naturalistic inquiry into more highly social and collaborative ways of working. The complicated collaborative and social roles of both "researchers" and "subjects" are taken up in the next two essays. Shirley Rose and Janice Lauer speculate on the obligations, risks, and dilemmas researchers face when they are committed to the enactment of feminist methodology in their work. Yuet-Sim Chiang extends the analysis by examining the western framework in which research in composition is conducted. Using examples of her own teaching, scholarship, and research, Chiang suggests ways in which constructs of race, color, and gender can transform the dialogue among researchers, theorists, and practitioners. In an attempt to understand and resolve some of the tensions arising from these configurations of stance and role, Ellen Cushman and Terese Guinsatao Monberg propose a new stance for research in which scholars reposition themselves in relation to others for whom they presume to speak. Susan Romano then comments on the shifts taking place as a result of the internet explosion. Drawing a distinction between textual production and rhetorical analysis, she proposes that we have not developed a legitimate space to raise questions about rhetorical education on computers, education in which analysis plays a much stronger role. Ruth Ray and Ellen Barton end this section by exploring research on the functions of personal writing in nonacademic institutions, such as nursing homes. They argue that moving into such contexts causes composition researchers to identify and be challenged by their own biases and those of our profession (including the primacy of texts).

Part Four, "Remaking Knowledge and Rewriting Practice," concludes the book with a critical examination of the ways in which new teacher/scholar/theorists are brought into the field. Wendy Bishop begins the section by examining the nature and functions of teacher talk (lore, story, narrative research, testimony, literacy autobiography). She dismisses the question of whether such talk creates knowledge and expertise, and instead explores how it does this and what the political and social implications are of valuing it. Kathleen Blake Yancey then moves the discussion into the context of a methods course in which the students are invited into a new way of experiencing the learning of teaching—as a process of lifelong reflection. Shifting the focus from learning communities to written representations of research, Nancy Maloney Grimm, Anne Frances Wysocki and Marilyn M. Cooper explore various strategies of representing scholarship (storytelling, multiple voices, hypertext, and multiply-authored texts). They critique the institutional resistance to these alternative modes. Gail Okawa brings the volume to a close by offering a representation of work with students and teachers of color, showing how elements of autobiographical narrative creates and mediates both representations of the self and a learning community.

In choosing and editing pieces for this volume, we have strengthened our belief that while never more self-critical, composition's authority has never been stronger. We find a field willing to continually reconsider itself, to investigate difference and contradiction, to include research subjects beyond the composition classroom as agents, to use the local to call into question the general, to reflect on failure as well as success, to make new knowledge about composition in all three intersecting locations—theory, research and practice. We find disciplinary activity that continues to invite others into conversations that open up space for renewed and revised belief, critique, and change.

We would like to thank Art Young for his support of this project from the beginning and Michael Spooner, whose enthusiasm saw it through to the end. Thanks also to Alice Eads for her computer expertise and to our spouses Bill Rasch and Gean Anson, and our book-loving children, Alison Rasch, and Ian and Graham Anson. We dedicate this book to our fellow compositionists working at the intersections—may we keep one another from getting run over.

PART ONE

The Research/Theory/Practice Relationship

CHAPTER ONE

Theory, Research, Practice, Work

Christopher Ferry

Well, I'm thwarted by a metaphysic
Puzzle
And I'm sick of grading papers—that I
Know.

Jonathan Larson, "Rent"

PAULO FREIRE, LONG AN IMPORTANT INFLUENCE ON COMPOSITION STUDIES, argues that education must be a process by which students and teachers help each other become "more fully human" and, at the same time, "transform reality." Central to this process is the phenomenon he calls "praxis," the inter-action between reflection and action that results in the transformation of the world. For Freire, praxis can be authentic—that is, can accomplish its trans-forming work—only when it includes both components. Without action, for example, reflection becomes mere "verbalism," shooting off one's mouth, while action without thought becomes "activism," "action for action's sake." In either case praxis, the work of changing the world's material conditions, of eradicat-ing oppression, injustice, illiteracy, for example, the labor of helping each other become more fully human, cannot occur (1993, 68-69).

I want to use Freire's concept of praxis as a starting point to examine the relationship among theory, research, practice, and work in composition stud-ies. Specifically, I want to explore the position of work in our field: what is the nature of our "work" within institutions of higher learning? Compositionist has entered the professional lexicon, a neologism that signifies what people in rhetoric and composition "do." Just the same, the question of what we "do" remains open. On one hand if one peruses the professional literature, our work seems to be researching and making knowledge in a "scientific" way, a method supported by the American academy. Certainly, this situation seems to be what Richard Braddock, Richard Lloyd-Jones, and Lowell Schoer had in mind when they compared research in composition to that in chemistry and, by extension, all (hard) scientific research:

> [S]ome terms are being defined usefully, a number of procedures are being refined, but the field as a whole is laced with dreams, prejudices, and makeshift operations. Not enough investigators are really informing themselves about the

procedures and results of previous research before embarking on their own. Too few of them conduct pilot experiments and validate their measuring instruments before undertaking an investigation. (1963, 5)

Compositionists might be said to research and construct a meta-discourse, a totalizing narrative that explains "writing"; in other words, we create a "theory" of composition. On the other hand, discussions of work—by which I mean the material conditions of the "labor" of teaching composition—are not always welcome at professional sites removed from those material conditions. Consider, for example, the editorial policy of *The Journal of Advanced Composition:* "*JAC* does not accept articles describing classroom techniques unless the author clearly demonstrates how such practices derive from current theory and research and how they can be applied to the advanced composition classroom in general" (1996, n.p.).

Stephen M. North calls Braddock's *Research in Written Composition* composition's "charter" as a field of study (1987, 17). North's argument turns on Braddock's assumption that composition's domain should be research and knowledge-making in a "scientific" way. I support the importance of this task; I also believe, however, that we pursue it at the expense of seeing composition as an intellectual endeavor located in classrooms with students. In other words, what we have in composition now is an unbalanced praxis, one that seems focused on reflection at the expense of action (or to put in more appropriate terms for this essay, a praxis focused on theory at the expense of work). It may indeed be true that we are, as Kurt Spellmeyer has argued, "knowledge workers" (1996, 961), that the "product" of our work is knowledge, or the way we construct composition as a discipline is through the knowledge we make. Certainly this model seems to be the one approved by the academy which, as we all know, bases professional advancement on scholarship. The prominence of scholarship, David Damrosch notes, leads to "a real decrease in the diversity of forms of academic work" (1995, 42, his emphasis). I want to make a case that in composition our focus on theory leads us to overlook the teaching of writing—the material conditions of our work as teachers—an endeavor for students and with students.

When we map the shape of composition, one thing seems plain: theory and practice are separate. North foregrounds this idea and makes it a central argument in *The Making of Knowledge.* As composition coalesced into a discipline or field of study, theorists (knowledge-makers) staked claims that ignored and ridiculed the work of "Practitioners," writing teachers and writers, "so that, despite their overwhelming majority, they [Practitioners] have been effectively disenfranchised as knowledge-makers in their own field" (1987, 3). Indeed, North's representation of "lore" as "practitioner knowledge" divides composition into those who do and those who think about, make knowledge about, theorize about doing. Patricia Harkin revisits North's claim in "The Post-Disciplinary Politics of Lore," in which she tries to recuperate lore as a means of knowledge production. Her map not only separates theory and practice but depicts theory hierarchically, as a foundational "top" that informs research and practice below it. One can think about theory, she argues, as a "metadiscourse, a generalized account of a practice [in this case, teaching writing] to which all instances of that practice can be referred" (1991, 134). Her mechanism to recover lore is a "series of conferences that asks us [Compositionists] to work up from the practice of lore, not down from a theory of writing" (136, emphasis added). Instead of seeing theory and practice as either separate or hierarchical, I want to examine them as points on a "discontinuous continuum": theory informs and is informed by research which informs and is informed by practice. Even so, as in a hierarchical relationship, practice is not just a genteel way to say work; instead, practice elides discussions about actual work by abstracting it from its material conditions. For this reason, then, the continuum is discontinuous.

THOSE WHO CAN, DO. THOSE WHO CAN'T, . . .

James Sosnoski argues that the division between theory and practice, at least in English departments, developed recently (1994, 162). This may be true inasmuch as "theorists" gained professional cachet and began to be hired during the 1960s; but the gap between "scientific" knowledge-makers and teachers has far deeper roots. Laurence R. Vesey's *The Emergence of the American University* documents the evolution of higher education in the United States from 1865 to the early twentieth century. Whereas colleges had focused on preparing (mostly) young men for careers in law or the ministry, emergent universities focused on scientific research. Colleges gave way to universities for various historical and socioeconomic reasons, including industrialization (and concomitant need for "research"), newly acquired national wealth, and American envy of European intellectual achievement (1965, 1-18). As universities and the knowledge created therein grew in importance, however, there occurred a change in the psychology of the faculty, a paradigm shift if you will from teaching to research. Vesey describes this change as an "emotional absorption" of the "spirit of inquiry":

> One had to believe that the unknown was worthier of attention than the known, perhaps even that once an area became a part of the widely agreed upon body of knowledge research in it would lack a certain glamour. More fundamentally, the researcher had to believe that he was making contact with 'reality' itself—in other words, that gold as well as dross existed in the universe and that his special training made him capable of knowing the difference. The gold of reality lay in particular phenomena which could be isolated and then systematically investigated. . . . Research thus demanded a close respect for the unique, nugget-like fact—especially when such a fact violated a previous theory. (135-136)

One implication here is the appearance of disciplinary knowledge, "sheltered," as Vesey says, in "specialized departments of knowledge." Another is the displacement of teaching as the primary act of work by the pursuit of these nuggets of fact: "The most pronounced effect of the increasing emphasis upon specialized research was a tendency among scientifically minded professors to ignore the undergraduate college and to place a low value upon their function as teachers" (143-144).

David Damrosch notes a third implication, the paradoxical position of the academic professional vis-a-vis society at large. Knowledge-makers position themselves and their institutions as social resources, forums "for research and training in the growing complexities of the modern world" (1995, 31). Nevertheless, universities become tangential to the everyday world, even to the extent of providing refuge from it; departments become nations with fiercely defended frontiers, and disciplinary discourse, "self-enclosed and often self-confirming," becomes a professor's native tongue (37). Searching for nugget-facts attracts alienated people, Damrosch argues, people who detach from the world, see it through the lens of scientific objectivity. And while such a psychology may, in fact, be valuable, it also serves to construct the academic institution as a home for "perturbed souls, a place where they can work through their sense of unease with society as they find it" (78). Further, the training of academic professionals reifies social detachment and introversion. We write our dissertations, after all, the culminating experience of our professional formation, in isolation. The "publish or perish" mentality has become something of a cliché as a way to describe contemporary academia. The work that garners recognition—publication, tenure, promotion—is the work of knowledge-making, theorizing. And the inherent isolation lies, I think, at the heart of the theory/practice division. I also think, however, that it helps explain the position of work-as-labor on the discontinuous continuum: We are talking, finally, about a gap between a knowledge-making "professional" class and a teaching working class.

The isolation inherent in academe may well keep professionals cloistered from the cares and concerns of everyday life. In this connection, Jerry Herron argues that professional academics have never worked in the usual sense of the term: "Fundamental to the discourse of academic professionals is the distinction between real work and our work, between the real world and the academy" (1988, 47). Moreover, when academics refer to their "work" they typically refer to their writing, their knowledge-making, rather than to teaching (or serving on committees or performing community service). Why should this be the case? To bring my argument back to the teaching of writing, why do compositionists seldom discuss work? Why is so little said or written about the labor of being with students and for students (to paraphrase Paulo Freire), or of reading student papers, and thinking of things to write in response? Herron argues that such topics are "unprofessional" and that writing instruction, moreover, is part of the academic "working class": "The important fact about writing, then, is that it is working class; and the important thing for the other members of the profession is that it should remain so. Otherwise, their own supervisory security might be in jeopardy" (1988, 56). In other words, the current professional structure configures work as déclassé. Meanwhile, institutional spoils—prestige, advancement, power, private offices—go to knowledge-makers, the professional theory-class. An article in *The Chronicle of Higher Education,* 13 February 1998, reinforces this point. In a feature entitled "Bad Blood in the English Department: the Rift Between Composition and Literature," Alison Schneider reports on the status of compostion within English departments and argues that, "Composition is a service course, and, in the hierarchical world of academe, service courses are the province of the proletariat." Schneider interviews David Bartholomae, who opines: "As a professor, you're not identified with something of great cultural value, like Shakespeare or the English novel. . . . You're identified with the minds and words of 18-year olds'" (1998, A15).

PRACTICE, PRACTICE, PRACTICE

There have of course been attempts to reclaim the value of teaching. Unfortunately, these attempts originate in a hierarchical model; rather than breaking the hierarchy or making the continuum continuous, they marginalize work and workers further. Consider, for example, the focus on lore in composition studies. Stephen M. North identifies lore as the "accumulated body of traditions, practices, and beliefs in terms of which Practitioners understand how writing is done, learned, and taught" (1987, 22). "Practitioners" gather lore: anecdotes, bromides, in-class exercises, writing assignments, course syllabi—a chaotic collection of "what works." Nevertheless, lore cannot count as "theory" or "research"; it is neither unified nor replicable. Patricia Harkin calls for a critical recuperation of lore as "postdisciplinary," an antidote, so to speak, for the extant top-down theory-model: Lore "avoids[s] the unfortunate aspects of disciplinarity, particularly its tendency to simplify to the point of occulting its ideological implications and making us think that its narrowness is normal" (1991, 135). North and Harkin both seek to valorize lore as a legitimate way of knowing; yet neither admits the centrality of work (or workers)—of being in classrooms with students, of handling and reading reams of student papers—to lore's production. One way to make a place for work in composition studies, I think, is to consider it and theory in the context of Paulo Freire's liberatory praxis.

PRAXIS, PRAXIS, PRAXIS

Paulo Freire's liberatory pedagogy and liberation theology emerged simultaneously in late 1950s and 1960s Latin America in response to social, religious, and political upheaval. Freire worked closely with the theologians, and the tenets of liberatory pedagogy are often indistinguishable from those of liberation theology. Such is the case with praxis which, as it is most broadly conceived, denotes the practical application of a field of study.

Strictly speaking, theology is reflection upon a faith so as to deepen one's understanding of that faith. Theological work is typically insular and textual, performed by clergy (or sometimes learned lay people) and directed toward an audience of clergy (and/or learned lay people). Liberation theology, on the other hand, offers a radically new way to understand Christian faith, a way that grows from the lived experiences of dominated peoples. It rejects "traditional" European theology because the latter tends to address social problems abstractly, on a philosophical level, rather than with transformative action. Liberation theology is not, therefore, simple reflection on faith; instead, it is Christian action upon the world—Christian praxis to transform unjust and alienating social structures—followed by theological reflection upon that action. Faith generates the praxis.

Gustavo Gutierrez, a founder of the movement, writes: "From a perspective of faith, what prompts Christians to participate in the liberation of oppressed people and of the exploited social classes is the conviction of the radical incompatibility of the evangelical exigencies with an unjust and alienating society" (1973, 145). In other words, when oppression confronts people of faith, these people, because of their faith, must act. Liberation theology typically describes oppressive social conditions in the context of critique—often a Marxist critique—of developed—that is, capitalist—nations and their exploitation of the Third World. The transformative action liberation theology calls for is in part emancipation from developed nations' capitalist systems. One's understanding of the faith is deepened first through action upon the world (Christian action) and second through reflection on that action. Theology-as-reflection thus becomes the necessary "second act," a reflection ancillary to Christian praxis: the church's profession of faith "is—at least ought to be—real charity, action, and commitment to the service of men. Theology is reflection, a critical attitude. Theology follows; it is the second step" (1973, 11, his emphasis).

Whereas in traditional models, theological work is conducted by an elite corps of scholars or—um—theorists, in liberation theology all people everywhere who endeavor to create justice and equality "do" theology. Liberation theology replaces the received textual mode of conducting theological work (theology as "reflection" or, more precisely, as "contemplation," from the ancient Greek *theoria*, to contemplate) with work in the field, so to speak, labor to transform the world's material conditions. Now, does liberation theology's reconfiguration of theory as secondary to action dis theory? Does it follow that liberatory praxis is a-theoretical? anti-theoretical? anti-intellectual? Freire's commentary on liberatory praxis shows that it is not. Freire's language in *Pedagogy of the Oppressed* echoes Gutierrez's. The "banking method" of education, he argues, may lead students (and, by extension, all oppressed people) to "discover through existential experience that their present way of life is irreconcilable with their vocation to be more fully human" (1993, 56). Freire and liberation theology stress education for critical consciousness (or conscientization), critical self-insertion into reality, as a fundamental agent of liberation. No matter what its name, however—education for critical consciousness, cultural action for freedom, pedagogy of the oppressed, education as the practice of freedom, reading the word and the world—conscientization is praxis, transformative action upon the world, mandated by God. According to Freire: "The process of conscientization leaves no one with his arms folded. It makes some unfold their arms. It leaves others with a guilt feeling, because conscientization shows us that God wants us to act" (1974, 29).

For Freire, then, praxis denotes more than a fancy way to say practice. Indeed, praxis is a distinctly human activity that occurs only at the nexus of reflection and action. Praxis is a dialogue—between reflection and action, yes, but also between humans to name and transform the world. Praxis-according-to-Freire renders human existence as a state of becoming, a dynamic, creative process, rather than as a static and rigid state of being. Moreover, it demands conversion, what Freire calls an "Easter experience": "The old Easter of rhetoric is dead—with no hope of resurrection. It is only in the authenticity of historical praxis that Easter becomes the death which makes life possible" (1985, 123). The educator who would engage in praxis must die to her assumptions about reality and be reborn in communion with her students: "Conversion to the people requires a profound rebirth. Those who undergo it must take on a new existence" (1993, 42-43). This notion may sound familiar to many of us in composition studies. Ann E. Berthoff, an early admirer of Freire, takes "begin with where they are" as one of her favorite maxims for teaching (1993, 49). Rather than interpreting students' struggle as resistance or intransigence, then, critical teachers should study, understand, and "convert" to students' experience of reality. Rather than forcing students into some preconceived theoretical model, such teachers must work with and for students to understand the reality they share, then to construct a theory together that will change that reality.

To return to my earlier questions, if theorizing—the reflection—follows, does it also follow that this phenomenon is anti-intellectual or a-theoretical? No. Teachers must make some reflective assumptions before the praxis, namely, they must be converted to the people, the students; they must begin with students' reality. What this means for theory-work is that it, like all elements of human existence, is reconfigured as a process. Because the context that creates theory always changes, theory occurs in a constant state of becoming rather than as a totalizing narrative. One consequence for teaching is that each class becomes a "culture in progress"; teachers must experience Freire's Easter with each new class, with each new section, and thus become part of the evolution of the culture in progress.

THEORYRESEARCHPRACTICEWORK

Workers in composition inhabit a unique place. They—we—identify our own site-specific problems and invent solutions on the spot. Does theory inform this work? Or does the work create theory? Both, of course. Theory and work are, or should be, inextricably bound, a serpent swallowing its own tail. Further, configuring theory and work as continuous poses some urgent questions. For example, why does so much composition continue to be taught by untenured and untenurable part-time faculty and/or graduate students? These people belong not just to the academic "working class" but to the "under class" as well, and the shabby treatment they often receive at the hands of the institution damages us all. We might also question the status of literature specialists who've "done an exam area" in composition but who have no particular stake in teaching writing. Do these people resent the labor-intensive "service" they must perform for the institution, and if so, how are students affected? Is it possible, finally, to free composition studies (and Compositionists) from the service ghetto?

Seeing the classroom as a culture in progress and as the ground for theory-work may also lead us to transform our relationship to students. If we replace the "us versus them" model that now prevails with a more collective one, we will certainly break down received power structures. Classes will be "ours"; that is, they will "belong" to teachers and students. We might redefine "student writing," which now exists only inasmuch as we assign, read, and respond to it. Students will understand composing in writing not as a required, school-sponsored task, but as integral to being human, reading the word and the world, as Freire says. Student voices might take active places in "professional" settings, speaking for themselves rather than being spoken about. Surely these are worthy goals, indispensable to knowing and doing composition.

CHAPTER TWO

Composing
Composition Studies
Scholarly Publication and
the Practice of Discipline

Peter Vandenberg

R HETORIC AND COMPOSITION AROUND THE END OF THE NINETEENTH century has been described as "an academic desideratum . . . to be escaped as soon as practicable" (Connors, 1991, 55). As we approach 2000, it is one of the fastest growing academic fields in the university.

The Spring, 1994 issue of *Rhetoric Review* announced empirical evidence suggesting something of a golden age. Data complied by Stuart Brown, Paul Meyer, and Theresa Enos indicated a doubling in just seven years of "core rhetoric/composition faculty in US doctoral programs"(241), a phenomenal rise in the number of associate and full professors in the field, and a 123% increase in the number of PhD-seeking students specializing in rhetoric and composition. According to Brown, Meyer, and Enos these data reflect "an increased disciplinary viability" (240), a "profession . . . coming of age" (248).

Although that special issue includes articles critical of this burgeoning growth and its implications (Moneyhun, Schilb, Slevin), the data that Brown, Meyer, and Enos gather reflects a growing emphasis on connections among disciplinarity and the professionalized reproduction of the field's professoriate. Implicit in such an emphasis is an increasing marginalization of the act of teaching writing in the work of those whose first obligation is to "the discipline" of rhetoric and composition. As the Program Chair's theme statement in the 1997 CCCC *Call for Program Proposals* suggests, the field is increasingly aware of the "growing gulf between research faculty and teaching faculty" (Selfe). *Teaching* and *research*, when they are discussed together, are often grossly generalized in order to demonstrate their apparently equal importance and self-evident interrelationships. Quality teaching, the argument goes, is dependent on research, and research presupposes its teaching; "to achieve a balance in which the two activities actually complement each other is one of the most important contributions we can make" (Commonwealth 79 –80). What typifies such formulations, however, is a failure to account for the profoundly powerful institutional and disciplinary structures that lend *teaching* and *research* practical definitions as neatly hierarchized workplace activities.

To "work in rhetoric and composition" means either to publish or to teach; well aware that those who publish typically teach as well, my argument is that the "disciplining" of rhetoric and composition insures that those who do much of one do comparatively little of the other. This bifurcation constitutes an economy that serves those who are at its head; publishing scholars, whose work is defined by acquiring and advancing the specialized literacy of heavily theorized professional discourse, assume a professional-client relationship with those whose work is defined predominantly by teaching a more basic literacy—first-year English. My purpose here is to describe in specific terms how rhetoric and composition's publishing professionals have clientized writing teachers through the declaration of expertise, and to locate that expertise not in the possession of knowledge *necessary* to the task of writing instruction but in the rehearsal of privileged literate practices and their resulting products, "research." Further, I want to suggest that this ideology of research obfuscates its own historical appearance and sustains its dominance.

MANAGEMENT AND THE SCHOLARLY WRITING PRODUCT

The emergence of rhetoric and composition mirrors the professionalization of most academic disciplines, in particular literary studies, following the late nineteenth-century adaptation of the German research university to American higher education. Already by 1840 a hierarchy of productivity was visible across German higher education, and over the next several decades, as specialization shaped the field of classical studies into philology, a tightening circle of archival researchers bound by a single method distinguished themselves from those engaged primarily with pedagogy (Turner). Scholarly publication aimed at a broad non-specialized audience was not only out of fashion, but the subject of ridicule. In confluence with the state, the research university had redefined the concept of knowledge production as the activity of specialists, and had come to occupy the center of that activity. Archival textual research framed within a self-conscious methodology (philology), and written directly to specialist colleagues through the journal article would define acceptable academic work (Diehl). The former authority of the textbook—and those who wrote them and taught from them—was subverted by the specialist publication. Senior professors, in concert with the state, controlled the means of scholarly production: the largest libraries necessary for the newly favored archival research, the seminar training that would function as a screening device, and the modes of knowledge dissemination, scholarly journals.

The explosion of students in the last third of the nineteenth century, many of them Americans like Henry Adams, provoked the hiring of unranked and unsalaried instructors in all fields. The process of achieving professorial standing, which could take as many as twenty years, could rarely be survived without private income. So acute was the poverty of aspiring professors that many depended on the excess food and clothing of their mentors (Thwing 420). As appointment and promotion became increasingly tied to publication, reputation among specialist colleagues replaced local, collegial standing as the determinant of academic success. Locked into localized contact with students, the vast majority of unranked German faculty never achieved distinction outside their own institutions.

While this system originated within classical language study, by the time most American students were enrolled in German universities and institutes (1880s to 1890s) it had become orthodoxy in natural philosophy (the sciences) as well. A combination of an intense work ethic and Platonic epistemology, this system provided a neat ideological fit with the needs of early American capitalists willing to infuse huge amounts of money into research efforts leading to increased production and lower costs (Veysey, 1965; Oleson and Voss). The emerging class of university administrators found in this system a ready-made arrangement for the division of labor. As Burton Bledstein points out, administrators themselves emerged in the generation after 1870 as a specialized group of men pursuing individual careers, and they succeeded as professionals when they were able to assert their authority.

That administrative authority came not in the form of direct intervention in the process of creating or discovering knowledge, but in the institutionalization of the German system of academic reward within the new American research universities of the late 1800s. While the ongoing critique of positivism continues to foreground disparate sets of discursive practices, values, methods, and assumptions across the university, we tend to forget that some twelve decades of meticulous corporate organization are responsible for making these differences "academic." As Veysey (1979) writes, "[t]he kingdoms may have been separate and diverse, but nearly all of them came to be governed by the same kind of rules" (51). Most salient to the discussion at hand is the rule for separating university employees along a particular standard of productivity. This was accomplished quite effectively by ignoring multiple and widely discrete methods, practices, and processes and attending exclusively to the commodification of "results." The outcomes of diverse methodological operations constitute "research" when they are "written up" in a form suitable for dissemination.

Within such an arrangement faculty can rather efficiently be sorted into categories of "productive" and "unproductive," with comparatively little or no attention given to teaching. The present grounds of this division of labor can be discerned in the rhetoric of those who initiated its management—Wisconsin president Charles R. Van Hise, for example, insisted in 1916 that each faculty member should "resolve that he will become a recognized scholar in his field and begin at once some piece of productive work" (qtd. in Hawkins 291). Given the related assumption that the very purpose of teaching is to disseminate the "findings" of a field's research to students, the university, across its disciplines, assumes a professional-client relationship between researcher and teacher. Thomas Newkirk locates the origins of this top-down arrangement in the application of industrial management to schooling: "Students are the raw material—essentially inert—waiting to be 'shaped.' Teachers are the workers . . . who carry out the plans of their superiors, those who make the specifications and outline procedures for meeting those specifications" (120).

It is within this closely managed dichotomization of labor that English departments were formed, primarily based on a desire to study fiction and poetry in the vernacular. This, after all, was the very focus of Prussian philology, and with a fervor as great as any displayed among their counterparts in the natural sciences, the first American literature professors distanced themselves from pedagogy at the outset. Those present at the first meeting of the Modern Language Association in 1883 unanimously adopted a resolution directing it toward the goals of study, scholarship, and discipline. Articles about teaching writing diminished markedly in the *PMLA* until 1903, when the Pedagogical Section disappeared entirely; according to William Riley Parker, by 1911 "the MLA had become so absorbed in the advancement of research in its field that it was ready to leave to others all talk of teaching and enrollment" (32). Working within recently constructed standards of academic competence and success, the new department of English had organized itself according to disciplined, professional criteria. It had narrowed its focus of inquiry to a canon of older, "difficult," "literary" texts; solidified its dominant mode of inquiry, the "scientific" approach to historical philology; and carefully constructed a system of reproduction, in which prospective scholars were trained in the canon, method, and assumptions of the discipline. On a more visible level, English studies—literary studies—engaged in a constant process of self-legitimation and preservation through its professional organizations and academic journals.

This is a story that readers of contemporary rhetoric and composition scholarship know well, owing in particular to the privileged work of its most celebrated historians, Robert Connors (1984, 1991), James Berlin, and Winifred Horner, all of whom owe some degree of debt to Albert Kitzhaber. As Berlin explains in his monograph, the epistemological alignment of literary study, philology, and the emerging research ethos helped to diminish attention to student writing and the teaching of student writing (25), resulting in a literature/composition duality that already by 1984 Connors insisted he "need not rehearse in any detail" (160). Yet these histories of composition, in their construction of "heroes" and "villains" (Connors 1991, 54), serve a community-building function in the present as they shape a view of the past. By its very title Horner's book, *Composition and Literature: Bridging the Gap*, asserts the primary goal of rhetoric and composition scholars over the past twenty years—institutional legitimacy. Her "Historical Introduction" turns not on epistemological hierarchies, but on professional ones; it stands as an implicit claim on academic territory. Metaphorically, rhetoric and composition is elevated there to the same plane as its perceived oppressor; if rhetoric and composition is to become part of the "serious business" of the English department,

it must do so according to the standards already established by literary scholars, and the bridge between the two fields is comprised, in part, by the privileged scholarship of her collection's contributors.

Horner's book demonstrates in retrospect that the route to institutional
legitimacy for rhetoric and composition looked remarkably similar to the one
traveled by literary scholars seven decades earlier. The professional discourse
of rhetoric and composition, however, continues to remain attentive to the two
fields' differences rather than the ways the larger institution enforces their similarities. "[I]ntellectual and 'practical' moves toward equality for composition,"
Susan Miller writes, "reproduce the hegemonic superstructure . . . . [T]hey are
politically unified attempts to become equal in, and to sustain, a hierarchy that
their supporters often claim to be overturning" (51). The short history of composition studies has been one of appropriation—appropriation of the same
disciplinary categories and attitudes that seemed oppressive when used to
characterize literary studies. By continuing to recite histories based on a hierarchized literature/rhetoric opposition, like the frenzied character in Robert
Frost's "Home Burial," rhetoric and composition continues to go forward
"looking over [its] shoulder at some fear." And in so doing it has stumbled into
the academy's disciplinary memory, reconstructing a class-based system of
inequality in (re)claimed institutional space.

DISCIPLINE AND THE PRIVILEGE OF "RESEARCH"

The reorientation of some compositionists and rhetoricians from "hapless
bottom feeders" (Connors, 1991, 72) to endowed chairs has come about, in
part, by the privileging of *research*, a signifier vacated of specific meaning for
the purpose of establishing its necessity and, therefore, the necessity of those
who produce it. As Cheryl Geisler explains in *Academic Literacy and the Nature
of Expertise*, "the separation of knowledge production from knowledge use led
to an internal stratification of the professions into academic and practitioner
wings" (74). George H. Daniels, in a 1966 article published in *Isis*, locates the
professionalization of an academic field and this seemingly inevitable stratification identified by Geisler in a process he terms "preemption." This procedure
takes place in a "period of emergence" in which a task that has "customarily
been performed by one group or by everybody in general comes into the
exclusive possession of another particular group. This automatically occurs
when the body of knowledge necessary for the task becomes esoteric, that is,
when it becomes obviously unavailable to the general scholar" (152). At first
blush, Daniels' Preemption model seems suitable to explain the emergence of
"rhetoric and composition" from the anti-discipline of pre-1960s composition
teaching. In interpreting Albert Kitzhaber's scolding address at the 1963
Conference on College Composition and Communication as a defining
moment in the "emergence" of rhetoric and composition, Stephen North
seems to implicitly recognize Daniels' process of preemption:

Kitzhaber's challenge calls . . . for the exertion of authority over knowledge about composition: what it is, how it is made, who gets to say so and why. What made that so difficult a challenge to meet . . . was that [the CCCC] never really had the means to do so: it had no such control over knowledge, no *mode of inquiry* by which such order might have been imposed, nor whose findings would have been acknowledged by the wider profession. The school subject, composition, consisted almost entirely of knowledge produced by Practitioner inquiry . . . . And what marks [rhetoric and composition's] emergence as a nascent academic field more than anything else is this need to replace practice as the field's dominant mode of inquiry. (15)

The apparent correlation between Daniels's framework for professionalization and North's extended account of emergence are overshadowed by a significant difference. North establishes that preemption, in the case of rhetoric and composition, did not "automatically occur" through the expansion of an autonomous "body of knowledge" somehow capable of demonstrating its own necessity. On the contrary, North confirms that preemption is better understood as a political exercise by the institutionally motivated. Although North is unable to demonstrate that "practice" indeed functioned as a "mode of inquiry," let alone a dominant one, he makes it clear that composition teachers lost their tenuous *potential* for control in a struggle for institutional power among academic professionals. North claims that the research/teaching dichotomy is held in place through an intermethodological battle for supremacy—publishing academics depend on the degraded status of composition "practitioners" to justify their claims to superiority. Yet in defining the research/teaching dichotomy strictly in terms of methodological warfare, North disregards the tacit unification of proponents of competing methodological camps by an overriding set of professional criteria. Those he refers to as practitioners are not generalized and then degraded strictly on the basis of their fidelity to something called "practice as inquiry," but because their primary activities fall outside what James Sosnoski has called the "standard career template" (3).

During the preemption of writing teachers' authority by publishing scholars, a process begun in the early 1960s, perhaps *how* writing teachers "know" has been far less important than simply what they have read: "research." With the introduction of *Research in Written Composition* in 1963, Richard Braddock *et al.* used the term to designate the results of a clinical or empirical method. In this rather specific usage, *research* was implied, Thomas Kerr finds, "to make substantial that which otherwise lacked substance in the form of scientific credibility" (201). Long since, however, the term has lost its specific "scientific" referent; most often, as in this segment from a 1990 issue of *College Composition and Communication*, it signifies any text authorized by academic publication: "Many of the liveliest debates in the field have taken place between proponents of different theories of composition *research*, such as cognitivists versus contextualists. Because of the varying theories and methodologies governing this *research* . . ." (Durst 395). While this increasing generalization appears to have drained the term of specific meaning, its rhetorical power of authorization has hardly abated. As Kerr shows, figured as a "diverse phenomenon," *research* has been cast "as an arbiter, even a hero, of near-mythic proportions, ready and able to repudiate past ignominy" (202). What it has often been used to repudiate is the work performed by teachers of writing, who have been found to lack its supposedly profound corrective influence.

Throughout the 1980s, published articles, "research," in rhetoric and composition often reflected an implied reader easily disgusted by the conditions of composition pedagogy and intensely motivated to rectify the situation. Paul Heilker (1996a) shows that the workplace of the composition teacher—the first-year English classroom—has often been constructed "as an empty space notable for its various lacks, as an absence" (108), and the teachers themselves as helplessly dependent on the professional discourse. Heilker suggests that a typical rhetorical strategy begins with the formulation of "a hyperbolically bad teacher of the past or present away from which the writer's contribution will help readers move" (1996b, 232). In this way, rhetoric and composition researchers, exploiting the seemingly immutable ideological confluence of literacy and research, have declared their work indispensable to the "productivity" of writing teachers.

Consider a 1982 *College Composition and Communication* article, "The Winds of Change: Thomas Kuhn and the Revolution in the Teaching of Writing." Maxine Hairston declares here an impending "paradigm shift" in composition studies finding, not surprisingly, the "most promising indication" in the work of "specialists who are doing controlled and directed research on writers' composing processes" (85). Hairston's repeated use of the term *research* implies no methodological distinction, but her article is instructive in the conviction with which the research/teaching hierarchy is revealed. Teaching is systematically denied its active, inventive, transformative potential and recast as a void that can be filled and made productive only through consumption of research. Adding insult to injury, writing teachers, astonishingly, are lumped together with the very class of managers who inevitably restrain them for their lack of privileged productivity: according to Hairston, the group of "people who do most to promote a static and unexamined approach to teaching writing . . . probably includes most administrators and teachers of writing."

Hairston declares that writing teachers who can't or don't read the professional literature are "probably doing more harm than good" (79). Teachers without knowledge of the professional literature are teachers without knowledge: "they are frequently emphasizing techniques that *the research* has largely discredited" (80, my emphasis). Hairston's claim does not privilege any one theory or method, it recommends that effective teaching demands knowledge—possession—of the professional literature itself. According to Hairston, because most writing teachers haven't read Elbow or Bruffee they have no way of knowing that their students might benefit far more from small group meetings with each other than from the exhausting one-to-one conferences that the teachers hold. They both complain and brag about how much time they spend meticulously marking each paper, but because they haven't read Diederich or Irmscher they don't know that an hour spent meticulously marking every error in a paper is probably doing more harm than good. (79)

The subordination of "local" values, primarily teaching, to professional values reflects the degree of importance placed on the primary material incentive for advancement, scholarly publication; and it is published scholarship that defines the dichotomization of labor in rhetoric and composition. As Alain Touraine argues, a social hierarchy based on the possession of knowledge replicates the economic system in which it is contained. "At the head . . . are those whose knowledge is greatest and, who are above all, apt to develop furthest. They constitute a capital that bears interest, for they are constantly producing new knowledge" (140). Academic publications in rhetoric and composition have been likened to poker hands (Connors, 1984) and naval vessels (Hashimoto), yet their direct relationship to advancement and monetary success recommends understanding them as professional currency. Once legitimized by the approbation of the field's "epistemic court," the knowledge products of individual professionals are transformed into marketable currency, and therefore power, for the individual professionals who compose them. The very materiality of a textual product promotes its exchange value. Itself an extension of other texts, every published article is a potential locus for continued profitability as an artifact to be possessed and assimilated in later ventures.

Defined by what they are not/have not, non-publishing writing teachers are the economically disadvantaged. The vast majority of those who each year teach writing to four million freshman students are neither producers nor consumers; they do not engage in the exchange of valid academic currency. Their work is transitory and predominantly oral; when they write, they write, literally, in the margins—of students' texts. They are evaluated chiefly by those defined by their very lack of knowledge, students. "Regarded as temporary, as amateurs, sort of Kelly-person teachers" (Penfield 20), they teach without benefits, merit pay or the possibility of promotion, most of them in two-year and four-year colleges. The objectification and exploitation of their collective labor has been thorough enough to motivate Dennis Szilak to declare the "disposable composition teacher . . . the greatest labor-saving and money-saving device since the folding chair" (qtd. in Heilker, 1996b, 234).

There is a danger of course in romancing the poor. The historically abysmal employment conditions of writing teachers have sometimes provided a shelter for the unqualified, uninterested, and unmotivated. In addition, defining the teaching/research opposition strictly along the tenure boundary obfuscates the "tokenization" of most tenure-track writing teachers who pursue careers in teaching while married to a reward structure designed for the consumption and value-added re/manufacture of literate products. Those who have no time to produce significant "research," regardless of their academic rank, become the *de facto* clients of those who do.

In the years since the publication of Hairston's "Winds of Change," few such overt instances of beating the poor have been recorded. The condition that North described in 1987—researchers "find out what there is to know, and then pass that knowledge along to Practitioners" (331)—has become tacit in rhetoric and composition as a sort of institutionalized clientism. When Elizabeth Rankin, for example, describes the sort of teacher to whom she would lend credence, it is not surprising to recognize precisely the situation North has articulated: "[W]hen an experienced, enlightened composition instructor—say one who's been teaching six or eight years and keeps up with *CCC, College English*, and *Rhetoric Review*—tells me that writing groups 'work' in her classes, I'm likely at least to pay attention to her claim" (266). While immensely more generous in her estimation of the "practitioner community" than Hairston, Rankin confirms that educational certification, the satisfaction of hiring criteria, and teaching experience are finally sanctioned only through the influence of publishing professionals.

Clearly the clientization of writing teachers has been crucial to the field's formation. Yet as rhetoric and composition has solidified as an academic field, the need to destabilize teaching in order to create a market for "research" has subsided; those once defined as ignorant due to their location in the division of labor are as likely now to be seen as simply unimportant. The ultimate pre-emptive or disciplining act is to remove teachers of writing from the discourse about writing. As *Journal of Advanced Composition* editor Gary Olson said in 1992, "What I'd like to resist is the tendency to suggest that all theory or scholarship has to necessarily have some relation down the line to something practical. I don't think that is what most academic disciplines are about" (qtd. in Vandenberg). Confidently free from the pedagogical imperative in which "one of the requirements always seemed to be that you make some kind of connection between your research and the teaching of writing" (Witte qtd. in Goggin 1997), researchers have found a space where they can theorize the abolition of the first-year writing requirement—and the thousands of jobs it supports— (see Connors 1995) as well as further elaborate the nuisance that the work of teaching writing represents to publishing researchers, particularly those, according to Maureen Goggin (1995), who prefer the title *rhetorician* over *compositionist*. Like the economic system that contains it, the publishing industry in composition functions as a mechanism for the maintenance of social distances. To the extent that the publishing authors can be said to manage composition—not through "actual" control over the teaching of writing, but through control of the institutionally authorized discourse about that activity—they define the objectives and direction of the "discipline" in terms of their own professional function.

28   *Peter Vandenberg*

DISSOLUTION: RESISTING DISCIPLINE

The professional discourse of rhetoric and composition functions at present as a center of authority, what Richard Weaver referred to in *Visions of Order*, his 1964 treatise on culture and discourse, as a "tyrannizing image." The published discourse of rhetoric and composition and the image of the publishing professional, the ideal of its own excellence, implicitly sustains a hierarchy that enforces conformity to that ideal. Like the societal and institutional systems that contain it, rhetoric and composition is grounded in class stratification; and as is the case elsewhere within those larger social systems, there is a consistent and irrefutable alignment of class privilege with the creation, distribution, and constructed necessity of particular literacy practices and textual products.

Those who submit or subscribe to the tyrannizing image "view the world in a particular way; they act, order, and believe in relation to the image" (Cushman and Hauser 321). In contemporary rhetoric and composition, to act, order, and believe in relation to the dominant image is to understand the published, professional discourse as a kind of sacred well, and the publishing professional as a *representation* of excellence to which the field subscribes, strives, and submits, an embodiment of its most prominent beliefs and values. This image operates tyrannically *between* believers and experience, framing concerns and potentializing responses to them like a lens.

This ideology of research and its resulting hierarchy of productivity has been so seamlessly naturalized within the academy that virtually everyone accepts her role, and her relative status, without question. In *Token Professionals and Master Critics*, James Sosnoski keenly maps the extent to which "humiliations and injustices" within the academy are "thought to be the necessary accompaniments of discipline" (xxiv). Detailing the division of labor in literary studies, Sosnoski describes the way in which a template of the ideal academic as publishing "master critic" is used to contain the vast majority of "token professionals" whose teaching loads and departmental commitments will not allow them to realize the ideal. As a matter of routine the token professional "accepts standards that will invariably insure her failure" (Sosnoski 4).

These conditions are virtually self-sealing owing to the pervasiveness of literate values within the university at large; the entire enterprise of higher education is geared toward the production of text—by students and "ideal professionals." As David R. Olson argues, "literacy in general and schooling in particular are instrumental in the construction of a *particular* form of knowledge that is relevant to a *particular* set of socially valued activities" (67). However, it is a fact that, despite being judged on their in/ability to do so, the vast majority of writing teachers simply are not employed for the purpose of producing text; their function within the academy is to sustain the privilege of publishing professionals through the consumption and further dissemination of their ideas to students. *The very privilege of literacy within the academy works to mask the fact that those who do the most to promote it are prevented by conditions of their employment from fully utilizing it.*

Worse, challenges to the system seem inevitably swallowed up by it. The very appearance of a published critique, such as this one, smacks of privilege. Such a analysis unavoidably yields symbolic capital for its author and invites charges of hypocrisy; worse, it sustains the system in the most aggravating fashion by demonstrating the system's ability to both provide for and nullify its own critique. Robert Markley's maxim holds that efforts at resistance through publication are exercises in co-optation: "[W]e all, when given the opportunity . . . wind up perpetuating the system instead of attacking it" (81). Like literacy, which tacitly legitimates itself (Stuckey), by its very function the academic publishing system appropriates the claims of its authors, implicitly re-authorizing them in a larger, institutional context. And every disseminated text carries within itself the potential for self-justification; as Janice Lauer argues, if research "does inspire action and change . . . this action in turn provides a type of validation" (24). However, this gratifying cycle of professionally automated confirmation may be little more than a disciplined reflex action—the "technical fix error." Scholarly publishing is a system, and the seemingly self-evident presumption that systemic error will yield to systemic solution, a version of what Pierre Bourdieu calls the "epistemocentric fallacy," is rarely called into question.

To believe that a "solution" to the deeply embedded class differential held in place by that system will emerge from that system—from this chapter—is a tacit expression of the ideology of research. What writing teachers have consistently lacked in the sluggish, one-hundred year march toward the professionalization of rhetoric and composition is the privileged work of producing text authorized by the university's class-making system. Given that the particular literate conventions of researchers are framed as the ideal, and that the working conditions of most writing teachers prevent the acquisition of the ideal, disrupting the system through the dissemination of text appears to hold little promise. If the *working conditions of writing teachers*—not the disciplinary status of rhetoric, composition studies, or whatever one chooses to call the privileged institutional arrangement built on the backs of writing teachers—are to change, they will change as a result of physical and symbolic action *outside* the order of academic publishing. In any case, to the extent that the top-down relationship of "research" to teaching appears natural, logical, or self-evident rather than historical, contingent, and economically determined, the present division of labor in rhetoric and composition and the university at large is certain to persist.

CHAPTER THREE

Toward a Theory of Theory for Composition Studies

James Thomas Zebroski

I. THE CONTEXT OF THEORY

*I*N THE MID-1980S, I WAS STILL HOPEFUL THAT ALLIANCES MIGHT BE NEGOTI-
ated among the theoretical communities emerging in literary studies and
those scholars in composition studies who saw a value in doing composition
theory. As different as these theoretical discourses seemed, I believed that there
were strategic and ethical reasons for pursuing conversations with literary theorists. I thought that we shared a critique of traditional scholarship in literature,
composition and the humanities, and that we both in our respective ways were
reacting to and moving beyond the limits of formalism, whether of the New
Critical variety in literature or of a product orientation in writing. I shared some
common roots with these academic second cousins, after all. I had studied with a
scholar who himself had worked with, and then reacted to, John Crowe Ransom,
Robert Penn Warren and Cleanth Brooks at Kenyon. He had found an alternative theoretical community first in transformational linguistics and then in
Marxist theory. I too saw parallels between literary theory and language theory,
between theory of the French sort (Barthes, Derrida, Lacan, Althusser, Foucault)
and theory of the Russian sort (Vygotsky, Leontiev, Volosinov, Bakhtin).
Language for the theorist, whether literary or compositional, was far more complicated and dynamic than the prevailing communication models pretended;
context was far more determinative of text than formalism would allow. Surely, it
was in our mutual interest to work together to transform English departments
and scholarship on language, to support each other's efforts to reform the curriculum and the canon, and to endorse each other's candidates for tenure and
promotion against the status quo arrayed against theory of any sort.

After five years of trying to forge such alliances, I wrote "The End(s) of
Theory" and concluded that both locally and nationally trying to bring literary

and composition theory together was a mistake. I discovered that my attempts at dialogue were met with expectations that I should submit to poststructuralist and postmodern theory (Theory, capital T, I named it) while not a single Theorist I knew or worked with (or their graduate students) ever read any of the theory that I had been pursuing. The implicit narrative seemed to go something like this: composition theory is primitive and backward. It is unaware of the important work of the last twenty years. It is obsessed with the mundane and the ordinary tasks of writing, with the administering of writing (and of thought), and is impatient with the intellectual work that serious thought requires. It is simpleminded in its conception of the political. It is conservative, if not right wing, in its politics. It will be years, if ever, before it catches up to current advances of poststructuralist and postmodern Theory. It is eminently critique-able.

Clearly, there were differences between the work of the two theoretical communities, and, obviously, there were always a sufficient number of examples in composition that one could easily point to for confirmation of that narrative. Still, the narrative had too much the whiff of the orthodox decrying the Gnostic heretics, projecting their anxieties and fears onto a convenient other, regardless of the lack of evidence supporting such claims. Such characterizations did not do justice to the complexity of thinking that occurs when a composition teacher works with a student on the production of a text, or when the composition theorist collaborates with colleagues in the discipline to produce knowledge about writing. Even more surprising was that this narrative ignores some of the key facts of disciplinary history and the role of theory over the last thirty years.

Usually theorists track poststructuralist literary theory in the U.S. back to the 1966 Johns Hopkins Conference. That same year however, a conference of American and British scholars met at Dartmouth, and the impetus for at least some of composition theory can be tracked back to that conference. It is significant that the field of composition appropriated theory far faster than literary studies if we take these two conferences as emblematic beginnings. Historically speaking, composition led the way during the 1970s for theory in English departments. Dartmouth eventuated in the work of James Moffett, among others, whose *Teaching the Universe of Discourse* appeared in 1968 and in later editions throughout the seventies. Dartmouth made American teachers aware of the work of James Britton whose 1970 *Language and Learning* introduced teachers to Vygotsky's theory of language and thought. But there were also many other developments in composition theory outside of the work of Dartmouth. James Kinneavy's *A Theory of Discourse* was published in 1971; Frank D'Angelo's *A Conceptual Theory of Rhetoric* in 1975. Both were works of sophistication and synthesis. Richard Young, Alton Becker, and Kenneth Pike's *Rhetoric: Discovery and_Change* came out in 1970. Their idea—that it was important to teach writing heuristics and structures of creativity—was taken up and seconded by Janice Lauer and disputed by Ann E. Berthoff in *College Composition and Communication* in 1971. The decade after Dartmouth was a rich one for theory in composition.

During this same period, however, literary studies ignored and then resisted Theory. It is instructive to go back and look at the early issues of the journal *Critical Inquiry* which began publication in 1974 to see how little the Johns Hopkins Conference, and Theory, had influenced literature. The first few volumes showcase work by Ortega Y Gasset, E.D. Hirsch, David Daiches, Wayne Booth, Henry Nash Smith, traditionalists all, Theorists nary a one. The closest thing to Theory is work by Murray Krieger and mention of the work of a young upstart named Stanley Fish. By the later seventies, the most theoretical part of *Critical Inquiry* are its advertisements for *Social Text* and *Glyph*. Only by 1980 and 1981 do we begin to see what we today recognize as Theory in the work of Leitch, J. Hillis Miller, Spivak, Derrida, Knapp and Michaels, Foucault. So while literary study basked in the failing light of a thirty year old New Criticism or occasionally toyed with the exotic ideas of a Northrup Frye or a Norman Holland, the foundation of composition theory had already been laid. This cursory review is supported by the testimony of the compositionists who at this time tried to publish what today we would call composition theory and who found the literary apparat of journal editors, program chairs, as well as department colleagues and tenure committees at best uninterested in composition theory, and, at worst, antagonistic to it, finding theory—and composition—a sacrilege, a committing of social science or philosophy foisted upon the literary. The revisionists would erase this history or minimize it, just as they would minimize the sort of theory that composition does and the sort of theorizing that goes on every day in the composition classroom or in composition publications.

All of this brings me back to the "The End(s) of Theory" and to my belief that, although composition missed an opportunity to influence literary Theory for the better, our contribution to that dialogue might have helped Theorists avoid the dead-end that Theory has now become. Compositionists now must pursue their own kind of theory which arises from the grassroots of composition, rather than submitting to what amounts to re-colonization once again from literati. We need to resist the land rush in certain quarters of composition to appropriate postmodern Theory and convert composition as quickly as possible to what in literary studies is already outdated. How can we construct concepts that will allow us to make use of insights of postmodern Theory, but that still preserve a space for us to learn about and teach writing? This requires a theory of theory in composition. Such a theory of theory emerges from a philosophy of internal relations.

II.EXCURSUS ON THE PHILOSOPHY OF INTERNAL RELATIONS

Poststructuralist and postmodern theory in literary studies (i.e. Theory) often scrutinizes its relationship to structuralist and modernist theory. It wouldn't be quite correct to say that Theory necessarily views itself as a radical break from its predecessors. Rather it theorizes that relationship or lack of one. To be sure, from the perspective of other philosophical stances, it is difficult to see how Theory is not right smack dab in the middle of the mainstream tradition of Western philosophy and twentieth century language study. In its more evangelical moments, this is exactly the all encompassing claim made in Theory, that it thinks itself "beyond" (or "in" or "through") the very categories and moves of Western logocentricism that underlie twenty-five hundred years of thought. In critique, Theory tries to reach truth by denying that it is possible to reach it. Philosophy itself is discovered to have been the problem all along. Still, it is curious that so many philosophical systems since Hegel have named themselves the last word on philosophy, the "end" of philosophy (or history), often by discovering the original sin and fall from grace somewhere in Classical Greece. Why else Heidegger's obsession with the pre-Socratics and rhetoric's current gesture toward the sophists?

I just never can see things as quite as monolithic and singular as Theorists do, I have to confess. As a son of the working class, I experientially know that whole traditions with elaborated ways of knowing, constructing, and living in the world have existed and continue to exist, and even thrive, apart from (thank the gods) this single stream of history and culture. All around us in the most conformist of times, we see vibrant alternative traditions that track their histories alongside this "line" of philosophy, itself a fallacy of projected linearism. Michael Murphy in his recent dissertation "Camp Happens: Modernity, Post-Modernity, and Recycled Culture" critiques this sort of misplaced reductionist linearism which ignores the vibrancy and relative independence of other less elitist movements and traditions. Murphy, starting from a neo-Frankfurt School philosophical stance, critiques recent Theory as being contradictory in its decrying of the elitism in traditional art including the institution of the museum, while at the same time being ultimately complicit with the museum in the construction of the avant garde. Such a contradictory stance makes it necessary to ignore, for example, art deco and the role it has played in this century's history. Unlike the elitist art that Theory deals with, art deco has had far reaching effects on architectural design and practice, bridging elitist and popular traditions through a process Murphy terms "camp."

Even in composition, the very idea of modernism as a single thing is complicated if not contradicted by the variety of counter philosophies, whether of the New Abolitionists (Petraglia 1995) and the Externalists (Kent 1993) who draw from Donald Davidson, or of Ann E. Berthoff (Berthoff 1981, 1990, 1991, 1996) who presents a strong case for the alternative hermeneutic tradition based on Peirce, James, Whitehead, Sapir, Cassirer, and Langer which is at best marginal to the "line" of philosophy fantasized and projected by Theory. So too my notion of theory draws heavily on an alternative tradition which Bertell Ollman calls a philosophy of internal relations.

Ollman in his *Alienation: Marx's Conception of Man in Capitalist Society* sets forth the concerns and approaches of a philosophy of internal relations that he sees alive and well in Marx, Hegel, Spinoza, and others. I reduce his superb discussion to the following principles, losing, for the sake of efficiency, much of the subtlety and richness of his account.

It is curious how few contemporary Marxists (or postMarxists) seem to feel any obligation to read Marx; this is too bad because, if they did, they would be immediately presented with a reading problem. Karl Marx's *Capital* for instance, just doesn't seem to follow the conventions of either Marx's discourse community of a century ago, or our current conventions of scholarly writing. His categories, at first reading, seem repetitious, vague, undefined. The order of topics eludes our conventional notions of what is a properly arranged piece of discourse. What is going on in these important texts? How can we interpret them? Bertell Ollman argues that Marx is a notoriously difficult and slippery read because he works out of a philosophy of internal relations while we live in a capitalist society that privileges positivist sorts of knowledge.

A philosophy of internal relations approaches concepts *ecologically* (my term not Ollman's), that is, a concept is seen as coming out of an environment, a social formation with its histories, and the concept retains traces of that ecology and, in fact, is still a part of that ecology when we appropriate it. [1] Ollman notes:

> What is unusual in Marx's statement is the special relation he posits between categories and society. Instead of simply being a means for describing capitalism (neutral vehicles to carry a partial story), these categories are declared to be "forms," "manifestations," and "aspects" of their own subject matter. Or as he says elsewhere in this Introduction, the categories of bourgeois society "serve as the expression of its conditions and the comprehension of its own organization . . . the story itself is thought to be somehow a part of the very concepts being told." (*Alienation*, 12)

Ollman continues:

> Three conclusions stand out from this discussion: that Marx grasped each political-economic concept as a component of society itself, in his words as an 'abstract one-sided relation of an already given concrete and living aggregate'; that it is intimately linked with other social components to form a particular structure; and that this whole, or at least its more significant parts, is expressed in the concept itself. (*Alienation*, 13)

Let's take up each of these conclusions in turn.

Each concept is a component of society itself. So a concept comes out of, in fact is still part of, an environment. The social formation structures possible forms of language. It shapes the range of options available. And a major facet of the social formation is its material effects. Thus a concept or an idea is a material form which is not just a neutral or arbitrary stencil put onto the world, but is an actual part of a social, economic, and political ecology that carries the concept's value. The social formation expresses itself, partially to be sure, in the concept. We might term this the *macro* side of a concept.

A concept is intimately linked with other social components to form a particular structure. A concept is termed a "Relation" in Ollman. All words, signs, things, people, processes, activities, cultures, histories, are or involve Relations. The idea of a Relation keeps our concepts dynamic and constantly presents us with an anti-foundational world which we can nevertheless encounter through mediations. A tree is a Relation, a computer is a Relation, a person is a Relation, an author is a Relation. Capital, of course, is the key Relation in our society.

Now "Relations" (R) are made up of "relations" (r), but these same relations are also the interconnections (r) between Relations (R). In other words, the relatively stable entities called Relations (R) are made up, consist of, internal relations, (r) which are processes within the relatively stable entity. At the same time, these internal relations have their basis outside the Relation, the entity and these outside connections are also relations (r). The philosophy of internal relations, then, asserts and assumes that all inner processes are parts of outer processes, that, in fact, outer and inner are only relative terms in a dynamic and constantly changing world.

So, for example, a tree is a Relation that is made up of, expressed through, relations. So the tree (R) might be functionally defined as that Relation which has as its internal processes photosynthesis, reproduction, growth, sugar storage, etc. But these inner processes or internal relations (r) are clearly part of and influenced by external relations, for example the soil, sunshine, the climate, the location the tree occupies on the Quad., other trees and other living beings. The philosopher of internal relations goes farther and asserts that these external relations are actually a part of the internal relations. They are both little r's. So the tree, seen relationally, is partly about *other* trees and *their* internal processes. The tree's own internal processes are part of the other trees (other R's) and their internal processes (other r's) and the connections between trees (also r's).

The seemingly external factors are in diminished and changed form to be sure, a part of, internal to, an expression, of the tree. We know the tree through these relations "internalized." We might term this the *micro* side of a concept. Now all the Relations are tied to each other through relations for a time and form relatively stable wholes (structures).

These relative wholes and their internal relations are expressions themselves of the social formation. This whole is expressed in the concept itself. My very idea of treeness is specific to this social formation and to those relations that are internal to it. It is an effect of capitalism as much as photosynthesis. This tree is on the Quad. after all, not in an untouched forest. There are none of those anymore. To an extent, this tree and its concept are capitalist trees and capitalist concepts. As "natural" as this tree seems, indeed the very epitome of nature naturing, it is a product of a commodity culture that expresses itself over and against nature as a subject to an object, as cultivator to the cultivated, as master to slave, as owner (the university) to commodity, as the sum total of owners, property, relations of production, forces of production, that is capital, to commodity. Through this analytic process, we begin to see a transaction between the macro and the micro concepts. Marx in *Capital* goes through a similar, if far more complex, sort of investigation of the seemingly simple concept of commodity and discovers its relations to other Relations, including labor and labor power.

We might represent this philosophy of internal relations schematically as Figure 1, in which "R" represents the Relation as a relatively whole structure, and "r" stands for the connections between and within Relations.

Figure 1

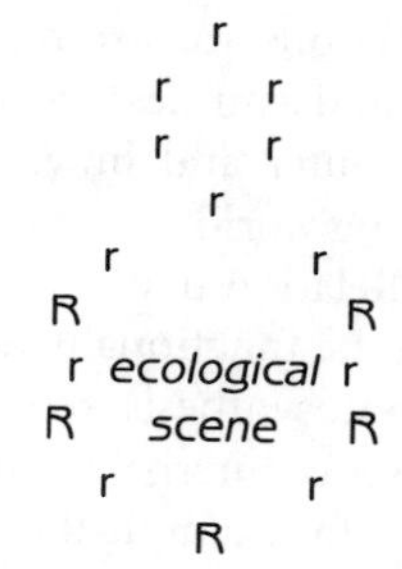

```
                    r
                 r     r
                 r     r
                    r
              r           r
           R                 R
             r  ecological  r
           R     scene      R
             r           r
                    R
```

In effect, a philosophy of internal relations tracks changing connections and disconnections in time. The very thing we think with, the concept, is a changing part of our changing culture, and carries with it necessary limits. Concepts taken too far from their niche either break and don't do the work for us, or if they are ripped out of their environment but survive, distort the thing they are being used to understand. As Robert Frost noted "there are roughly zones" and, not just for peach trees, but also for concepts.

Now it is true that Marx and Ollman are concerned with concepts for social analysis. Still, I think that the concept of "theory" in this case is closer to their political economic categories than "tree" seems to be. Applying the philosophy of internal relations, one might begin by acknowledging the embeddedness of the term theory. We might view as significant theory's rise at a particular juncture in twentieth century capital's development. Theory is an expression of the social formation, mediated through many Relations and relations. Theory is an effect of the social relations of this historical moment. Theory is about the failure of formalism in literary and composition studies in the early 1960s, the twenty year, great depression in the academic job market from about 1973 on, the need to recycle canonical studies in seemingly new ways, the turn to the political right which began with Richard Nixon's landslide and basically has continued unabated to this day, the economic and intellectual need of a new generation of scholars to establish themselves in contradistinction to their departmental elders, the need for the newly emerging discipline of composition studies to establish itself as a proper object of study in the middle and late 1970s, and to declare its independence from the literati in the late 1980s and the early 1990s. Theory, however, is not a freestanding concept in isolation from other concepts. Rather, in a philosophy of internal relations, theory itself must be seen as an effect of and as having effects on related Relations in an ecology of practices.

III. THEORY IN AN ECOLOGY OF PRACTICES

The presupposition of the following section is that most compositionists want to see what sort of relationships might obtain between theory and practice, and that we need to understand if, and when, theory and other kinds of scholarship feed into teaching about writing and learning to write, and what the consequences of such interrelations are. Among many scholars, this is an increasingly unpopular stand. The literati in the person of Stanley Fish warn us that there are no consequences of Theory and that it is an illusion named Theory-hope, to expect Theory to solve our problems, to help us to understand, implement, or transform our practice. (See Mailloux 1989 for the best discussion of theory, Theory, Theory Hope, and fishy consequences.) In composition a group of scholars has arisen called the New Abolitionists (NA). Ironically, they share some of the same thinking as Newt Gingrich. Both would appear to believe that the best way to deal with institutional structures—for Newt, the federal government, for the NA, freshman composition—that regulate and hem in the expansion of their entrepreneurial ventures, whether corporate or scholarly, is abolition. Such abolition will supposedly free us—though it is always somewhat unclear exactly when and how this freeing will take place, what it will consist of, and who exactly "us" is. Clearly, however, for the New Abolitionists the practice of the first year required composition course is a fetter. As Maureen Daly Goggin notes:

> The new abolitionists' position, although attractive to some, is quite unacceptable to compositionists who continue to define the the discipline solely within the boundaries of first-year composition. For them, abolishing the course amounts to professional suicide. Yet, the problem with this position is that although in some instances composition classrooms may serve to generate research problems and also serve as research sites, these instances represent just one strain of scholarship in the field. Restricting our disciplinary enterprise to the composition classroom severely restricts the kinds of problems, questions, and objects of study that we validate for study, and thus severely restricts the shape of the discipline. (43)

I will let pass the unwarranted claim that there is a group of so-called compositionists who define the discipline solely in terms of the first year course, to focus on the scholarly and disciplinary enterprise (itself a significant word choice, given the milieu where business-like practices are god-terms) spoken of in the second part of the quote. While I do see a value in keeping the required first year course, I do not see that as the only thing I do. Nor do I see my teaching, whether of freshman or any other "required" composition course, as an unrelated expenditure of energy taken from a more important activity of scholarship or research. Who is excluding whom here? Instead, I would question what passes in this argument for research and what relation that has to any teaching. And I mean teaching in the broadest sense. Teaching, after all, occurs in all kinds of settings and institutions besides colleges and schools. Still, what is it about a required course that is necessarily so antithetical to research? Isn't that expression of antagonism between research and teaching precisely the problem, that for an entire century teaching has been looked upon in the university as different from, even secondary to, research, that teaching is seen as a fetter on research? This is hardly a new idea; it is the reigning idea. Our whole tenure and promotion system is based on this assumption of separate and unequal. The "new" idea is that of Ernest Boyer, among others, that we need to break out of this trap and view research and teaching in relation. I would add, in no simple relation, to be sure, but in an ecology. As I noted in my book *Thinking Through Theory: Vygotskian Perspectives on the Teaching of Writing*:

> Theory and practice are involved in each other in ways far more complicated than the usual pairing of these terms in discussion among composition teachers and scholars would indicate. Both theory and practice arise out of some broader, richer, and more dynamic life activity. (9)

I do, then, want to view the relations and Relations of theory to practice, including teaching practice, though in positing these concepts and stating my aim, I also want to take care not to reduce one to the other. The philosophy of internal relations discussed in the previous section allows me to do exactly this.

> For these reasons, I generally do not use the term "dialectic" to describe theory and practice relations, partly because I don't think the term always leaves room for the possibility that theory does not necessarily connect with my teaching, not in any conscious, short-termed way. I do theory of a certain sort; I teach in a certain style. What connects them is that they are separable in principle, but that they are also answerable to each other over time. Like the relation between art and life, theory and teaching should not be reduced to each other, but they are involved together in a whole set of changing relations over time. They have histories. (*Thinking Through Theory*, 10)

I see this position, then, as a moderate's position, a realist's view, that eschews all-or-nothing dichotomies.

Of course, the very binary theory/practice is itself problematic. What I ought to do here is, as implied by my first quote, mediate the two terms with a third, in this case the Vygotskian psychology concept of activity (*deyatel'nost*), but because that will only add complications of introducing that scholarship, and because the primary danger, as I see it, in academe is philosophical ideal-ism—the notion that ideas, knowledge, and theory are somehow independent of and above the material, corporeal fray, somehow more truthful then mere practice, let alone mere teaching—I instead will focus on practice to emphasize the connections among, and the materiality of, practices, including, theory which I now reconceptualize as "theorizing practice." Theory is not the oppo-site of practice; theory is not even a supplement to practice. Theory is practice, a practice of a particular kind and practice is always theoretical. (*Thinking Through Theory* 15)

So imagine theorizing practices as one Relation among a circle of Relations, all in a certain ecology. Theorizing practices, then, are related to writing prac-tices, teaching practices, curricular practices, disciplinary practices and profes-sional practices. Each practice is a cluster of practices, i.e., a Relation (R) that both "contains" these relations (r) in internalized and reduced form, and has "connections" (relations, little *r*), to other Relations. We might picture these practices as in figure 2.

Figure 2

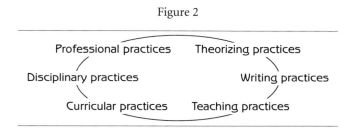

All of these categories obviously are aimed at composition. This list is somewhat arbitrary, as there could be any number of practices in relation to theorizing practices.

Writing practices. These are writing activities that could occur in or out of school environments including note taking, marginal comments on reading, transcribing, journaling, some homegrown rather than professional "creative writing," and some informal invention and discovery techniques (brainstorm-ing, lists of various sorts), and editing, revising, proofreading techniques. A quick way to begin to observe writing practices that occur apart from school or work contexts is to keep a regular watch of the shelves devoted to writing in a good bookstore. Such sections have exploded over the last decade from purely reference sections (grammar handbooks, dictionaries, thesauruses, etc.) to full blown writing for yourself sections, though few scholars in composition seem aware of these dramatic and important developments. It is, for example, stun-ning that at the same time that so-called expressive writing has been banished from college composition, which has been over-committed for a decade to the teaching solely of academic discourse, expressive discourse has seemingly taken over the shelves at bookstores and fills our email flickerings across the World Wide Web. But there are many other writing practices in life besides so-called expressive discourse. Most letters fit here, as do planning writing practices, everything from income tax preparation to grocery lists.

Teaching practices. I am concerned in this case with common practices for teaching writing which are deployed mostly, but not solely within the college classroom. More formal invention techniques like tagmemics surely fit here. Much of the conferencing and group work we do fits as well. Reading in order to write, class discussions of both readings and assignments in order to write, lectures, lessons on grammar and usage, research papers, processes of reading papers. commenting on papers, teachers' corrections, grades, assessment and evaluation processes, portfolios, peer editing, assignment sheets, syllabi and policy documents, all are teaching practices. Obviously, some of these activities and documents can function both as teaching practice and curricular practice.

Curricular practices. These are mostly departmental practices that reproduce, but also sometimes reform composition teaching, but go beyond simply involving the individual teacher and the individual classroom. These are shared practices within a department and among a faculty, in effect the culture of the department. The work of committees which set policy for composition courses fits here. Their lists of acceptable textbooks, examples of official syllabi for new teachers, the lists of criteria for acceptable writing or goals for the various courses, also fit. Curricular practices are often involved in controlling teaching and writing practices. So the collection of syllabi each term, class observations, teacher groups that work on curricular change, or on new teacher assimilation, or on overall evaluation (holistic scoring or portfolio reading, or placement or exit exams), as well as in house publications, conferences, orientation sessions, workshops, are located here and tend to promote uniformity across classrooms and up and down the curriculum. Yet probably the most important curricular practice is not directly or necessarily concerned with departmental consistency. It is teacher talk and lore that circulates in the local community, occurs regularly and almost always goes on unnoticed in the hall, in the lounge or in the mailroom. Such talk and lore forges bonds among teachers across the department, beyond each individual teacher and classroom, that often resist departmental policies.

Disciplinary practices. These are the formal ways of knowing and displaying knowledge in the discipline. I would label most of the practices that Stephen North studies in various methodological communities in composition in his book *The Making of Knowledge in Composition* as disciplinary practices. Writing across the curriculum and within the disciplines (WAC and WID) often get at these sorts of practices in other subjects, but WAC/WID scholars have done strangely little work on such practices in our own discipline of composition studies. I would include teacher lore as North describes it, as a disciplinary practice, but only when teachers are consciously working together to produce, circulate, and consume knowledge about writing and teaching beyond their own individual departments. I think this happens often at our conferences, as well as in networks like whole-language support groups or collaboratives like the Bay Area Writing Project. But this model distinguishes such lore from that which is constructed and circulated for local purposes. Finally, the process of writing and submitting articles and books to publishers lies on the border between disciplinary and professional practices.

Professional practices. These vocational or career related practices are epitomized by the activity of reading a paper at a professional conference, something that it is virtually impossible to explain to nonprofessionals. (Reading at someone is an infrequent practice these days, confined mostly to religious and legal institutions. Even journalists and politicians pretend they aren't reading at the listeners through the use of TelePrompTers, cue cards, and other devices.) Professional practices also include a version of talk and lore that corresponds to teacher talk and lore, and which has itself gone largely unnoticed and unstudied. But also, paying membership dues to be in national, regional, local professional organizations and attending their meetings, receiving and reading professional journals and books, serving on professional boards, reviewing articles for editors in the field, editing a journal, chairing a conference and putting together a program, editing a monograph or volume series, doing external tenure and promotion reviews, appearing on a television or radio program or writing popular accounts or responses for the media, all count as professional practices. Documents about class size, student language, the job market for new doctoral graduates, appropriate preparation for teachers, fit here.

Theorizing practices. Theory includes an array of possible practices from the reflective practice of Donald Schön, to a synthesizing sort of theorizing that integrates new information into a broad, preexisting frame (James Kinneavy's *A Theory of Discourse* is the classic example of this sort of theory), to a more analytic theorizing that takes an uncharted realm and tries to sort it out and in that process derives a theoretical frame (the work of Louise Phelps especially in *Composition as a Human Science* is an good example), to the more prevalent critiques that burrow into a subject or topic to demonstrate its materiality, or its embeddedness in discourses of class, race, gender, sexualities.

We can imagine these practices arrayed on the circumference of a circle as in Figure 2. This indicates both the fact that these practices are related and that this circumference is a kind of spectrum on which any number of new (or unmentioned) practices might be placed. The six practices then indicate a general vicinity in the ecology of composition practices as Relations, rather than any single static genre. Each practice changes relations with itself and with other practices across time—history and time being the key missing dimension here. (See Zebroski, "Writing Time" 1994, for a reconceptualization of temporality which needs to be factored in here.) We might more accurately envisage this circle of practices as a three dimensional cylinder, though again that makes this all too symmetrical and geometric. Some practices will expand in an historical moment while others contract. What is important is that in this ecology even the slightest changes in one Relation (i.e. practice), will necessarily have effects on all other Relations and relations in this ecology. Sometimes these effects are minor or nearly nonexistent.The changing Relations are distant. The effects are indirect, mediated, through other practices. But a single change will in the last instant effect the internal relations of the Relations and of the system as a whole. This allows us to focus less on whether or not change has occurred and simply accept the proposition that change always occurs even when we do not notice it. A consequence of this view is that it inverts ideology from being a means of keeping things the same, that is an instrument of reproduction, to ideology being a means for modulating, controlling, and slowing time, that is, as a way to domesticate changes that are inevitably happening on a daily basis in our classroom, the curriculum, the discipline, the profession, and our lives. Change rather than stasis becomes the assumption.

Now the scheme is too neat and tends to veil the fact that Relations are functions, that is, what a thing is depends on what it does. Function itself depends on location in history. The same Relation may well change function at different moments in history. The classic Marxist example is that the principle of steam power was well known by the ancients where it was employed to open temple doors. Steam power in the Classical period functioned as a toy of the elite, whereas the "invention" of the steam engine early in the industrial revolution functioned differently as a instrument of production. Likewise, literacy was a Relation which functioned differently in Classical society of the first century of our era (see Henry Gamble 1995 who takes a fascinating approach to ancient literacy while still extensively citing and using the more standard works) than it did in the industrial revolution and than it does now. To see these Relations functionally will help prevent us from essentializing them, but it will also give us some relatively stable concepts with which to work, something that the usual critique of essentialism and foundationalism fails to do.

This scheme, then, demands a study of history if we are to begin to understand how Relations develop, but also how they function. It is exactly for this reason that Marx in *Capital* seems to shift willy-nilly between theory (what is a commodity?) to history (how has the working day changed? what happened in England in the 1400 and 1500s that readied it for the industrial revolution?) to empirical work (notice in *Capital* the extensive use of contemporary governmental reports and newspaper accounts of capital and labor). For Marx and for the theorist coming from the perspective of a philosophy of internal relations, there is one recursive process at work here: one theorizes the current categories, then one takes the results of this unfreezing of categories and searches for interconnections, and begins to historicize them. This results itself in further theorizing and reworking of categories—so we can expect that commodity and capital and labor as they appear early on in *Capital* will look considerably different from how they look toward the end of *Capital*. And, at the same time, as one begins to see historical shifts and the changing functions, one needs to begin connecting such insights to the contemporary scene and the need for empirical work arises, which itself, when factored in, sends one back to do more theorizing and historicizing work.

This scheme does not allow us to easily see all that. Still, it does begin to make the philosophy of internal relations a bit more accessible to composition theory. As a heuristic, it begins to suggest some implications, one might even say some consequences, of all this theory.

III. IMPLICATIONS OF UNDERSTANDING COMPOSITION AS AN ECOLOGY OF PRACTICES

Composition studies, as a relatively new disciplinary formation, finds itself at a moment of both confirmation and crisis. The last three decades have established a firm basis not only of scholarship and research on writing, but also of all the other practices distinguished by this theory. By every statistical measure, composition has made great strides. We are a success story. Yet this is also a moment of despair and anger. Like American society at large, the volume on controversial issues in composition has gone way up. Some quarters of the society of composition, as Stephen North once called us, seem intent on making their views (theories and practices) hegemonic regardless of the cost. Toleration, which still, perhaps more than any other academic speciality, charactizes our conferences and professional dealings with each other, is being called into question. Certainly disagreement and contestation of arguments is essential to intellectual work; I do my share of that in this very article. And yet in this essay, I am not calling for the abolition of a segment of the field or discipline (I even see some value in the work of cognitivists, empiricists, externalists, and New Abolitionists, which are the farthest removed from my interests or commitments).

Recently, there also has been a too easy move in the discipline to categorize people and movements (expressivism is one example) and then to hold up an entire group or even generation for easy ridicule. (See the Shamoon and Wall Colloquy 1995—especially Schwegler—and the Lauer-Varnum exchange 1992–93, though the practice is much more widespread than these instances). I think there are solid economic and material reasons for such discourse and behavior occurring at this particular moment. It is not accident (Zebroski 1996). But I also believe that we can try to be ethical, that we can be careful about how we judge history and those first generation compositionists who under great duress started work in this discipline thirty year ago. They made some honest mistakes, but we need to keep in mind that we may not stand up nearly as well when the history of our time and deeds is written and we are judged. Perhaps the greatest advantage, then, of this theory of an ecology of practices is that it integrates an understanding of a large number of practices, and the communities which attend to them, into a tolerant, but not eclectic, theory. There is a place for nearly every sort of practice in our field and discipline in this theory and there is even room for great distances between some of them (we don't all have to live in the same neighborhood) and still there is the overall, integrative framework and worldview. It's a small field and discipline, and a small planet. We would do well to see the advantages of integration and nonviolence.

There are, of course, other implications of this theory of theory. Let me simply list some.

1. This theory dissolves what Berthoff (Berthoff 1990) calls killer dichotomies, in this case, theory versus practice, scholarship versus research, research versus teaching. By beginning with the concept of practice, we see these activities as related, though in no way identical, practices. Stephen North's work following the contours of the discipline suggests a scholarship versus research split. But this is not simply an epistemological binary. I would argue that the great fault in composition is between the disciplinary practices (but also some teaching and writing practices) that have funnelled into composition from English and the humanities (i.e., scholarship) and the disciplinary practices funneled into composition through education, especially English education, from the social sciences (i.e., research). This model sees both domains as part of a more encompassing category of disciplinary practices. So too, this theory clearly makes an important place for teachers and their lore without relegating their work to the bottom of a ladder. (King Arthur decided to array his knights around the Round Table for good reason after all.)

2. This theory reminds us that we too, as a field and discipline, have disciplinary and professional practices, and that these practices ought to play some role in our courses, especially our upper division courses. To an extent, the New Abolitionist argument descends from a decade of overemphasis in composition on academic discourse. At least one exponent of discourse community theory, Patricia Bizzell, has always insisted that inculcating students into academic discourse needs to be paralleled with introducing students to critique as a way to mitigate (perhaps transform) assimilation (perhaps indoctrination) pure and simple. In contrast, some of the New Abolitionists seem to simply want to keep the inculcation side of the dialectic. And then it seems logical to simply extend the study of academic discourse into the specific disciplines and then on into the professions. Yet, aside from the dangers of leaving out any sort of politically critical content in this process, a danger that seems to lead to rampant vocationalism and over specialization, there is something peculiar about this logic. The logical end of this thinking in biology is to introduce (or indoctrinate?) students into biological disciplinary and professional practices, in physics to physics disciplinary and professional practices, in sociology to sociological disciplinary and professional practices. Why should composition be any different? It is unclear to me why composition courses must submit entirely to every other discipline or profession on or off campus. This

is not to say that WAC, WID, and WIP (writing in the professions) is to be abolished. Rather, this model suggests we need to do all of these practices in some coherent way and that we should not neglect disciplinary and professional practices in composition itself.

3. This theory goes beyond a live and let live philosophy and contends that there are effects of one sort of Practice on all the other sorts of Practices. But it widens the possibilities while simultaneously characterizing effects in a qualitative way. So theory has effects on teaching in this model, but the question becomes from what direction do these effects come—is it through professional practices or writing practices? or somewhere else? how direct? and how strong are the effects when they leave theory and how strong are they when they reach teaching? And how is theory already an internal relation within teaching practices? So the questions change.

This theory of theory also suggests that we ought to be looking at the ways theory influences professional practices or how theory influences writing. In fact, a whole series of relational pairs emerge. The relations between Theory-Writing, Theory-Teaching, Theory-Curriculum, Theory-Profession, make us wonder which Practices have been most influenced by theory and when and why.

4. The thinking of the last sentence moves us into historical questions. I began to make the case at this article's start that composition was a rich environment for theorizing practices in the early 1970s. Why was that?

Recent work (Mack 1996) has responded that composition theory of the 1970s was related to, in fact preceded by, a renaissance, a virtual explosion, in the practices of teaching writing in the late 1960s and early 1970s. This study shows effects both ways, from teaching to theory, as well as theory to teaching. And the preliminary work suggests that a critical mass of teaching practices had to be reached before critical theory could develop. In essence, changing teaching practices changed theorizing practices, which changed the field and discipline as a whole.

I would speculate a bit and argue that, in a relational view, one can go even further. This relational model suggests that composition teaching led composition theory which probably led literary theory which is only now beginning to lead literary studies teaching. What an irony that the very folk castigated by some High Theorists, those lowly writing teachers of the 1960s and early 1970s, might well have started a "chain reaction" that made Theory possible!

5. In investigating historical change, this model suggests a way to begin to talk about temporalities of change. The tempo at which change occurs is a part of that change, and while metaphoric, this model can begin to get at such tempos by reconfiguring the order of the Relations (the Practices) at differing historical moments. Then one could begin to examine the rapidity and strength of effects, the assumption being that some Practices are "nearer" to (or "farther" from) the Practice which we are focusing on, than others. The flow of processes and connections in composition from teaching to theory, for example, seem "nearer" in

the 1970s in composition than the flow from theory to professional practices. So too at the very time that a huge amount of disciplinary work was taking place in the early 1980s, professional practices lagged far behind, something to which many of us who were around then could well attest.

For example, during a time of burgeoning disciplinary practices, there were extremely few outlets for all of this work. The few journals were not hospitable to disciplinary work, unless it was of a cognitive sort and only then sporadically. It was unheard of for entire books on composition to be written by a single author and, for many years, it was nearly impossible to get such single authored books on composition which were not textbooks accepted by publishers. There is a whole history that needs to be written about the publishers who were willing to take the chance with those first single-authored volumes on composition and why. It is interesting that the first advertisements for non-textbook volumes, with only a few exceptions, appeared in *CCC* in 1981 and 1982 and were lists of books published by Boynton/Cook Publishers. So the flow in one relation (teaching to theory) was fast and strong in the 1970s, while the flow in the other relation (disciplinary practices to professional practices) was nearly nonexistent in the 1970s and was slow and weak in the 1980s. What might account for this? Such questions this theory poses.

6. Finally, my model provides a way to distinguish the disciplinary origins of composition studies from the teaching or study of composition as a field. Robin Varnum (Varnum 1992) raises some good points about the inadequacies of recent historical descriptions of composition in the first half of the century. Yet starting from this theory, I see Janice Lauer as being more precise in describing her experience in the 1960s and 1970s as disciplinary. In fact, my model suggests that composition is a discipline and independent profession only when professional and disciplinary practices are as fully developed as the other practices, and the accompanying social apparatuses are material realities in an ecology of composition practices. As long as either the apparat or the practices (writing, teaching, curricular, disciplinary, professional) are undeveloped or uncontrolled by those "in " composition studies, then no discipline has formed. This argues for a relatively late date for disciplinary social formation in composition, regardless of how many generations of great teachers and curricular practitioners or even scholars went before. It also implies that much "history" is retrojected narrative of current forces, material conditions, and anxieties. In this view, it is obvious that the rise of disciplinary histories in the 1980s was less about "history" than about the emerging discipline of that moment.

A theory of theory in composition, like all theory, is a thinking device, as Yuri Lotman calls it, a speculative instrument as Ann E. Berthoff, citing Richards, names it. It is a heuristic that suggests some directions and some implications, but that guarantees nothing. The compositionist can use and extend such concepts and discover the truths in them, exactly to the extent that such devices suggest insight. (*Priem* is the Russian word for device, which also can be translated as *method, way* or *trick*). This is not in any sense Grand

Theory or High Theory. The end is there in its beginning—to get back to the richness, the materiality, the dynamics, the ecologies of life activity, in our case, the writing moment. My doctoral advisor put it best:

> the use of theory as basis of evaluating what we do: learning in the process of work, praxis; testing what we do against our theoretical beliefs; challenging the status quo. Theory becomes the medium through which the actual relations and connections in the world, the culture, the society, are discovered. *Theory as a medium of discovery; theory as a heuristic.* (Bateman 1996)

NOTES

1.   The reader, seeing the word "ecology" and "practice," may assume that this essay is extending or revising or critiquing the work of Louise Wetherbee Phelps (1991, 1988) regarding knowledge in composition, which uses similar terms. Such an assumption would be a mistake. Our work inhabits two virtually unrelated universes of discourse. Phelps does phenomenological theory; I see my work as critical theory. Phelps is concerned with knowledge, I with social relations and the circulation and distribution of power. Phelps finds value in Aristotle; I prefer to go to what is left of Heraclitus. Phelps tries to think ahead of the status quo. I try to think around, that is, to resist it. Phelps, I believe, though I have not consulted her about this, sees her work as being broadly centrist, if it can be said to be political in any sense, while I, a scholar of the left, would argue that Phelps's work has serious potential import for the political right of the future, of the twenty-first century.

All of this can be summarized be looking back at the word "ecology." Phelps uses the term often in her *Composition as a Human Science,* as well as in other contexts. She notes the importance of Urie Bronfenbrenner's *book* in this regard. But she also adds to her concept of ecology the idea of self-regulating systems derived from chaos science and the work of lifespan developmental psychology, which is explicitly, forthrightly, Hegelian. On the other hand, my use of "ecology" comes out of a qualitative research educational seminar I was taking in the fall of 1978 in which we read Bronfenbrenner's *article* in *Educational Researcher.* What struck *me* about that article was Bronfenbrenner's interest in, quotation and use of, the work of A. N. Leontiev in Soviet psychology. After all, Bronfenbrenner, among many other accomplishments, did impressive cross cultural research on American versus Soviet educational systems. So I saw, and see, a political import, a left politics, in that idea of ecology.

Having lined up some of the intellectual differences, let me be quick to assert that I think that the work of Phelps has been rudely and radically under-appreciated, that it is just about the only work in composition that I would tempted to label brilliant, and that there is (or ought to be) an important niche for her kind of work in the field and discipline of composition studies. This may seem inconsistent, but as I take up in the last section of this essay, toleration is *not* eclecticism. We need toleration and preservation of differences in our disciplinary and professional ecology. Calls for abolition, for orthodoxy and its necessary twin, heresy, and for politically motivated purges, only hurt ourselves in the end. This view does not arise from an easy going pluralism and celebration of the other, but rather is very much a strategy of self-preservation a la Bakhtin. It is part and parcel of a radical doubt about knowing, in the short run, precisely what the consequences of one's actions can or will be and thus, taking care of self.

PART TWO

Critiquing Theories in Practice

CHAPTER FOUR

The Dialogic Function of Composition Pedagogy
Negotiating between Critical Theory and Public Values

Rebecca Moore Howard

*I*N ANIMATED BATTLES OF THE 80S AND 90S, TEACHERS AND SCHOLARS OF composition have defended themselves and their discipline against what they variously describe as the hostility, contempt, or indifference of the literature faculty. Unlike most other internecine English contests, usually only one side of this debate is waged in public print: whereas compositionists' arguments are a familiar form of scholarly publication in composition studies (see, for example, Little and Rose; Miller), contradictory beliefs held by scholars of literature seldom find their way into print. Instead, the arguments of literature faculty are typically expressed in semiotic silences (e.g., Marshall Gregory's description of English departments being composed of literary theorists and teachers of literature, without any mention of compositionists)[1] or in performative silencings (e.g., denying tenure to compositionists). The arguments of literature scholars can also be traced in the college catalogues that list advanced offerings in literature but only required normative courses in composition; in the dominance of tenured faculty in the teaching of literature but adjuncts and teaching assistants in composition; and in comparisons of salary and advancement for literature and composition faculty.

In this agonistic climate, some scholars of composition have endeavored to assert that the work of composition and rhetoric should not be measured by the standards of literature. Composition, so goes this reasoning, is different from literature and should be measured by its own standards.[2] Others have endeavored to demonstrate that composition actually does measure up to the values of literature. One strand of this reasoning asserts that composition and literature are inextricably linked (e.g., Horner 1983). Another asserts that composition pedagogy is a form of theory. A familiar variant of this assertion is one described by Peter Smagorinsky and Melissa E. Whiting: behind all pedagogy is theory, articulated or unarticulated. To teach, therefore, is to practice theory (Horner 108).

This essay offers what I believe is powerful counter-evidence to that assertion, counterevidence emerging from my explorations into how the figures of the author and the plagiarist are described and represented in our culture and especially in our pedagogies. In those explorations, I have found that composition scholarship, especially in its discussions of collaboration, appreciably accords with the "new" author emerging in critical theory, the author who neither is nor can be autonomous and originary. Composition pedagogy, in contrast, continues to uphold and reproduce the "old" author inherited from Romantic literary theory, the author that still prevails in lay culture. In a variety of articles and books, Martha Woodmansee and Peter Jaszi have endeavored to demonstrate that the public, including copyright law, persists in clinging to the Romantic author, notwithstanding critical theory's challenges to it. In matters of the author, I find that composition studies comports with the lay public rather than with the discipline of textual studies. In at least the arena of representing the author, composition pedagogy is *not* a form of theory—or, rather, its "theories" are lay rather than disciplinary theories.

This is a troubling statement for me to make, for it undermines an argument by which many hope to win better treatment for composition and rhetoric.

I am indebted to the composition faculty at Southern Illinois University at Carbondale, and especially Ronda L. Dively, for increasing my understanding of how readily my argument can be co-opted for the purpose of demonstrating the inferior status of composition studies. That appropriation and distortion is indeed possible if one is measuring composition pedagogy by the standards of literary theory. In this essay, however, I am urging that composition pedagogy be measured by its own standards—which, I am proposing, include a dialogic function. I find myself taking an argumentative tack paralleling that of W.E.B. DuBois in *The Souls of Black Folk:* nineteenth-century African Americans suffered from a racial "double consciousness" in which they could fully appraise themselves neither by their own standards nor by those of white people. Composition studies labors in a state of intellectual double consciousness, trying to demonstrate its value by asserting its identity with literary studies.[3] The relation, however, is not one of identity. Rather, the two are separate though related disciplines within the larger category of "English," and each needs to be evaluated by its own standards.

COMPOSITION PEDAGOGY'S "DIFFERENCE"

Those standards must in part be derived from an appreciation of difference. An examination of three descriptions of citation—one from a critical theorist, one from a composition theorist, and one from a composition textbook—reveals significant divergences that, as I will show, can lead to an informed appreciation of the work of composition pedagogy.

In her 1991 *Crimes of Writing,* critical theorist Susan Stewart investigates transgressive forms of writing such as forgery and graffiti. When she says, "An ideal . . . device of citation would be a full (and necessarily impossible) history of the writer's subjectivity"(25), she emphasizes how arbitrary must any practice of citation be, since none of "our" words or ideas are "our own." We cannot fully cite our sources, Stewart says, because to do so, a writer would have to limn his or her own intellectual history. In *Crimes of Writing* Stewart herself does engage in citation, but she acknowledges the contingency and arbitrariness of the practice.

Composition scholar Elizabeth Rankin strikes a similar chord when, in her 1994 book *Seeing Yourself as a Teacher,* she enumerates tenets of her theory of authorship:

> that the idea of 'authorship' is problematic indeed; that language itself is inherently dialogic, shot through with voices of all those we have read and met and spoken with and listened to; that all our theories are socially constructed, sometimes of the most unlikely and incongruous materials; and that the stories we tell about teaching are really theories in themselves. (83)

Rankin then goes on to declare, "And besides, the simple truth is that I couldn't begin to name all the sources of my own theoretical thinking" (84). For her, as for Stewart, complete citation is impossible.

I remember my own pilgrimage to full citation. One of my first essays about transgressive authorship, an essay that was eventually published as "Plagiarisms, Authorships, and the Academic Death Penalty," was initially rejected by journal reviewers. One of their criticisms was that I cited too much. They wanted to hear the author's "own" voice. One reviewer even said that the essay sounded too much like the students' patchwriting that it was describing.[4]

Today I cite much less. Part of my maturation as a scholar has been to learn that full citation is not actually a desideratum for professional writers; equally important is the appearance of autonomy, of having one's "own" words and ideas.

Composition students, however, are urged to engage in full citation. Although acknowledged by scholars such as Rankin and Stewart, the impossibility of full citation is suppressed in composition textbooks, as is the desirability of limiting citations. Rise B. Axelrod and Charles R. Cooper provide a typical textbook statement on plagiarism:

> Writers—students and professionals alike—occasionally misuse sources by failing to acknowledge them properly. The word *plagiarism,* which derives from the Latin word for "kidnapping," refers to the unacknowledged use of another's words, ideas, or information. Students sometimes get into trouble because they mistakenly assume that plagiarizing occurs only when another writer's exact words are used without acknowledgment. . . . So keep in mind that you must indicate the source of any ideas or information you have used in your research for a paper, whether you have paraphrased, summarized, or quoted directly from the source. (602)

Axelrod and Cooper then list three causes of plagiarism: ignorance of citation conventions, sloppy note-taking, and students' "doubt[ing] their ability to
write the paper by themselves." These pitfalls can be avoided, though: "This
chapter *makes clear* how to incorporate sources into your writing and how to
acknowledge your use of those sources" (603) Like most other composition
textbooks, *The St. Martin's Guide* elides the complexities of citation and plagiarism; all can and will be made "clear." It then becomes the student's responsibility to adhere to those clear guidelines, notwithstanding the belief among
composition scholars and critical theorists that this clear task is actually very
murky, indeed. If composition pedagogy is a form of theory, why do its representations of student authorship, revealed in its injunctions against plagiarism
and in favor of citation, contradict those of composition scholarship?[5]

These contradictory representations of authorship demonstrate a disjunc-
tion between composition theory and composition pedagogy. We need not,
however, assume that lack of unanimity between composition theory and
composition pedagogy signals a fissure in the discipline; rather, it may signal
the discipline's commendable attention to its remarkably varied and powerful
audiences.

CRITICAL THEORIES OF AUTHORSHIP

In representations of the student author, composition scholarship accords
much more closely with critical theory than with the composition pedagogy
expressed in and guided by rhetoric textbooks. The status of the author has
been a focus of attention in twentieth-century criticism, with New Criticism
insisting that the text and not authors' intentions are the origin of meaning.
(Already a difference between composition pedagogy and critical theory is
apparent, since composition pedagogy aims to help student writers articulate
and pursue what are represented as their own intentions.) In "The Intentional
Fallacy," one of the landmarks in this strand of criticism, Wimsatt and
Beardsley declare that the author's intentions should not be a criterion for critical evaluation of a text. Such declarations distance New Criticism from the
Romantic textual theories that dominated the nineteenth century, when the
author—solitary, autonomous, free of influence, and shouldering the responsibility for what Stewart calls "an unbearable originality" (22)—invested texts
with an intentionality that governed not only the meaning of the text but also
the evaluation of the author's character.[6]

In 1968 Roland Barthes contributed to the undermining of the Romantic
attribution of divinity to the author when he combined it with the
Nietzschean declaration of the death of God: if the author is divine and God is
dead, then the author, too, is dead. If the author is dead, then intentionality is
not only inappropriate for evaluating a text but is unavailable for interpreting
it. But whereas Foucault a year later would offer fresh proposals for the text
itself as the source of meaning, Barthes locates meaning in the reader:

Thus is revealed the total existence of writing: a text is made of multiple writings, drawn from many cultures and entering into mutual relations of dialogue, parody, contestation, but there is one place where this multiplicity is focused and that place is the reader, not, as was hitherto said, the author. The reader is the space on which all the quotations that make up a writing are inscribed without any of them being lost; a text's unity lies not in its origin but in its destination. (129)

And that reader, Barthes declares, is without history; he or she can only be described in terms of the person reading at the moment of reading, not in terms of that reader as a collective or unified, transtemporal subject.

Foucault, too, attests the death of the author: "It is obviously insufficient to repeat empty slogans: the author has disappeared; God and man died a common death" (Barthes 121). His essay "What Is an Author?" focuses on the name of the author and how readers construct from the text an "author" that may have little or nothing to do with the person who composed the text. An author's name differs from other proper names in that it functions as a means of classifying texts and establishing relationships among them: a change in how we view an author's works accomplishes a change in the meaning of the author's name (Barthes 122–3). This "author-function" is not attributed through naming but is instead a rational entity constructed through a complex process that includes our projecting dimensions of our "way of handling texts" upon an individual author-function, as we assign qualities like "profound" or "creative" to it (Barthes 127). So Foucault, too, attends to the role of the reader, but for him the reader is a collective that constructs an author-function from the text.

Although Jacques Derrida's work is often "misconstrued as radically anti-intentionalist," Séan Burke's reading of *Grammatology,* Book II, finds Derrida "actually resist[ing] the polarities of the debate" (1995). Derrida acknowledges that intentionality matters but denies that it fully controls the text; the text can have signification beyond the meaning intended by the author.

The successors to Barthes, Foucault, and Derrida have developed these ideas even further. Much of contemporary critical theory focuses not on the reader but on the author—but for the purpose of debunking the Romantic ideology of individual, autonomous, originary authorship (e.g., Piglia; Randall) This line of reasoning is not without its adherents in composition studies. Conducting a rhetorical analysis of a "developmental" student's writing process, Glynda Hull and Mike Rose conclude that patchwriting, which is commonly regarded as a too-heavy appropriation of language from a source text, is actually a valuable writing strategy whereby inexperienced students learn unfamiliar discourse. Working from the theories of Derrida, Mikhail Bakhtin, and Jacques Lacan, Mary Minock laments the gap between postmodern composition theories of the author and Romantic composition pedagogy. She undertakes the task of bridging that gap. Students' imitation, she says, is always creative, if for no other reason than that it places the passage of text into a new context (499). "Repetition presumes alterity; the more a text is repeated and altered, the more it is committed to unconscious memory, and the more the power of its words and syntax is there to be imitated" (501). Minock therefore encourages her students to patchwrite, unfettered.

COMPOSITION THEORIES OF COLLABORATION

Hull and Rose's and Minock's treatments of patchwriting go only a little beyond representations of collaborative authorship that are widely endorsed in composition scholarship. Anne Ruggles Gere's 1987 book *Writing Groups* represents an important transitional position between the notion of individual authorship and the vision that all authorship is collaborative:

> Theories of collaborative learning . . . build upon an opposition to alienation and to the highly individualistic view inherent in traditional concepts of authorship and emphasize the communal aspects of intellectual life. In the collaborative view individual genius becomes subordinate to social interactions and intellectual negotiations among peers. (75)

Gere's description very much accords with critical theories of authorship, lending credence to the unity of composition and literature. Nor is hers an isolated voice; collaborative theory increasingly questions the possibility of autonomous authorship, as John Schilb suggests when he says that collaboration is valued for its challenge to "the misleading image of the isolated writer" (1992, 107). In the same volume, John Clifford denies the possibility of scholarly autonomy: "Academics have never existed as autonomous agents outside disciplinary or institutional discourse" (1992, 174). Edward M. White offers this cautious 1995 composition theory of collaborative authorship:

> In one sense, all writing is collaborative: Every writer needs some kind of audience, some conversation, some reading, some responding. The peer groups that are now part of many writing classes serve as sounding boards for initial ideas, responders to drafts, and even editors for presentation copies of final drafts. The picture of the writer as a solitary genius, holed up in an attic, emerging on occasions waving a manuscript that expresses his or her inner self, has not been a useful one for writing instruction. (139)

In a much earlier article that might qualify him for the title of "transdiscursive author" if not "founder of a science,"[7] Kenneth A. Bruffee observes that collaborative learning seems a comfortable pedagogy until we recognize that it is "not merely a better pedagogy" but also a model of "how knowledge is generated, how it changes and grows" (1984, 647). It is that model, made increasingly explicit in the accretion of collaborative theory, that brings composition scholarship on collaboration so close to contemporary critical theories in which authorship is not autonomous and cannot be originary and in which a writer's text cannot clearly be differentiated from its sources: a writer's text *always already* functions as a repetition of its sources. In its representations of the author, composition theory accords very closely with critical theory.

COMPOSITION TEXTBOOK REPRESENTATIONS OF PLAGIARISM

Composition pedagogy, on the other hand, evidences great discomfort with such theories. It's all well and good to assign a paper and then place students in peer response groups; that makes collaboration a useful means of developing an individual student's paper, and it defines *collaboration* as an activity that takes place face to face between one living writer and another. It's quite another thing, though, to suggest that a student writer "collaborates" with her precursor texts, and that "her" text cannot be differentiated from "theirs." That's when proposals such as those of Hull and Rose and Minock pose dangers from which most composition pedagogy recoils.

Critical theorist Martha Woodmansee succinctly describes the notion of authorship that prevails outside English studies: "In contemporary usage an 'author' is an individual who is solely responsible—and thus exclusively deserving of credit—for the production of a unique, original work" (1994, 36). But this vision of the author prevails *inside* English studies, as well: it prevails in pedagogy's representations of plagiarism and citation.[8] The excerpt from Axelrod and Cooper's *The St. Martin's Guide*, with its assurance of clear guidelines for citation, is typical of pedagogical representations in which no blurring of "my" text and "theirs" is necessary or permissible. Linda Anstendig and David Hicks' textbook implies a similar clarity when it observes, "Most of the cases of student plagiarism arise because of uncertainties about, or insufficient attention to, correct research procedures" (54). The uncertainties to which they refer are not in authorship itself but in the student who doesn't yet know "correct research procedures."

Emphasizing the need to make major rather than minor changes when appropriating the language of a source text, Ramage and Bean's *The Allyn and Bacon Guide to Writing* places the issue squarely in the "realm of ethics" (561). Mary Lynch Kennedy, William J. Kennedy, and Hadley M. Smith also focus on the need for substantial change, and their *Writing in the Disciplines,* 3rd edition, provides extensive guidelines for successful paraphrasing, including the suggestion that what's needed is for the student author to achieve distance from the concrete language of the source text (24). The rhetoric section of Sheridan Baker's *Practical Stylist with Readings and Handbook* also emphasizes the need for students to make major changes:

> The solution is, again, to take down and mark quotations accurately in your notes or to summarize succinctly in your own words, words as far away from the original as possible, keeping the two as distinct as you can, so that nothing from your source will leak through your notes, unmarked, into your paper, arousing your reader's suspicions. (408)

Baker's passage is notable in its allowing the possibility of ambiguity: first, the student is to keep self and source "as distinct *as you can*," and second, it is readers' suspicions rather than some transcendent textual purity that governs the effort. Far more than most textbooks, Baker's pedagogical treatment of student authorship suggests the ambiguity of interpretation that is intertextuality.

Brenda Spatt devotes more than the usual page or two to plagiarism; her instruction on the issue appears in six different passages of *Writing from Sources,* 4th edition. Like other textbooks, hers urges students to speak in their own voices, and it imagines paraphrase as an exact linguistic translation: "When you paraphrase, you retain everything about the original writing but the words" (117).[9] But Spatt doesn't limit her injunctions against plagiarism to legal or ethical admonishments; she also points out that plagiarism prevents learning (116, 119). She's right; if we only repeat verbatim the words of others, we don't necessarily understand their ideas. If, however, we can rephrase the words of others, we are forcing ourselves to understand those ideas, especially if the rephrasing is done in the absence of the original text.

These textbooks propose a variety of reasons for not plagiarizing: ethical considerations, the need to avoid readers' punitive actions, the need to learn. But they all advance the possibility of authorial autonomy, the possibility of something called "your own" words. Proper writing from sources is an act of paraphrase and citation, and the paraphrase is an exact translation of the source's ideas into significantly different words.

The difficulty is that one doesn't readily leap from unfamiliar ideas in an unfamiliar discourse to the ability to rephrase those ideas. The typical intermediate stage is appropriating the words in which those ideas were originally expressed; the intermediate stage is patchwriting. It doesn't take much, in fact, to assert that all our writing at all "stages" is patchwriting. Describing collaboration, Charlotte Thralls says,

> According to Bakhtin, "The word in language is half someone else's." Language is never the purview of the individual only, but always an interaction of the individual with *others* because language is, in Bakhtin's words, "not a neutral media that passes freely and easily into the private property of the speaker's intentions; it is populated—overpopulated—with the intentions of others." (66)

Insofar as composition pedagogy urges students to a heuristic translation, then, it contradicts neither composition theory nor critical theory. But when pedagogy invokes students' "own" words and "own" ideas and declares that patchwriting is unethical, subject to punishment, or countereducational, a great chasm opens. Patchwriting, according to composition theory and critical theory, is at the very least a necessary stage in learning new ideas. By many accounts, it is how all of us write all of the time. Hence patchwriting is not an ethical transgression but a natural function of academic life, and citation is not a separation of self and source but a research trail, a gesture toward language and ideas encountered recently enough that the writer can still identify the source. The question is not whether we patchwrite; we all do, all of the time. The question is only whether we do so clumsily, or with panache.

COMPOSITION PEDAGOGY IN THE CONTACT ZONE

Why is it so difficult for composition pedagogy to embrace these critical insights? Drawing on the work of Peter Stallybrass and Allon White, Susan Miller, Pierre Bourdieu, and Sharon Crowley, I have argued elsewhere that it is intellectual hierarchy that makes the plagiarist such a perennial, persistent figure in composition pedagogy's representations of student authorship. In "The New Abolitionism Comes to Plagiarism," I review two related phenomena in the American academy: the nineteenth-century emergence of composition pedagogy and the early-twentieth-century emergence of students' plagiarism as a perceived social problem. Both of these phenomena derive at least in part from intellectuals' need to differentiate themselves from those who are only functionally literate.[10] The recently educated masses of the nineteenth century were reading trashy novels and newspapers and failing to appreciate the esoteric texts of the intellectuals; composition instruction endeavored to change their tastes. The masses were also gaining access to institutions of higher education from which their forebears had been barred; labeling patchwriting (which had previously been considered an acceptable textual practice) as unethical plagiarism established an intellectual hierarchy within the academy. By virtue of their patchwriting, students were on the bottom of that hierarchy; and by virtue of patchwriting's ethical transgression, they could be ejected from the academy altogether.

One constructive response to this chilling scenario is to advocate the decriminalization of patchwriting. "The New Abolitionism Comes to Plagiarism" urges that patchwriting cease to be categorized as plagiarism and instead be treated as a natural part of academic writing—that students be taught how to write sophisticated intertextual prose. This is, I believe, a satisfying and plausible pedagogical remedy.

My present task, though, is not to describe sound pedagogy but to explore disciplinary quandaries. What does it mean that, despite the mid-century emergence of the discipline of composition studies and despite the late-century assertion of composition scholarship that no writing is ever autonomous, composition pedagogy nevertheless continues to sustain the inherently hierarchical binary of the autonomous author and the unethical, ignorant, plagiarizing patchwriter? Although I believe my own argument in "The New Abolitionism"—that intellectual hierarchy is a significant factor in the early-twentieth-century criminalization of patch writing—that argument provides only an aetiology. It does not explain why the ideal of the autonomous writer persists in the face of contradictory scholarship.

Ironically, it is composition pedagogy that provides a plausible explanation. We teach our students to be attentive to audience. Composition studies, in the aggregate, also has an audience to which it must attend. In making this assertion,

I should identify not only who it is that I consider to be the "audience" of composition studies but also what I believe the discipline's relationship to that audience to be.

We can think of the audience of composition studies as compositionists; thus scholarship in the discipline functions as a sort of talking to oneself, when "composition studies" is described in the aggregate. Indeed, that is how most academic disciplines conduct business; for the most part, the audience for their work is the participants in the discipline. Yet this phenomenon of disciplinary audience has, strangely, become a target for attack since postmodern perspectives emerged in textual studies. Journalist Richard Bernstein's incredulity after visiting a Modern Language Association convention is just one among a plethora of critiques (16). From the perspective of Bernstein and many others, the language—and hence the ideas—of textual studies should be transparently accessible to all educated persons. Somehow an analogy between textual studies and, say, chemical engineering does not occur to commentators like Bernstein. Somehow textual studies is different from other academic disciplines, in that many inside as well as outside the discipline believe that textual studies should be accessible to a non-expert audience. And it is specifically postmodern textual theory—the very discourse in which the autonomous author is challenged—that is rancorously charged with the sin of exclusionary language.

When one considers the history of composition studies, a subfield or at least a relative of textual studies, this avowed necessity of a public audience seems not so strange, after all. Composition scholarship speaks not just to compositionists, and composition pedagogy speaks not just to its students. Both of them speak to the public that demands college composition instruction. Composition studies arose not just as an esoteric search for knowledge about writing, but as a way of relieving a social problem, the problem of appropriate literacy for the newly-educated masses. Composition pedagogy continues to be funded in colleges large and small because of a public perception (a "public" that includes a group as diverse as the professor of physics, the neighborhood real-estate agent, and the state legislator) that literacy, normatively conceived, is important to American citizenship and economic and social advancement and that it is the business of college composition to assure this normative level of literacy. So the audience for composition studies includes compositionists (both composition teachers and composition scholars); composition students; and a larger, concerned public (both inside and outside the academy). The students of composition and the larger public are primarily concerned with composition pedagogy; their complaints about esoteric textual studies may well be rooted in a hope that textual scholars will not lose sight of what the public defines as the paramount mission of transmitting normative literacy skills.

Composition scholars' relationship to this diverse audience often tends to operate on very traditional notions of conflict and persuasion. In *Ancient*

Rhetorics, an undergraduate writing textbook drawing upon precepts of classical rhetoric, Sharon Crowley describes the classical notion of audience as those whom the rhetor will sway to her point of view. Cicero in *De Oratore* notes that the rhetor must consider whether the audience enters the rhetorical situation as "hostile, indifferent, or accepting." The audience's willingness to change its mind relates directly to the extent to which personal identity is tied to the argument, along with "the emotional intensity with which [the audience] clings to an opinion" (124).

A good deal of composition's interchanges with the larger public, notably in writing-across-the-curriculum programs, works this vein, endeavoring to persuade that public to what compositionists consider to be enlightened viewpoints about literacy instruction. Corollary to this endeavor is a resistance to and even a demonizing of public values. Those who espouse textual values that conflict with those of composition theory are often depicted as the enemies of composition studies, enemies who must either be persuaded to more enlightened viewpoints or be vanquished. Thus Bruce Horner's allusion to teachers' work being coopted by social pressures and his allusion to "powerful others committed to the use of composition courses to police and exclude students from higher education" draw on a commonplace in disciplinary discourse (522).

In the classical notion of audience, argument is a one-way affair, involving persuasion rather than negotiation and exchange. The rhetor is not among the persuaded; if she changes her mind as a result of the exchange, she and her argument have failed. This is not, however, the only model of audience and argument available. "Clearly," say William Covino and David Jolliffe, "real communication does not operate on such an immediate, one-way, agonistic street" (13). The "real" communication of which Covino and Jolliffe speak is multi-directional, dialectic; when successful, it results in change for all parties concerned.

Accountable only to its discipline-internal audience, composition theory can recoil in horror from the hierarchical assumptions underlying public perceptions of college literacy instruction. Instead of running the risk of being affected by those perceptions, theorists can engage in New Abolitionist calls for the end of normative instruction altogether.[11] But introductory college composition pedagogy must account for and respond to its audience; it must uphold the values of both composition scholarship and the academic and lay public. My studies of the representations of student authorship suggest that when those values conflict, composition pedagogy aligns itself with public values, not those of composition theory. This unfortunate reflex not only renders composition pedagogy a-theoretical—fueling the long-held suspicion that composition studies is not "real intellectual work"—but it also places a growing distance between composition pedagogy and the increasingly theoretical orientation of composition scholarship.

But if we can think of argument not as persuasion but as negotiation, perhaps we can engage arguments about literacy instruction—including arguments about the functions of patchwriting—that will put composition pedagogy in the salutary position of reconciling the values of composition theory and the lay and academic public. Introductory college composition can involve composition theorists in negotiations with a larger public, negotiations that compositionists cannot and should not necessarily expect to "win." Composition pedagogy is *not* the same thing as composition theory; theory can maintain the illusion of its disciplinary autonomy (even while denying the possibility of individual autonomy), and pedagogy cannot—even that pedagogy which offers models of autonomous authorship to its students! Composition pedagogy and its dialogue with the public is what has made composition studies such a difficult place to live; all too often that public does seem a "powerful other," and all too often composition pedagogy *is* simply coopted, estranged from composition theory. Yet that dialogue is also what makes composition studies such an exciting place to live. Pedagogy is the contact zone in which theory talks with (not to) that larger public.[12] If as a discipline we can imagine that conversation in dialogic terms, perhaps we can converse in such a way that we cease capitulating to or running from public values that contradict those which our theories have developed, and instead build syllabi and curricula that engage the ceaseless process of honoring and negotiating the values of both.[13]

Does this mean that composition teachers need not be composition scholars? No, it does not. Distress over the chasm between composition scholarship and composition pedagogy was expressed by Maxine Hairston, who, as 1982 chair of the Conference on College Composition and Communication, called for all composition teachers to be composition scholars. The assumption underlying Hairston's call is that composition pedagogy should be guided by composition scholarship. Yet despite a proliferation of Ph.D. programs in composition and rhetoric, together with an increasing number of professional journals and regional conferences, the great majority of composition teachers today are not composition scholars by anyone's definition; it is even possible today for a college's writing department to include no composition scholars at all.

It would, however, mean that composition teaching and composition scholarship are not the same thing. It would instead mean that composition teaching is responsive both to composition scholarship and public values. As a composition theorist, I am horrified by the figure of the plagiarist that persists in composition pedagogy. But as a writing program administrator, I see a certain dialogic wisdom to it. It signals composition pedagogy's continuing respect for public values. The danger comes, I believe, when pedagogy goes too far in either direction, toward scholarship or toward lay values; then its dialogic function ceases. Composition pedagogy performs a unique, remarkable function in higher education in America. Coming to an understanding and appreciation of that singular function may do more than anything else to establish an honorable place for composition studies in the academy and in English departments. And that, in turn, may enable composition pedagogy to accomplish its dialogic function, rather than converging with one pole while ignoring the other. Then, instead of simply continuing to endorse the notions of plagiarism and authorship valued by the public, pedagogy could be the site at which the findings of critical theory have the opportunity to influence those values—and vice versa.

NOTES

1. Gregory's argument appears in "The Many-Headed Hydra." In a reconsideration of the article, Gregory calls the omission of composition and rhetoric a "neglect occasioned mainly by space requirements" and not a "principled neglect" ("Marshall Gregory Responds," 92).

2. This line of reasoning has been used in support of establishing separate departments of writing and English. Separationism has gained enough adherents that the Conference on College Composition and Communication now includes a Special Interest Group on free-standing writing programs.

3. The comparison here is theoretical rather than cultural. I am not suggesting that the situation of composition studies compares with that of African Americans at the turn of the century. Rather, I am suggesting that Du Bois' analytic framework can be applied in more than one situation.

4. *Patchwriting* is a term defined in a still earlier article: "Copying from a source text and then deleting some words, altering grammatical structures, or plugging in one-for-one synonym-substitutes" (Howard, *"Pentimento"* 233).

5. Although the distinction is seldom clear in college composition textbooks or in college policies on academic integrity, patchwriting is quite a different activity from purchasing a term paper. Nor is the difference simply one of intention, as is so often asserted. Patchwriting often derives neither from ignorance of citation practices nor from an indifference to textual ethics, but from an effort to understand and enter difficult, unfamiliar discourse. The conflation of patchwriting and ghostwriting, together with the erroneous beliefs that intention separates the two and that either ignorance or immorality causes patchwriting, makes end-of-the-semester writing program administration a needlessly complicated, onerous job.

6. See, for example, Ralph Waldo Emerson's *Nature:* "A man's power to connect his thought with its proper symbol, and so to utter it, depends on the simplicity of his character, that is, upon his love of truth and his desire to communicate it without loss" (IV 2).

7. The terms are Foucault's, and they are useful for marking texts that have wide-ranging influence upon succeeding scholarship. The difference between the two is not always obvious, Foucault acknowledges, but he does identify Freud and Marx as transdiscursive authors, or "initiators of discursive practices." These authors differ from, say, Anne Radcliffe, who made available to her successors analogies upon which the Gothic novel was built. Transdiscursive authors make not only analogies but also differences available to their successors. They are to be differentiated from the founder of a science (e.g., Galileo, Saussure), in that the latter function as successors to their predecessors, and their followers refine, test, and

prove their theories. The work of the initiator of a discursive practice, in contrast, provides the measuring-stick for the work of his or her successors. A return to origins is not uncommon among practitioners of such discourses, e.g., Chomsky's return to Descartes. In these returns, practitioners examine the interstices of the text—its gaps and omissions—and enrich the discourse. The discoveries and rediscoveries made in these returns "reinforce the enigmatic link between an author and his works." "These returns, an important component of discursive practices, form a relationship between 'fundamental' and mediate authors, which is not identical to that which links an ordinary text to its immediate author" (131–6). Within the relatively modest realm of composition scholarship on collaboration, Kenneth Bruffee surely occupies a transdiscursive position.

8. In this essay, I take composition textbooks as an index of composition pedagogy. The two are not, of course, identical. But textbooks do reflect what are commonly considered pedagogical ideals, even though they may not always describe what actually takes place in the classroom. And the reports that I have read of teachers' attitudes toward student authorship accord closely with the textbook representations that I describe here. For an enlightening collection of teachers' commentary about student authorship, see the September 1994 issue of *The Council Chronicle,* which offers teachers' definitions of plagiarism.

9. Translation from one voice to another thus approximates translation from one language to another, which is a time-honored pedagogy. (See Edward P.J. Corbett, "The Theory and Practice of Imitation in Classical Rhetoric," *College Composition and Communication* 22 (1971): 247.) But, as Mary Minock explains, we should not assume that it is only the language that changes; "even a *faithful* interlingual translation of an original involves a series of interpretations along with ruptures and gaps" (497).

10. An oft- and long-contested feature of composition pedagogy—the gatekeeping impulse variously manifested in assessment and evaluation and especially in ability grouping—is clearly a function of this same hierarchical ordering of pedagogy.

11. Robert J. Connors argues that attitudes toward composition pedagogy alternate between two poles: the reformers who want to improve composition pedagogy, and the abolitionists who want to do away with it altogether. Connors' argument offers considerably more nuance than this one-sentence summary can provide.

12. Mary Louise Pratt originated the term *contact zone* and its attendant concepts. The contact zone is where two cultures encounter each other, "often in context of highly asymmetrical relations of power" (34). In the contact zone a number of phenomena occur, including *autoethnography,* transculturation, oppositional discourse, and resistance.

13. I appreciate the readings of drafts and the conversations in which Gary Tate has urged me to articulate some of the implications of composition pedagogy's dialogic function.

CHAPTER FIVE

Keeping Honest
Working-Class Students, Difference, and Rethinking the Critical Agenda in Composition

David Seitz

O VER THE PAST FIFTEEN YEARS, MANY GRADUATE PROGRAMS IN COMPOSITION have been influenced by theories that are critical of the relations between discourse, knowledge, and multiple forms of power. Yet while composition studies often claim to privilege practice, our programs rarely allow these theories to be informed by practice. Few researchers have looked ethnographically at how undergraduate students from particular class and cultural backgrounds respond to writing classes structured by these theories of culture and language. As composition teachers and theorists, we need to continually engage in this research to keep ourselves honest with our claims of theory that may organize our graduate education and teaching behaviors.

These critical pedagogies tend to emphasize issues of resistance and hegemony to dominant American ideologies. Yet when writing teachers privilege this agenda, they may misinterpret implicit social meanings embedded in students' language that sounds like mass culture ideology. And when these students are from working-class backgrounds or are recent immigrants, we can miss out on views from outside middle-class institutions that imply valuable critiques to these theories and their application in the writing class.

Ethnographic research can try to relate these students' social and discursive positions to the community practices of groups at the local and socio-economic levels with which they identify. I believe, in the long run, this is one way to find out what different communities think of us as "critical teachers." We may better understand why many of our critical positions hold little internally persuasive authority for some of these students in the classroom, or more importantly, in the practice of their everyday lives.

"DIFFERENCE" AND THE CRITICAL AGENDA IN COMPOSITION

One strand of critical teachers' agendas that has grown in American composition classrooms is the critical valuing of difference over unity and consensus. Most American students may be receptive to pedagogies emphasizing difference(s) because they can more easily accommodate dominant perceptions of individualism, compared to cultural studies' critiques of individual success and material consumption. For example, Donna Qualley ("Being Two Places") argues that a postmodern emphasis on difference for her white middle-class female students can bring out a "radical brand of individualistic feminism as exemplified by such pop icons as Madonna" (32).

Composition theorists who have emphasized the term "difference" in their teaching generally define it as a socio-political term, useful for developing critical reading and writing. University and business administrators often speak of "diversity," connoting a level field in which all contributions are equally welcome. In contrast, difference as a term among critical academics evokes issues of hierarchies and power relations. Thus when composition theorists have foregrounded a politics of difference in their courses and writing programs, they have generally developed their teaching practice in two ways. One, the practice may encourage students to explore subject positions, primarily gender, race, and class. In this writing class, "difference" may be the explicit course content (e.g., Penticoff and Brodkey, "Hard Cases") or the course may press students to explore issues of difference in their own lives (for example, Fox, *Social Uses*). In any case, the implicit pedagogy here poses an inquiry into the dominant myth of the American individual divorced from socio-cultural and economic factors.

Two, the teachers' practice may favor a postmodern valuing of dissensus, believing that efforts toward total consensus (or possibly majority rule) inevitably suppress the voicing of differences within the individual subject. Similarly, the necessity of consensus or majority rule can inhibit potentially productive conflicts that exist in a social group. Thus, this practice means to challenge the valuing of unity as the basis for group identity and action. Composition theorists have mostly used this critique to rethink classroom collaboration and consensus (e.g. Trimbur, "Consensus and Difference" and Myers, "Reality, Consensus, and Reform") but also as a way to reconsider the social positioning of privilege and power between students as well as with their teacher (see Jarratt, "Feminism and Composition" and Bizzell, "Marxist Ideas").

Through participant-observation in another teacher's classroom at the University of Illinois at Chicago and ethnographic interviews outside it, I have been looking at how students from working class backgrounds respond to these theoretical assumptions in the writing class.

Rashmi Varma's research paper course at the University of Illinois at Chicago titled, "In Our Own Words: Women In the Third World" pressed students to investigate the politics of their research approaches as well as the ideological positions of the course readings. Since Rashmi's course endeavored to complicate most students' comparisons of third world and first world women, talk of difference was prevalent, often in discussions of cultural relativism. The students were mostly urban commuters, primarily African-American, Asian (of different nationalities and generations of immigration) and ethnic white of working-class background. While Rashmi's course emphasized a global perspective, the critical approaches had much in common with American cultural studies critiques that have gained popularity in composition studies.

For her course, Rashmi sought to raise issues of difference and identity politics within a systemic critique of global capitalism. She believes, as do I, that multicultural agendas in American education can often allow students to maintain a kind of cultural relativism warranted by consumer-based ideologies of individual choice. This relativism lets students off the hook when it comes to developing and taking positions on complex and contentious issues of culture and power relations. Lester Faigley (*Fragments of Rationality*) has argued critical postmodern assumptions of difference may be particularly suited for the culturally and economically diverse student population that is fast becoming the norm at many urban universities. And in Rashmi's class at UIC, most students displayed appreciation for what they saw as academic recognition of their situations. At the same time, participants in the class rarely used the term "difference" on their own.

To examine these applications of theory into composition practice, I will focus on two situated interpretations of difference built around two respective cultural themes from some students: the individual and unity. Critical pedagogies routinely interrogate the dominant meanings of these ideological terms, making them taboo. Consequently, teachers reading their students' texts (and possibly the students themselves) through these critical assumptions may be more likely to gloss over some students' more local meanings. I believe these working-class students' thinking and behavior drawn from their neighborhood communities pose complicated questions for a critical pedagogy in the urban university. To illustrate some of these questions, I will first discuss Diana's and Mike's frames of reference in the context of one class discussion, and then draw out Lilia's perspectives in talk with me and her writing for Rashmi's class. What's valuable here is the contrast of positions and languages of these students in and out of this institutional context and what they can suggest.[1]

PERSPECTIVES ON WORKING-CLASS INDIVIDUALISM

Diana is from a staunch Greek orthodox background, a biology major who describes herself as traditional, wanting the role of home mother. Her parents own and teach in a Greek school in Berwyn, one of Chicago's suburbs that has, from the view of Diana, changed demographically from old word European to a primarily Latino population. She described neighbors' occupations as "assistants to somebody or secretarial work, blue collar." Mike is South Side Irish from a family of cops. He identifies his neighborhood as the "last good part of Chicago" for cops and firemen who have to live in the city by law. When I first met Mike he was considering journalism as a career, as he does work at a newspaper. Now he is talking about becoming a cop like his dad and grandfather. Although Mike and Diana differ in their positions toward academic acculturation, here I will focus on their common ground.

Three months after Rashmi's class ended, I taped a discussion I had with Diana, Mike's and two of Mike's neighborhood friends who also attended UIC. Earlier near the end of one particular class, the white working-class students had expressed their differences from the dominant values of their neighborhoods, which they saw as racist. Since I was interested in issues of acculturation and conflict, I asked if they would share their neighborhood stories with me. But instead of explaining their separation from the community's values, as their classroom discourse led me to believe they would, their talk displayed hard class solidarity along traditional lines. They railed on about affirmative action, the ties between race and crime in their neighborhoods, capital punishment, and the general disempowerment of working people. They initiated all these topics in response to my general questions about their schooling and neighborhoods. Because they displayed such discontinuity of positions in and out of the classroom, I asked them about a class discussion on homosexuality where I thought they did not reveal their felt opinions.

That class I asked about was a discussion of Gloria Anzaldua's "Towards A New Consciousness" that occurred late in the semester. Some composition theorists and anthologies have embraced Anzaldua's metaphors of borderlands and the mestiza. Min Zhan Lu ("Conflict and Struggle"), Richard Miller ("Fault Lines"), and others see Anzaldua's figures and multi-voiced writings as a way for students to explore political and rhetorical positions of identity and language. In these two scenes of talk for Diana and Mike, who gets to define "identity politics" in the public sphere is the implicit issue in and out of the classroom.

Once after class I had overheard Diana proclaim her disgust with homosexuality, claiming it was against God's intent. I wondered then how Diana would talk about Anzaldua's praise of gay identity scheduled later for class reading and discussion. For Diana endeavored to speak *in every class*, whether or not she had done the reading. Just before this transcript excerpt, several students began to question the role of gay identity in Anzaldua's theories of borderlands, opening a teaching moment for Rashmi (see transcript excerpts 1 and 2 below).[2]

1) Classroom Talk 4/6

> Rashmi: How is she using the concept of gayness to understand culture and to understand identity?
>
> Diana: I think that *as homosexuals as something that's different and multicultural as something that's different*, they make a connection between the two

because they can relate to something, someone who *knows how it feels to be an outcast, because everywhere homosexuals are considered, you know,* "Oh my god, they're so weird."

2) Discussion after term 6/8

(with Diana, Mike, and two of his friends)

Diana: I think its become a FAD now in the United States. *It's become good to be weird. Everyone wants to be like a freak* . . . it's become so cool to be bisexual or dress up in drag. *Look at the TV, all the talk shows, all of a sudden there's a great outbreak because its cool to bring attention to yourself.*

Mike: I don't go and march every year and saying, oh, I'm heterosexual.

Diana: Yeah! we don't have a heterosexual parade, why should they do that?

Diana's themes and language in both contexts are similar even though their social meanings intended for their audiences were radically different. She correctly reads the theoretical problem posed by Rashmi's question and responds to that, all the while maintaining her conservative community's disapproval. She recasts all that she condemns, when with a like-minded group, as linguistic currency for the academic marketplace when in the critical classroom, whether knowingly or not. While the discourse outside class (excerpt 2) mocks issues of difference as fodder for Geraldo: "Everyone wants to be a freak," in the class (excerpt 1), Diana's language grants Anzaldua privileged cultural knowledge: "someone who knows how it feels to be an outcast." In class, she positions the voice of repulsion outside of her subjectivity to a faceless realm of "everywhere."

When I asked Diana and Mike if they expressed their own views during this class discussion, Diana was quick to respond, "I'm homophobic and I hate them. Not that I hate them it's just wrong." Her language choice, "homophobic," implies an awareness of how others who value sexual difference might define her. She knows their critique and perhaps accepts it as the authoritative discourse necessary for traveling in some privileged verbal-ideological worlds. Yet her quick use of the word "hate" and her belief in the godly origin of AIDS suggests this more critical discourse of homophobia is not internally persuasive.

Soon after Diana's comment in class, Rashmi synthesized the students' talk of gender constraints Americans face into a more systemic category of "threats to the norm." She suggested there is also a backlash against immigrants because they are perceived to threaten the definition of being American. As a response, Diana then postulated why others may see homosexuals as a threat "because they are willing to speak for what they want" (see transcript excerpt 3 below).

3) Classroom Talk Continued 4/6

Diana: Uh I mean on t.v. a lot of times when you see people who are homosexual, *they're very outspoken. They kind of say what they want to say.* They don't, you know, b.s . . . that's kind of a stereotype too, but the ones I have heard on TV, or whatever, or in plays, or whatever, *you always see very blunt*

> *people. And I think that threatens because they are willing to speak for what they want.*
>
> Rashmi: So its become a *political, category,* to be gay—
>
> Diana: *Its become everything,* become all (threatening)—
>
> Rashmi: Okay, any other response to this article?

Here it is unclear whether Diana was still distancing this talk from the positions she had voiced outside the institutional context with like-minded people and me. Rashmi told me later that although she recognized Diana's rhetorical turns here, she used them for her own purposes as the critical teacher. Once Rashmi has gotten Diana's assent to her metaphor, a political category, she cuts her off. She believes that Diana took so many contradictory positions in the class depending on the situation, that she admitted to no position.

Nevertheless, Diana's response to Rashmi, "its become everything," suggests a glimpse of the values and attitudes she engages when she is with others who identify with white working-class concerns. In our discussion after the term (excerpt 2), Diana's talk reduces homosexuality to a fad along with other alternative cultures, a point she stressed several times in this conversation. Yet more importantly, Diana's talk here links her view of homosexuality with a resentment of those who *publicly* claim difference, those who seek action based on claims of marginal status. Mike explicitly takes up this view in the same after term discussion (see transcript excerpt 4 below): " What I don't like are people who go out there and make a spectacle of themselves just because they're gay, they're black . . . " Perhaps then Diana's comment in class, "Its become everything," refers to this larger category of identity politics and difference within the public sphere. In discussion after the term, Mike's talk linked this resentment of identity politics to working-class ethics.

In our talk, Mike repeatedly stressed to me his neighborhood value of work to judge the integrity of an individual, what his father and others had taught him. "I think the big difference between groups, where culture comes in, is that you've got people who are willing to work for it, and I can respect these people, but not someone who sits around and complains about how they are being oppressed . . . sure things are against you, but you have to work against that."[3]

This view of work and the public domain expressed by Mike suggests that the individual is on his own. Collective action of any public nature seems to go against this deep cultural code of personal integrity historically rooted in material necessity. Yet Mike's perspective also resembles the peer solidarity network of white working-class young adults in two other researched communities. Among the group of mainly working-class high school "burnouts" in the suburban outskirts of Detroit (Eckert, *Jocks and Burnouts*) and a cohort of more economically successful youth of working-class "Cityville" on the edge of Boston (Steinitz and Solomon, *Starting Out*), class solidarity is ultimately valued over more middle-class values of individual prestige.[4]

In Eckert's study, the burnouts resented the more middle-class "jocks," those students who identify with extra-curricular roles in the high school institution. In the burnouts' view, the jocks sought social gain through the school's hierarchies in implicit preparation for corporate life. Eckert points out that the burnouts' parents act similarly in the work world, "avoiding job changes that will put them in subordinate positions to their peers and separate them from their solidarity peer networks" that have sustained them (138). In this context, arguing that individuals each need to prove themselves by their hard work is also a way of speaking against those who negotiate for power within more hierarchical social structures. It is an adversarial position toward institutional powers that are organized by individual advancement.

Many of the more successful white working class young adults in Steinitz's and Solomon's study echo this attitude. They reject their more status-conscious classmates in school who, "make sure they serve their own interests first. Being different just for the sake of being different" (31). These students hope to "remain oneself while still becoming somebody" (30). To do this, Steinitz and Solomon argue, they tacitly value and practice family and neighborhood inter-dependence over individual competition. They seek economic mobility while rejecting, or remaining ambivalent to, social mobility. So while they may often implicitly practice an ethics of solidarity in an effort to maintain a community self, there is often a talk of individualism that can give them hope against their political cynicism.

Like the Cityville young adults, Mike sought in our conversations to erase the differences between his college world and non-academic friends in his neighborhood, even those who Mike views as "racist skinheads."

> Well in my neighborhood, I'd go to school, I'd come home, I'd hang out with my buddies, jerk around a little, throw some rocks at some cars, or we'd play baseball. We didn't think of anything. That was our life. Even now what do I do, I go to school, go home. I don't, like march in rallies, you know? I just have friends, just hang out with them. Even with my friends who are racists, we don't sit around and go, "I hate niggers," and I say, "Well, you're wrong." We don't talk about stuff like that. It's just not brought up, so there's really no influence."

Here, Mike demonstrates he cares more about maintaining long-time social networks, regardless of their political stance. The social ties are more important than explicitly practicing a "politically correct" politics that would, among other things, imply an interest in social mobility.[5] But this strong sense of a community self paradoxically expressed by language of the individual and work is only part of Mike's and Diana's community view of identity politics.

In her dissertation on argument as rhetoric in a working-class bar, Julie Lindquist contends that the culture of working-class whites can be between a rock and a hard place. Because of their subordinate social class, they haven't the economic or political power. And because of their "race," they can't claim a marginalized status as an "other." Or most tacitly refuse to do so because their racial identification grants their only tie to the dominant American culture. Diana articulated this frustration in our talk when she lumped O.J. Simpson's treatment in jail with the rich who can buy their way out of corruption. "The people who have the money, those political people or whatever . . . they get treated like kings because they have money, right? There's so many political things, scams going on . . . and they get away with it just because they have a . . . place. Know what I mean?"

Moreover, much of Diana's and Mike's language play during their discussion implies how they think groups with presumed marginalized status might characterize them. Here Mike is explaining why he hid his opinions when he did speak during the class session on Anzaldua (see transcript excerpt 4 below).

4) Discussion Continued 6/8

Mike:	What if someone was in there and I go "gays suck." I don't want to say all my opinions and-
Diana:	I hate 'em all. I want to kill 'em.
Mike:	-and hurt someone else. I'm not saying gays suck but I mean, *what I don't like are people who go out there and make a spectacle of themselves just because they're gay, they're black* . . . Its almost like, okay, you're gay. That's just something you are, you can't help it, just like a birthmark, I don't go parading, I got a birthmark, I wanna be, I want my own parade, because its part of me. Or I have blonde hair so I wanna march.
Diana:	Do you want to have a blonde parade for all the blondes? (laughs)
Mike:	I want to have a blonde parade. That's stupid, you know. To have a parade or anything for that matter for the fact that-
Diana:	I hate blondes.
Mike:	You know-
Diana:	I want to kill them all (laughs)
Mike:	I'm not actually blonde. I'm sandy blonde.

Diana parodies her own position—playing the role of rabid bigot. Her humor implicitly criticizes those who would see her as solely intolerant, that would deny her humanity. But this play also functions to trivialize more legitimate claims of difference, making it a non-issue, compared to critical teachers wanting to make an issue out of everything.

How then might a composition teacher trained in critical theory read and respond to Diana and Mike in these situations? While Diana's ability to slip in and out of these roles may imply a postmodern subject shaped by late-capitalist culture, her comparison with a former friend complicates this view. She describes his return from college with white hair, tattoos, and writing on his head. "I understand you can wear whatever you want and do your hair however you want, but they start changing their IDEAS, about everything, about religion, the acceptance of things, just changed completely and I'm like why?

Because they don't have the family supporting them, they don't have the right upbringing."

Thus for students like Diana and Mike a pedagogy of identity politics may ultimately lack persuasive authority as a means to investigate self and society, reading and writing. Nor can the critical teacher finally theorize their valuing of individualism as "speaking the hegemonic discourse." Mike's and Diana's talk indicate that their understandings of individualism may have more to do with complex issues of white working-class solidarity and resentment than general manipulations of mass culture most often addressed in published narratives of the critical classroom.

DEFINING THE NECESSITY OF UNITY FOR URBAN LIFE

Diana's and Mike's frames of reference provoke other ways of seeing white working-class students' discourses of individualism. Similarly, Lilia's social and discursive positions that emerged in her talk and writing for the course can challenge postmodern critiques of unity. Lilia describes herself as a Latina who rejected the Catholic tradition, though not the Mexican culture, to become a disciple in the Chicago Church of Christ. In this respect, she is clearly not typical of most Latinas who do attend urban schools. But neither are her beliefs typical of this fundamentalist church. In conversations with me, she repeatedly associated her beliefs with the ideals of Rashmi's course: feminism, the political power of speaking out, social critique, and activism. At the same time, these positions were often in tension with concerns for unity that some critical theorists might dismiss as naive.

Unlike most of the students in Rashmi's class, Lilia sought to incorporate into her writings some of the course's most explicitly theoretical positions on difference, race, class and women's struggles. For their first response paper, Rashmi had required students to write about their "politics of location" using Chandra Mohanty's essay, "Cartographies of Struggle: Third World Women and the Politics of Feminism." which the class had discussed. More than half the students summarized Mohanty's position within their first paragraph, and did not return to this reading, except in their closing sentences. Understandably uncomfortable with the article's density of post-colonial feminist theory, they often emphasized Mohanty's individual experience as the major source of her views.

In contrast, Lilia sought connections using Mohanty's theories of social geography to view her own heritage as a Mexican Latina and the value of all women gaining—in Lilia's and Mohanty's words, "a voice to fight against 'exploitative structures.'" At one point, Lilia writes, "Women [who] are shaped by their culture, and find themselves in different locations do have a similar struggle that brings them together despite their differences. The struggle to describe themselves and express themselves freely in society." When Lilia and I discussed this paper weeks later, she told me she was thinking about her roles with other women of different colors and ethnicities in her church, what she termed her "sisterhood.":

> To have that one purpose, as a Christian, to love God, to be a disciple with other women, that really binds us together, that really creates incredible unity, despite their opinions even. And you do, you get to express yourself a lot.

Throughout our conversations, she stressed women's necessity to have both a spiritual and a political voice, though as a Christian disciple, she values the spiritual life over the material world: "your whole eternal being." For Lilia, the spiritual and the political came together in her mid teens, when she dismissed her family's Catholic traditions for a fundamentalist discipleship, thus challenging her parents' expected role of the submissive Mexican daughter. In our interviews, she compared herself with other Latina women who never become politically involved. "They are a great part of society but are silenced, in this world, here in this country. I thought about the many grandmothers and aunts who are so caught up with their families, their jobs, their home, that they don't even, are aware of the political world." In her second paper, a required summary of a journal article outside the course readings, Lilia refers to the global exploitation of women's labor in her conclusions. Talking with me, she identified her religious beliefs with those church organizations who voice dissent against local governments that condone these practices. Yet she never spoke of her own Church taking these kinds of political actions. Lilia's favoring of a kind of liberation theology, though she never called it that, is definitely rare for a fundamentalist Christian disciple.

For her final research paper, Lilia wanted to concentrate on the prospects for "global feminism" despite the power relations structured in different women's situations of races and nations. Her title, "From a Larger Perspective," explicitly seeks unity over difference and implicitly invokes the language of her religious faith. One paragraph suggests the frustration she felt reading articles in Rashmi's class that critique the possibility of a global "sisterhood." "I believe that's what it strives for [,] that's what women hope for, but that's not what many articles in English 161 have proven to say." And further on: "Much 'difference' among one another when there are internalized and extroverted 'differences' crush the spirit of 'sisterhood' and cause discord among women." She had expressed similar discomfort with these feminist scholars' "negative critique" in the conclusion of her second paper: "Recognizing the false assumptions and their development is just the beginning of effective research. Soon lets write about research expressing fine productive, edifying results and solutions to the crisis women in the third world countries face today."

Unlike Lilia's previous papers, her final paper reads like a hybrid genre of sermon and opinion page calling for unity within women's common struggles, rather than an argumentative researched inquiry into an issue. Lilia clearly rushed this paper more than her earlier course writings. She threw in quotes as examples, including biblical references to Esther and Ruth, but did not develop their implications. Yet her driving concern for speaking out—as she stressed in conversations with me, for directly addressing a positive message of unity tied implicitly to her religious beliefs, may have also worked to overpower the expected critically academic discourse.

The critical teacher informed by cultural studies might primarily attribute Lilia's discourses of unity within diversity to the "manipulations of mass culture," as in the "United Colors of Benneton," or to a monologic discourse in her church. Yet in our interviews this view of unity emerged most often when Lilia compared the problems of her west-side neighborhood and early schooling to the haven she found in the local Boys and Girls club. "When I look back you realize that a lot of your friends are really not involved in a lot of good things, like drugs, gangs, or crime or abuse. In the neighborhood and where I went to school, there was a lot of crime." By Lilia's account, she now thinks 50-65% of her former friends in the larger neighborhood of the school were caught up in gang activity or other dangers. Like many other students from particular Chicago neighborhoods, she could describe to me several incidents of violence that happened to her or her friends. When she moved to a supposedly accelerated high school program near the Cabrini Green housing projects that was not primarily Latino youth, she witnessed more racially motivated violence. Consequently, much of this schooling dealt with physical discipline, "keeping us down." Fortunately she was able to transfer to an accelerated school less hampered by these problems.

During these tough periods, Lilia found refuge in the local Boys and Girls Club where she was part of a tumbling troupe:

Lilia: I basically grew up there, going to the classes, volunteering, doing summer work there, very involved until I was like seventeen or so.

David: Do you think the Boys and Girls club took the place of what school might have been otherwise?

Lilia: In a sense, yeah, they always had activities going for kids to nurture them. And their logo or motto, their theme was "we get along." Unity, united, a unit, we're a unit. And even like their Logan Square club tee shirts had like these figures of people holding hands. It made you feel important that you could become someone, you could stay off the streets, you know stay away from the drugs, the strangers, bad company, could stay in here.

Lilia's comments also reflect the conclusions of a five year ethnographic study of inner-city youth organizations headed up by Shirley Brice Heath and Milbrey McLaughlin (*Identity and Inner-City Youth*). 90% of these organizations judged effective by the teens involved are not organized around ethnic interests. Rather they are built around youth-based projects, often in team athletics or arts troupes, that develop a "core of personal efficacy achieved as a member of a close and personally collected group" (23). For these youth whose neighborhoods are in socio-economic turmoil, ethnic and gender tensions could present "one more boundary that could, if flaunted, add to gang, turf, or girl-boy struggles ever ready to erupt into violence." (32). Ethnic and gender identity needed to be embedded in achievement, responsibility, and an immediate support network not often available anymore through their schools or immediate environment.

While Lilia's situation was not as dire as the youth in Heath's and McLaughlin's research, she clearly speaks for them in relation to her experiences. After we talked about her neighborhood, I asked Lilia what she saw as the cause of these problems. I wondered if she would provide a systemic critique, as she had in her early papers from Rashmi's class, or a more individualist perspective.

> Lot of people say its the lack of education, lack of money, lack of socialism? You know family units. Could be a little of everything, you know. I think it needs teamwork, people working together, building that unity, making it— owning it, making it their territory, making it a right territory, a safe place to grow up in, for older people to feel safe in . . . You really also need to let the ones they want to push out, feel welcome. Because if they did, they wouldn't cause trouble. They also want to feel part of society and that's the point of like boys and girls clubs.

Here, Lilia doesn't dismiss the socio-economic factors, but perhaps she does see that these critical (more academic) perspectives may be ineffective at the local level of social change. Or perhaps these critiques remain too negative for someone who must live within them. Like the organizations Heath and McLaughlin have participated in, Lilia views solutions of team unity in the *doing*, "rituals, processes, and structures that make room for building identities" (10), rather than abstract exclamations of collectivity. In this respect, Lilia's implicit position does resemble a postmodern valuing of power developing from each respective situation. But since Lilia's language sounds so much like a "liberal hegemony" of the status quo, it might be overlooked by critical teachers thinking through theory.

Moreover, Lilia believes this unity becomes "even more important when you have a diverse group of people working together" as in the mixed group of blacks, whites, Latino and Asian people at her church. This work gains greater significance when it is not for money or personal ambition, but "because they like the task at hand and they want to complete it and work as a team. . . . That can mean a lot to someone who may have not had that before." This talk values difference as the diversity of contributions to the group. For Lilia, and others in similar situations, the problems can come when individuals over value difference:

> Lilia: I think it matters what you use the difference for. I think that's the biggest issue, what you do with it.
>
> David: Say a little more about that?
>
> Lilia: Yeah, can do with it is what happens every day, gangbangers hurting one another, because of difference, difference. Someone who thinks that

they're so different, might not want to relate to someone else? And might
just use it to keep themselves isolated from someone else or from people or
whatever.

David: Sort of what you were saying earlier about bearing a grudge?

Lilia: Holding back.

Lilia's view here indicates that when she encounters academically critical
arguments for valuing difference, she reads them through these tensions of
troubled experience and future hopes.

While Lilia's situation and critical values may be uncommon, her concerns
for unity in her world are not. Shianta, an African-American working-class
student in Rashmi's class who is deeply committed to her black church, spoke
through a similar language. She believes her church's values of unity can offer
one way to heal the divisions in her tough world and provide the chance for
economic mobility. Practically every semester I have taught at UIC, I have
encountered one or two African-American or Latina women, often religious,
who psychologically invest in messages of racial or inter-racial unity despite
their deep understandings of racism toward their community and sexism
within it. In some of their writings for my classes, there can be a clash of tones
between the critical inquiry I encourage and their calls for unity. Perhaps like
Chianta and Lilia, they require conviction, rather than critical uncertainty, to
face the odds against them.[6]

CONCLUSIONS: PRACTICES CHALLENGE PEDAGOGICAL "PRAXIS"

Several composition teacher-scholars have argued that cultural studies in
the composition classroom can offer ways for students and teachers to test out
and rethink cultural theories from perspectives outside the critical academy
(e.g., Harris, "Other Reader"; Schilb, "Cultural Studies"). Providing we allow
students space to "extend, or revise, or argue against what a particular critic
has to say" (Harris, 35), we can hear what individuals from different social
groups think of critical theories that often intend to speak for them. When
these students are from working-class backgrounds or are recent immigrants,
their positions may fruitfully question the sometimes middle-class assumptions of critical pedagogies based on critiques of dominant ideologies.

Nevertheless, we also know that writing and discussion in these contexts are
constrained within the institutional context, students' school histories, and different community values toward education. For instance, which students value
college primarily for hopes of economic mobility and which seek social mobility as well? And considering the historical situations of their backgrounds,
which students feel they can psychologically afford the practice of negative critique in some areas of their lives? As the situations of Diana, Mike, and Lilia
show, these contexts and values will shape different students' approaches to
these calls for critical engagement. While this is the advantage of more holistic
research, I am not claiming that the "truth" of what these students really think

lies outside the classroom. This research must continually try to understand the relations between their various ways of knowing and behaving in multiple domains. In this way, we may better recognize the limits of these pedagogies and their theories' persuasive authority for individuals of different social groups, and begin to work from there in our classrooms and in our graduate training.

NOTES

1. Before proceeding, I must make two caveats. One, while I situate particular students' views here, for the sake of brevity, I do not discuss here my role and subjectivity in shaping their interview responses. Needless to say their view of me as a white teacher and researcher colors the meanings of much of this talk. Two, although I discuss these students as primarily "working-class," they are definitely in-between the values and discourses of these communities and middle-class institutions.
2. I have partially edited all oral transcripts for readability.
3. Mike's and Diana's talk clearly drew from current anti-welfare discourse, but primarily because it fits their community's values. Both Mike and Diane saw themselves as sometimes prejudiced, but not racist compared to others they knew.
4. Like the values of any local social group, working class values are going to vary depending on region and historical circumstances. Mike's, and to a lesser degree, Diana's community situations bear some similarities to these studies' research sites.
5. I had not solicited Mike's views about possible racism in his neighborhood at that moment. I had simply asked what was it like growing up in his neighborhood. I believe his response suggests his unspoken view of the context of Rashmi's class and my research which spurred a defense of his investment in his friends and social networks.

    In contrast, Diana claimed her boyfriend and his friends within the Greek community continually make racist arguments which she either argues against or concedes, finding they have tapped her own community prejudices.
6. Nevertheless, I cannot finally say whether these students assumed their school expected more positive conclusions. For example, Valerie Balester (*Cultural Divide*) shows how some black students with a religious background call upon the African-American rhetoric of "talking respectable" when faced with controversial topics in school. For some of these students at UIC, their expressed views toward unity may be both conviction and rhetorical strategy.

CHAPTER SIX

Rethinking the Personal Narrative
Life-Writing and Composition Pedagogy

Deborah Mutnick

The testimonies of the people as they express in a thousand ways
their tribulations and their hopes are more eloquent and beautiful
than the books written "in the name of the people."

Eduardo Galeano

*I*N A RESEARCH PAPER COURSE I RECENTLY TAUGHT WITH POPULAR CULTURE as its theme, a newly arrived Russian immigrant, Dmitriy, combined a review of personal narratives by contemporary multicultural writers—Leslie Marmon Silko, Adrienne Rich, Richard Rodriguez, Fan Shen, Dorinne Kondo, and Yelena Khanga—with his own story. Dmitriy began his project by asking: "What is the effect of culture on different people's identities? How do people, especially writers, with different ethnic background, race, and language explore identity? . . . At the same time, answering this question involves me in finding out who I am." In the first draft of his exploration of his own identity, he wrote lyrically about Odessa, his hometown, "a beautiful port city on the Black Sea in Ukraine . . . where the waves broke against the huge rocks and the tide crept far over the sand during summers." But his elliptical explanation of why he left his beloved city—"because of Soviet politics"—raised questions for me and his classmates.

Although I knew he was referring to anti-Semitism, I wanted him to go beyond generalities to reflect on his individual experience in the larger sociohistorical context of "Soviet politics." As the granddaughter of Jewish immigrants from Odessa whose son—my father—had been radicalized in the 1930s and remained a leftist for the rest of his life, I was especially curious to know what Dmitriy thought about both the Soviet Union and his hometown. As for his classmates, except for two other Russian students, the gap in his explanation was even more enigmatic. In the habit of visiting my office frequently, eager to get a good grade so he could enter the university's physical therapy program, Dmitriy brought me his next draft before class. He had explained that anti-Semitic policies in Russia limited Jews' opportunities for higher education, good jobs, and promotions. More intriguingly, he wrote: "That system 'taught' me to look in my passport, and see fifth graph, a line where it said my nationality. It defined me as a Jew, although I didn't get a real sense of it. For me, that graph meant that I didn't know who I was and didn't have a bright future."

I begin with this anecdote because it epitomizes my evolving sense of the importance of personal narrative in college writing classes not only as a pedagogical device but as a contribution to our collective knowledge of diverse experiences and points of view. The more I reflect on recent debates on personal writing and academic discourse,[1] the more I am convinced that to champion one or the other does students a disservice by truncating writing instruction, ignoring both research findings and classroom practice in the field of composition. In this essay, I argue that both a process orientation to teaching writing and ethnography—the one a defining disciplinary conception of writing, the other a newer but increasingly popular mode of research and instruction—are widespread practices implicitly and explicitly critical of mainstream educational and social institutions, and that each, in different ways, supports the use of various forms of life-writing in college composition. To draw categorical boundaries between "academic discourse" and "personal writing" impedes writers' development by imposing artificial limits on attempts to make sense out of complex experience. It contradicts descriptions in composition research of the uneven, recursive, constructive nature of writing as well as interest across (and outside) the disciplines in blurred genres and experimental writing. And it opposes efforts of social activists and scholars to redefine knowledge mediated by a dominant white male perspective through the recovery of suppressed or silenced points of view and experiences, a project uniquely suited to college composition classes—"contact zones"—in a multicultural era.

WHOSE "I" COUNTS?

Notwithstanding the debates on the personal narrative, its persistent use in the composition class, along, more recently, with ethnography, attests to a larger cultural fascination with autobiography. Autocriticism, autoethnography, cultural biography, biomythography, autography, *ecriture feminine, testimonio*: if nothing else, this plethora of self-/life-writing calls attention to itself. In advanced industrial societies like the U.S., the spectacle of autobiography from academic autocriticism to Jenny Jones might be read as deeply narcissistic, a form of cultural pathology, a retreat from social activism. At the same time, autobiographies by postcolonial, ethnic, and women writers reflect struggles for socioeconomic justice and a transformation of traditional views of knowledge and truth that have excluded the experiences of vast numbers of the world's people. The potency and stakes of these struggles are evident in the recent intensification of political attacks on affirmative action, immigration, and welfare.

Autobiography, however, arguably casts doubt on historical metanarratives and binary oppositions like those I have just suggested by providing a more fine-grained account of experience. It could be said that one strand of autobi-ography delineates a white male Western tradition starting with Augustine, while another consists of testimony by cultural outsiders of collective suffer-ing, aspirations, and social change. But as Françoise Lionnet (1989) argues in *Autobiographical Voices: Gender, Race, and Self-Portraiture*, even these tradi-tions are far more interconnected than conventional scholarship suggests by its artificial separation of entities into "discrete units . . . that, if studied together, would teach us far more about the status and function of our own subject positions in the world" (7). This complex weave of culture—what Lionnet calls *"metissage,"* a type of *briccolage* or "cultural braiding"—can be seen in tradi-tional as well as modern literature when we "re-vision" the past and recognize the cultural borrowings and blurred styles erased by previous interpretations.

Writers like Gloria Anzaldua, Michelle Cliff, bell hooks, Maxine Hong Kingston, Guillermo Gomez-Pena, Trin T. Minh-ha, Adrienne Rich, and Patricia Williams utilize the first person to reconfigure oppressive notions of gender, racial, ethnic, and class identity imposed on them by the dominant culture. Linked directly or indirectly to larger social movements that have chal-lenged (with partial success) such injustices as racial and sexual discrimina-tion, colonial rule, and repressive dictatorships, these writers try to work through the problem of self-determination defined by successive national and transnational struggles for liberation. They speak, often audaciously, from per-sonal experience to counteract the negative impact the dominant culture has had on their lives. They tell stories of their own encounters with racism, sex-ism, and other forms of domination as they struggle to deal with the "split consciousness" of the colonial subject, the lesbian poet, or the black woman law scholar, rewriting both "self" and history.

But their work is eclipsed by myriad negative images of "cultural others" that pervade every social sphere and circulate through mainstream media on a daily basis to construct subjectivity through what Althusser calls a process of interpellation. Thus, even though these resistant voices can now be heard—read—in books available in mega-bookstores and are routinely taught in col-lege literature and composition classes, they alone cannot restructure identities that "hail" us in a cultural hall of mirrors from which there is no escape. That work must be done on a more grassroots level, giving ordinary people the opportunity to "write" themselves, or, as Michelle Cliff (1988) puts it, "mix[ing] the forms taught us by the oppressor, undermining his language and co-opting his style, and turning it to our purpose" (59).

Complicating the political question of whose "I" counts in autobiography are two philosophical problems underscored by recent poststructuralist cri-tiques: the notion of a unitary self and the relationship between objective and subjective knowledge. Although a review of these large questions is beyond my scope here, let me briefly show how they relate to contemporary life-writing. Both psychoanalytic and deconstructive theories have interrogated the notion of a unitary, rational, fixed self. But the view of the self as a linguistic construct, fragmented, indeterminate, and irrational, has not always served the interests of marginalized groups like women who have been historically denied self-hood. Consequently, many feminist and critical theorists, though persuaded that identity is mainly constructed and always multiplicitous, have nonetheless opted for a "strategic essentialism" that recognizes the need to identify with and/or as members of groups struggling to speak and write themselves into history. The articulation of "I" and the autobiographical impulse, in this sense, are never purely individual acts in that they insert the writer into public discourse, creating new social spaces for all group members.

The second, epistemological problem of the relationship of objective to subjective knowledge also has implications for autobiography. The omission of the "I" in written discourse achieves an effect of objectivity, omniscience, and authority. Through the elimination of agency, statements assume a facticity, a presumption of truth, that more subjective discourse self-consciously calls into question. Although the use of "I" by no means necessarily alters the substance of an argument, it does foreground the interpretive, rhetorical dimension of all communicative acts. While the postmodern challenge to scientific objectivism has in some cases been taken to an absurd extreme, it serves to remind us of the dialectic between knower and known and the implications and limits of objectivist thought. These ethical and political considerations have encouraged writers of conscience to examine their assumptions more carefully and situate themselves in their writing (albeit, sometimes insipidly, as in recitations of cultural markers like white, female, etc.). Together with psychoanalytic and deconstructive theories of self and multivocal (re)constructions of self by subaltern writers, the critique of objectivist discourse invites us to explore the parameters of "I" more closely. Although these perspectives do not necessarily lead to autobiographical writing, they create the contexts for such writing inside and outside the academy.

In addition, the autobiographical turn reflects popular obsessions with celebrity status, self-help techniques, the cult of the body (diet fads, eating disorders, fitness clubs, tattoos, body-piercing), talk show confessions, and images of success, beauty, glamour, and other always unattainable attributes that constantly assault us in the media—in contrast to fleeting news clips of Somalian refugees, Serbo-Croatian war victims, or homeless families in the U.S., which lose meaning in the "infomercial" stream of TV consciousness. From philosophical and literary investigations of subjectivity to everyday spectatorship and consumption of popular culture, the turn to personal discourses reveals an attempt, however effective or futile, to overcome feelings of fragmentation and deracination endemic to postmodern culture.

THE PERSONAL NARRATIVE IN WRITING PEDAGOGY: GIVING VOICE TO NEW WRITERS

In his introduction to *Confessions of the Critics*, a compilation of autocritical essays by well-known academics, H. Avram Veeser (1996), a new historicist, gives examples of two "performative writing traditions," *ecriture feminine* and "pedagogical theories of expressive writing" (xiv). Veeser's sound bite description of writing pedagogy is useful here because it condenses voluminous material from the annals of composition into a few sentences, giving us a view of the discipline from the outside. Having posed the question relative to *ecriture feminine* of "whether a particular sort of writing can be assigned to the biologically female subject," he links expressivism, process, open-admissions students, and gender in a revealing encapsulation of recent composition history. Veeser writes: "Expressivist composition pedagogy—the 'process' theory of writing—also defended the rights of the weak, including the open-admissions students who flocked to public universities. Expressivism embraced the idea that writing was a gendered practice" (xv).

Veeser's outsider's version of the teaching of writing in relation to autocritography, though superficial, reflects three aspects of contemporary composition pedagogy relevant to the role of autobiography in the writing class. First, his equation of expressivist pedagogy with process theory suggests that self-expression is inherent in a process approach to writing. Second, Veeser connects expressivist/process pedagogy to the policy of open admissions in the 1970s. And third, he associates expressivist writing with gender, an area of research in composition studies linked in various ways to the feminist credo that "the personal is political." This construction of college writing instruction shows how process theory and expressivist rhetoric became entwined with the social and educational movements of the 1960s and '70s. Yet none of the contested positions at the Dartmouth Conference in 1966, as outlined by Joseph Harris (1991) in his review of the transatlantic meeting's legacy, dealt explicitly with the crisis of mass education—specifically, with public school desegregation and open admissions. Rather, they focused on student growth, the definition of the subject of English, and its legitimation as a discipline.

It was the mainly British [2] "growth" and "expressivist" camps that advocated most vigorously for students' rights, giving value to their stories and respecting their home cultures and languages. And later it was the research of scholars like Sondra Perl and Mina Shaughnessy, which focused on the writing of unskilled college writers, that established writing-as-a-process as a cornerstone of composition instruction. Although the critics of these educators and the process theory that evolved from their work point, perhaps rightly, to an absence of context, a vacuum in the regimen of drafting, revising, and editing, they often lose sight of the political undertones—however liberal, sentimental, and often unarticulated as a class issue—of their advocacy for students. I believe that the unfortunate schism between process and social epistemic approaches remains so deep, in part, because the underlying issues of class and racial discrimination have never been adequately addressed by either camp. Instead, these issues, which drive both educational failure and reform, have been masked by theoretical and methodological differences that overlook or universalize the socially marginalized students whose educations and lives, as Jonathan Kozol so eloquently describes, continue to be at risk.[3]

But critiques of composition pedagogy's valorization of the personal narrative also raise troubling questions: what subjectivity does the personal essay construct (Faigley 1992); does an instructional focus on personal writing fail to prepare students for the demands of academic discourse (Bizzell and Herzberg 1986); to what extent does such writing reify personal experience and reinforce liberal humanist assumptions (Bartholomae 1995); do process writing and its reliance on the personal revive an elite, belletristic tradition (Trimbur 1994); what instructional ends are served by the evaluation of student writing as "authentic" and "truthful" (Faigley 1992); and does an emphasis on the individual subject depoliticize resistance to oppressive social structures (Berlin 1988)? Without a critical edge, the "naturalness" of process pedagogy can serve to reify the transience of everyday life and authenticate experience on the basis of its cultural capital rather than its multiplicitous or resistant features. To presuppose an inner life apart from or opposed to social structures and discourses promotes an individualist ethos and a view of writing as innate and ideologically neutral instead of cultural, learned, value-ridden. Expressivist rhetoric is thus more likely to reinscribe stereotypes and prejudices than challenge them; rather than express one's "true" or "authentic" inner self, such writing may uncritically reproduce discourses that claim authenticity by virtue of their first person status; or it may simply be dismissed as unscholarly and self-indulgent by dubious readers across the academic disciplines.

The critiques of process and expressivist pedagogies reveal their ideology and limitations, underscoring the importance of critical discourse to a liberatory pedagogy. As Daniel Mahala and Jody Swilky (1995) point out, however, such critiques "also tend to ignore ways personal writing might be used in classrooms to help illuminate the self as a sociohistorical subject" (368). For one of the best-known proponents of liberatory or critical pedagogy, Paulo Freire (1988), dialogue or problem-posing starts with the "present, existential, concrete situation, reflecting the aspirations of the people" (85) and asks the question of whose story gets told. If storytelling and self-writing are avenues of liberation for many writers, past and present, why close them to students? As observed by feminist critics in regard to female subjectivity, the poststructural critique of the self is ironic for those whose voices have historically not been heard. As a teaching tool at all levels, as well as in our own research, our own and other critically inflected personal narratives can help us make connections between theory and practice, knowledge and experience, as we learn to participate more fully in diverse social discourses as speakers *and* listeners, writers *and* readers.

For students on the social margins, the opportunity to articulate a perspective in writing on their own life experiences can be a bridge between their communities and the academy. Such student writing is also a potential source of knowledge about realities that are frequently misrepresented, diluted or altogether absent in mainstream depictions. To an extent, this view of college composition as a cultural repository is true of all students, regardless of social background. But the stories of subaltern students are comparatively scarce. In the context of the explosion of autobiographical writing, the personal narrative as an instructional mode is especially important in that it can give voice to these new *non*writers, making the classroom a more dialogic space and inserting the "I" of ordinary working people and their everyday struggles into public discourse.

PROCESS THEORY AND REFLEXIVITY: COMPOSING WORDS, COMPOSING SELVES

The work of self-reflexive writers like Adrienne Rich and Audre Lorde encourages a theorization of experience—both of everyday life and acts of witnessing, observing, reading. It supports not only a feminist practice and Freire's notion of critical consciousness but also social theories of language as dialogic and pedagogical practices like "writing to learn." In each case, a bifocal perspective on writing as social act stresses a rhetorical dimension in which we situate ourselves as writers in relation to reader, text, and context, and a phenomenological dimension in which we transmute perceptions into words. While neither aspect of written language necessarily produces autobiography (except in the broadest sense that authorship is always delimited by circumstance), both imply an autobiographical element in all writing—the writer's situatedness, her particular consciousness, what Joseph Harris (1997), in his discussion of "person, position, and style" in composition scholarship, calls a "disciplined subjectivity" (55).

The more closely one examines both our reliance on the personal narrative in the teaching of writing and our discomfort with it as too individualistic, expressivist, essentialist, or simply unacademic, the more clearly the substratum of process pedagogy emerges. Process theory stresses self-reflection and metalinguistic awareness through genres like journal writing, metatexts, and reader response; its conceptualization of writing as recursive and revisional is central to the emergence of composition as a discipline.[4] Insofar as these methods are predicated on a self-reflexive move that encourages students to examine the evolution of particular pieces of writing as well as themselves as writers, the schism between so-called "personal" and "academic" writing reflects not just a theoretical or pedagogical difference but an underlying schizophrenia in composition studies.[5]

Similarly, discursive and cultural hybridity—blurred genres—support the use of the personal narrative as a "mixable" form, a means of "writing the self" and giving voice to diverse writers that can be easily integrated into other modes of composition. Yet even Mahala and Swilky, in their incisive defense of personal stories in composition instruction, feel obliged to make the following disclaimer: "Indeed, we do not wish it to escape notice that our own discourse defending 'stories' closely follows dominant conventions of philosophical argument" (379). Their belief that such writing is more likely to be "heard" (published), though understandable—and even laudable if it produces more rigorous thought and scholarship—assumes that the discursive contradiction between their advocacy as teachers of storytelling and their adherence as writers to the traditions of "philosophical argument" is inescapable.

In fact, to feel so beholden to "philosophical argument" ignores the extent to which personal reflection suffuses composition pedagogy (and other forms of public discourse) and blurred genres and cultural hybridity already define much writing. As Clifford Geertz (1983) argues, we have developed multiple conventions of interpretation "built—often jerry-built—to accommodate a situation at once fluid, plural, uncentered, and ineradicably untidy" (21). That is, different modes of writing emerge and endure only insofar as they can be read, which is determined, says Roland Barthes (1968), by a break "at the precise moment when a new economic structure is joined on to an older one, thereby bringing about decisive changes in mentality and consciousness" (18). It is my contention that we are experiencing just such a moment in history, marked by a globalization of capital and culture that has painfully paved the way both for masses of students in higher education and the emergent literatures of subaltern writers. Were we to recognize these students as "emergent writers," we might, as David Bartholomae (1993) suggests, "see that writing as material for an ongoing study of American life and culture" (17)—a national archive of student "testimonies" written in their own names.

(AUTO)ETHNOGRAPHY AND SOCIAL TRANSFORMATION

Like autobiographical declamations of "selves" and "lives" that add new writers to literary canons and challenge traditional notions of universality and cultural hierarchies, ethnography, as James Spradley (1979) explains,

> offers all of us the chance to step outside our narrow cultural backgrounds, to set aside our socially inherited ethnocentrism, if only for a brief period, and to apprehend the world from the viewpoint of other human beings who live by different meaning systems. . . . It is a pathway into understanding the cultural differences that make us what we are as human beings. (v)

Nearly twenty years ago, Spradley termed the growing popularity of ethnography across the disciplines "a quiet revolution" as ethnographic methods previously used in anthropological fieldwork in nonwestern cultures were adopted by researchers across the disciplines in the industrialized world. On the one hand, the anthropological turn from the study of cultural "others" to one's own society reflects critiques of the ethnographer as a cultural colonizer. But the same asymmetry in power relations persisted in ethnographic research in the industrialized world, raising a similar set of questions about representation, privilege, and the ethics of research.

This tension between the understanding of cultural diversity as "one of the great gifts bestowed on the human species" (Spradley, p. v) and the enduring problem of who studies whom and to what end underscores the importance of autobiography. Even more collaborative forms like oral histories and testimonies, which are intended to give voice to those who cannot, for various reasons, write their own "life," raise questions about power dynamics. These issues have been at the forefront of much disciplinary and methodological reform, and much of the controversy revolves around acts of writing—issues of authority, control, point of view, the constructive power of language quite literally to order, structure, and interpret a life. Their impact has led to more self-reflexive ethnographic research as well as interest in hybrid forms like autoethnography, biomythography, and cultural autobiography.

In the field of composition, according to Stephen North (1987), ethnographic research on writing emerged in the early 1980s, along with a turn generally toward qualitative, descriptive, and naturalistic inquiry. As a qualitative approach, grounded in experience, ethnography and other naturalistic forms of inquiry gained popularity as researchers and teachers began to question positivistic and quantitative methods and to recognize the importance of social context in research on writing. As of 1987, North stressed the lack of "methodological integrity" in qualitative research in composition and pointed out a relative dearth of examples of ethnographies. Nevertheless, he underscored the crucial point for my argument here that the aim of ethnographic inquiry "is to enlarge 'the universe of human discourse'" (Geertz, qtd. in North, 284). That motive has permeated composition research and practice since the 1950s, across rhetorical, cultural, and political differences.

In 1988, Lauer and Asher devoted a chapter to ethnography in *Composition Research*, characterizing it as a study of "writing in context" that focuses on "entire environments," "withholds initial judgments," and is reported "in the form of thick description" (48)—Geertz's terminology. This emphasis on descriptive research marks a shift in research methodology that Lester Faigley (1992), more recently, notes as part of the "interpretive turn" in the social sciences. Such types of scholarship, he states, including ethnography, "investigated the *situatedness* of writers within webs of meaning" (31, emphasis added). At the same time, ethnography was gaining support as a classroom practice. For David Bleich (1993), "university classrooms . . . were almost ideal locations for ethnographic research—for students as much as for teachers" (186). Bleich also compares ethnography to composition as "a cognate field of inquiry." Critical of the exclusionary tendencies of both ethnography and composition that lead us to assimilate dominant cultural paradigms and retain the privileged status of the observer, he calls for "socially generous research" that contributes to the welfare of the community. Bleich concludes that "ethnography and composition research have similar challenges: to include in the research initiative the responsibility to serve the population that would otherwise only be considered as 'data'" (181).

Critical ethnography, according to Linda Brodkey (1996), not only describes but creates "the possibility of transforming such institutions as schools—through a process of negative critique" (106), thereby contesting cultural hegemony. This perspective is echoed in Brodkey's autoethnographic essay, "Writing on the Bias" (1994), in which she reflects on her development as a reader and writer whose working class background ultimately positions her to resist the formalistic school writing to which—good student that she was—-she had succumbed, and understand the underlying social divisions it masked. To become conscious of one's bias, Brodkey maintains, requires a "conceptual" rather than a "perceptual" narrative stance. Borrowing Seymour Chatman's (1978) distinction between narrative and story as a shift in emphasis from the teller to the tale, she explains that perceptual narrative records events uncritically while conceptual narrative requires narrators "to interrupt their own stories" and subject them to conscious critique. Such research, which she assigns in the form of autoethnography in a graduate course called Ethnographies of Literacy, enables students to see that "personal histories are also cultural histories" (209).[6]

As writers, scholars, and researchers have become more aware of the pitfalls of ethnography, new forms have emerged that stress the location and subjectivity of the observer, exert a more critical perspective, and/or shift the act of telling/writing from the privileged researcher to the points of view of those who have, in the past, been objects rather than subjects of study. But these problems of representation and reification are not easily solved. In her illuminating book on autobiographical innovations of ethnic American working women, which focuses on "extra-literary" forms like cookbooks and labor histories, Anne E. Goldman (1996) examines the relationship "between the desire to speak autobiographically and the pressures ethnography exerts upon this desire" (xv).

Concerned by a tendency among some autobiography theorists to substitute a collective for an individual perspective, Goldman argues that ethnic, working class women have often been pressured into a particular kind of writing that has presented opportunities for them and that "for women of color, especially, such openings have often taken shape in an ethnographic publishing context that ignores the specificities of individual voices in order to draw general and abstract claims about the way 'culture' operates" (xx). This desire to render lived life and cultural realities in their full complexity is expressed again and again in critiques of both autobiography and ethnography. On the one hand, narrative interruptions of a story can "refer to some of the complexity of experience that any story necessarily reduces" (Brodkey, 12). On the other hand, "the move toward 'story' and writing from 'personal' experience can reveal conventionally suppressed contextual conditions that mold a discourse" (Mahala and Swilky, 365).

Increasingly, as working-class, women and/or nonwhite academics enter the professional ranks and practice ethnographic methods, the contradictions between privileged observers and those they research become more sharply apparent. For Sofia Villenas (1996), a Chicana doctoral student conducting research on the educational life histories of Latina mothers who had immigrated to a small rural community in Pennsylvania, being both "colonizer" and "colonized" creates a dilemma. As she puts it: "I am the coloniz*ed* in relation to the greater society, to the institutions of higher learning, and to the dominant majority culture in the research setting. I am the coloni*zer* because I am the educated, 'marginalized' researcher, recruited and sanctioned by privileged dominant institutions to write for and about Latino communities" (714). It is her recognition of her own complicity with mainstream social service and school professionals in framing the Latino community as a "problem" that forces her to reflect on the fact that she was "hiding [her] own marginality in relation to the majority culture" (715). Ultimately, Villenas repositions herself as a "citizen-scholar-activist" and vows to "facilitate a process where Latinas/os become the subjects and the creators of knowledge" (730).

This desire for self-determination reverberates in the historic struggles for social justice that define the modern era. In light of our heightened awareness of the role language plays in constructing social realities, autobiographical writing can be seen as a terrain for the partial enactment of such struggles. Autobiographical writing and theory can lead us as researchers and teachers to question our assumptions and change our practice to reflect the importance of letting others—students, informants, community members—speak and write for themselves. Depending on our own social location, such goals require different strategies. For Villenas, she must confront both "my own marginalization and my complicity in 'othering' myself and my community." But Villenas also challenges "majority-culture ethnographers . . . [to] call upon their own marginalizing experiences and find a space for the emergence of new identities and discourses in the practice of solidarity with marginalized peoples" (729).

In his discussion of autobiographical collaborations, including the practice of ghostwriting, Philippe Lejeune (1989) shows how the autobiographical signature both challenges the assumption that the ghostwriter functions simply as a translator of another's life and reveals the extent to which all autobiographies are fabricated. Ethnography and oral history depend on investigators tied, not unlike Villenas, to elite institutions, often motivated by nostalgia and curiosity, whose writing is an ambiguous "act that fixes and preserves the memory of an 'oral' society, at the same time it alienates it, recovers it, and reifies it" (209). According to Lejeune, this "ethnological gap" is compounded by the alienation of working-class autobiographers whose intellectualization uproots them from their working-class communities. Lejeune writes:

> From the moment when the peasant and working-class milieus accede to the practice of writing (and in particular to the life story), they will do so with images of themselves that have already been formed. . . On the other hand, the fact of taking in his hands his own life story (and eventually trying to publish it) will be more or less voluntarily an act of social ascension and of assimilation into the dominant culture, even if it is within the framework of a militant struggle destined to arouse class consciousness" (199–200).

Despite this overdetermined view of working-class writers, Lejeune concludes that the solution to the problem of identification with the dominant culture depends on the degree to which studied groups themselves internalize the skills of researchers in order to "reappropriate and use for their own ends the [dominant culture's] means of knowledge and the instruments of analysis" (214). The ultimate logic—the "real revolution"—would be a reversal of roles in which the researcher became the model observed from a different point of view.

THE DOCUMENTATION OF ORDINARY LIFE

The *Journal of Ordinary Thought* is a publication of work by men and women involved in a parent writing program in local elementary schools in Chicago aimed at increasing community involvement in education. Editor Hal Adams (1995), who describes himself as "the outsider from the university," describes the writing workshops he leads for parents as predicated on the belief that "every person is a philosopher." Influenced by Antonio Gramsci, Paulo Freire, and C.L.R. James, Adams says he invites community members to explore their personal experience in order to draw conclusions about the world that serve their own interests rather than those of the dominant culture. In addition to hoping the parents will contest the powerful corporate and political interests that control their lives, Adams agrees with James that "the artistic expressions of ordinary people contain truths essential for social change" (9). As Adams states, "The parents were intrigued by the idea that it is people leading ordinary lives who understand the world most clearly and create the truest meaning of their situation" (10).

Among the writers he cites is a woman who describes a "bad day" in which she traipses around town failing to get her welfare check, a medical card, and food no longer on sale, returns home, cooks dinner with what she has—not enough for both her and her family—and goes to bed hungry. As part of the parent writing program, she reads her piece to her daughter's first grade class. The children's comments, observes Adams, reflect their understanding of the writer's "subtle message" that bad days are hard but can be survived with dignity as well as that literacy is "an everyday, important part of their community" (12). Several male writers, astonished that they are neither dead nor in prison, document the precariousness of their lives as young black men. They insist on calling their magazine *Through the Eyes of a Villain*, to which Adams initially objects as sounding "evil" but comes to understand as ironic, a title that appropriates and challenges the mainstream perception of black men in a racist society. One man notes that he woke up one morning "unemployed, but not without work to do"; another describes a violent police search in an alley that leaves him feeling "raped" and his dissatisfaction with his elders' advice not to "hang" with his friends and stay out of the alley—"My alley!" he exclaims. The writing groups eventually become a grassroots think tank that involves members in school board and community politics in a dramatic enactment of Gramsci's notion of "organic intellectuals."

Although the university writing class is a different venue, more socially diverse and driven by institutional goals that often contradict the critical practice to which Brodkey, Villenas, and Adams subscribe, it can function in similar ways to encourage students to write themselves into history. For mainstream students, such writing can foster critical awareness of their own privilege and power as well as their own stories of marginalization as female, disabled, or otherwise objectified. It can counteract the numbing, conformist, homogeneous images of pseudo-selves that dominate the media as well as the super-alienated confessions of talk show guests whose dysfunctional lives both mirror and absolve our own. For working-class, African American, Latino/a, and other students whose lives have only recently been reflected in the curriculum, there is an even greater need for opportunities to explore and document their own experience, illuminate the borders between the academy and their communities, and make conscious choices about how they will position themselves in their professional and civic lives.

As Michael M.J. Fischer (1994) argues, "autobiographies, carefully interrogated, can provide *one* important data base for reconstructing social theory 'from the bottom up'; they provide fine-grained experiential loci of the interaction of changing social forces" (92). Both autobiographical and ethnographic writing probe the cultural complexity of contemporary life; their place in the composition class has been established through decades of practice, though not always with the critical goal of enabling the emergence of new hybrid discourses, voices, and cultural and personal histories. As my student Dmitriy writes, summing up what he has learned from Rich, Rodriguez, Shen, Silko, and Khanga:

> Most of my appreciation I should render to these writers who help me to define myself according to what nation I belong and my ethnic history. Furthermore, I think rereading these authors will lead me to have a different perspective. This perspective will push me forward and make me realize the feeling that I have of being split at the root between Russian, Jewish and American culture. Finally, through the ideas of the stories told by these authors, I will learn how to be able to find in myself the ability to be a storyteller who will pass on to the next generation the cultural values of our Jewish heritage, keeping them alive.

Although I would have liked Dmitriy to develop the idea, borrowed from Rich, of being "split at the root," and to deal more directly with the conflicts between national and ethnic identity and the complexity of the multicultural scenes of New York City to which he now belongs, I am impressed by his articulation of both impulses—to preserve his cultural traditions and to "push forward" to explore his contradictions. It is also interesting to note that he omits from his narrative but includes at the end of his journal an apology for the quality of his work, which he explains may have suffered due to late hours of study. He has had to stay up late, sometimes until three in the morning, to complete his schoolwork as a result of the "new politics" at the public assistance office which requires students to work at least 52 hours every two weeks and may ultimately prevent Dmitriy from completing his education. I believe we need to encourage students to tell such stories—whether about old "Soviet politics" or the "new politics" of the Gingrich era—and help ensure an audience for them.

92   *Deborah Mutnick*

NOTES

1. The most highly publicized version of this debate took place between Peter Elbow and David Bartholomae in a packed session at the 1991 Conference on College Composition and Communication and was subsequently published in 1995 in *CCC*.

2. As Harris (1991) points out, there were in fact a number of American proponents of the "growth" model, including Benjamin DeMott and, most notably, James Moffett.

3. In a recent *CCC* article, Bruce Horner (1996) laments the depoliticization of basic writing as a "movement for cultural democracy" and warns against its institutionalization as a discourse that naturalizes and fixes writers on a developmental scale.

4. Sharon Crowley's (1996) assessment of the status of process-oriented writing pedagogy is that it never displaced current traditional methods. She says further that the Enlightenment value of rationalism is the flip side of expressionism, and that both modes reflect the "politics of liberal humanism." Crowley also points out that it was composition's identification of its subject matter, not as rhetoric but the composing processes of freshmen students, that gave it disciplinary status.

5. Indeed, Joseph Harris (1997) suggests that while it is appropriate for students to write autobiographical essays as a means of reflecting on "the complexity of the relationship between language and experience," it is inappropriate for scholars to do so because they "impose too much" on their readers (51).

6. Literacy autobiographies have become fairly standard assignments in many graduate and undergraduate composition courses. In her chapter on rhetoric and composition in an introduction to language and literature studies for undergraduate students, Andrea Lunsford (1992) suggests that students conduct "a retrospective study of their own writing and reading histories, trying to map the development of their own literate behavior." Keith Gilyard's *Voices of the Self*, Victor Villanueva's *Bootstraps*, and Mike Rose's *Lives on the Boundary* are often used to generate discussion and writing on literacy acquisition. The propaedeutic value of asking students to reflect on their own experience of language and literacy, as Villanueva (1993) puts it, "is to provide a problematic based on sets of experience: an experience which leads to a theory, a theory that recalls an experience; reflections on speculations, speculations to polemics to reflections—all with an aim at affecting what might happen in classrooms, the sites of action" (xvii).

CHAPTER SEVEN

What Difference the Differences Make
Theoretical and Epistemological Differences in Writing Assessment Practice

Brian Huot and Michael M. Williamson

INTRODUCTION

*T*HIS ESSAY LOOKS AT THE RELATIONSHIP BETWEEN THEORY AND PRACTICE in writing assessment. While this volume recognizes the many connections between theory, practice and research in composition, scholars in composition who work on writing assessment have not always shared an awareness of its theoretical assumptions and beliefs. Moreover, such recognition or awareness is crucial, we believe, if writing assessment is ever going to be an important component of composition as a discipline and in the practices of composition teachers and writing program administrators. The topic of theory and practice in writing assessment is especially important to us because a 1986 conversation about "holistic scoring being a practice without a theory" spawned a series of conversations, which in turned spawned three dissertations (one written by Brian and all three directed by Mike), several conference sessions, an edited collection, articles and book chapters we've written individually and together, and this essay. It's interesting, then, for us to go back to the site of our initial interest and curiosity about writing assessment. It is a site that we have revisited in our work about writing assessment in a general attempt to excavate the theories, epistemologies, beliefs and assumptions that support much practice in writing assessment. Of course, the intersection of theory and practice is important beyond its personal significance, since we believe that to change the way writing assessment is designed and implemented, we must alter the way it is theorized and constructed as an intellectual space.

It's worth noting that writing assessment procedures were not always recognized as even having an intellectual space. Nearly two decades ago, Anne Gere (1980) lamented the lack of an articulated set of principles for writing assessment. Five years later, Faigley, Cherry, Jolliffe and Skinner (1985) made a similar statement based upon the same rationale. According to this line of reasoning, we had simply been too busy trying to assess writing to spend time developing a theory upon which our emergent practices might be based. We should note that in the early 1980s, holistic scoring and other *direct* forms of writing assessment (assessment that included the evaluation of student writing) were just emerging. While writing had been assessed regularly since the 1800s,[1] the technology of direct writing assessment was formally developed in the 1960s after decades of work by the test developers at the College Entrance Examination Board (CEEB) and later by the Educational Testing Service (ETS).

As most of us interested in writing assessment are now aware, procedures developed by measurement professionals at ETS and CEEB outside the field of English Studies and the field of rhetoric and composition were supported by beliefs and assumptions from classical test theory within a positivist epistemology. Within such a belief system, there exist discernible truths which we can, if rigorous and objective enough in our methods, discover. The basis, then, of our first conversations about writing assessment proved groundless because holistic scoring has always been a theory-driven practice (Huot 1996; Williamson 1993). Such a discovery, however, merely took our conversations about theory and practice in new directions and provided new insights. For example, it became clear that the major so-called debate over the efficacy of indirect writing assessment (multiple choice tests) versus direct writing assessment was not really a debate between measurement specialists and teachers as it had been constructed (White 1993) because both sets of procedures aim to create the reliable measurement of student writing, and the achievement of that reliability was the central issue not only in this particular debate but within the central tenets of psychometric theory and the procedures this theory spawned. The debate over multiple choice tests versus essays was conducted by the measurement community over principles defined and articulated according to the theoretical basis of their intellectual community. Writing teachers were certainly interested in the outcome, but we were not active participants who advanced ideas and ultimately developed the procedures. This is an important point because some scholars in writing assessment (Scharton 1996; White 1994) advocate that composition teachers become more familiar with psychometric procedures, so that they can be taken more seriously in conversations and debates with the measurement community. While we will take up this particular point about the importance of scholars in rhetoric and composition learning statistical operations associated with a psychometric approach to writing assessment, we do believe that work in writing assessment needs to be interdisciplinary and to draw upon theories of teaching, literacy and validity in educational measurement. In this chapter we outline some basic tenets in validity theory because, as Pamela Moss points, out "the field of college writing assessment appears seriously isolated from the larger educational measurement community" (1998, 113). Our outline of validity and its implications for writing assessment permits us to look at competing models for writing assessment theoretically as we conclude the chapter with a comparison of the different theoretical and epistemological positions supporting such practices and an examination of the significance of these differences.

IMPLICATIONS OF VALIDITY THEORY FOR WRITING ASSESSMENT

Any interdisciplinary consideration of writing assessment needs to consider the concept of validity in educational measurement. While the implications validity can have for studying writing assessment are extensive, validity is not a subject most of us in Composition are familiar with. We hope to provide a concise discussion on the nature of validity itself and on its evolution over the last several decades as a way not only of showcasing the interdisciplinary nature of writing assessment but of providing a useful set of ideas for understanding the way writing assessment can best work within the context of Composition. Like most theoretical constructs, validity continues to be redefined, debated and implemented within a changing world. This evolution is especially important for writing assessment because recent changes in validity mirror the many changes in the social construction of knowledge that have affected the way language and literacy are studied, theorized and taught in the late twentieth century. The literature on validity is extensive, dating back several decades, though its current theoretical orientation began in the early 1950s (Shephard 1993).

In its simplest terms, validity is concerned with how accurately an assessment hits a target. Reliability is concerned with the ability of an assessment to continue to hit the target. To be accurate over time, an assessment has to be reliable. That *reliability is a necessary but insufficient condition for validity* is an accepted maxim in traditional notions of writing and educational assessment. Thus, contemporary statistical procedures that examine the accuracy of an assessment consider its precision or reliability. Any deviations in reliability were considered to be sources of error, detracting from the overall validity of a measurement. These sources of errors were aggregated to produce mathematical calculations of validity. Initially, the literature in direct writing assessment was dominated by the issue of reliability although in the last few years this has begun to change as work in writing assessment has begun to move beyond the establishment of the procedures themselves. Traditional procedures for evaluating the validity of an assessment procedure are built upon an axiom that all data are distributed normally, that is, that they form the shape of a bell curve when plotted in geometric space. When data do not distribute normally, that is, when the range of the data is restricted in some way, the variance, a measure of how spread out the data are, is constrained. The more constrained the data, the lower the reliability. This phenomenon emerges from the mathematical fact that greater variance tends to produce greater reliability, all other things being equal. Thus, writing assessment procedures that create normal distributions of students are more reliable than those that create more narrow distributions. For example, a multiple choice test with a large number of items is going to have a potentially larger range of scores than a holistically scored essay that only has four score points. Validation processes are designed to help tests create a normally distributed set of scores. Items are selected for a test precisely in order to insure that students are spread out over a range that is close to a bell curve. Thus, the mathematical axiom becomes a self fulfilling prophecy. Because a normal distribution is assumed a natural phenomenon in mathematical theory, tests are constructed to uncover that characteristic. Consequently, because tests are believed to be more valid when they are more reliable, they are constructed to be more reliable.

In their now classic statement of test theory, Frederick Lord and Melvin Novick (1968) are very clear about the limitations they see in the various educational and psychological assessments that had been developed in the previous part of this century. They argue that all tests which measure mental phenomena of real interest have little reliability, while all reliable tests measure trivial mental phenomena. Lord and Novick's ideas are important beyond just a historical sense of the field of educational measurement because their position provided the support for later theorists like Lee Cronbach (1988) and Samuel Messick (1989), who would eventually revolutionize validity theory. In an important sense, then, "comparatively high reliability is neither a necessary nor a sufficient condition for establishing the validity of a measure" (Williamson 1994, 162). This distinction between the value of reliability and validity is crucial for those of us who work in writing assessment because of the dominant force reliability has been in the creation and design of writing assessment procedures. However, the importance of validity in educational measurement cannot be overstated, since the concept of validity furnishes the fundamental rationale for taking test results seriously and using them to make important educational decisions. In a nutshell, validity is the essential way in which a measurement is judged, what Pamela Moss (1998) has called "the test of a test." The changing nature of validity reflects the changing values of those who work in education. Initially, validity meant whether or not a test measured what it purported to measure.

Traditionally, validity has been conceived as a three-part concept: content validity, criterion validity and construct validity. For a measurement to have content validity it must contain content and use procedures relevant to the phenomenon of interest. Essentially, the domain of the content being measured needs to correspond to the material used in the assessment. Criterion validity refers to the values and performances the assessment is designed to assess. For example, one type of criterion validity could be predictive validity, which means that a measure is able to predict how well a student will perform in some future context. SAT and ACT tests are said to have predictive validity, since they can reasonably predict student success in the first year of college. Writing assessment for placement into first-year writing courses would also need to have predictive ability because a reader examines student writing to make a judgment predicting where that student would most profit from instruction. Other kinds of criterion validity include concurrent validity which stipulates a measure to be valid if it correlates well enough to another valued measure. For example, multiple choice tests of usage, grammar and mechanics achieved status as valid *indirect* measures of writing because scores on such tests correlated highly enough with scores given on holistically scored essays. Criterion validity can take many forms depending upon the assessment purpose and location. Within the trinity of content, criterion, and construct, construct validity was considered the most important of the three but also the most illusive. Early conceptions see construct validity as a net of relations that are connected nomologically (Cronbach and Meehl 1955) in consistent fashion to produce an adequate construct of the ability to be tested. More recent ideas about construct validity relate it to the conformity of a measure with a model or theory of the phenomenon of interest (Anastasi 1986).

It is important to note that validity does not reside within a test itself, but that "one validates not a test, but an interpretation of data arising from a specified procedure" (Cronbach 1971). The three-part nature of validity allowed claims about the validity of a particular assessment to be meted out piecemeal, so that something like a multiple choice test could be considered a valid measure of writing ability based upon the simple fact that scores on such tests correlate to a specific degree to scores received on holistically scored essays. This notion of validity as three separate entities often allowed validity to be conceived in rather limited terms. For example, Lorrie Shephard notes that during a thirty-year period from 1920–1950, "test-criterion correlations became the standard for judging test accuracy" (1993, 409). Writing in 1946, J.P. Guilford states that "a test is valid for anything with which it correlates" (1946, 410). Of course any of us who has had even an introductory course in statistics or rudimentary training in scientific methods understands the basic fallacy of confounding a correlative relationship with a causal one. This problem with reifying validity into its component parts was recognized in the 1974 version of *Standards for Educational and Psychological Tests* which is issued periodically by the American Psychological Association, the American Research Association and the National Council on Measurement in Education[2]. These aspects of validity (content, criterion and construct) can be discussed independently, but only for convenience. They are interrelated operationally and logically; only rarely is one of them alone important in a particular situation (1974, 26).

While this made sense theoretically, in practice, separate camps within the measurement community continued to privilege one form of validity over another, allowing such practices as the validation of multiple choice tests for writing ability. In fact, writing as late as 1984, Peter Cooper draws upon this notion of validity in his statement about writing assessment: "From a psychometric point of view, it does appear that indirect assessment alone can afford a satisfactory measure of writing skills for ranking and selection purposes" (1984 27). By the 1980s Lee Cronbach (1988) and Samuel Messick (1989) began to write a series of essays that changed the direction of validity study away from strictly technical and statistical considerations to a consideration of a range of social and environmental factors important in determining the validity of decisions made because of tests and in the formulation of a theory of validity as a singular concept. In this sense, validity can no longer be considered in three separate properties. Instead, in order for a test to be assumed valid it must meet standards for construct validity. Construct validity, then, subsumes matters of content and criterion, so that to speak of construct validity itself is to speak of validity. Lee Cronbach (1988), who has been influential in the evolution of validity theories since the 1950s, views test validation as the construction of an evaluation argument for the soundness of a particular set of inferences to be derived from a specific measurement. Validation speaks to a diverse and potentially critical audience; therefore, the argument must "link concepts, evidence, social and personal consequences, and values" (Cronbach 1988, 4). Cronbach's emphasis on audience and argument lends a rhetorical feel to validity that resonates with those of us who work in writing assessment. Cronbach's rhetoric of validity also resonates with current conceptions of language and literacy as he stresses the importance of the "social" and "personal," recognizing that validity (as does rhetoric) contains "consequences" and values" crucial to groups and individuals.

Cronbach's insistence on linking the conceptual with the evidential foreshadows and mirrors Samuel Messick's emphasis on the combination of empirical and theoretical concerns in test validation. In Messick's definition, "validity is an integrated evaluative judgment of the degree to which empirical evidence and theoretical rationales support the *adequacy* and appropriateness of *inferences* and *actions* based on test scores or other modes of assessment" (1989, 13). This definition of validity combines empirical and theoretical perspectives in constructing guidelines for making sound judgments based upon a particular measurement. In this sense, Messick is calling for a theorized practice of assessment in which theory and practice are inseparable from each other. This fusion of theory and practice is also central to the discipline of rhetoric and composition. James Zebroski (1994) articulates the centrality of the theory/practice connection:

> Theory is not the opposite of practice; theory is not even a supplement to practice. Theory is practice, a practice of a particular kind, and practice is always theoretical. The question is not whether we have a theory of composition, that is, a view or better, a vision of our selves and our activity, but whether we are going to become conscious of our theory. (15)

In this sense, validity requires that we become conscious of our theory of assessment and of the theories that support the educational practices and decisions the assessment is designed to measure.

This intellectual move to become more conscious of the theoretical implications of our practices and the practical implications of our theories has important consequences for the kinds of writing assessment procedures we build now and in the future. Pamela Moss notes that "Where the mainstream literature in validity theory (and program assessment) falls short, in my judgment, at least in practical emphasis if not in intent, is in encouraging a kind of critical reflection about its own taken-for-granted theories and practices" (1998 112). This critical reflection is even more crucial for writing assessment, since a full understanding of its issues and practices requires an interdisciplinary approach involving a multiple theoretical understanding. For example, in delineating a systems approach to validity, Fredericksen and Collins (1989) refer to work done in writing assessment to highlight the forward-thinking nature of composition and language arts teachers in linking educational outcomes and environment to assessment in writing. In general, this fusion of practice and theory can highlight the importance of pedagogy with educational measurement and promote the kind of dialectic that Moss (1998) and others like Donald Schön (1983) call for in conceiving appropriate professional activity as reflection-in-action. This discussion of multiple theories and practices in understanding writing assessment brings us back to an earlier point we mentioned about the importance of English teachers learning statistics or psychometrics to be able to carry on conversations with measurement specialists (Scharton 1996; White 1994). It should begin to be clear from our discussion of current theories of validity that English teachers' understanding of the importance of rhetorical principles and the integration of theory and practice in composition positions them to carry on fruitful conversations with the measurement community. Although we don't mean to ignore the statistical side of educational measurement, it is a misnomer to highlight statistics as the fundamental property in educational or writing assessment. Instead of emphasizing statistics, we would rather advocate a working knowledge of a few fundamental principles in validity theory for those English teachers who work in assessment, because emerging theories of validity have the potential to pressure measurement specialists to consider the importance of composition theory in writing assessment design and implementation.

COMPETING MODELS OF ASSESSMENT

Current traditional forms of writing assessment, like analytic, holistic, or primary trait,[3] share common assumptions from traditional forms of measurement theory and practice. These procedures were developed by the CEEB and ETS during the first half of the twentieth century and were widely adopted during the 1970s. All three require that readers be trained to agree and to score papers according to a common rubric that describes numerical points. Each paper is given two different scores, and the scores of more than one scale point discrepancy are mediated to produce a more overall reliable rate of agreement. Such procedures share many of the assumptions of logical positivism, including the importance of technical and statistical rigor. The emphasis is on creating procedures in which readers can consistently score the same paper. Rates of agreement are calculated and monitored because without a high enough rate of reliability, scores cannot be considered valid. Student writing is scored because it is assumed that student ability in writing can be communicated numerically. There are no restraints on the guidelines used to describe specific score points. Recent writing assessment programs like, the statewide assessment program in Georgia from 1989 to 1990, used a scoring guideline that was predominantly focused on language conventions (Englehard, Gordon and Gabrielson 1992). The scoring guideline for the assessment of state-mandated portfolios in the State of Kentucky uses the exact same score criteria for portfolios scored from students in elementary, middle, and high school grades (Kentucky Department of Education 1994), even though writing at these three different levels is likely to be quite different in terms of subject matter, skill, audience and purpose. Such consistency is in keeping with the purposes of current traditional writing assessment procedures like the trend sample of the writing portion of the National Assessment of Educational Progress, which attempts to measure and compare generations of students' writing ability.

These traditional procedures, and the theoretical and epistemological rationales which highlight the importance of consistency and standardization, assume that these qualities can and should be maintained across temporal and environmental contexts. Traditional forms of writing assessment like holistic, analytic or primary trait are clearly supported by traditional notions of validity that focus on determining that *a test measure what it purports to measure* and that the consistency of a test be maintained at all costs. Lord and Novick's (1968) concern from thirty years ago seems poignant in the consideration of the two examples of state wide tests from Georgia and Kentucky. Both testing systems provide an efficient means of examining a large number of students' writing, and there is every reason to believe that this examination is consistent across grade and school district boundaries. What is not so clear, however, is how robust a version of writing ability is actually being examined. Can we assume in Messick's (1989) terms that the large-scale assessment of student writing undertaken at the state or even national level provides the empirical and theoretical rationales for adequate and appropriate decision-making about student writing? Is there enough high-quality evidence to construct, in Cronbach's (1988) terms, an evaluation argument for the validity of important decisions based upon these measures? Of course, a responsible answer to such questions would require research beyond the scope of an entire chapter in a single book. We do think, though, that the disjuncture between newer versions of validity and current traditional notions of writing assessment are clear and indisputable.

Recently, we in composition studies have begun to develop writing assessment procedures based upon our understanding of literacy and its teaching (Allen 1995; Durst, Roemer and Schultz 1994; Haswell and Wyche-Smith 1994; Smith 1993). Newer versions of writing assessment that do not share either the assumptions of traditional measurement theory or the practices of current traditional writing assessment have been appearing the literature for the last five years or so. William L. Smith developed one of the earliest of these new procedures for placement of students in the various courses in the composition program at the University of Pittsburgh. Smith's design deviated from traditional procedures in that he hired his readers according to the classes they most recently taught. Instead of scoring student writing on a numerical scale, readers made one of two decisions, whether or not students should be placed in their course, or whether the student writing should be referred to the readers for the course above or below their own. This system involved no formal rubrics or training procedures, since readers made decisions about particular classes based upon knowledge they already had. Smith reported that this method allowed a more accurate and efficient placement of students than did holistic scoring, which had been used previously. Smith's method has been adapted at the University of Louisville in a pilot program that uses students' state-mandated portfolios for placement, and it has been found to work well with portfolio placement (Lowe and Huot 1997).

The placement program developed by Richard Haswell and Susan Wyche-Smith (1994) at Washington State University involves having only one reader examine all student placement essays. This reader decides whether or not a student would profit from the composition course designed to meet the needs of most enrolling first-year students. Sixty percent of all students are placed into the most heavily enrolled course based upon this singular reading. The other forty percent of students have their writing read a second time by a group of readers who were expert in all courses in the first-year composition curriculum. This multiple "tiered" reading, as it has been dubbed, has been extended to create a portfolio junior-level writing assessment program for all students (Haswell 1998). Again, these programs have proven to be more efficient and accurate than those they replaced which depended upon rubrics, training, interrater reliability, numerical scoring and the other trappings of what we call the technology of testing.

We now consider one last model in which students writing is read to make important decisions—this one from the University of Cincinnati. This program is designed to ensure that all students who move from one course to another have the necessary skills envisioned and demanded by their writing program. Competency programs, even those using portfolios, are not that rare these days. What makes this program worthy of mention is that student writing is read by three-teacher teams known as trios. Each teacher brings her students' portfolios to be read together as a group. These trios make decisions about whether or not student writing is at a level commensurate with program standards. In addition to providing accurate decisions about students' ability to move from one course to another, this program also provides important benefits to the program itself: "portfolio negotiations can serve as an important means of faculty development, can help ease anxieties about grading and passing judgment on students' work and can provide a forum for teachers and administrators to rethink the goals of a freshmen English program" (Durst, Roemer and Schultz 1994, 287). Such an assessment program meets the concerns of newer forms of validity that educational assessment have a positive influence on teaching and learning. Just as it would have been irresponsible of us to claim any sort of invalidity for more traditional writing assessment measures, it is equally problematic for us to claim any kind of validity for these newer writing assessment practices. However, we believe it is clear to see how these new programs attempt to combine the accurate generation of assessment data with an understanding of the ways in which student writing is read, evaluated and taught within acceptable educational contexts. It is conceivable, for example, that we could make an evaluation argument for some of these newer forms of writing assessment that links "concepts, evidence, social and personal consequences and values" (Cronbach 1988).

One implicit contention we hold about these new forms of assessment is that through the use of specific readers for specific educational decisions or the use of teacher collaboration to make decisions about program standards and values, what emerges is a type of writing assessment that links the making of decisions about written texts to specific contexts. The importance of context in meaning making through literate practices has its roots in various literary, linguistic, and rhetorical theories and theorists (for example, see Derrida; Halliday; Perelman). This theoretical grounding is also important to informed pedagogy in the teaching of writing that helps students define purposes and locate audiences for their own writing. As we have seen in our examples of newer forms of assessment, audience and purpose also play an important role in writing assessment. Our last example of writing assessment outside of a traditional theory of assessment also comes from outside an educational context and looks at the ways people in the publishing industry go about making important decisions about writing. Over the last decade or so Janice Radway has done a series of studies about the Book of the Month Club (BOMC). Much of Radway's study has come from her focus in critical theory and literature about the way in which competing cultural values get inscribed and replicated in people's reading habits as exhibited in the kinds of texts BOMC offers to its readership. What we are interested in, however, is the part of the study in which Radway describes how decisions are made about what books get chosen for the club itself. The assessment task the club faces is quite daunting: "its editors sift through more than five thousand manuscripts annually to choose approximately two hundred and fifty books that the club eventually offers to its membership" (1989, 260). What makes this task even more complicated is that the club offers selections in "several informally defined categories," so that the selection process is not just about choosing the best books. Like the newer forms of placement we reviewed above, readers are choosing texts that "serve . . . different kinds of readers who use books for different purposes and thus judge them according to different criteria" (1989,

261). Just as traditional forms of writing assessment describe specific numerical points on a rubric, the BOMC isolates texts with specific criteria for its diverse readership. However, unlike traditional forms of writing assessment, the Book of the Month Club does not choose its books according to a set of articulated criteria, nor does it train its editors or stipulate that they code their decisions about texts into numeric rankings. Instead, editors read and select books, writing descriptions of their selections for the BOMC catalogue that is sent out to its readers on a regular basis.

> With little more to go on than a paragraph or two of description and a few sketchy plans for future publicity, they must "place" the book, evaluate it, and decide whether they can convey their enthusiasm to a potential reader in a description that is routinely two hundred to three hundred words long and no more than one thousand. Their reading is governed finally not only by their own preferences and training but by the fact that the club is a business designed to sell books to others. They are always trying to read as they believe their members do. (1989, 262)

It's interesting to note that these procedures resemble in some striking ways the newer forms of assessment we have been describing, even as they differ from traditional forms of assessment. The judgments of the editors for BOMC are based upon their experience and expertise as readers, as editors, as employees of a particular company, and as writers who must take their judgments about texts and convey them successfully to the readers who will ultimately purchase the books and eventually ratify the accuracy of such judgments. What makes the comparison of the way BOMC editors make decisions about texts so interesting to us is that while the similarities between new forms of educational writing assessment and differences from traditional forms are so striking, the situation and outcome of the decisions are so radically different. What appears to emerge here from a consideration of the assessment of texts from both an educational and professional context is a sort of professional ability to read texts for various purposes and to make important decisions without the need to articulate standards or ensure standardization.

These competing models of assessment, it seems to us, are based upon competing models of the way people arrive at judgments about written texts. Traditional measurement theory is based upon a Platonic universe and positivist epistemology in which there is an idealized universal truth that assumes a single correct answer. New forms of assessment assume the importance of context and purpose in the process of reading written texts, student or professional, to arrive at a specific judgment, whether that is the suitability of a book for a particular readership or whether or not a student should be placed into a specific class or exited from another. Regardless of the decisions in mind, there is an assumption that professional editors or teachers are qualified to make these types of decisions based upon their experience and expertise without the need of special training or monitoring. The ability to make appropriate decisions is in the expertise and experience of the readers, not in the external technology of a specific methodology or set of procedures.

WHAT DIFFERENCE DO THE DIFFERENCES MAKE?

Before we can answer the question that this concluding section of our essay asks, we need to articulate what the differences, indeed, are. The biggest difference, it appears to us, is the use of different terms which reflect different attitudes and assumptions about the way writing is assessed. Holistic, analytic and primary trait scoring are about what *scores* students get or raters give. In newer writing assessment schemes teachers *read* student writing to make decisions about writers. While traditional forms of writing assessment are based upon a *theory of scoring*, new forms of writing assessment are based upon a *theory of reading*. Scoring, as we have already discussed in our section about the theoretical basis for traditional writing assessment procedures, assumes a knowable, ideal, single account of writing quality that requires a specific technology like training, rubrics, etc. to make that assumption a reality. Reading, on the other hand assumes a divergent approach to meaning making, since different readers are capable of multiple accounts of a given text, depending upon the context of the reading and the position of the reader. Wolfgang Iser (1978) coined the term "wandering viewpoint" in his book *The Act of Reading* to describe the flexible nature of a reader's ability to comprehend various types of written discourse. Whether we consider literature from psycholinguistics like the work of Frank Smith (1982) or from reading theory like Richard Anderson and P. David Pearson (1984) or literary theory like Stanley Fish (1980), the current characterization of the act of reading is one of fluidity, adaptability and divergence. Each of the various newer methods for assessing student writing as well as the BOMC procedures are all based upon a notion of reading that privileges the individual reader who has the necessary expertise, experience and authority to make accurate judgments about written discourse. The key to the kind of reading given by an individual is the specific context within which she reads. In newer forms of writing assessment and the method used by the BOMC, the reader is given a rich context within which to read. Conversely, in traditional forms of writing assessment, raters are restricted to the limited context of the rubric and training they receive to agree with other scorers.

Edward Wolfe's (1997) research into the scoring processes of highly reliable holistic raters indicates that they employ a more focused and limited reading process than less reliable raters. Inherent in the difference in context provided by the different methods for assessing student writing is the amount of control given to individual people or sites. There is a reluctance, we believe, on the part of traditional procedures to let such decisions about writing assessment be based upon such authority as an expert reader and his or her local community. Standardizing procedures and limiting context is another way to ensure control for assessment, standards and values with a central authority.

Radway notes that although BOMC editors did successfully choose books for the club, these decisions are not based upon extensive market research or surveys of readership taste or preferences.

> The editorial decisions upon which the present study are based were still grounded predominantly in hunch, intuition, and luck. This is not to say that the editors knew little about their audience, only that the knowledge they had of it was not in quantifiable form but existed as the tacit, relatively unconscious product of long personal experience. (1989, 264)

Radway's language here is revealing. In her use of such words as "hunch, intuition, luck," she relegates these important, accurate assessments of texts to a sort of second class status because "the club's past editorial operations have been based on surprisingly little hard data" (264). Her classification of these judgments parallel the reactions some have had about new forms of writing assessment.

A couple of years ago at the University of Louisville, we were contacted by an employee of the Kentucky State Department of Education who had heard we were using state-mandated portfolios to place students into first-year writing courses. She offered to train us according to the holistic rubric and methods the state uses for scoring the portfolios. We told her we were adapting William L. Smith's method, and when she questioned the lack of a rubric we referred her to literature on the reading processes of holistic raters (Huot 1993; Pula and Huot 1993; Smith 1993) which seems to indicate that readers have an internalized rubric that they use to read and rate student writing regardless or in spite of any holistic training they might receive. Not too long afterwards, we heard through the office that acts as a liaison for the university to the public schools, that the State Department was concerned that we were letting teachers use their "intuition" to score writing portfolios for placement. Of course, we took great pains to correct what we saw as a misconception of our procedures. Our lack of comfort with characterizing our teachers as using their intuition points out the suspicion with which teachers' decisions are often viewed and the lack of authority accorded to their expertise and experience. In fact, Edward White (1995) sees direct writing assessment as a way to control for the problems inherent in teachers' readings of their students' writing. In our specific case, we were aware that the design of our procedures was based upon research into the ways teachers read student writing in holistic scoring sessions; we were also aware of the ways in which standardized methods of assessing student writing are privileged over more local ones. What we also see at work here is that local, contextualized knowledge about the way people read and arrive at judgments about that reading is not considered to be as good or appropriate as procedures that are more standardized, that appear more scientific, objective or quantifiable. Even though we could argue for the validity of localized procedures within Cronbach's ideas of validity as argument (1988), ultimately we have to argue against the continuing perception of superiority for standardized methods for assessing writing. In other words, argument for newer forms of writing assessment are often not about the new methods but about ingrained perceptions of what assessment *ought* to be[4]. Like Radway, we at Louisville were uncomfortable with characterizing important evaluative decisions about text as based upon intuition. While perceptions for assessment continue to rely upon more technological and scientifically based procedures, those of us promoting a new agenda for writing assessment need to recognize the power of an expert reader's "intuition, hunch or luck."

The critical importance of theoretical and epistemological differences between traditional and emergent writing assessment practices seems too large and important for a single essay. Clearly, the differences in praxis point out completely different theoretical and epistemological orientations, not to mention the important ideological question of where the power and control lie in these different versions of assessment. Our hope is that this discussion of theory and practice in writing assessment helps to bring to the surface the important task of looking past assessment practices to the theories that inform them. It is paramount, we believe, that those of us who teach student writers gain some control of the way student writing is assessed in and outside of the classroom. Calls for state and national assessment programs continue to be an important political rallying point for school-reform movements as well as for the advancement of individual political careers. Continuing the conversation about writing assessment which we have hoped to begin in this chapter is an important way for English teachers to have some say about educational reform and about the ways writing will not only be assessed but what about what kinds of written communication we will be able to value and teach in our classrooms. Conversations about assessment theory and practice need to continue and flourish, and these conversations need to include English teachers and writing program administrators. As we highlight the importance of theory and practice in composition studies as a whole, we also need to make a conscious effort to include such conversations about theory and practice in writing assessment.

NOTES

1. In her book *Institutionalizing Literacy,* Mary Trachsel (1992) examines the history of the essay examination in higher education in America and explores its impact on writing assessment and writing instruction.
2. These guidelines are published periodically to provide a set of professional principles for those working in educational assessment. These standards are currently under revision because of recent calls to make professional standards of practice in assessment relevant to more current theoretical understandings of validity and its subsequent effect on decisions and inferences based upon educational assessments.

3. Comparison studies of holistic, analytic and primary trait scoring show that all three procedures correlate fairly well (Freedman 1984; Veal and Hudson 1983). Holistic scoring has become the procedure of choice mainly because it is more efficient. (Veal and Hudson 1983). Actually primary trait was adapted from analytic scoring by a group working outside of the CEEB or ETS who were trying to implement an examination of writing for the National Assessment of Educational Progress. See Richard Lloyd-Jones (1977) for a description.

4. We are reminded of an experience we had at a meeting about writing not too long ago. After we described some procedures we had been using, one of the participants asked us what rubric we had been using. When we replied that weren't using a rubric, his response was, "Oh, this is just a subjective assessment." We, of course, pointed out to him and the rest of the audience that writing out criteria for assessing did not necessarily make an assessment more objective.

PART THREE

Refiguring and Relocating Research

CHAPTER EIGHT

Voices of Research
Methodological Choices of a Disciplinary Community

Susan Peck MacDonald

*T*HE FIELD OF COMPOSITION STUDIES—PERHAPS PRE-DISCIPLINARY BEFORE the 1980s—made a simultaneous move toward disciplinarity and the social sciences in the 1980s. In the 1990s, however, a significant portion of composition studies has moved once again resolutely toward the humanities. With an influx of theorizing from the humanities and an assortment of intellectual influences from postmodernism—calls for multi-vocal texts, the "interpretive turn," distrust of science, a reassertion of the value of the local—composition studies today has in some ways turned away from empirical research and knowledge making. In so doing, I will argue, the field of composition studies undermines the possibilities of developing as a form of social science while encouraging a type of scholarship found more often in the humanities. The purpose of this essay is ultimately to argue for conceiving of the field of rhetoric and composition as an enlightened, flexible social science and, more specifically, to examine one area of debate about how to write research in the field of composition. My focus will not be on the truth or falsehood of research findings derived from one methodology rather than another or on the ultimate goals of different methodological choices, but on some of the implications methodological choices have for us as a disciplinary field.

Key theoretical or methodological discussions in the humanities have recently focused on "the subject position." There have been calls for more multi-vocal or polyvocal texts to represent more voices within the texts we write as scholars or researchers. There have also been calls for scholars or researchers to include a more personal voice or to write in a more narrative manner. I am eliding many distinctions in this brief characterization, but such eliding is necessary to get to my starting point, which is this: there are, in general, three kinds of voices potentially heard in any scholarly text:

- the voice(s) of the author/researcher
- the voice(s) of the "subjects" of research
- the voice(s) of other members of the research community

I will begin by reviewing, briefly, what might be called the default mode of academic writing—the epistemic repertoire, as I call it—in which the voices of other members of the research community are represented through citations and discussions of others' research. I then review some of the confusions implicit in justifications currently offered for alternative ways of academic writing: for including the voices of the "subjects" of research and the personal voice of the author/researcher(s). After this review, however, I return to the epistemic voice, discussing (1) what it looks like as text and (2) what consequences it has for the disciplinary community.

EPISTEMIC ACADEMIC WRITING: VOICES OF THE RESEARCH COMMUNITY

The cluster of postmodern impulses leading to calls for multi-vocal texts or more narrative stands in opposition primarily to the epistemic repertoire. Considerably simplified, the epistemic ethos is this: An academic field gains its identity by some sort of cumulative work on a knowledge problem in the field, by a number of different academics adding to the field. There will be agreements and disagreements, both of which have to be sorted out explicitly by writing about them. There are widely accepted norms by which academics cite others' research, referring to others in their field both as a courtesy and because their mutual academic work depends on some degree of collaboration. These norms, as proponents of the epistemic repertoire might argue, reflect—possibly even enforce—a sense of fair play among academics and in that way have ethical consequences. More importantly, perhaps, these norms help the knowledge-making activities of the field: they help researchers in the field keep up with the work their colleagues are doing in order to build on that work, suggest corrections where it seems wrong, negotiate over its implications, and use it to create new knowledge. In this view, referring to and representing one's colleague researchers should promote the welfare of the field as a knowledge-making endeavor.

In my 1994 study of professional academic writing in literary studies, history, and psychology, I distinguished between two kinds of sentence subjects used in academic knowledge making: "epistemic" and "phenomenal" sentence subjects. Phenomenal sentence subjects consist of nouns and noun phrases referring to what the researcher is studying. Epistemic sentence subjects, by contrast, consist of nouns and noun phrases referring to research and researchers in the field or conceptual tools and specialized terms used by the field to conduct its knowledge making. Within both general categories—phenomenal and epistemic—further distinctions and subcategories can be made, but the general distinction between phenomenal and epistemic is related to the distinction I will develop further below between looking *outside* the discipline to consider how we represent the "subjects" of our research and looking *inside* the discipline to consider the representations we make *within*—and *for* and *of*—the research community in which we are doing research.[1] It may currently seem retrograde to many academics in the humanities to think positively about disciplinary boundaries or negatively about transcending, disrupting, or moving outside those boundaries, but that is, in fact, one implication of my argument.

I will return to a more concrete discussion of what the epistemic repertoire looks like as text and how its "voices" may function in comparison to the alternative voices currently urged by some postmodernists. But first, I review the arguments for these alternative voices.

THE RATIONALE FOR INCLUDING THE VOICE(S) OF THE "SUBJECTS" OF RESEARCH

Calls for including the voice—or voices—of the "subjects" of research have been made implicitly or explicitly in opposition to the epistemic model on the assumption that composition researchers may be hearing too much from scholars or researchers and too little from our "subjects." Some of the reasons given for including such voices involve problematic assumptions, I will suggest, about what might be achieved by new ways of academic writing versus what might or might not be achieved through the epistemic repertoire.

A first type of reasoning comes from Patricia Sullivan, who has argued that a female graduate student whom Stephen North characterized as repeatedly failing exams might have been better understood if her voice were heard:

> Nowhere in North's account is the woman herself allowed to speak. We simply do not know what she would say if she could tell the story for herself, how she would interpret her three failures or her eventual success. Hers is an untold story, a story we're not permitted to hear, an "other" perspective we're not allowed to share. (47)

Sullivan understandably envisions the woman's problems as related to gender; the implication is that better understanding might have helped the woman learn better and sooner how to succeed as an academic writer. This reason is grounded, then, in the desire to know better how to do what we as a field are trying to do. There is no conflict here between Sullivan's goal for this research case and the goals of epistemic research. Any discrepancy—leading Sullivan to propose including the woman's voice—comes from the assumption that composition could do its traditional work better (know better what to do with this woman) if we heard from her.

From my point of view, however, there are two potential problems—not with Sullivan's goal, but with her concrete proposal. First, the woman herself may not know how to interpret her problem; she may be resistant to the notion that gender matters or may assign the wrong interpretation to *how* gender matters. In that case, adding her voice may contribute nothing. Analogous phenomena have been noted by several anthropologists, and since many of the calls for multi-vocal texts in composition have been influenced by discussions of multi-vocal texts in anthropology, compositionists should be aware that anthropologists have noted the possibility of misguided informants.[2]

A second potential problem with Sullivan's proposal involves the role of the researcher and research field. We are entitled to ask whether the epistemic repertoire might operate just as efficiently—or more so—in achieving the very goal that Sullivan hoped to obtain. Even in the years since North published his research in 1987 or Sullivan hers in 1992, we have seen growing interest in gender and writing. Is it not the fault of the researcher (North) or the research field itself if a plausible variable like gender was not examined in a research study during the 1980s? Empirical research has ways of dealing with variables such as gender so long as a research field acknowledges that gender may be an important variable. I would argue, then, that the problem Sullivan points to in that particular instance lay in the research field at the time of publication, rather than in the silencing of the voice of the woman student.

I began with Sullivan's 1992 example as representing a rather conventional goal that could be shared within the epistemic model. However, not all proposals for multi-vocal texts arise from similar goals. For Blakeslee, Cole, and Conefrey, including the voices of research "subjects" has social consequences either independent of or equally important as the more epistemic rationale Sullivan gives for including the woman's voice. Here are two key pieces of Blakeslee, Cole, and Conefrey's rationale:

[1] Rather than being arbiters who, in formulating interpretations, cast judgments on and exercise authority over the sites and subjects we study, we will become collaborators and mediators engaging with and involving our subjects more fully in our research and in our writing. (142–143)

[2] Feminist perspectives also advocate an antihierarchical approach to research in which subjects are not seen as objects to be studied, observed, or written about, but as co-originators of our inquiry (Rich 135). By allowing subjects to speak for themselves and to clarify or correct our interpretations of their ideas, we reduce the possibility of misnaming, misrepresenting, burying, or confusing our subjects' voices and perspectives. (147)

In these statements, I see at least three kinds of assumptions: (1) that subjects speaking for themselves may clarify or correct our misinterpretations, (2) that it is better for researchers to be collaborative and anti-hierarchical than not, and (3) that silencing our subjects' voices is harmful. The first of these three reasons seems similar to the one in Sullivan's example above—and it seems vulnerable in the same way Sullivan's example is vulnerable. Discussions of the value of multi-vocality are often carried on in this general way as if what is valuable in one research setting is likely to be valuable in another. But if our "subjects" happen to be wrong or confused or resistant in what they are thinking, then adding their voices to our research may contribute little of importance to the knowledge developing in the field.

The second reason, however, rests on an ethical claim: that one type of behavior by researchers is preferable to another not because of the knowledge that ensues but because it is preferable to foster some types of people rather than other types. The third reason is also ethical: that we owe our research "subjects" a hearing not because—or not solely because of—what they can contribute to our knowledge making, but because it is good to let people be heard.

Important though it is to consider the ethics of our professional lives, I suggest that part of our professional ethics should require us to scrutinize carefully ethical claims like those I have quoted. One quick way of making certain we do not silence our "subjects" would be to forego having "subjects." If we do no research, we will not engage in hierarchical activities, will not set ourselves up as authorities in relation to others who are not our equals. Another way to give voice to our "subjects" would be to devote our research to the project of giving voice, but if that is our goal, we might do just as well to become newspaper reporters, tabloid TV hosts, social workers, or psychological counselors. The rationale for research itself disappears and perhaps the safest research is no research at all.

Consider this hypothetical situation, using the sort of example Sullivan discusses. Let us say that woman writer X has had writing problems that may have something to do with gender. Let us say, also, that—like Stephen North's "subject"—she has finally succeeded in passing exams and that therefore research on her problem is motivated less by concern for this particular woman's future as a writer than by concern for future women writers and writing instruction in general. In such a case, my question is: Whose concern is this? And my answer tends to be: the concern of the research community. If the woman's privacy is not violated and her future as a writer is not jeopardized in the way that a patient's taking a placebo might jeopardize her health in a drug comparison study, then it does not seem to me that we should focus our ethical or text-forming questions on whether the subject's voice is heard. Instead of turning our attention outward to the "subjects" of our research, we should, I am arguing, turn our attention inward to our research community. We should care less about the woman herself—mindful of the caveats I have mentioned above—and more about developing research which is increasingly informative, convincing, and helpful among those who are professionally committed to teaching writing and understanding more about writing.

THE RATIONALE FOR INCLUDING THE VOICE OF THE AUTHOR/RESEARCHER(S)

Recent arguments for including the voice of the author/researcher are related to arguments for including the voices of our "subjects," but they nevertheless deserve separate discussion. I refer here not to older expressivist preferences for the "I" or the personal "voice," but to more recent postmodern, feminist, or political rationales for narrative and recognition of the personal.

In the 1998 convention program for the Conference on College Composition and Communication (CCCC), the number of convention sessions listed under the category of "Personal Writing/Identity" overwhelms the number devoted to more traditional epistemic research subjects in composition. Here is a *partial* list:

Assessment—13 sessions
Empirical Research Methodologies and Reports of Research—17 sessions
Rhetorical and Textual Analysis—9 sessions
Teaching of Writing and Rhetoric—194 sessions
    Grammar and Style—2 sessions
    Public Discourse—3 sessions
    Personal Writing/Identity—36 sessions
Writing and Difference—51 sessions
    Issues of Gender—18 sessions
    Teaching in a Multicultural Environment—25 sessions

These numbers offer a reflection of our current professional concerns—and confusions. I see a professional identity crisis lurking behind our devoting eighteen times as much attention to "Personal Writing-Identity" as to either "Grammar and Style" or "Preparing for the Workplace," four times as much attention to "Personal Writing-Identity" as to "Rhetorical and Textual Analysis," or over three times as much attention to "Personal Writing-Identity" as to "English as a Second Language."

One of the seminal arguments for the personal came from Jane Tompkins in 1989:

The problem is that you can't talk about your private life in the course of doing your professional work. You have to pretend that epistemology, or whatever you're writing about, has nothing to do with your life, that it's more exalted, more important, because it (supposedly) *transcends* the merely personal. Well, I'm tired of the conventions that keep discussions of epistemology, or James Joyce, segregated from meditations on what is happening outside my window or inside my heart. The public-private dichotomy, which is to say, the public-private *hierarchy*, is a founding condition of female oppression. I say to hell with it. The reason I feel embarrassed at my own attempts to speak personally in a professional context is that I have been conditioned to feel that way. That's all there is to it. (122 –3)

The reasoning here seems to contain three premises: (1) that any dichotomy between public and private implies a *hierarchy* in which public is the preferred term, and that is, in Tompkins' view, bad; (2) that such a hierarchy contributes to female oppression; and (3) that we would include the private were we not conditioned (by *what* or *whom* exactly Tompkins does not say) to do otherwise. Each of these premises seems arguable, but the first is perhaps most interesting for my purposes here.

That Tompkins—or others following her—can make unsupported claims for the benefit of combining the private and public may well show the strength of our commitment to the private, rather than our obsession with the public. It may show a particularly persistent, though frequently mutating anti-intellectu-alism in American life that makes us consider expert knowledge undemocratic.

We should note that Tompkins uses the term "public," rather than a term like "academic" or "knowledge making," in opposition to "private." This sug-gests that she has little sense of there being a body of *disciplinary* knowledge that might have some worth *within* a discipline. Her opposed terms—public and private—exclude the existence of disciplinary work that might be relevant or important to disciplinary practitioners for the work they do independent of either their private lives or their public lives.

Confusion about Forums and Purposes

I offer Tompkins, then, as one influential example of how advocates of the personal voice may confuse four possible forums and purposes.

First is the classroom forum in which students learn to write—for purposes that composition researchers or scholars appear not to agree upon. Some of us may be concerned about the student's ultimate proficiency as a writer in upper division courses, the workplace, or the public arena, but the 1998 session sta-tistics I have cited suggest that we are currently even more concerned with helping students work through identity issues, overcome past traumas, or learn to think in ways we consider more liberating. The liberatory intents of some of these pleas for the personal may have their origins in other disciplines; anthropologist Ruth Behar, for instance, claims that "Personal writing repre-sents a sustained effort to democratize the academy" (Behar 1994, B2). In any case, claims for the liberatory effects of the personal are now frequently found among compositionists:

[W]e wish to highlight the move towards a practice of storytelling and the "per-sonal" which deliberately challenges the boundaries of this reserved space of Western culture for aesthetic self-reflection. Increasingly, the work of a number of minority and third-world writers reflects a sense of storytelling as the marrow of a heritage that can revive dispossessed cultures and experiences, and make possible a newly critical relationship with the dominant culture. (Mahala and Swilky 363)

In author-saturated texts . . . there is a better chance for engaging a reader in our sometimes confusing and always modest cultural journey. . . . Ethnography is subversive—it challenges the dominant positivist view of making knowledge. It demands attention to human subjectivity and allows for author-saturated reconstructions and examinations of a world . . . . (Bishop 152 & 153)

Both examples, the first from Daniel Mahala and Jody Swilky and the sec-ond from Wendy Bishop, imply that at least some significant part of our pur-pose in teaching writing should be to affect what sort of human beings our students become. Writing proficiency has dropped from view as a key purpose. There might be little role for research on student writing if writing proficiency is not the key purpose of the writing classroom.

Second is the forum of the professional literary critic or other academic who is writing critical reflections—either for him/herself or for others who wish to share such reflections. For instance, Frank Lentricchia, in 1996, announced his "Last Will and Testament of an Ex-Literary Critic." In it Lentricchia recounts how in 1983 he "was convinced that a literary critic, *as a literary critic,* could be an agent of social transformation" (60) but that more recently he has stopped reading literary criticism "because most of it isn't literary" and that "it proceeds in happy indifference to, often in unconscionable innocence of, the protocols of literary competence" (60). Arguing that "Imaginative writers have but one agenda: to write beautifully, rivetingly, unforgettably" (65), Lentricchia recounts turning his back on graduate teaching and criticism in order to concentrate just on appreciating literature in his undergraduate classroom. In other words, Lentricchia seems to see little or no need for a professional forum dedicated to research and knowledge making about literature. The only role he sees for discourse about literature is that of sharing and deepening each others' reading and aesthetic experiences. Lentricchia identifies, in my view, one legitimate purpose for discourse about literature, but its purpose is not scholarly or knowledge making, and so he sees no need for a professional forum.

A similar view underlies this view from literary critic Marianna Torgovnik:

> It seems pretty clear to me that if all we want to do is to write for professional advancement, to write for a fairly narrow circle of critics who exist within the same disciplinary boundaries as we do, there is nothing really wrong with the traditional academic style. In fact, it's the right style, the inevitable style, because it says, in every superfluous detail and in every familiar move, You don't need to read me except to write your own project; I am the kind of writing that does not want to be heard.
>
> But when critics want to be read, and especially when they want to be read by a large audience, they have to court their readers. (27)

Torgovnik here seems confused in a number of ways: She seems unable to understand that there might be some reason for professional writing other than personal advancement. She seems to think that the epistemic style is characterized by *superflous* detail. She uses the metaphor about "not wanting to be heard" in a way which leaves me uncertain whether she thinks written knowledge making has an obligation to be pleasing to the ear. And she seems not to understand why some particular knowledge-making activity—lung cancer research, for instance—might legitimately have a smaller set of readers than the a novel or a newspaper report.

If composition scholars saw themselves as coming from a distinctly separate professional area of the academy than literary scholars, they might decide to accept Lentricchia's or even Torgovnick's view of literary forums while holding a different view of professional forums about writing. However, since many composition scholars are trained by and housed with literary scholars in the university, literary views of professional forums are frequently adopted by compositionists. When Mahala and Swilky argued for "reviv[ing] dispossessed cultures and experiences" they used a quotation from Trinh Minh-Ha—not a composition researcher—and an appeal to ethics from African American legal scholar Patricia Williams, who argues that the turn toward the personal will enable "a more nuanced sense of legal and social responsibility" (quoted in Mahala and Swilky 365). Similarly, Bishop takes the term "I-Witnessing" from anthropologist Clifford Geertz when she argues for "author-saturated texts" and the subversiveness of ethnography (Bishop 152 & 153). The fact that such justifications and the goals appealed to (e.g., a sense of "legal responsibility") are often drawn from outside the disciplinary context of composition scholarship shows how far the "discipline" of composition studies is from having much consensus on its disciplinary purposes or identity.

Third, some imply that there is a public forum that academics disregard when they write for other academics. Perhaps this is the source of Torgovnik's confusion—that she thinks there should be a wide public audience for our musings about literature. In any case, the 1998 CCCC session breakdown suggests that we do not seem likely to resurrect a public forum, for there were only 3 sessions on "Public Discourse" next to the 36 on "Personal Writing/Identity." And there might legitimately be no real public interest in all sorts of knowledge-making research where professionals in some relatively narrow field share their research and negotiate disciplinary knowledge. I see writers like Tompkins and Torgovnik as gripped by the dichotomy between private and public while ignoring the role of professional forums.

Fourth, then, professionals might write to build knowledge or resolve disciplinary knowledge issues for each other, envisioning some sort of ultimate good to come out of disciplinary knowledge—a cure for lung cancer, better understanding of how students learn, and so on. This fourth forum is the one that interests me, the one whose purposes I call "epistemic," and the one in which the epistemic voice has evolved. Anyone who intends to create or build on existing knowledge about how writers learn, what writing is, or how different kinds of writing are received ought to recognize the close fit between the epistemic voice and its goal of making knowledge. The confusions come, then, when academics privilege some other goal over the goal of making knowledge.

We see confusion about purposes mixed in with confusion about forums. For instance, Mahala and Swilky, relying on frequent references to Tompkins, argue that the personal voice will allow emotion back in to "the process of attaining knowledge" and will thereby enhance women's authority (371). Yet students are not, ordinarily, *producers* of knowledge in our composition classes, and Mahala and Swilky seem to see no difference between professional knowledge making and the learning that we usually hope for in our undergraduates.

THE EPISTEMIC TEXT

Faced with these challenges to the epistemic repertoire, it is important to consider concretely what the epistemic repertoire looks like *as text* and what consequences it may have for a research community committed to developing its own epistemic repertoire. Following are samples of epistemic sentence subjects from recent empirical work in composition.[3] The sentences come from an article by Danette Paul and Davida Charney, "Introducing Chaos (Theory) into Science and Engineering: Effects of Rhetorical Strategies on Scientific Readers," published in *Written Communication* in 1995. It is a strongly epistemic article, and since Charney has offered a recent exposition and defense of the virtues of empiricism, it serves as an exemplar of what empirical research in composition may look like as text.

These, then, are sentences from Paul and Charney demonstrating three categories of sentence subjects crucial to the epistemic repertoire:

References to research or other researchers

Sentence subjects naming other researchers or referring to other studies in the same field serve, first of all, to locate Paul and Charney's research within a pre-existing disciplinary conversation. John Swales's earlier research on article introductions forms the explicit background context within which Paul and Charney build their discussion of how very new scientific ideas may be presented within the context of previous work. The following sentences occur in their introduction:

> *Kaufer and Carley* (1993) described a paradox in the accumulation of scientific knowledge. (396)
> Over the last 10 years, *some rhetoricians of science* have attempted to answer this question by . . . (397)
> *Paul* (1991) has argued that . . . (398)
> *Swales* found this pattern was quite frequent in the 158 articles he examined across a variety of academic disciplines. (398)
> *Other studies* have also found that migrants to another field often try to sound like insiders (Blakeslee, 1993; Law & Williams, 1982). (400)

Each of these sentences serves to place Paul and Charney's research within a larger disciplinary problem and to differentiate which piece of the problem they are working on from the other pieces that other research has addressed.

Their research is both dependent on and distinct from prior knowledge others have developed. Theirs is not an adversarial relation to prior work, but their frequent references to other work allow for careful distinctions to be drawn. Here, for instance, fully conscious of Swales' concept of "gaps" in previous research that later researchers announce in their introductions (see the first example below), Paul and Charney describe gaps in previous research:

Unfortunately, *none of the studies* we have cited (and here we unabashedly dig our own gap) focused specifically on introductory moves, and *none* have compared revolutionary articles to later articles to see how introductory strategies develop from the point when an approach is launched to the point when it gains a stable place in the literature. (401)

Although Kaufer and Carley's model underscores the importance of tying new work to the best possible old work, *they* did not distinguish citations in the introduction from those in the article as a whole. (401 –2)

Few studies have been conducted of scientists reading and evaluating articles in their professional literature, and *none* that we are aware of have focused on how scientists read introductions. (402)

The *few direct observational studies* of scientists' reading processes have not focused specifically on rhetorical strategies. *Wyatt, Pressley, El-Dinary, Stein, Evans, and Brown* (1993) cataloged a large number of comprehension and evaluation strategies used by social scientists but did not associate those strategies with particular textual features. (402)

It is worth stressing here that Paul and Charney are not writing adversarily in differentiating their research problem or results from the problems addressed or results presented by other researchers. Instead, they use others' research to build their own and to allow them to take a relatively small part of the research problem for inquiry, rather than have to stake out entirely new ground.

Some of the feminist defenses of the personal voice and critiques of the epistemic repertoire have been based on the assumption that the epistemic repertoire is adversarial. Olivia Frey, for instance, writes:

> What does the adversarial method look like? . . . It is the necessity of establishing credibility or cognitive authority. It is the "Critics to date have ignored _____" or the "Critical opinion about _____ differs considerably, betraying how badly _____ has been misunderstood. (511 –12)

But Frey herself is missing important distinctions. If a disciplinary discussion has no cooperatively defined disciplinary research problems and no cumulatively built body of work on those problems, then adversarial or performative gestures may serve for self-promotion. But that is not the case in the sort of research Paul and Charney represent.

Paul and Charney could not ask the questions they ask if they were not building upon previous research—Swales' work on introductions, as well as work by Charles Bazerman, Carolyn Miller, Greg Myers, and others. So Paul and Charney use Swales, but they also draw distinctions from Swales made possible only by Swales' first having laid out the possibilities. Without such communally defined and worked on problems, the alternative is to recycle or constantly rehearse the same testimonials in every new article—as much composition research taking its cues from literary theory and anthropology seems to do.

Reasons, concepts, procedures, or analytic tools belonging to the research field

Sentence subjects referring to reasons, concepts, procedures, or analytic tools of the research field itself are a second crucial category of epistemic sentence subjects.

> *Our selection* of the early articles and their authors was in part predicated on . . . . (414)
> *These procedures* allowed us to investigate . . . . (415)
> *The tapes of the reading-aloud sessions* were transcribed and segmented into commenting episodes. *Most episodes* were bounded by . . . . (416)

While these sentence subjects do not represent the voice of researchers in the field, they illustrate how the presentation of research is filtered through the lens of the field's characteristic reasons, concepts, procedures, or analytic tools. The researcher does not approach the phenomena under study in an unmediated way—face-to-face with the phenomena, naked of conceptual filters—but with communally constructed filters belonging to the research field.

References to Paul and Charney as "We"

A third important category of sentence subjects refers to the researchers themselves (Paul and Charney) and distintinguishes their voice as researchers from the other research they draw on:

> *We* begin to address these questions with . . . (401)
> *we* identified two prominent scientists whose work . . . (403)
> *We* found evidence that readers did recognize . . . (422)
> *We* also observed that all were . . . (423)

This is a real, though collective *we*, not the vaguely general—and sometimes coercive—*we* academics sometimes use to characterize a broad group of readers. Paul and Charney's epistemic *we* performs specific work in making distinctions, spelling out methods, and introducing findings.

These three types of sentences dominate Paul and Charney's article. The only phenomenal sentence subjects occuring frequently in the article are those in sentences which refer to the scientists under study, aspects of the scientists' prose, and the participant readers—the phenomena under study. It is typical of social science writing—particularly in the Methods section of an APA report or its equivalent—to use phenomenal sentence subjects of the latter kind to describe the subjects of research, but it is also typical for a preponderance of the other sentence subjects to be of the three epistemic kinds I have listed above. [4]

These three kinds of epistemic sentences perform crucial disciplinary work. The first kind—sentences naming other research or researchers—situates new research within a disciplinary context, offers recognition and respect to disciplinary colleagues, and makes visible differences of opinion. The second kind makes the claims and warrants of the researchers' reasoning visible and, in the process, makes it possible for other researchers to scrutinize, critique, agree with, or refine the original researchers' reasoning. The third kind—sentence subjects referring to the researchers themselves—allows researchers to tell what they have done and what they have found. It allows them to distinguish between their results and other researchers' results, and it allows them to draw attention to possible shortcomings in their results. Within the epistemic repertoire, this third kind of sentence subject is where the "self-reflexivity" valued by postmodernists enters in. It may not look like the self-reflexivity that most postmodernists think they have in mind, but it serves that purpose.

THE CONSEQUENCES FOR A RESEARCH COMMUNITY

Compositionists' recent calls for more personal voices, more voices of our "subjects," more activist research, more subversion of dominant academic styles, and more empowerment of those whose writing we study in the end look like a form of disciplinary identity crisis or a form of anti-intellectualism long familiar in American society but now turned by the academy against itself. When we focus on goals like empowerment, activism, or social change, we implicitly deny the value of research or of a discipline which already may seem weak or pre-disciplinary to many academic colleagues. Ultimately, borrowing ideas from postmodern work in other fields, denigrating the value of knowledge making, and constantly turning away from our field toward what lies outside the discipline will mean that no disciplinary work of compacting and coalescing and articulating our own disciplinary questions and methods can develop. But by focusing more attention inside the discipline instead—paying scrupulous attention to our own epistemic voices, questions, and methods—we can marshall the effort required to build a cumulative body of knowledge suited to our goals as students of rhetoric.

NOTES

1. I am aware of the amorphousness of defining a discipline when a discipline may consist of many subfields. It is really the subfields that most interest me: the sets of scholars or researchers interested in roughly the same knowledge problems and therefore motivated to read each others' research.
2. See, for instance, Margery Wolf or Katherine Borland.
3. In each case I have italicized the sentence subject, but eliminated inessential parts of sentences in order to make the epistemic patterning stand out more clearly.
4. In a case study of academic writing in psychology, I found approximately 61% of the psychologists' sentence subjects were epistemic but that in their Methods sections, they might use a high percentage (42%) of phenomenal sentence subjects (See *Professional Academic Writing*, chapter six.)

CHAPTER NINE

Grounded Theory
A Critical Research Methodology

Joyce Magnotto Neff

*I*N HIS LAST BOOK, *RHETORICS, POETICS, AND CULTURES*, JAMES BERLIN TALKS about the social and political "formations and practices" that are always "involved in the shaping of consciousness, a shaping mediated by language and situated in concrete historical conditions" (1996, 169). Berlin reviews composition research that examines the production of texts within historical and socioeconomic power structures. He then encourages researchers to consider "production-based studies, text-based studies, and culture-as-lived activity studies," studies "situated within the institution . . . that sponsored the examined activities . . . , [studies that are] related to the ideological—the arena of language, idea, and value" (170).

We as compositionists have been heeding Berlin's advice by theorizing, analyzing, predicting, and arguing with one another in an ever-increasing number of articles and books. What we have not done as prolifically or as well is to account for the methods we use to generate our predictions and reach our conclusions. We do not always critique the assumptions that drive our research, nor do we publish the data bases that support our empirical studies. As Huberman and Miles note, research reports from the 60s, 70s and early 80s rarely contain enough data for "readers to follow how a researcher got from 3,600 pages of field notes to the final conclusions" (1994, 428). Huberman and Miles repeat their lament for the late 80s and early 90s: "It is still unlikely that a researcher could write a case study from a colleague's field notes that would be plausibly similar to the original" (1994, 428). Such a state of affairs indicates to me a need for publishing not only our research conclusions but also our justifications for the methodologies we select to reach those conclusions, especially if the methodologies are relatively recent ones as is grounded theory. Furthermore, a conversation about *how we work* as well as about what we find can help us engage others in a dialogue about composition research. To invite such a dialogue, in the following pages I explain grounded theory and review its application to composition studies. Then I argue two points: (1) we have not made enough progress in developing methodologies that interrogate distinctions between composition theory and the teaching of writing, and (2) we have not studied our research methodologies as social practices in themselves. I look forward to vigorous response.

GROUNDED THEORY AS A METHODOLOGY

In the 1960s, Barney Glaser and Anselm Strauss developed a systematic methodology for qualitative research and for the "discovery of theory from data" (1967, 1). They called the methodology "grounded theory" because the results of the research are "always traceable to the data that gave rise to them" (Strauss and Corbin 1994, 278). Grounded theory requires the researcher to use a specified set of procedures to code data in a series of passes (open, axial, and selective). Data are examined for dimensions and properties, compared with similar phenomena, regrouped and reconceptualized until a provisional theory emerges inductively from the analysis and is further tested through theoretical sampling. Codes are recorded in code notes, integrative memos, visuals, and balancing matrices. Grounded theory is based on "systematically and intensively analyzing data" not just to order them, but to examine conceptual relationships and to *generate theory*. The theories that result consist of "plausible relationships proposed among concepts and sets of concepts" (Strauss and Corbin 1994, 278). The iterative nature of the methodology leads to findings that are rooted in precise analytic procedures and to theory that is fluid, open, and provisional. Grounded theory produces sophisticated representations of complicated social practices (such as writing and the teaching of writing) while it leaves a paper trail of memos and visuals documenting the researchers' paths through the data.

Strauss and Corbin stress this point: "Grounded theory methodology insists that no matter how general—how broad in scope or abstract—the theory, it should be developed in that back-and-forth interplay with data that is so central to this methodology" (1994, 282). This "grounding" of theory suggests that the methodology can support composition research that crosses the border between local and general knowledge. Grounded theory also offers a means of meta-analysis across case studies. In addition, grounded theory is excellent for long-term research agendas that aim for a full theory of composition as defined by Richard Fulkerson in his seminal article on the subject.

Of course, grounded theory is not a panacea. The processes of interviewing subjects, collecting data, cycling findings to participants, negotiating meanings, and returning to the data for theoretical sampling are both recursive and intensive. One project can require months and even years to complete. Likewise, grounded theory produces so much data that physically managing them and intellectually manipulating them is difficult even with software programs for assistance. And for researchers (myself included) who were originally trained to be solo interpreters of texts, the methodology requires some epistemological shifts. Grounded theory is best done collaboratively; it is field-based, uses coding systems derived from the social sciences, requires graphic as well as textual reporting of results, and tests theory through negotiation. On the other hand, grounded theory does not require the researcher to simplify the complex acts of teaching and learning or to choose between description and theory. My experiences with it convince me that grounded theory is a promising methodology for composition studies.

HOW GROUNDED THEORY IS APPLIED IN COMPOSITION STUDIES

The ERIC database from 1982–1996 lists twelve entries about grounded theory and writing. All are about perceptions of the subjects under study, e.g., how sixth graders define themselves as readers (Guice 1992), how veteran teachers reconceive the value of dialogue journals when confronted with student responses to the journals (Gross 1992), how a novice researcher redefines herself as she produces a dissertation using grounded theory (White 1992), and how two researchers perceive their collaborative efforts (Smith 1982). Dissertations Abstracts Online lists additional studies that use grounded theory to explore relationships among teacher training, curriculum decisions, and writing instruction (e.g., Pippen 1991; Weitz 1995).

These studies underscore the reflexive nature of grounded theory which forces researchers to remain aware of their situatedness within the methodological paradigm. Grounded theory requires a questioning stance up to the end of a research project and beyond. Those applying the methodology must learn to live without closure.

Another phenomenon that occurs when grounded theory is the prime analytic methodology is the use of multiple data collection and reporting methods. Triangulation in data gathering and creativity in reporting of the findings are logical outcomes of constant comparison and the active search for disconfirming evidence. For example, in her study of peer writing groups, Candace Spigelman combines historical and textual methods with naturalistic methods of data gathering. She uses grounded theory to analyze the whole data base and then reports her findings in a reasoned argument combined with a case study narrative. Spigelman explains her use of grounded theory as both philosophical and pragmatic. She sees it as a systematic method that offers "an important corrective to [her] vested position in the research," a methodology that lets her move beyond description to "some level of generalization [about] . . . ownership values in writing groups—for which there are, at present, no theoretical claims." Spigelman believes that "any discussion of educational settings and practices must involve critique and recommendations for change" (1996, 133 –34).

In the research seminar that I teach, graduate students apply grounded theory to various "sites and scenes" of writing. For example, one student studied the writing processes of a local author, another analyzed the pedagogies of teachers who are active writers themselves, a third theorized about students who initially fail the Virginia Passport Literacy Test and then pass it after attending special writing classes, a fourth studied how the public perceives educational documents published by an AIDS Task Force, and a fifth analyzed

Department of Defense consultants who write under security-clearance constraints. In these types of studies, researchers use more than one method of data collection (field study and surveys; statistics and classroom observation) and then report their findings in combinations of genres (case study/theoretical statement; feature story/research report; management proposal/narrative).

A Closer Look at One Application

In a recent study of student and faculty perceptions of televised writing instruction, I used grounded theory to investigate how participants are constructed as "students" and "writers" in the virtual and material spaces of a televised composition course, and to theorize about the impact of distance education on composition pedagogy (Magnotto 1996).

Grounded theory allowed me to complicate previous generalizations about the influence of electronic pedagogy on higher education with specific findings about televised writing instruction. Some of my findings follow:

1. Interactive television (ITV) constructs the student as an educational consumer by packaging courses as products to be purchased, presenting the site director as a sales representative for those courses, and using market research to assess satisfaction with products consumed.
2. ITV constructs students as producers as well as consumers. Texts become commodities of value.
3. ITV redefines "presence" and "absence" for students who can be present and absent simultaneously in this medium.
4. ITV creates a virtual, postmodern space in which students can imagine multiple subjectivities, one of which can be a "writerly self."
5. ITV places intermediaries, filters, screens, and interpreters between the instructor and the student. These mediating elements can both enhance and diminish the construction of students as writers.
6. ITV does not preclude a liberatory pedagogy.

The time between my shaping of the research questions and my writing of the findings was filled with long sessions of recursive data analysis. In the next section of this chapter, I explain grounded theory methodology in more depth and use the television study to detail components of the research paradigm and its appropriateness for situated, local studies of writing and the teaching of composition.

HOW TO DO GROUNDED THEORY

Miles and Huberman, in their landmark volume on data analysis, examine a range of approaches to qualitative research: interpretivism or hermeneutics, ethnography or field research, critical ethnography or action research. The common features across these varied approaches include coding, constant comparison, returning to the field to further test emerging patterns, working toward a small set of generalizations, and constructing theories to explain the selected phenomena (1994, 9). Grounded theory uses the same strategies. As Glaser and Strauss explained it 30 years ago:

> Joint collection, coding, and analysis of data is the underlying operation [in grounded theory]. The generation of theory, coupled with the notion of theory as process, requires that all three operations be done together as much as possible. They should blur and intertwine continually, from the beginning of an investigation to its end. (1967, 43)

Spigelman explains coding procedures by defining them as "numerous intellectual maneuvers for grouping data and for naming the relationships among the groups or categories thus derived. In open coding, data are disassembled and categorized; in axial coding, data are regrouped in terms of their conditions, contexts, and so on; and in selective coding, a kind of 'story line' or interpretive frame is created. Finally, a workable theory emerges" (1996, 132–33).

My study of televised instruction serves as an illustration. Data analysis began with sorting and labeling data into types and then applying open coding methods to data sets, starting with my teaching journal, moving to videotapes, and then on to other types of data such as students' papers. As categories emerged, I further developed them through axial coding, and I wrote *coding memos* recording each category and examples of it from the data base. I continued to interview students, faculty, and staff associated with the televised course and to ask for their responses to my early categories. I kept a research log as well. As coding memos accrued, I reread them periodically and drafted *integrative memos* to record salient concepts and issues and to develop the codes that would shape the "story line." (See Appendix)

Naming Assumptions

All research is based on assumptions. What is critical in grounded theory is the researcher's obligation to closely examine those assumptions as the research progresses. For example, my work on televised instruction is based on a social constructivist epistemology and on two findings that emerged from a previous study of writing centers: (1) students are rarely constructed as writers in school settings, and (2) when they are constructed as writers, they make progress as writers (Magnotto 1991, 1995). The television study is also based on the assumption that successful writing classes provide a setting in which students *can be* constructed as writers who produce as well as consume texts. In the final report of a grounded theory, each assumption is explained in detail.

Collecting Data

Most of us who have studied classroom teaching or writing center tutorials have used multiple approaches to data collection, hoping through triangulation to capture some of the complex interactions that occur in settings where writing/teaching are primary. Data collection methods such as surveys, interviews, talk-aloud protocols, and field notes have been explained quite well in other sources (Denzin and Lincoln 1994; Miles and Huberman 1994).

These methods of collecting data are not easy to carry out, but neither are they mysterious. Data analysis, on the other hand, is slippery. What goes on in the researcher's mind when she analyzes extensive amounts and varied types of data? How does she actually "do" data analysis?

Analyzing Data

In grounded theory, the three main techniques of data analysis—coding, memoing, and diagraming (drawing visual representations)—require excursions into several sub-routines at the same time that the researcher is continually pushing for integration of all previous analyses. In the final phase, multiple analyses are drawn together to produce new theory, and that theory is disseminated in a research report, the writing of which also plays a critical part in the study. In other words, grounded theory gives writing its due as a knowledge-making process.[1]

The following scenario describes a data analysis session that followed the taping of a writing center conference between a faculty-tutor and a student enrolled in an economics class. The student was working on a paper about John Kenneth Galbraith, and she was thoroughly frustrated by her instructor's response which was "I stopped reading after the second page because this paper is giving me a headache." As the researcher, I have before me the audio-tape of the conference, the student's draft, and the student's and tutor's responses to my interview questions. How do I incorporate these data with those from the 20 other tutoring sessions I have witnessed?

The first step is to quickly read through the day's data collection and to listen to the audiotape (using fast forward as often as necessary). I read/listen to get an overview of the event, a holistic sense of the data set. The second step is to reread the data set, jotting notes in the margins as I go along. The third step is to write myself a preliminary, descriptive memo of my responses to this early reading of the data. Most of the memo is a list of notable moments in the data set. "Notable" is operationalized as that which I, with all of my experience in writing centers and as a writing teacher, deem important—things which jump out at me *because of*, not in spite of, my expertise.

Coding of data is the next procedure and takes place the following day after I have transcribed parts of the audiotape. Open coding, analogous to brainstorming, is the most creative coding. I read the data set word-by-word and line-by-line trying to name *concepts* that emerge from the reading. For example, when the student says, "I can't write," "I'm not good at writing," and "I hate writing," I brainstorm a code list which includes: negative attitudes, lack of confidence, learned helplessness, deliberate self-effacement to gain sympathy, ploy to get tutor to write paper, writing resistance—and as many additional concepts as I can think of to name what might be happening.

Open coding serves as a springboard to later analysis because even though I begin with the student's words, I also play around with hypothetical codes and questions that address larger issues. I'm not worried about some of the codes being far-fetched because later analytical procedures will require ample empirical evidence if a concept name is to survive additional rounds of analysis.

In my next work session, I pick some of the most promising concepts developed through open coding for a closer look called *axial coding*. Axial coding forces me to examine each concept in terms of conditions, interactions among actors, strategies, tactics, and consequences. For example, when "negative attitude toward writing" seems to hold up as a concept, I reexamine the data base for information about the conditions surrounding similar statements of negative attitude, for interactions between students and tutors when negative attitudes are voiced, for strategies students use to convey attitudes, and for consequences of voicing attitudes (Does the tutor take a different tact? Does the talk turn to affective matters rather than rhetorical ones?). I am examining relationships across and within concepts, making concepts denser, giving them more texture to see if they hold up as conceptual codes or have to be dropped. Eventually, this close examination helps me determine the important *dimensions* of the concepts that will become *core categories*.

In *selective coding* I systematically and deliberately go through the full data base looking not only for additional examples of core categories but also for examples that *defy* core categories.

All the while that I am doing various types of coding, I am generating and refining my hypotheses, and I am recording these hypotheses and syntheses in *coding memos* that I write to myself and to other team members if the research is collaborative. In addition to memos, I am drawing visuals—diagrams, matrixes, tables, and graphs—to capture the current state of the analysis and to use as heuristics for further analysis.[2]

At periodic intervals during data analysis I confer with others about the "fit" of my emerging findings. For instance, I play the audiotape of the conference on the Galbraith essay to three writing tutors as they follow along on the transcript. We then discuss the tape, and I ask for their responses to the core categories.

Writing the research report draws the analysis to a close. It is important to note that in grounded theory, the act of writing is considered part of analysis, not a separate "translation" of the logic, proofs, or warrants of prior activities. Often the memos written earlier will become significant sections of the report just as the act of putting findings into words is part of the research itself.

LIMITATIONS

Naturalistic research methods in all their various guises share similar limitations as Denzin and Lincoln and Miles and Huberman, among others, point out. But the need for situated studies of writers remains strong (Broadhead and Freed 1986), and to achieve such studies, composition researchers continue to import naturalistic methodologies from other disciplines (ethnography from anthropology, discourse analysis from linguistics, case studies from education). Given the hybrid sources of naturalistic methods, it is not surprising that some of the same compositionists who represent themselves as proponents of naturalistic research still seem conflicted about choosing naturalistic approaches over experimental or rhetorical ones. For example, even though "time" is a component of all these methodologies, Broadhead and Freed lament the two years it took to complete their naturalistic study of the writing processes of management consultants. They also voice their reservations about coding methods that produce non-quantifiable results and suggest that future researchers change the method:

> Interviews with writers should be more structured, so that more information can be accumulated earlier to guide coding and subsequent analysis of texts. At the same time, single texts should be coded by several researchers working independently, so that the coding (and hence the analysis) can depend less on decision by consensus and more on decision by quantifiable measures. Finally, a greater number of texts and writers should be analyzed, so that statistical tests of reliability may be applied to the apparent similarities and differences. (1986, 127)

If naturalistic researchers take these injunctions to heart, I contend they risk building their studies on a methodological house of cards. At the base of Broadhead and Freed's complaint is the lack of generalizability of case studies. To make this point, they say that Nancy Sommers' conclusion that writers revise recursively rather than in a process of stages is only applicable in certain contexts. Broadhead and Freed find that management consultants may revise quite successfully by using a more or less linear process rather than a recursive one. In other words, they find that the local writing situation critiques theory, yet it is long-term, situated research (such as case studies) that accounts for local writing situations. Broadhead and Freed are up against the powerful scientific research paradigm which valorizes generalizability more than it does local knowledge. Grounded theory is a possible solution to this dilemma because it works for formal theory building as well as for substantive theory building. That is to say, a researcher can apply grounded theory to several case studies and use those studies as the empirical basis for a meta-analysis across cases.

WHY GROUNDED THEORY?

I begin this section with two claims: (1) we as compositionists have not made enough progress in developing methodologies that interrupt the theory/practice binary, and (2) we have not studied our research methodologies as social practices in themselves.

The Theory/Practice Distinction

To address the first claim, let me point to the characteristics of grounded theory that contribute to its usefulness to both theory and practice. For one, the methodology is inclusive. The team approach provides opportunities for those individuals who describe their primary work as teaching and for those individuals who describe their primary work as research to collaborate on projects. Likewise, the team approach extends easily to include graduate assistants and others who wish to theorize about their practice. Second, grounded theory is interpretive. It was developed to study scenes of complex human interaction (pain treatments in hospitals, for example). The methodology encourages multiple mind-sets, yet is rigorous because each stance is interrogated by other stances. The analyses that survive are never simplistic. Third, the methodology is dialogic. It works through consensus and negotiation. As team members move through the recursive cycles of data analysis and theory building, they interrupt (and thus inform) one another (see Silverman and Torode 1980). Finally, the methodology is proactive in intent. As Patti Lather reminds us, research should lead toward emancipatory knowledge and purposeful change. Grounded theory develops agents for change through the inclusion of participant-researchers, and it opens up spaces for action and reciprocity.

Grounded theory "explains" and "predicts" and thus is useful for practitioners. It goes beyond description and is recursive in nature. Additional data can be used to enrich the explanatory power of a particular grounded theory. Furthermore, as Glaser and Strauss note, "the form in which the theory is presented can be independent of this process by which it was generated. Grounded theory can be presented either as a well-codified set of propositions or in a running theoretical discussion, using conceptual categories and their properties." (1967, 31) Glaser and Strauss choose to emphasize *"theory as process*; that is, theory as an ever-developing entity, not as a perfected product."* (32)

Grounded theory is, itself, a critical research practice with the potential to help compositionists work the borderlands between scholarship and teaching. It is open and ongoing as a research methodology, and the written reports produced during and after a grounded theory study are also open and ongoing. One memo is absorbed into the next; a 'completed' visual becomes a heuristic for the next visual. A published research report doesn't necessarily signal the end of the project. Glaser and Strauss in their study, *Time for Dying*, state the following:

> The discussional form of formulating theory gives a feeling of "ever-developing" to the theory, allows it to become quite rich, complex, and dense, and makes its fit and relevance easy to comprehend. On the other hand, to state a theory in propositional form, except perhaps for a few scattered core propositions, would make it less complex, dense, and rich, and more laborious to read. It would also tend by implications to "freeze" the theory instead of giving the feeling of a need for continued development. (qtd in Strauss 1987, 264)

Methodology as Social Practice

My second claim is that we as compositionists have not studied our research methods as social practices in themselves. Our methodologies too often remain traditional, patriarchal, and exclusionary. We tout composition as a democratic discipline, but we maintain a researcher-practitioner hierarchy that can be seen in the marginalization of teacher-researchers and graduate students. We continue to reward the solo researcher over the collaborative one. And, we continue to send researchers into the field to study "subjects" as "objects." Nowadays, of course, we describe and quote our "subjects" in our research reports, but we rarely invite our subjects to join us as researchers. In contrast, grounded theory is self-consciously critical. Through triangulation, analytic recursiveness, and inclusion of subjects as agents, it invites others into our disciplinary conversations. As an empirical and naturalistic methodology, it offers us a timely opportunity—a means of grounding our theory in our practice.

In their preface to *The Discovery of Grounded Theory*, Glaser and Strauss point to "the embarrassing gap between theory and empirical research," a gap which has been addressed from the research side of the chasm by "improvement of methods for testing theory" (1967, vii). However, not much progress has been made from the "theory side." Glaser and Strauss define grounded theory as "the discovery of theory from data." They claim it works by "provid[ing] us with relevant predictions, explanations, interpretations and applications" (1967, 1). In contrast, logically deduced theory comes from *a priori* assumptions that may or may not be based in empirical research and thus may have less "fit" and "working capacity" to explain things to expert researchers and practitioners:

> [O]ne canon for judging the usefulness of a theory is how it was generated . . . . other canons for assessing a theory, such as logical consistency, clarity, parsimony, density, scope, integration, as well as its fit and its ability to work, are also significantly dependent on how the theory was generated. They are not, as some theorists of a logico-deductive persuasion would claim, completely independent of the processes of generation. This notion of independence too often ends up being taken as a license to generate theory from any source—happenstance, fantasy, dream life, common sense, or conjecture—and then dress it up as a bit of logical deduction. (1967, 6–7)

Grounded theory promotes the teasing out of political and social components affecting writing/teaching. It does not require the hiding or demoting of certain features to make points about other features. As conditions such as gender or power or technology claim a place in a researcher's agenda, grounded theory is able to incorporate their impact because the analytic procedures require asking "What is power [or gender or ethnicity] in this situation and under [what] specified conditions? How is it manifested, by whom, when, where, how, with what consequences (and for whom or what)?" (Strauss and Corbin, "Grounded" 276). As an added feature, research reports that make use of balancing matrices allow the researcher to display multiple factors and conditions so that readers can view complex relationships simultaneously.

CONCLUSION

Whenever I read the memos and logs generated by researchers using grounded theory, I am struck by how these texts blur the line between doing research and writing up research. The practice of grounded theory is a stunning example of the fusion of thought and language. It forces the researcher to create connections from the investigative scene to the interpretation of that scene, but more importantly, it forces the researcher to document those connections. As composition matures as a discipline, this state of meta-analysis seems ideal. It promises to interrogate the distinctions between theory and practice that limit our current ways of understanding the complex human activities of writing and teaching writing. It makes us accountable to ourselves, to the writers and teachers we study, and to our field.

NOTES

1.   Glaser and Strauss (1967) explain these techniques, but Lincoln and Guba (1985) operationalize them in a series of steps that are "user-friendly." See also Strauss and Corbin (1990).
2.   For an update on the advantages and disadvantages of software programs that store and sort data, see Richards and Richards (1994).

APPENDIX:
INTEGRATIVE MEMO: ACCULTURATION TO MEDIATION OF DISTANCE

As I start to reread the early memos and to think about my conversations with JB and H, I realize the following things come between the instructor and the student in TT. They are like sliding screens:
the camera,
the elmo,
the site director,
the crew,
the mail room people,
the *tv screen which reduces my size and the size of my words,*
the transmission mechanism which may make my voice fuzzy or intermittent.
the desk I sit behind
the raised dais
the microphone I wear and the ones students use
material delivery thru the mail—I don't physically hand out papers nor do students return them directly to me

voice mail and email conferences versus face-to-face

copy center—if they don't get the course pack and syllabus together the way you want it or don't get it to sites on time (do they mail it?), or even the way they put the fac. member's name in small print on the cover, gives them a roll as intermediary

One consequence of these intermediaries is the highs/lows I felt after (and before) each class. Another consequence is *distance* (it makes sense that this is called distance learning). How far apart are students and I? Time distance, physical (spatial) distance, emotional distance, intellectual distance.

Again, these things are related to how students are constructed as students by the distance ed system which now shapes them as much as an individual teacher does. The *distance system becomes the virtual as well as the material institution within which we shape and are shaped as teachers/learners/etc.*

My sheer force of will and my belief that students learn partially because of *who I am changes* on TT because I am as virtual as my students are!! I can't look students in the eye (JB saying that's why he refuses to teach on TT). Thus, if the force of my "self" (including my experience, my knowledge, my credentials, my people skills) is dissipated by these intervening screens, how will I motivate students to learn? Do I give up on motivation? Are the students in TT self-motivated (there may be a difference between studio and site students in this regard)? Will the material do it? (Probably not in a junior level required course). I will go back and look at evals for TT 327 and classroom 327.

Does this say a lot about my assumptions for teaching writing—the coach metaphor, mentor metaphor, or editor metaphor imply a "personal" relationship between two people (actually between 2 stable individuals). Maybe TT is the postmodern answer to fractured selves. Whatever the cause, the consequence is a learning curve that is very noticeable. The virtual/material dichotomy needs to be deconstructed. We know one by virtue of there being the other. Is this a continuum? It seems to be, especially since the concepts of virtual and material are themselves socially constructed.

CHAPTER TEN

Feminist Methodology
Dilemmas for Graduate Researchers

Shirley Rose and Janice Lauer

*I*N THIS ESSAY WE WILL EXPLORE THE IMPLICATIONS OF FEMINIST METHODOLOGY for composition researchers. Specifically, we will discuss the obligations, risks, and dilemmas a composition researcher committed to enacting a feminist research project can encounter in the processes of conducting an empirical research project, including defining a research question, choosing a research site, designing a study, negotiating a relationship with participants in the study, and making public the results or outcomes of the inquiry.

Though our own inquiry in this essay is speculative rather than descriptive, we draw upon our experiences as writing teachers, program administrators, and researchers to think through the possible consequences that conducting an inquiry consistent with principles of feminist methodology might have for both the individual researcher and the community which is the site of the research. Given our own positions—as director of an introductory writing program that is a likely site for research employing feminist methodology and director of a Ph.D. program in rhetoric and composition that is likely to produce several researchers interested in conducting such an inquiry—we are especially interested in explicating the politics of our own location, examining the issues raised and problems posed by our own situation. However, since our concerns are not unique, we will also locate these in the broader context of composition studies in general.

SITUATING OURSELVES

We begin by acknowledging the situation of our inquiry and ourselves as authors, for inquiry is always situated. In "Beyond the Personal," Gesa Kirsch and Joy Ritchie (1995) advocate a "politics of location" for composition research, arguing for a feminist methodology that is self-conscious about the researcher's own motives, beliefs, and experiences as well as being participatory and emancipatory for subjects. Kirsch and Ritchie identify the requirements such a politics of location makes of researchers: they must recognize their own subjectivity, adopting a reflective and critical stance; they must investigate the relations between the knower and the known, exploring the possibilities of collaboration with participants; they must be open to change themselves; and their efforts must lead to research centered on the local and individual while acknowledging that the research has social consequences in the world.

Identifying the positions from which we write and the commitments which guide us, we recognize that in the process we are constructing these positions and enacting these commitments. We are a Director of Composition for a large introductory college writing program (Shirley) and a director of a well known Ph.D. program in rhetoric and composition (Janice). These positions are constituted by commitments and responsibilities to both local institutional constituencies and broader professional and disciplinary communities. In the following descriptions, we do not attempt to characterize the broad scope of our own academic experiences and interests, but to characterize the expectations of anyone who holds these positions.

As Director of Undergraduate Composition, Shirley is responsible to the thousands of undergraduates who take composition courses, the larger Purdue University academic community, the taxpayers who contribute to the support of this public university, and students' future employers for providing well-prepared and knowledgeable teachers and a coherent curriculum of writing instruction that remains consistent with the best social, educational goals of a land-grant university at the end of the 20th century while contributing to a critique of ways in which the institution may fall short of those goals. She is also responsible to the broader disciplinary community of rhetoric and composition studies for contributing to a practical critique of its research and theory.

As director of the graduate program in rhetoric and composition, Janice is responsible to the profession of English Studies that expects quality doctoral education and especially to the discipline of Rhetoric and Composition whose doctoral programs help to shape it as a field, and to whose changes and developments a program must contribute and be responsive. At Purdue, she is responsible to ensure that graduate students receive an education that prepares them well for professional lives in English Studies in its current shape, and that enables them to become competent and competitive as both scholars and teachers in a difficult job market. These responsibilities entail helping students become publishing scholars, prepared to pursue original, significant research and to publish as an integral part of their professional lives.

Preparing theoretically informed and experienced teachers whose knowledge of research about writing is transformed into understanding in action or reflective practice becomes the joint venture of the graduate and undergraduate programs. At Purdue, Rhetoric and Composition graduate students have the opportunity to teach or tutor in several programs in addition to introductory writing: writing lab, business writing, professional writing, and technical writing. Each of these is directed by a composition specialist who guides these graduate instructors or tutors as they enact major theoretical understandings about writing in diverse pedagogies.

Since good graduate programs also need a critical mass of highly qualified students who have an intellectual community of peers, Janice has worked to facilitate that community, providing a communal lecture series, supporting collaborative meetings while students are writing dissertations, sponsoring an annual reunion dinner at the CCCC, and publishing a periodic newsletter that is circulated to faculty, graduates, and current students. Further, as director she has paid attention to the position of the graduate program within the department, school, and university. To make connections, Janice has offered an annual Interdisciplinary Lectures Series, inviting colleagues (linguists, literary scholars, philosophers, communication specialists, historians, psychologists, anthropologists, and so forth) to speak of their scholarship that bears on written discourse.

The differences in this ordering of commitments—from the local, specific concrete institutional context to more dispersed, generalized abstract professional community for a director of an undergraduate program vs. the reverse ordering for a director of a graduate program—reflects conventional priorities and values often taken for granted. This essay will, to some extent, call these into question.

Each of us also contributes to the program that is the primary responsibility of the other. Each year, Janice is the mentor for the eight or nine new Rhetoric and Composition graduate students who are teaching assistants in the Introductory Writing Program, sharing responsibilities for the preparation of teachers for this program. As a member of Introductory Writing Committee, she shares in decision-making about goals and directions of that program. Shirley participates in the graduate program as an occasional instructor for graduate courses and as a member of dissertation committees and graduate examination committees. This definition/description of our roles and responsibilities represents our specific, particular institutional site as well as our individual interests and commitments, though these are not necessarily unique to our institution or to the two of us.

In representing our roles as we must inevitably do in this essay we are very much aware of the risks we take and the obligations we must fulfill, as well as the constraints under which these place us. Our institutional roles define us as representatives—our actions and words are understood as representative of our programs just as our programs are seen as representations of ourselves, whether or not we wish this to be so. In making these representations we risk seeming to codify institutional practices that are always undergoing negotiation and change, to fix circumstances that are continually changing, and to oversimplify theoretical and ideological positions that are continuously contested from within and without. We have obligations to other members—students and faculty—of the communities we represent: to acknowledge their contributions to defining and realizing our programs' goals; to understand and respect their intellectual, ideological, and experiential differences from our-selves; to recognize the legitimacy of their goals and purposes and their work toward them when these are not entirely in concert with our own.

Why are we engaging in this elaborate discussion of ourselves? We are con-vinced that such an elaboration is consistent with the points we wish to make about the effects the politics of location have upon research in composition. The questions and issues we address here reflect problems posed to us as direc-tor of an introductory writing program that is a site of research employing feminist methodology, and director of a Ph.D. program in rhetoric and com-position that educates the researchers who conduct this inquiry. As a Director of Composition and a Graduate Program Director, we are always involved, given the duties of these positions, in needs assessment and evaluation research—"action research" projects that might be characterized as feminist in perspective.

THE SITE OF RESEARCH: UNDERGRADUATE AND GRADUATE PROGRAMS

The Introductory Writing Program at Purdue might be expected to be a popular site of composition research projects, given its location, size, and diversity. Because all students in the rhetoric and composition graduate pro-gram teach for at least one year in the Introductory Writing Program, it is a context with which they are familiar and find conveniently at hand. Their con-current pursuit of advanced studies in composition and rhetoric not only enables their reflective practice of teaching writing, it also provides the theo-retical grounding and intellectual tools they would need in order to undertake informed, systematic classroom-based research with their own students.

The size of the introductory writing program also creates conditions favor-able to research with other teachers and students: in a recent, not atypical fall semester, over 6500 students were enrolled in 263 sections of first-year compo-sition taught by 162 different teachers. The 70 percent of Purdue's students who are from Indiana come from a variety of economic, ethnic, and cultural backgrounds and a broad range of academic preparation and expectations. Our in-state student population is no more diverse than the rest of our student body, which includes students from every state in the U.S. and nearly every country in the world. Most of these students are required by their respective Purdue schools to complete either the courses in our two-semester sequence or a one-semester accelerated first-year composition course; about two percent of our students are required to complete our developmental writing course prior to enrolling in the two-semester introductory writing sequence. The TAs and lecturers who teach our courses employ many different pedagogical approaches to a variety of writing curricula within program-wide guidelines. A college writing program of this size and complexity generates an enormous number of very diverse teaching and writing events and texts that are, at least theoretically, potentially available and subject to study.

The graduate program in Rhetoric and Composition, begun in 1980, has nine Rhetoric and Composition faculty, two associate faculty in English Education who specialize in writing, and 67 currently enrolled graduate students (63 doctoral students and 4 masters students). Forty-four are on campus; twenty-three are finishing dissertations off campus. Our graduates (61 Ph.D. and 30 MA) remain an integral part of our Rhetoric and Composition community. Our curriculum includes a required core of five courses: contemporary composition theory, historical work on issues of written discourse from the sophists to early twentieth century (two semesters), empirical research on writing, and composition issues and postmodern theory. Other courses include studies of computers and composition; cultural studies and composition; discourse analysis; ESL writing; ethics, rhetoric, and writing; gender issues in composition studies; literacy studies; professional writing theory; qualitative studies of writing; reading and writing; writing program administration; and writing across the curriculum. Students also have a second field concentration (four courses) in such areas as cultural studies, professional writing theory, literary theory, and linguistics. As a part of this comprehensive background, feminist theories, pedagogies, and research designs are studied within each of the core courses and in most of the second fields. Thus many students bring to their own research an interest in feminist issues and methodologies. The question posed here is to what extent they can activate these interests if they choose to do qualitative studies, especially in the introductory composition program.

FEMINIST RESEARCH ACROSS THE DISCIPLINES

Before suggesting several fictional scenarios, which present a range of dilemmas faced by feminist researchers in composition, we will review characterizations of feminist methodologies that have been recognized as appropriate for composition studies research. Since it is not our purpose to develop criteria for determining an inquiry project's feminist orthodoxy or fidelity to a particular feminism, our characterization of feminist research approaches will be fairly inclusive. We will briefly summarize and review a number of descriptions, definitions, and discussions of feminist methodology, epistemology, and ontology that have helped us to recognize a feminist agenda in the inquiry projects considered, planned, and undertaken by our students.

We've found Shulamit Reinharz' descriptions of feminist methods especially useful for appreciating the diversity of feminist approaches. After reviewing hundreds of projects, for which the chief criteria for inclusion was the researchers' own identification of their inquiries as "feminist," Reinharz reached the following conclusions:

   a. Feminism is a perspective, not a research method.
   b. Feminists use a multiplicity of research methods.
   c. Feminist research involves an ongoing criticism of nonfeminist scholarship.

   d. Feminist research is guided by feminist theory.

   e. Feminist research may be transdisciplinary.

   f. Feminist research aims to create social change.

   g. Feminist research strives to represent human diversity.

   h. Feminist research frequently includes the researcher as a person.

   i. Feminist research frequently attempts to develop special relations with the people in the studies (in interactive research).

   j. Feminist research frequently defines a special relation with the reader. (1992, 240)

Many of Reinharz' conclusions are consistent with Patti Lather's discussion of feminist methodologies in *Getting Smart* (1991). Lather explains the ways in which feminist methodology is emancipatory: it acknowledges the subjective as valid and acknowledges the impact of the researcher on and in the research situation; it privileges natural as opposed to laboratory settings; it operates from a holistic perspective that doesn't exclude some details as irrelevant; it retains a sense of the uniqueness of what is studied; it operates inductively and it recognizes that data from inquiry conducted by humans is value laden.

In "Feminist Praxis and the Academic Mode of Production," Liz Stanley (1990) describes the dimensions of "unalienated knowledge" that is the goal of feminist research: "the research/theorist is grounded as an actual person in a concrete setting; understanding and theorizing are located and treated as material activities and not as unanalysable metaphysical 'transcendent' ones different in kind from those of 'mere people'; and the 'act of knowing' is examined as the crucial determiner of 'what is known'" (12). Stanley summarizes: "academic feminist unalienated knowledge is that which concretely and analytically locates the product of the academic feminist labour process within a concrete analysis of the process of production itself" (12). She explains that

> "feminism" is not merely a "perspective," a way of seeing; nor even this plus an epistemology, a way of knowing; it is also an ontology, or a way of being in the world. What is distinctively "feminist" about a concern with research processes is that this constitutes an invitation to explore the conditions and circumstances of a feminist ontology, with all its slips and contradictions certainly, but a feminist ontology none the less. (14)

In another essay, Liz Stanley and Sue Wise (1990) recommend that characterizations of feminist research be based not on method, but methodology, including epistemological and ontological considerations. They define five "related sites" where "feminism" can be located within the research process, reflecting feminist epistemological principles: "in the researcher-researched relationship; in emotion as a research experience; in the intellectual autobiography of researchers; therefore in how to manage the differing 'realities' and understandings of researchers and researched; and thus in the complex question of power in research and writing" (23).

These various characterizations of feminist approaches might be synthesized and summarized into three principles: reflexivity, attention to the affective components of the research, and critical attention to the situation at hand. We can identify at least two reasons for the reflexive nature of feminist approaches, especially their explicit discussion of process: 1) the logic and reasoning used in new or unusual methods sometimes needs to be made explicit because it cannot be taken for granted that readers will understand it implicitly; and 2) feminist research approaches often counter traditions of research and knowledge production that ignore the politics of the research situation, thus they must be scrupulous in examining their own politics.

Because feminist research is prompted by a desire to change the status quo, it necessarily is concerned with the outcomes and effects of the inquiry. It gives attention to affective components of the research, because its goal is unalienated knowing. Feminist inquiry characteristically makes use of the situation-at-hand because the inquiry is usually motivated by a desire to understand and in some way alter the circumstances of the inquirer. That none of these characteristics is perceived as the exclusive domain of explicitly feminist projects is perhaps a measure of the achievement of the feminist agenda to resist social and cultural oppression by transforming institutional practices.

RELATING FEMINIST RESEARCH AGENDAS AND PRACTICES TO RHETORIC AND COMPOSITION RESEARCH AND PRACTICES

Several composition scholars have begun to explore the potential contribution feminist methodologies might make to composition research. Patricia A. Sullivan (1992) cites three of the characteristics of feminist research identified by Sandra Harding that she finds relevant to feminist research in composition: this research is generated from the perspective of women's experiences; its goal is to provide women with needed explanations of social phenomena; and it requires the researcher to place herself or himself within the framework of her/his representations of what has been studied. In "Rabbit Trails, Ephemera, and other Stories: Feminist Methodology and Collaborative Research," Rebecca E. Burnett and Helen Rothschild Ewald (1994) discuss their experiences as collaborating researchers and explore ways feminist methodologies might help them to understand conflict in collaborative research groups. Gesa E. Kirsch and Joy S. Ritchie (1995) discuss the contributions of feminist theory and methodology to composition research, with reference to their own projects for examples of strategies and difficulties, in their essay "Beyond the Personal: Theorizing a Politics of Location." They argue that what can be learned from feminist theory and women's experience "can become a location for reconsidering what counts as knowledge and for revitalizing research in composition" (8).

In addition to this characteristic agenda for explicitly feminist research in composition, there are a number of features which feminist methodological approaches share with composition research in general. Both are multi-modal and pluralistic (see Lauer); both recognize the importance of attention to process; they share an awareness of the significance of the rhetorical strategies used for "writing up" an inquiry project; both are interested in praxis, or the consequences of the knowledge-making activity; and both are relatively new and have occupied marginal positions in research traditions, yet have a potential for radically altering those traditions.

RELATING FEMINIST RESEARCH AGENDAS AND PRACTICES TO INSTITUTIONAL TRADITIONS AND PRACTICES

As a means of discussing the expectations engendered in our graduate student researchers by their study of feminist methodology, we will introduce two scenarios of graduate student research. After briefly characterizing these projects, we will discuss the dilemmas posed by the constraints of their situations. These dilemmas are largely based in actual research experiences of two graduate students with whom we work. We have made some changes, however, partially fictionalizing these scenarios for exploring the dilemmas here for two reasons. First, we are acutely aware of our own obligations toward these students. To describe actual projects under consideration, in progress, or recently completed would be to risk anticipating the outcomes of those projects and the students' own eventual publication and to subject these students' work to a premature critique. Second, it is possible for us to imagine research projects that are appropriate to our students' interests and training but have not been undertaken because of the institutional constraints we discuss here.

Scenario #1

During Susan's MA work, she became interested in the relationship between students' revising and the kinds of responses they received, especially from their instructors. During her first year of teaching at Purdue she used an analytic type of response to student drafts. Wondering about what students were making of her feedback, she speculated that perhaps certain kinds of responses might impact student revisions differently. For her dissertation, she decided to conduct a qualitative study of the revising of selected students in the introductory composition course, studying their affective responses, their interpretations, and their negotiations of comments. The director of the undergraduate program agreed with her decision. She prepared a prospectus for her four-member committee, arguing for the value of the project, its theoretical authorization and underpinnings, and its methodology. She explained at her defense of the prospectus that she needed student subjects who were high, low, and mediocre revisers, defining each category. But she had trouble deciding how to make this determination. After conferring with her committee about which of several bases she would use, she decided to ask some teachers who had taught the first semester course to identify strong and weak revisers in their classes. Here was her first point of negotiation with her peers.

Having gained the cooperation of several teachers, Susan then began the time-consuming task of contacting these students to gain their agreement to be subjects in her study. One of the requirements was that the student had to be enrolled in a second semester course in which written feedback was going to be given by the instructor. Not only did the student need to be enrolled in such a section, but the instructor had to be willing to share her responses to students' drafts with Susan. Given these constraints, Susan obtained nine students as subjects. So far her project had now entailed several negotiations: with her committee, her first group of teachers, her student subjects, and her cooperating teachers for the study itself.

Although she had learned from feminist methodology and pedagogy the value of engaging subjects in planning the study, she was puzzled as to how to accomplish this because she did not want to influence the way students later dealt with their teachers' responses nor to reveal that some of them were selected because they were poor revisers. Further, the kinds of revisers and bases for determination were settled before any students were invited to join. Thus she found it counterproductive to involve the students in the development of the design. She did not want to intervene in the study by promising them benefits like providing additional help with revising because this too would skew the results. One of the risks of her study was the fact that she would inevitably examine and evaluate the responses given to the students by their instructors.

Her research was further complicated and constrained because her students were distributed in several sections during the second semester. She therefore had to adjust her plan to visit classes to gain some acquaintance with the context. Another frustration was the fact that two subjects dropped out, leaving her with seven.

After her defense of her dissertation, she planned to submit an account of her study for publication. But could she share the results with the program in which she had done the research? Of course, her dissertation would be on file in the department, but because her husband's work drew them to another state, she left the university while she was still analyzing the data, thus making it difficult to communicate her results. By the time she herself left, four teachers had already gone. The director of composition had changed, hence her dilemmas.

Scenario #2

Laura became interested in the relationship between student collaboration in the classroom and authority. In order to study these two factors, she decided to observe a group collaborating in an introductory composition class. After conferring with the chair of her dissertation, her committee members, and the Director of Composition, she was approved to observe a composition course. She wanted to examine the impact on collaboration of three loci of authority: instructor, composing strategies, and gender. She further wanted to study collaborative groups during both planning and after drafting. In her prospectus defense, she negotiated this project, its value, supporting theories, and methodology. She was encouraged at the prospectus defense to locate the origin of her project in her personal experience as a teacher-writer; yet, she later wondered how this narrative could fit in the dissertation itself.

One of her crucial efforts was to find a willing instructor who was using collaboration during planning and after drafting. Her second negotiating challenge was to gain consent from this instructor to sit in on the classes, taking field notes, to study a group within the class, and to examine students' written planning and papers. She was able to secure such consent. She worried, then, about the extent to which she should plan her research with this instructor. She did not want to influence his strategic pedagogy or his use of collaborative groups but rather to observe them. Because she did not plan to select the group she would study in depth until she had observed the class for a while, she was unable to engage the students in designing the study. She wanted to observe their interactions in the group as it met, stimulated only by writing strategies and the teacher's expectations. Within the group, she hoped to be as unobtrusive as possible. Clearly she had to gain the group's consent to observe them and to collect their work for study. But she had trouble figuring out what benefit she could offer them or the instructor for their cooperation. She did plan to share her findings with both of them after the dissertation was finished and before she left the university, hoping her results would give them another perspective on collaboration. Because, however, she was not conducting an experimental study, she could offer no definitive account of a causal relationship between her three variables (gender, strategies, and teacher authority) and effective collaboration.

One of the risks in her research was the stability of the group during the semester. Normally in that instructor's pedagogy, groups could stay together during the semester if they wished or they could request changes. In fact, one member of her three-person group did migrate to another group. Thus she faced the dilemma of whether to adjust her study to accommodate this change or start over. With the advice of her committee, she adjusted her project. This kind of dilemma rests in the conflict between the feminine principle of reciprocity and the traditional fear of contaminating data. Clearly, as she visited every class period, she was communicating to the students that some aspect of their instruction was under scrutiny. Although she explained that she was researching collaboration, she hesitated to reveal the variables she was observing, especially teacher instruction, writing strategies, and gender (the instructor was male). Other elements worried her. If she ultimately concluded that the instructor's authority had some adverse connection with the group collaboration, should she reveal this in her writing? In a public report? To the instructor? To the students? If the writing strategies appeared to interfere with collaborative efforts, should this be made public at the university? Would she ever be able to find the students in her study to later share the results with them?

CREATING AN ENVIRONMENT FRIENDLY TO FEMINIST RESEARCH

Despite the constraints of our roles in an institution that is, like many others, traditionally conservative, hierarchical, and masculinist, we are compelled to explore ways of meeting the challenges and contributing to solutions to these dilemmas. We will begin by exploring the possibilities for developing programmatic guidelines that might be defined for research for which the Introductory Writing Program is the site. Such guidelines could act as a larger research framework, helping researchers to plan a study within a community with guidelines already developed.

Any such set of guidelines would probably include requirements that the researcher specify and negotiate the needs and expectations of the introductory writing students and faculty who are subjects/participants in the research as well as the needs and expectations of those graduate students and faculty who are considering undertaking these inquiry projects. For example, the researcher might describe and attempt to accommodate the subjects' rights, which are granted by conventional inquiry projects, among them the expectations for privacy and for informed consent. Further, the researcher might articulate how these expectations fit within feminist principles, e.g., the guideline that the subjects participate in the design of the research and contribute to the interpretation of findings, and/or the expectation that they critique the study's design, methods, and conclusions.

These expectations need to be reconciled with those of the graduate rhetoric and composition students and faculty designing, directing, and supervising research who have expectations that they can define the problem they want to study, that their design can be carried out to meet their objectives, that they can resist possible coercion from subject/participants into ineffective methods or premature discussions of the implications of their studies, and that, as active researchers, they can contribute to the process of defining guidelines for inquiry in their community of researchers.

Likewise, according to feminist theory, both subjects/participants and researchers should articulate mutual expectations. These might include researchers' expectations that participants will honor the explicit and implicit contracts they enter into when they consent to participate, and the participants' expectations that the researchers will involve them in the inquiry to the extent that it is appropriate for the research design. In addition, at the beginning of the research it ought to be clear that if the results of the inquiry project are eventually to be made public, researchers should make efforts to share their conclusions and interpretations with and invite critique from the participants in the study and, if possible, from the introductory writing program community, given that these results will necessarily include representations of some part of the introductory writing program.

Another way such feminist principles might be facilitated is to give official value to sharing conclusions and inviting critique from the subjects' community.

For example, the formal process of review of a dissertation project, from prospectus to final defense, might require review by the subjects/participants. These changes would probably entail discussing issues of authority; that is, agreeing on who should be involved in endorsing research in the undergraduate writing program. At Purdue, this dilemma is frequently solved by inclusion of the Director of Composition on the dissertation committee. This solution may be problematic elsewhere if undergraduate directors have little experience with empirical research and its constraints. Further, such multiple loci of authority increase the number of hurdles for doctoral students' research by adding a stage of review that may deter them from choosing such sites altogether.

Moreover, for the harried doctoral student, inviting critique is currently given no value in the community of participants. There are no formal awards or recognition for contributing to the local composition community's knowledge of about or understanding of what it does—specifically, writing and instruction in writing. Finally, invoking feminist expectations for the research of some students and not for others (assuming feminist research principles are not the only ones) might end in holding a double standard for doctoral research. This in turn raises the question of determining when feminist criteria would be appropriate and who would make this decision—-the researcher, the doctoral committee, or the Director of Composition. Though our graduate students at Purdue are introduced to feminist methodologies in our research methodology courses, they may feel they have to find their own way methodologically, epistemologically, and ontologically—even when they have predecessors to follow—because of the invisibility or small amount of other feminist work in their area of study, or because of their limited reading/ experience in the field (and other disciplines) due to their relative novice status. Furthermore, many of the undergraduate writing program's teachers are graduate students in areas of study other than rhetoric and composition and therefore may not recognize classroom-based research as intellectual work or its "results" as intellectual capital because of its difference from the traditions of their own scholarly research.

We have asked ourselves and our colleagues, if we were to desire to do so, how we might go about committing institutional resources—human and material—to establishing a system of opportunities for sharing research processes and results and to establishing rewards for doing so in a way that would allow us to be accountable for the use of those resources.

We have asked, first, why there are no existing such guidelines and recognized that some of the same issues arise for us (authors/researchers of this issue) as for graduate student researchers. For example, developing these guidelines—especially if the process involved the whole community—would be time consuming and require intensive effort. The value system of the academy does not reward site-specific or local research, as Louise Phelps (1991) has demonstrated, defining it instead as service rather than as a scholarly contribution. There is no pre-existing institutional precedent for developing such guidelines and no formal system of review—human subjects research guide-lines aside, and also proving our point since procedures for these reviews are often confused and are interpreted in a variety of ways.(While most research institutions now have human subjects research guidelines, lines of authority and procedures for conducting these reviews rarely include the involvement of the participants.)

There are logistical and practical barriers as well. At Purdue, for example, the large size of the Introductory Writing Program's student body and instructional staff doesn't make sharing easy. In addition, we can identify several other poten-tial practical difficulties a feminist graduate researcher might anticipate. For example, because feminist inquiry projects often invite participants to con-tribute throughout the process, from design through interpretation of findings, the evolution of the project may not conform to the process implied by the con-ventions of the dissertation prospectus. While dissertation directors and com-mittee members can and do in fact reassure and even caution graduate researchers that the research process is messy, the formal conventions of the ultimate dissertation favor clear representations of the ultimate research design and the results. Doctoral students may also perceive conflicts between answer-ability to their dissertation committee and accountability to participants.

Often the timelines required by feminist projects do not mesh with the expected timelines for completing requirements for a graduate degree. Typically, graduate students can expect to receive only a few years of financial support for their coursework and dissertation research. For example, at Purdue, Ph.D. students are usually limited to five years of support; even those who can count on extended terms of support at other institutions may experi-ence financial pressures due to heavy student loan debts or family obligations to finish their dissertation research in as little time as possible in order to find a full-time faculty position. Because feminists' projects often dictate longitudi-nal designs and frequently involve human participants who understandably give priority to their own agendas and commitments, these projects can seem to take too long to finish.

Graduate feminist researchers may also find it difficult to meet their obliga-tions to share the results of their projects with their participants and the broader community. At Purdue, students sometimes are offered and accept full-time faculty positions before their dissertations are completed. It is not unusual for their dissertation defenses to be scheduled during the summer months, when the participants and the members of the larger community are out of town. It is not surprising that the graduates leave town to honor their obligations to their new local, institutional communities rather than stay behind or return to explore the implications of the conclusions of their inquiry projects for those who remain at the site of the research. They have, from the beginning of their work for the degree, been schooled to view their connection to IWP community as a short-term one and to expect their con-nection to the broader disciplinary community to be a long-term one.

In this essay we have begun to explicate some of the issues that we have encountered as well as to articulate some of our assumptions and values entailed in developing feminist research practices at our own site. By examining some of the dilemmas faced by feminist researchers in our local institutional community, we hope to contribute to a broader understanding of the ways their inquiry projects challenge and are challenged by conventional research methodologies. We also hope an examination of these experiences helps us to remove obstacles from the paths of graduate feminist researchers, creating an environment that encourages them to pursue research consistent with their theoretical commitments.

CHAPTER ELEVEN

Insider/Outsider/Other?
Confronting the Centeredness of Race, Class, Color and Ethnicity in Composition Research

Yuet-Sim D. Chiang

Complex global conversations . . . take into account European desires, but also exceed them . . . . A starting point for careful participation in these conversations is the recognition that theories cannot be abstracted . . . Scholarly theory cannot be separated from local dilemmas and propositions which it engages in dialogue.

Anna Lowenhaupt Tsing
"In the Realm of the Diamond Queen"

My own writing is invested with the same values as my teaching. In aiming to delight as well as to teach, I will rewrite and rewrite and rewrite . . . to bring order and clean, well lighted prose from a fragmented and chaotic universe of discourse. If these characteristics mean I am middle class, so be it.

Lynn Z. Bloom
"Freshman Composition as a Middle-Class Enterprise"

I WAS TROUBLED WHEN I READ LYNN BLOOM's (1996) ESSAY ABOUT FRESHMAN composition being a "middle-class enterprise." Bloom's literacy equation left very little room for many of my linguistic minority students where writing was learned not as a way "to delight" or "to teach," but rather as a way to stake a tenuous place for themselves in a post-colonial English-speaking world. I was troubled because Bloom's argument seems somewhat capricious in light of the changing demographics in English literacy and the growing membership of students from non-traditional, non-white backgrounds.

Bloom's equation of her literacy journey with "Peter Pan collars, and full skirts that reached to the tops of [her] bobby sox," also brought up the ghost of my early years of literacy unrest as I, clad in ill-fitting outfits and wearing red plastic slip-ons that never quite fit my sockless fee, went in search of that illusive white picket fence and the dog, Spot. But unlike Bloom, who exercised her reading and writing around the "right to complain, and [the] energy to improve matters," I never imagined such luxury of rights, at least not until the last ten years. To me and many of my students, using English "to teach" and "to delight" was only the prerogative of the white man, part of the unspoken colonial (post, albeit) curriculum which we were subjected to, but never invited to question.

My purpose in sharing the dissonance between Bloom's articulation of mainstream literacy and mine, and my students', is not to dismiss her—Bloom does have a point. My intention is, however, to use it as a way to embody the larger dis-ease in composition inquiry where constructs of race, class, color, gender and ethnicity are often decentered, undertheorized and/or homogenized. More significantly, I share my reflections in the hope that they point to the white-privileging of textual production in composition research, particularly in matters related to positionality and situatedness in identity politics. My response is also to name the chronic fissure I experience as a linguistic minority/English teacher/teacher-researcher whose lived realities in English are often relegated to ethnic studies, cultural studies, and leftist feminist critiques. In mainstream composition, I am often the outsider, "the Other."

The purpose of this paper is twofold: to respond to the particularities and situatedness of race, color, gender, and ethnicity in the textual production of composition theory and practice, and to argue that "[s]cholarly theory cannot be separated from local dilemmas and proposition which it engages in dialogue" (Tsing 1993, 18). To do so, I will locate my critique within my own practice as an Asian American/immigrant composition researcher. In particular, I will look at two sites of research and describe how identity politics both impeded and expanded my scholarly pursuits. I will then theorize the implications and argue for a critical inquiry that not only addresses identity constructs, but also embraces their centeredness, including their intersubjectivities, in composition research and practice.

OUTSIDER INSIDER OTHER: AN AWAKENING CONSCIOUSNESS

> *The class was a turning point for me . . . I could not pretend that what I was doing was just an "experiment" or a dissertation project, an institutional requirement. I was caught in the language experience of my students which reverberated in my own. And because of this emotional and linguistic bonding, I could not be just a "teacher-researcher" looking in—observing them, and analyzing them. I was one of them.*
>
> Yuet-Sim Chiang
> "The Process-Oriented Workshop"

> *Composition scholars need to develop a sophisticated understanding of the methodological, ethical, and representational complexities in their research.*
>
> Peter Mortensen and Gesa E. Kirsch
> *Ethics and Representation in Qualitative Studies of Literacy*

When I began my teacher-researcher study of a group of non-native English speakers in a process-writing workshop, I had just completed two ethnographic studies of an English methods class and a first-year writing workshop. Methodologically and theoretically then, I felt confident and well-equipped to embark on a third study, except this time around, I was interested in working with a group of linguistic minorities. My past research projects had revolved around white middle class Nebraskan teachers and students (for many of whom I was their first "teacher of color"). My development as a composition teacher, including the reclaiming of my writer's identity, was centered around Western-oriented epistemologies. However, none of this worried me; these factors, in fact, helped catalyze the study. I wanted to contribute to the paradigm shift that was evolving in composition study, particularly from a non-mainstream perspective.

The twenty participants in my studies consisted mainly of immigrant and international students. When I began the study, I saw myself as "outside" them. I was a doctoral candidate, their instructor. They were first-year college students, my students. English is my *primary* language; English defines my literacy. English is their *second* language; native/mother-tongue defines their literacy. These linguistic labels, along with the carefully framed institutional boundaries, separated me from the students and reassured me of a rigorous study. In my researcher's naiveté, I saw these boundaries as sufficient to buttress me, the researcher, from my students, the *subjects* of my research. I had assumed, furthermore, that the categories defined in my study—teacher-researcher, process-writing workshop, and non-native English speaking students (institutionally categorized as ESL students)—were clearly defined and well-packaged. Armed with a rigorous methodology, I genuinely believed that I had all the risk factors under control, and that my study would proceed on its orderly course.

The study, however, did not proceed as anticipated. Instead, the boundaries that I had initially perceived to help "contain" the study were the very things that shifted the textual production. The borderlands of race, class, color, and ethnicity became germane as I dug deeper into my analysis. What emerged from the study was a compelling recognition of the students' and my own identity constructs and their intersubjectivities on composition inquiry. More specifically, my study revealed how these labels were not tidy, neatly compartmentalized constructs that could be safely contained within the parameters of cognitive, expressionist and social-epistemic rhetorics. Instead, these identity constructs drove, shaped, and reshaped my scholarly inquiry that semester, highlighting, in the process, the multilayered issues of ethics and representation in ethnographic research that is just now being acknowledged by composition theorists (Mortensen and Kirsch 1996).

The study brought into sharp focus my close affiliation—emotionally, culturally, and politically—with students' struggles for recognition as authentic language learners, where English too was a meaning-making tool despite the "non-native" label. I empathized and personally identified with these students' linguistic oppression and their deep struggles as "colonized" language users learning to use English to name their lived realities. And in this study, I was forced, for the first time, to relive my literacy history as students yearned, in their accented writings, to write and speak English like "the white man"; linguistic imperialism that demanded these students to accord an uncontested authority to their white peers had likewise dictated my linguistic identity. That semester, I struggled with my students across the rough and ill-defined emotional terrain of split identities—linguistically English, but culturally ethnic. The ghost of alienation came back to haunt me again and again as I read students' poems about the "English walls" that kept them apart from their home culture and loved ones.

Unlike the Nebraskan students whose history and lived realities were historically, politically and culturally different from mine, the students in my teacher-researcher class were like younger (albeit less proficient) versions of myself. Consequently, I could not detach from these students with the same kind of ease I had when "analyzing" the small-town Nebraskan students in the two previous ethnographic studies. I could not *merely study* these "non-native" English speakers whose linguistic history and lived realities painfully echoed my own literacy journey.

The ethnographic stance I brought to the study thus became problematic. As I grappled with ways of capturing the unexpected upheavals, I was confronted with the manifold task of shifting in and out of focus—being like one of my students one moment and, in the very next, casting them as "others." As I plowed through my analysis, I soon realized that my major difficulty was the use of ethnography—a western construct—to delineate or "otherise" a group of people whose language experiences were, I found, increasingly webbed to mine because of the identity constructs of race, class, color and ethnicity. My students and I were distinct individuals; nevertheless, we were racially, culturally, historically and emotionally bonded at various levels: marginalization of our literacy journeys, schisms between linguistic and cultural identities, and an inexplicable emotional attachment to English (Chiang 1991; Chiang forthcoming). Not surprisingly, it became increasingly problematic to attain/maintain a teacher-researcher narrative voice where I could theorize about the students as "the other." Like many researchers who struggle as they enter "a world of subjectivity, to put into words, what [they] cannot say in words" (Chiseri-Strater 1996, 126), I also struggled. "I am one of them," "They are like me," "Yes, I too have experienced that . . ." criss-crossed the research log. In as much as I tried to distance myself from the study—to "objectify" it—the univocal researcher's voice that initially dominated my analysis soon evolved into an "outsider-insider-other" self-reflexive polyvocality.

Aided and encouraged by institutional boundaries—a doctoral student, an English instructor, a composition teacher-researcher—I embarked on the study with an ill-challenged sense of being an "observer," an outsider. But the identity constructs, along with their multiple and conflicting contact zones, shifted the faultlines of identity politics in the study; I had, very unexpectedly, become one of the "others"—the very people I charted out to study. The illusive (false, I would add) and uni-dimensional consciousness—that race, class, color and ethnicity could be safely contained or regulated—which initially framed my study, was now replaced by a tested consciousness of the competing tensions in the ethics and representations of identity politics.

INSIDER OUTSIDER OTHER: A CONTESTED CONSCIOUSNESS

"July 30, 1994; 9.15 p.m.; tired but restless; troubled but yet assured; hopeful yet uncertain" began my last semi-private class journal/letter to the group of minority students in a Summer Institute in Public Policy and International Affairs hosted by University of California-Berkeley. After listing them individually by their names in the letter (all 32 of them), I continued:

> Yes, I know it's easier if I have just said: "Dear WW Fellows" but in the context of what I'm trying to say in this letter, I feel a need to call you by name. After all, as much as I'm speaking to you all as a class, I'm also speaking to you individually. . . I'm not sure how to begin, or how to frame this letter. I guess I'll begin with sharing with you what I take away from this class, as a feminist teacher, as a teacher-researcher, as a person.
>
> As a teacher, I've been challenged to make my lessons real, my examples meaningful, to talk abut the "real" world that is in our class, that is in our everyday experiences . . . . I wondered about my own modeling, about my own stance towards affecting change, towards making a difference in the lives around me. This class has kept me working towards that, and has challenged me in unexpected or unplanned moments . . . There were moments when I felt I've encouraged you, have helped you to re-vision yourself, about your learning, and about your unique place in this world; but there were also moments when I felt that I've angered you, discouraged you, alienated you, made you doubt yourself. . . I'm made to confront my own definitions of teaching. What does it mean to teach? What does teaching entail? Where and when does self come in? How to locate one's selfhood (with its wants and needs) within the teaching process? . . . What are the constant dynamics in the teaching process—the teacher as a knowledge giver, the teacher as "the evaluator," the teacher as the facilitator, the teacher as the "more-experienced other?" When does the teacher become part of the whole? And just as importantly: How does one evolve as a teacher-researcher? This is especially critical in a class where much of my lived life is tangential to my students' realities; and where the teaching of the very subject—[English]—involves teaching the constructs of our world. Even more crucial is the question of how does the teacher disengage from the very subject that determines her realities?
>
> As a researcher, I've been challenged by the myriad of experiences I see embodied in this Institute. Daily, I'm confronted by issues that revolve around school socialization, school culture, school power and control. I'm challenged to make sense of . . .

classroom dynamics like power and control, hierarchies, student-student and stu-
dent-teacher relationships . . . I'm made aware of the politics of teaching and learn-
ing, politics of individualism, and politics of institutionalized and internalized
oppression . . . And although my research is about deconstructing multiculturalism,
the word "multiculturalism" doesn't mean a damn fucking thing if spaces are not
created to let students of diverse background negotiate with one another their oppos-
ing lived realities (ethnic, cultural, class, sexuality and [physical] ability). It has also
helped me to construct new ways of visioning multicultural America, and appreciate
the significance of each of our experience as a "minority" in the multiculturalism
dialogue. As I listened carefully to what the different ethnic groups are saying, are
not saying, are saying in their actions, but not in their words, are saying but not sure
if that's what they want to be saying, I'm confronted with the wide-spectrum of
issues we bring to our class. And how the commonalities and uncommonalities
within and between the ethnic groups at times enhance and diffuse one another. I'm
challenged to go beyond binaries, to see things neither as good or bad, but rather as
border-crossings, boundaries redefining and reshaping themselves.

Last but not least, as a person, Sim—"the English-educated Chinese woman
from Singapore"—I've been challenged to validate my own experience, to claim,
cherish, and celebrate my unique voice as a woman of two differing cultures, of two
distinctive landscapes, conflicting at times, but just as integral and significant to the
essence of my being. I've been challenged to see that there are ways that I can con-
nect with you all, in spite of the cultural differences, the age differences and the
imposed and problematic hierarchy of a traditional student-teacher relationship . . .
I've been challenged to reveal my vulnerabilities, my fallibility . . . As such, I've been
encouraged to keep on journeying in this adopted land.[1]

On July 30, 1994, when I wrote the semi-private class journal/letter (a
weekly practice I had with my students) we were one day short of completing a
seven-week long summer institute. The Institute was a well-funded, intensive
program set up to prepare third-year minority college students from across the
nation for careers in public policy and/or international affairs.[2]

When I joined the Summer Institute of Public Policy and International Affairs
in the summer of 1994 as a writing instructor, I was an enthusiastic teacher, and a
confident teacher-researcher. I felt my professional qualifications and the intellectual insights I had gained from my dissertation study had prepared me for a
summer of rich discoveries and insights to the highly complex nature of a multicultural class. I was especially excited because whereas the dissertation study
allowed me to engage with immigrant and international students, I was now
teaching native-born ethnic minorities. I believed their "U.S.-born" experience
would deepen my growing understanding of the complexities of identity constructs in the classroom. After being aware of the centrality of my own position
in a class of minority students, as indicated in the previous study, I now entered
the Institute study fully secure of my "insider" status—a status that was further
strengthened by an assured (although unexamined) belief that my own

minority background would offer an "inside" scope of students' experience in the Summer Institute.

My confidence was further increased by an acute awareness that, in addition to my professional qualifications and accomplishments, I was hired, as revealed in the long interview with the director of the program, for other reasons: I was a female Ph.D. holder with an immigrant background, and a member of the stereotyped "model minority." The director also reiterated that my accomplishments—a working class, first-generation college Asian woman who not only had risen above all odds, including racism, but had also secured a good job at one of the nation's top universities—would be an inspiration to my students. So, although my official role was course instructor, there was also an unofficial assumption about my obligations as a role model and mentor to my students, as well as academic and cultural bridge between the minority students and the university.

I was appreciative of the institutionally-inscribed and personally-sanctioned "insider" status. I saw in the third-year students younger, perhaps more street-savvy, versions of myself. Intellectually, I identified with the highly-articulate students' striving for academic success and excellence; emotionally, I was in tune with their personal struggles as first-generation college students. Many, like me, had experienced institutionalized racism in its various guises and, also like me, determined to empower themselves through education, through academic achievements, through their own re-presented voices.

Assured of the commonalities that had defined us, I did not contest that "insider" status nor the fact that we were all corralled together (read: homogenized) by the "minority" label. In fact, I was confident that the study would be enriched by the assumed shared realities I had with my students. After all, I did not see myself as *just* their instructor; I was their more-experienced fellow traveler on the political journey of making the academic and the larger world more egalitarian and accessible. But contrary to the previous summer pilot study in which the "insider" status offered a vantage point, and indeed connected me to my students in productive ways, the institutionally and personally-inscribed "insider" status was not so readily received nor accepted in the actual study. Not only was it seriously contested, but the integrity and authenticity of the "insider" status was also called into question.[3]

The identity constructs embedded in the "insider" status, which I had so readily adopted, became points of conflict and opened a dam of anger, unease, suspicion, and misgivings that were not present in the pilot study. At the heart of the "insider/outsider/other" battle—with me and among the students themselves—was the unspoken but operating hierarchies: immigrant Americans versus native-born; black minorities versus non-black minorities; marginalized minorities versus assimilated minorities; immigrant minorities versus involuntary minorities (Gibson and Ogbu 1991). "Institutionalized and internationalized oppression" and the "uncommonalities within and between the ethnic groups" prevented students from seeing me as "one of them." Further fueling the tension was a small group of highly articulate and vocal students who, having experienced their first public political awakening, were caught in the tension between political activism and political extremism.

Complicated by the mandated and institutionally-ascribed role as the instructor/evaluator of the program, my "insider" status became a sore point of unease and disaffection. Delineated and constricted by institutionalized hierarchies set within the university: the evaluator versus the evaluatee; the knowledge giver (read: teacher) versus the knowledge taker (read: the students); and faultlined along the multilayered hierarchies/tensions within minorities: the authentic versus the least authentic, the oppressed versus the least oppressed, the marginalized versus the least marginalized, I was deemed the "other." More specifically, the students saw me as the unofficial coordinator who was out to co-opt them, streamline their thinking. Students' inscription of me as the gate-keeper, weeding out the "fit" from the "unfit," was further complicated by my close working relationship with the white director whom they saw as the embodiment of the racist, oppressive establishment. In essence, many students felt that I, by not denouncing the friendship, had betrayed "our" solidarity as minorities fighting for legitimacy in mainstream discourse.[4]

My position as an instructor (with all its real or perceived power and privileges), and the unexpected "othering" shaped the textual formation in powerful ways. I began the study believing in the "solidarity" of race, class, color, and ethnicity but perhaps not in ways defined by students. My ill-conceived and naive consciousness of identity politics made me assume an "insider" stance that not only belied the situated realities of my students, but also denied their positionalities as minorities imposed by the term, "students of color." However, as the summer progressed, and as the political volatility heightened, I had no recourse but to submit to the hierarchies (in, between, and among the different minority groups) as they split open the social fabric of the class. I had to respond to the cacophony of voices—each demanding their rightful legitimacy—and acknowledge their colliding "innovation and structuration" within the boundaries of marginality (Clifford and Marcus 1986, 2). That summer, identity politics—with all its political and cultural intersecting spaces—reared its multifaceted head and became a bulwark in my teacher-researcher study.[5]

The tension and the hierarchies in the study revealed a very important finding: that empowerment of minority students through well-funded and culturally-sensitive academic programs was far more complex than simply inscribing students and the "model" minority teacher to the little-interrogated category of "people of color." What emerged from the study is that such programs need to renegotiate the spatial politics of positionality and situatedness, for the "observer" and the "observed," so as to allow for the ethical transcription of the blurring boundaries of race, class, color and ethnicity. In the study, to capture adequately the multilayered findings, I had to "reflect upon and write about how [my] situatedness or [my] terministic screens" influence my own textual production and reproduction of mainstream discourse. Along the way, I had to establish the "intersubjectivity between my informant's lives and [mine]" (Newkirk as qtd in Chiseri-Strater 126). In my "othered" position, I learned to transcribe the textual materials and transform my practice and realities as a composition teacher and researcher.

THEORIZING THE INSIDER/OUTSIDER/OTHER: THE CENTEREDNESS OF IDENTITY CONSTRUCTS AND POLITICS

> *Ethnography is actively situated between powerful systems of meaning. It poses its questions at the boundaries of civilizations, cultures, classes, races, and genders. Ethnography decodes and recodes, telling the grounds of collective order and diversity, inclusion and exclusion. It describes processes of innovation and structuration, and is itself part of these processes.*
>
> James Clifford and George E. Marcus
> *Writing Culture*

The two studies, along with other studies that I have done since then, have been pivotal in helping me relocate my own positionality in the "powerful systems of meaning" (Clifford and Marcus 1986, 2). My pursuits have also articulated for me the need to acknowledge "the grounds of collective order and diversity, [their] inclusion and exclusion" (2), and the interpolated subjectivity and the competing tensions of race, class, color and ethnicity. I have come to realize, like Chiseri-Strater, that "all researchers are positioned by . . . age, gender, race, class, nationality, institutional affiliation, historical-personal circumstance, and intellectual predisposition" (1996, 115). And like Chiseri-Strater who argues for an ethnographer's space to include one's own subjective reactions, I too am calling for space for my "reflexivity, subjectivity, and polyvocality" as a non-mainstream teacher-researcher who has chosen to live intellectually and emotionally in English (127).

My re-visioning as a composition researcher and practitioner also means contesting the binaries that pervade the discussion of race, color, gender, and ethnicity in composition inquiry. In particular, I think of the bipolarities that often exist in multiculturalism critiques: white versus nonwhite, ethnicity versus mainstream, oppressed versus privileged. The borderlands that circumference our realities, and which we often circumscribe to ourselves, are by no means static, or as self-contained, as my studies revealed. Instead, like osmosis, our public and personal borderlands are fluid—sometimes centering us, sometimes marginalizing us. This is demonstrated in my assigned roles in the two studies: Ph.D. candidate/Ph.D. holder, teacher/researcher, instructor/evaluator, valued and respected university friend/colleague. But in conjunction, I was also a woman of color, an immigrant woman, an institutionally categorized and defined "non-native" English speaker, a minority in mainstream composition studies and research.

Contesting those binaries also means seeing the sites of inquiry as a "room of mirrors" where visions of ourselves and of our "subjects" are simultaneously both at the center and in the margins (Sullivan 1996). I believe that it is the mirroring that will allow us to challenge the power relations created within the complicated spaces of race, class, gender and ethnicity; more importantly, it will also allow us to critique the ideological process and the spatial politics operating in the textual materials and production of composition research.

Clearly, the textual construction of the narrative self in the studies was implicated by who I was, and what I was. Just as I viewed the institutionalized non-native English-speaking students (ESL) as the "other," I was, paradoxically, also assigned to the "non-native" English speaker category by the larger discourse community; just as I was stereotypically, institutionally, and culturally viewed as a minority who shared common realities with students of color, I was "othered" by these very students because of the inherent and internalized operating hierarchies: immigrant (Fresh-off-the-Boat—FOB) versus native-born (American Born Chinese—ABC), exotic versus home-grown, marginalized versus mainstreamed, more oppressed versus less oppressed, the co-opted versus the activist, and the model minority versus the passive minority.

To counter such narrow and reductive dichotomies, our dominant epistemological framework needs to change to encapsulate a critical engagement of our own "discursive present" and how we inscribe, transcribe, and transform texts because of who and what we are. We need to examine how we are coding and encoding the "heavily nuanced conflicts" of our lived realities (Toni Morrison 1992, 6). As Mohanty argues,

> Difference seen as benign variation (diversity), for instance, rather than as conflict, struggle, or the threat of disruption, bypasses power as well as history to suggest a harmonious, empty pluralism. On the other hand, difference defined as asymmetrical and incommensurate cultural spheres situated within hierarchies of domination and resistance cannot be accommodated within a discourse of "harmony in diversity"(as qtd in Brady and Hernandez 330).

In other words, issues of positionality and polyvocality, as implicated in the constructs of the outsider/insider/other, must foreground our inquiry and practice. That is, we need to link the personal with the political, the personal with the academic, bridging the "asymmetrical and incommensurate cultural spheres situated within hierarchies" of race, color, and ethnicity in our critical practice. We need, as Sullivan reminds us, to learn how to "adequately transcribe and represent the lived experiences of others—inscribe an other's reality—in a text that is marked through and through by our own discursive presence" (1996, 97).

However, even as I theorize about how to re-inscribe an "other's" reality in our own research on the interpolitical and intercultural spheres of race, color, gender, and ethnicity, it is crucial that self-reflexive texts be judiciously guided by a sense of "a more responsible, social reflexivity." Like Ellen Cushman and

Terese Monberg, I, too, fear that a superfacial and superficial "awareness of our personal histories and social locations" may end in licensing us to immerse in "narcissistic or apologetic, navel-gazing prose" (this volume). That is, even as we respond to the identity constructs, and even as we take responsibility for our own discursive practices, we need to incorporate more than a sensitivity to these constructions. We need active and careful engagement with the nuanced subjectivity of identity representation. As Sherene Razack reminds us,

> Encounters between dominant and subordinate groups cannot be "managed" simply as pedagogical moments requiring cultural, racial, or gender sensitivity. Without an understanding of how responses to subordinate groups are socially organized to sustain existing power arrangements, we cannot hope either to communicate across social hierarchies or to work to eliminate them (1998, 8).

Recognizing power arrangements means acknowledging and contesting the historicity of the "white gaze" in traditional ethnographic research (see Cushman and Monberg). Inasmuch as ethnographic studies provide lenses for us to study ourselves and "others," we need to examine how these lenses are colored by our lived experiences and our literate past. For example, not only was I equipped as a researcher with a "western constructed" tool that simultaneously positioned me in the center and at the margins, I was also using a language—English—that is historically a stronghold in colonial subjectivity. I was at once both "it" (the researcher) and "other" (the researched). I needed to understand my "bi-focal-i-ty" before I could scrutinize the "power arrangements" implicit in ethnography and the use of English medium as its text medium. As Spivak puts it , "As a decolonized citizen you take a distance from them; you don't throw them away" (Spivak 1990, 76).

Because of the colonial subjectivity of anthropology of which ethnographic study is an off-shoot, it is even more imperative that non-mainstream and non-white researchers participating and engaging in English literacy studies be critically conscious of the double-edged linguistic tool. As captured in the study of immigrant students, colonization had brought about a buried alienation from my own native culture (Chinese Singaporean) which I had to learn to reclaim when confronted by my students' poignant literacy journey. But it was not until I learned to acknowledge that my "[s]ubjectivity is articulated in a foreign or second tongue" (Lim 1990, 189), albeit my adopted and only literate tongue, that I could realign myself within my ethnic Chinese culture and remember my linguistic rights within the larger cultural politics of English (Pennycook, 1994). I believe it is only when we recognize the potential complicity in such linguistic and textual productions that we can "write politically, with a sense of history and larger forces at work outside the subject" (Lim 1990, 188).

But as my study has demonstrated, intersubjectivities cannot be safely managed by the mere naming of a monolithic construct (in my case, a colonized literacy past) for intersubjectivity straddles all kinds of representations, superfacial and otherwise (Cushman and Monberg, this volume). We cannot "study" a construct without implicating others. For example, we cannot theorize about race without unpacking the "white gaze" (Mohanty, 1991; Razack 1998); we cannot uncover the cultural and political contours of color without raising the historical landscape of race and class (hooks, 1989; Mohanty, Russo, and Torres 1991); most of all, we cannot name the "other" without evoking the representations of selves in their myriad forms (Lee 1995; Moss 1992; Royster 1996; Spivak 1990; Trinh Minh-ha 1989).

However, lest these frictions be collectively reduced to relativism, I would argue that it is precisely such intersections that ensure the rich texturing of narratives in composition theory, practice and research. In fact, I would venture to say that we have no other choice. Unless we are able to intersect the personal with the public, the practice with the theory, the assumed with the lived, our epistemological and methodological frameworks will, at best, remain monolithic, and at worst, be oppressive, which we could ill afford in the increasing moral predicaments of composition inquiry.

LINKING THE PERSONAL AND THE PUBLIC: TRANSFORMING THE SPATIAL POLITICS OF COMPOSITION

> *The idea of neutral dialogue is an idea which denies history,*
> *denies structure, denies the positioning of subjects.*
>
> Gayatri Chakravorty Spivak
> "The Post-Colonial Critic"

I would be remiss if I do not include in this essay how the theorizing of the insider/outsider/other transforms the textual materials of my practice as composition researcher and teacher. At the risk of oversimplifying them, I offer the following:

1. I no longer engage in "neutral dialogue" (Spivak 1992, 72). Although I have a strong non-American accent, and used to wish that it would somehow go away (to the point of seriously considering taking an "accent-reduction" class), I now claim and celebrate it as part of my linguistic and ideological make-up. I consciously allow my post-colonial linguistic identity be part of the discourse transactions between me and my students, between me and my composition colleagues. I no longer try to "pass" or try to pursue unrelentlessly a "wholesome" American (read: white and mainstream) stance. In other words, I allow that linguistic marker to ground me, to platform my stance toward society in general, and composition inquiry in particular. I embrace the intersecting spaces that mark my history: English-educated, immigrant, Asian American, composition teacher and researcher. I do not run from the labels nor deny that my literacy journey in a post-colonial world (as seen in the alchemy of my Chinese/Singaporean/British/American accented speech) has shaped and is still shaping my realities. By locating myself within the intersecting distinctions, I find that it often results in honest talk and real learning, both in my teaching or professional exchanges, with students and colleagues.

2. I make issues of race, class, color, and ethnicity an integral part of my classroom but only in their complicated web. Whereas in the past when I tried earnestly to stay away from those "sensitive" issues, I now invite students to engage with these issues, particularly in their journal writings or in their dialectical reading journals. I also encourage students to locate themselves in texts that are written for a public audience. For example, when a student wrote a piece describing his ordeal when he was falsely arrested for a bank robbery, I asked that he identify his positionality (that of a black young man) instead of hiding behind a "colorless" narrative voice. I found myself asking, "Harry, what about your color? You're black. How does that feed/not feed into your narrative?" In the past, I would have, perhaps, responded to this student at the structural and rhetorical levels, but I no longer hide behind "safe" response. Instead, I encourage Harry to see that my reading of his text is also presupposed along the lines of identity constructs, whether consciously or unconsciously. In essence, I no longer practice a "race/class/color/ethnicity-blind" response, especially in literacy contexts where they are central to the textual formation.

3. I engage with students about the notions/constructs of the "other." Like Marian Yee who uses the question "Are You the Teacher?" (1991, 25) as part of the critique of dominant cultural narratives in her composition classroom, I also let the "othering" construct be part of my students' critical literacy journey in the class. For example, when I read a "non-native" English speaking student's work about his burdens as an "other" in the mainstream English speaking world, I allow my personal/on-going struggles and self-doubts to be part of the writing exchange/response/conference. In our exchanges, I consciously invited him to redefine his understanding of the "non-native" speaker, and the iconographic images that came to his mind when he talked about himself as "the other."

Did I influence the student's writing? I believe I did, but I no longer feel I need to apologize for it, for I believe it is exchanges like this that allow the teaching of writing to impact the world. As Rich points out, "[r]e-vision—the act of looking back, of seeing with fresh eyes, of entering an old text from a new critical direction—is for women more than a chapter in cultural history: it is an act of survival" (1979, 35). In other words, I revise what is often assumed, unspoken, and/or unacknowledged. I allow students' writing and the classroom text to be complicated by the dominant iconographic images of the "other." I do not necessarily recenter it but I do, however, invite students to problematize the notion of the "other" from multiple entry points, and to interrogate how this notion/construct shapes and reshapes our lived realities, both within the language classroom and in the larger society.

4. I see self-reflexive writing as an integral part of my development as a teacher and researcher. The "rich, thick" description of an ethnographer's stance now includes an interrogated "thick" description of my own process as I go about "studying" the cultures around me. How does who and what I am implicate the way I connect and understand my students and their writings?

Where am I in the context? Who and what is being centered in this context? Why? How? Where and how do I address the polyvocal realities as a teacher/researcher?

My self-reflexive writing also includes wrestling with that constant and ever-nagging awareness that I am using a "western construct" to deconstruct my understanding of my world. I am critical of the double-edged linguistic and research tool even as I use it to concretize the inherent contradictions, to counterpoint the dichotomies, the binaries, and the bipolarities that cross my path everyday, as an immigrant, a woman of color, a "model minority", a university composition teacher and researcher. In essence, I use it in the context and commitment of using "the master's tools to dismantle the Master's House" (Lorde 112).

These practices are not formulaic nor are they meant to be prescriptive, nor are they always predictable. In fact, I am often jarred and pained by the cultural, social and emotional complexities that come with my practices. Questions of my professional role and obligations (as defined by the university) and their inherent power structures often implicate my practice of linking the personal and the public. Finding my balance in the tight-rope of complicity in cultural hegemony and wholistic reconstruction in identity representation is never effortless—I worry about being compliant on the one hand, and being simplistically reductive on the other hand. However, I share these examples with the hope that they will put the "human voice and face" back into composition theories that have become increasingly highfalutin and removed from our daily realities.

CLOSING NOTE

I offer this discussion with a sharp sense that I am speaking from a position complicated by my colonial and immigrant background and my ongoing (no matter how tenuous it appears) linguistic affiliation with discourse communities that often "other" one another: mainly, English composition, English as a Second Language, and World Englishes (Chiang 1998). Indeed, part of my struggle in writing this paper is learning how to recenter myself within these various discourse communities that simultaneously see me as an "insider," "outsider," and/or "other." But I have discovered, in the course of writing, that rather than trying to distill these border crossers into unconstrained, manageable bits, I should instead let them form the framework; I should let the metalanguage used in the critique of intersubjectivities speak for itself. It is, after all, the essence of this paper.

As with other narratives in which the "I" is unapologetically pronounced, there is always the risk of having my work dismissed as essentializing, or undermined as "tentative and self-doubting" (Wolf 1992, 135); nevertheless, when there is such a scarcity of methodological and epistemological frameworks where ethics and representation of identity politics are ethically and democratically transcribed, I have no other recourse but to engage with such risks. I need, in writing the past, to "know it differently than [I] have ever known it, not to pass on a tradition but to break its hold over us" (Rich 1979, 35).

I also offer this self-reflexivity because like many of my feminist colleagues, I cannot see a return to an "unproblematic, unified, Cartesian subject" (Mortensen and Kirsch 1996, xxi; see also Behar and Gordon). Besides, as my studies demonstrate, the universal principle of the "classical boundary between the observer and observed" (Behar and Gordon 1995, 8) that originally guided my research, and which I subsequently had to re-vision, was no longer justifiable, nor defensible for that matter, in a multilingual and multicultural setting. After all, as Behar and Gordon argue, how can we "recite the mantra of gender, race, and class and go on with academic business as usual, handing difference over with one hand and taking it away with the other?" (1995, 7). Indeed, how could we when are truly committed to confronting the seduction of "empty pluralism" that mires much of current composition inquiry and practice.

NOTES

1. A discourse analysis of this journal excerpt revealed the complicated positions from which I was operating. Notice that I was simultaneously theorizing about the students and dialoguing with them. I was shifting "in" and "out" even as I wrote to the students. Although the letter was a form of personal closure, I could not extricate myself from the "researcher's narrative voice. Note in particular the lines "as a researcher, I've been challenged by issues that revolve around school socialization . . . by politics of individualism, and politics of institutionalized and internalized oppression." I was talking *about* them and *with* them at the same time. This constant shifting in positionality held true throughout the study.

2. The Summer Institute, funded by the Woodrow Wilson Summer Fellowship Programs in Public Policy and International Affairs, was hosted by the Graduate School of Public Policy, University of California, Berkeley. The Institute was committed to assisting minorities in a career in public policy and/or international affairs.

3. Several months after the study, I had a chance to visit with a couple of students who verified this observation. When I showed them my analysis, particularly about how they viewed me, one of the students said, "Yes, we couldn't trust you. We weren't sure if you were for us or against us. Especially when we came to talk to you about our problems with [the director], you didn't do anything about it. Instead, you told us to talk to [the director] ourselves. We thought you're one of us but we weren't sure after that, not sure we could trust you." I made the suggestion because I wanted the students to voice their concerns directly to the director, but students had put far more weight on their request than I had understood at that time.

4. In the self-evaluation at the end of the Institute, one student wrote, "I was disappointed to hear how many individuals in our debate group felt as though the "administration" was deliberately trying to instigate antagonism. Where did all of the conspiracy theories come from? Where did all of the distrust come from?

Was the amount of confrontation natural in this type of setting? Why were we so quick to judge and to make assumptions? Was it because of the dynamics of "our" group? ... Personally, I had a difficult time balancing my own individuality with the construction of a social norm that was manifested through the day-to-day interactions of the Woodrow Wilson participants. I felt as though this environment often times made individuals pressed into uncomfortable areas where one can easily take offense. Was this process a result of the 'administration?' [sic]. No. However, this process was a contributing factor which did create much of the antagonism that pervaded through the end of the program."

5.   This is succinctly captured in a student's self evaluation at the end of the semester. "I don't think I was completely successful at making myself heard there this summer. I guess the clearest example of this is that people talk about "zebra couples" around me. There was a note on the computer room board saying that zebra couples aren't welcome, Mary [a pseudonym] refers to herself as a yogurt (white and all mixed up with color), John [a pseudonym] frequently refers to people such as myself as Mulatto, etc. I personally find that kind of shit repugnant. Mulatto is a slave term. It comes out of a world full of words like "high yella," "Octoroon," "Quadroon," "red headed step child," etc. I am all of these things and I am none of these things. I am as much as "high yellow nigger" as everyone else in this program is a stereotype of their race ... How could I go to a dinner for black students when I see a message saying "No Zebra Couples." I am being excluded by my own race, and they don't even know that I feel this way."

CHAPTER TWELVE

Re-Centering Authority
Social Reflexivity and Re-Positioning in Composition Research

Ellen Cushman and Terese Guinsatao Monberg

*T*HIS PAPER STEMS FROM AN EXTENDED DISCUSSION AND EXPLORATION OF the ways we've tried to envision and enact a more socially responsible scholarship, one that builds bridges to facilitate border crossings. Where we come from, how far we've gone, what we still remain tied to—all remind us to make knowledge in ways that honor and respect and serve. Through social reflection, we look for ways to create an intellectual and social space for our own self-awareness, to inform and facilitate a mutually rewarding dialogic relationship with students, colleagues, and community members. We believe this kind of reflection, combined with an active repositioning of the self, can obviate one of the most pressing problems in current composition research: we're often socially distanced from the cultures we study. A socially reflexive scholarship is one that does not assume authority in representing others but negotiates that authority by creating "a different sort of social space where people have reason to come into contact with each other because they have claims and interests that extend beyond the borders of their own safe houses, neighborhoods, disciplines, or communities" (Harris 1995, 39). This kind of social reflexivity helps our work become more constructive than confrontational—helps us move beyond scholarship that merely makes cultural differences visible to us in the "comfort zone" of academe. Reflection can inform and facilitate the dialogue and negotiations that take place in this intersection of competing perspectives. Such reflection and negotiation, in fact, can build the bridges necessary for successful border crossings: those that allow people on both sides of the bridge to cross the border. As bell hooks argues, "to claim border crossing . . . as the deepest expression of a desired cultural practice within a multicultural democracy means that we must dare to envision ways such freedom of movement can be experienced by everyone" (hooks 1994, 5).

Social reflexivity and reciprocal dialogue also allow us to keep in mind the ever present risk of reifying boundaries, particularly when researchers assume authority in speaking for others (Royster 1996). We propose social reflexivity as one way for researchers to not only reflect upon the assumptions we bring to our work, but to challenge and change these assumptions through dialogue with others. We need to continually ask ourselves, what kind of work are we here to do, and who are we serving with it? The reflexive dialogue we envision acknowledges more complicated definitions of authority and identity, taking composition scholarship beyond the theoretical exploration of reflexivity, beyond self reflexivity, and toward a more socially responsible reflexive research.

In this essay, we argue that we must adopt a responsible, socially reflexive approach to negotiating our authority in composition research, one that truly facilitates the kinds of boundary/border crossings that begin to reduce social distance. We begin by highlighting contemporary issues related to authority and representation that have highlighted a need for more reflexive approaches, contextualizing these issues within historical and contemporary discussions in anthropology. Focusing on questions of authority, Ellen reflects on her role as ethnographer in an inner city neighborhood. She describes the many ways in which her authority as researcher/writer is socially constructed with the people in this community. She illustrates the ways authority to represent others does not come de facto from an academic position, but from the reciprocal and dialogic relations shared by scholars and community residents. With these dialogic relations in mind, Terese reads an essay by cultural studies theorist John Fiske, to highlight the risks involved when scholars assume or self-create their own authority in representing others. Her analysis highlights the tensions she experienced in reading Fiske's essay, based on the history of colonial-era ethnographies in the Philippines and her own history as a Filipina mixed-blood. Grounded in these histories, Terese illustrates some of the problems that arise when we use authority to create distinctions between ourselves and the people we study without questioning our sources of authority, without reflecting upon how we position ourselves in relation to others.

We find that a socially responsible reflexivity is an everyday practice that demands we continually reposition ourselves in relation to others and in relation to our own literate activities as scholars. When we position ourselves in a variety of social networks, we're more likely to break down some of the prejudices and misconceptions we hold about others and begin to identify with people outside of the "comfort zones" social distance reproduces. We propose a civically responsible composition scholarship that uses social reflexivity and reflexive identification as a benchmark for negotiating authority and facilitating social and cultural border crossings.

QUESTIONS FROM WITHIN: DECENTERED AUTHORITY

Recent discussions in composition scholarship have revolved around questions of authority, particularly questions of ethnographic authority. While recent moves in composition and cultural studies scholarship have encouraged academics to cross borders and boundaries, many of us have remained skeptical, protective, and hesitant. For example, Jacqueline Jones Royster, bell hooks,

Gesa Kirsch, Malea Powell, Janice Gould, and Patricia Sullivan, have all asked, warned, and/or demanded that scholars be more careful of where they step and for whom they speak. Royster writes, "we see the obvious need to contextualize the stranger's perspective among other interpretations and to recognize that an interpretive view is just that—interpretive" (1996, 31). Sullivan similarly comments that "[under] the pressure of postcolonial and feminist critiques, the grounds of ethnographic authority have been opened to ethical . . . scrutiny . . . . Who is telling the story, the researcher or the 'researched'?. . . . What gives her the right to speak for another, to tell another's story?" (1996, 104).

Questions related to authority, the politics of representation, and the colonial history of ethnography are not necessarily new questions. In the field of anthropology (and/or anthropology and education), it is more widely recognized that ethnography is a process of translating complex, ambiguous, cross-cultural interactions into textual form (McCarthy 1992). Since the 1960s, anthropologists from diverse theoretial approaches (such as Claude Lévi-Strauss and Clifford Geertz) have recognized the complex relationship between language and culture, acknowledging ethnography itself as an inscription. More contemporary theoretical and methodological discussions in anthropology have revolved around a "crisis of representation in the human sciences," highlighting issues of interpretation, questions of ethnographic authority, and new methodological directions (Marcus and Fischer 1986). In acknowledging that power components are present in any cross-cultural encounter, for example, James Clifford reminds us that an ethnographic account is only one version, one interpretation of that encounter (1986). In attempts to break-up ethnographic author(ity) and stress the interpretive factors involved with ethnography, many anthropologists have begun to experiment with conventional ethnographic forms of writing. These new forms, or "new ethnographies," may employ discursive dialogic techniques that are "polyphonic, playful, ironic, (and) confessional" (McCarthy 1992, 643). Ethnographers may try to include their subjects' voices and/or personal reflections on their experiences such as their initiation into the culture, the difficulties they've had translating the experience into (a specific) language (Clifford 1988), or how the encounter (inter)relates to their own history (Mascia-Lees, Sharpe, and Cohen 1989). In other words, ethnographers have for some time been experimenting with various forms of writing in an effort to portray the dialogic, complex nature of cross-cultural/intercultural encounters that surround the author(ity) of any ethnographic text.

As composition scholars wrestle with similar questions of representation and authority, we are also experimenting with the conventional forms in which we (re)present our data and our interpretations. For example, as Gesa Kirsch notes, we are seeing an increase in the number of multi-vocal or polyvocal texts. And while polyvocal texts may be produced with the intention of decentering our academic authority, these texts may undermine our very intentions. Kirsch offers several reasons why polyvocal forms of text may be undermining our efforts to decenter ethnographic authority: first, these texts require readers to "carry out much of the interpretive and analytical work usually done by authors"; second, these texts can easily "become elitist, leaving out a great many readers . . . who may find such texts confusing, annoying, and incoherent"; and third, multi-vocal texts "do *not* help scholars to come to terms with interpretive responsibility" (Kirsch 1997, 196 –197; her emphasis). To this list, we would like to add another potential problem with polyvocal texts: when ethnographers include long sketches of informants' voices in their writing (or even in conference presentations), these texts may end up decontextualizing informants' and participants' voices with the end result being an exoticizing of others. For example, Denny Taylor's polyvocal ethnographies, *Growing Up Literate* and *Toxic Literacies*, tend to showcase participants' lives and literacies as exotic others. Long stretches of quotes need careful interpretation and analysis so that readers understand the social and political context from which these informants hail. But in Taylor's writing, participants almost march in a decontextualized parade of literacy artifacts, stories, and fieldnotes with the disappointing effect that the complex social and cultural values of participants are relegated to the background while their literacies help create a sensationalized foreground.

Patricia Sullivan also recognizes the interpretive issues and risks associated with Taylor's polyvocal ethnographies. Sullivan explains that "Taylor routinely invites her informants—drug addicts, alcoholics, homeless persons—to share the stage with her" at conferences where participants tell stories they have written. Sullivan describes the scene in more detail: "Taylor's informants, her actors, seem strangely out of place on the conference dais from which they make their presentations, and they are visibly uncomfortable as they address their stories to the rapt academic audience" (Sullivan 1996, 104 –105). While Sullivan calls Taylor's work "performed ethnographies" (1996, 105), we see a real danger in these kinds of performances. These polyvocal performances often sensationalize the voices of informants for an awed academic audience who don't often see the way these voices have been, in very real ways, displaced from their context and culture. Rather than ask academics to move out of their comfort zones to understand others, Taylor extricates community members from their comfort zones so she can proudly display them in a museum-like contact zone with academics. While polyvocal texts have the potential for powerful cultural critique and to provide space for voices that have traditionally been excluded from traditional forums, these texts often risk exoticizing these voices.[1] While it may be important for us to hear informants articulate their experiences on their own terms, our scholarly responsibility also requires that we provide an interpretive context. But to provide an interpretive context also requires that we recenter and carefully negotiate our authority. Thus, as one response to current questions about representation, polyvocal texts often fall far short of reaching the admirable goal of decentering (our) authority.

Another response to current questions about representation and authority has been to produce texts that are more reflexive. The process of reflexivity is an attempt to recognize how one's personal history(s), ways of behaving and speaking, and social location(s) may be influencing methods of data collection and interpretation. Ideally, reflexivity sees these social and emotive influences as micro facets of larger social structures of power, illustrating the complex process of arriving at interpretations and explanations while also leaving room for alternative explanations or more "complete" understandings. In practice, however, many reflexive texts, rather than focusing on the process of arriving at explanations, have tended to focus too closely on the study of the self. Too often, reflexive prose becomes self-reflexive, confessional and apologetic. Unless personal reflection is tied back to larger social, cultural, political, methodological, or theoretical issues, we are hard-pressed to see what such self-reflection offers to us as readers, or to composition scholarship overall.

Anthropologists Francis Mascia-Lees, Patricia Sharpe, and Colleen Ballerino Cohen express concern that reflexive ethnographies have become autobiographies, stories of the ethnographer getting in touch with "'the other' in himself" (1989, 24). These anthropologists argue that when taken to the extreme (like polyvocal texts) reflexive texts may become obscure forms of ethnographic writing "difficult for anyone but highly trained specialists to dispute" (Mascia-Lees, Sharpe, and Cohen 1989, 10). While reflexivity is a worthwhile and necessary step to ethnographic validity and responsibility, not all attempts at reflexivity are equally "responsible." The strength of reflexive writing is to carefully delineate the context of our data and our interpretations. As Mascia-Lees, Sharpe, and Cohen remind us, it is a process that should prompt us to keep questions of purpose foregrounded in our minds: What is our purpose in studying a particular culture? How will we represent our subjects in our texts? How will we represent the ambiguity of our interpretations? (1989, 33). We see responsible, social reflection—reflection on ourselves as socially responsible beings—as a form that requires these questions to be answered with reference to those cultural practices we seek to honor and theorize about. Thus, in thinking about reflexivity, it has been useful for us to distinguish self-reflexivity from a more responsible, social reflexivity. An awareness of our personal histories and social locations should not immerse us in narcissistic or apologetic, navel gazing prose; it should instead inform our socially reflexive, everyday, border crossing actions.

NOT FROM WITHIN, BUT WITH: NEGOTIATED AUTHORITY

As a means for decentering authority, self-reflexivity and polyvocalism stem from a problematic assumption about power: power can best be understood in a hierarchical fashion where everyone occupies a position in the hierarchy. Self-reflexivity and polyvocalism both try to account for and complicate respectively positions on the ladder of power. This notion of politics works in top-down ways by looking to see who is above (the researcher) and below (the participants), which is why we so often hear dichotomies used to describe power: dominant/subordinate; liberated/oppressed; empowered/disempowered; study up/study down. Describing power solely in terms of positionality leads us to assess our research and writing too easily, politics at a glance: judgments based on the surface of a text or the face of a person—superfacial politics.

We need a definition of power that examines situated relations between people, a definition that allows us to ask: how do people willfully act out, push at, bend, shape, and subvert structures in their day-to-day activities? In other words, we argue that authority to represent others can only be judged through an assumption of power that sees the fluidity ofpower relations, as opposed to the bloodless, static, heartless, uni-dimensional way of seeing positionality. If we see power as fluid, as ever shifting and regenerated in our relations with others, we're much more likely to see how individuals consciously resist simple reproductions of structures, and how complicated and nuanced day-to-day living and literacies are. Using superfacial politics, scholars become invasive, dismissive and reductive and attempt to determine the positionality of the researcher and the participants.

At a recent conference an African-American woman asked Ellen to justify why she "as a white researcher from a prestigious institution had authority to represent African-Americans in an inner city." Ellen recalls:

The assumptions in her question alarmed me: as though I identify myself solely a white person; as though community members identify themselves as solely African-Americans; as though as researcher and participants we really could occupy such uni-dimensional, flat, bloodless, subjectivities. I told her I was no stranger to welfare offices, fighting roaches for my dinner, wearing the same bra held together with safety pins for months. I understood the need to steal, fight, and take drugs. I've had very unflattering mug shots taken of me. I'm the same gender as the people I have the most access too. "Many of these people migrated from the Carolinas and have Cherokee blood and ways. My family were some of the first listed on the BIA rolls in Oklahoma after the trail of tears," I heard myself say. I wanted to tell her I felt more at home in their living rooms than in the classrooms at Rensselaer, but I felt sick. I had already compromised so much of my own self by scrambling to reveal my positionality to her. Her question invaded me, probed around my own self looking for some justification to show I had the authority to represent others. I subjected myself to her scrutiny, made my identity naked for her inspection. I disgusted myself for compromising something very fundamental to my home culture: never talk about yourself, never set yourself apart from others, protect personal space—your own and others'.[2] Ironically, self reflexivity invades and colonizes the other as it tries to reduce the likelihood of invasion and colonization. Sometimes the medicine is worse than the disease.

We realize the need for reflexivity, but not so much self-reflexivity as social reflexivity. Social reflexivity contributes to a constructive scholarship that offers a "sense of how competing perspectives can be made to intersect with and inform each other" (Harris 1995, 33). That is, social reflexivity sees authority to represent as earned through the careful interaction and knowledge making with the individuals in the study, where we negotiate, through reciprocity, the power and status related to our positions. Social reflexivity demands that the researcher and participants openly negotiate their interdependent relations using dialogic interaction. We see authority as emerging out of relations with participants.

In the early afternoon of May 10, 1993, I finished tutoring in the Neighborhood Center where I first met children and teens in this neighborhood. Being spring, many community residents gathered together on front stoops. Cis and I sat together on the second step. She offered me a hit from the quart of Malt Liquor she sported in a brown paper bag. I took the bottle as she stood and motioned for me to follow her. We walked across the street to her front stoop and took a seat there: "I been put out," she said as she took a folded paper from her jacket pocket. I read the eviction notice she had been served earlier that morning by the County Marshall. When she went to court on the 13th of May, she found out that she was evicted because of the "traffic" in and out of her house and neighbors' complaints about her. Since she occupied the apartment on a month-to-month basis, she had only 30 days to find a new place to live. Her eviction notice was one of eight served to families over the course of this study. The literate and oral skills needed to overcome eviction, removal, and displacement became central to my study because it was central to so many lives in this area.

The mutually beneficial relations that community members and I shared stemmed, in part, from our dialogue together where we disclosed ways we identified with each other. Cis gave me permission to collect literacy artifacts related to her search for housing as I took her to see places and fill out applications for emergency assistance from the Department of Social Services and other agencies. I wrote a letter of recommendation for her to potential landlords and gathered housing lists from my university. Cis and I together scoured newspapers, met landlords, and did dumpster dives for boxes. We both knew how uprooting eviction felt. And we talked together: about how to get more cash for a moving van; how to ask utility companies to transfer service and renegotiate payments for past due bills. On one drive around town, she said, "you so young and without no kids. Why you know so much about [eviction]?" I told her about my mom who was the head of our household of 6; about the four evictions my family has been through: "once we were homeless for three months."

"Didn't that make her look bad?"

"With the neighbors?"

"Yeah."

"Not really. They didn't know. See, my sister had been saving her money from working at Burger King. She just gave it to Mom, we rented a Uhaul and drove out to California. We stayed with my brother in 29 Palms. Slept on his floor until we could find a place." On another day as we packed her boxes, she told me about her huge family, her move north, and her other evictions. I told Cis about going with Mom to court, to DSS for food stamps, and listening to her deal with utility companies she couldn't pay; about the "pack what you can, leave the rest, and shake out the roaches" moving days. Our dialogue worked in tandem with our

give-and-take during the data collection. We built an interdependent relationship with care for each other, for where we've been, for our families, for what we knew.

But reciprocity also enters into the analysis of data and writing of the ethnography as well. When I interpret data, I ask for criticism from the people involved in the piece of data under consideration. I summarize the area of work I'm responding to and then ask them to tell me how they link their actions to that theory. Often their insights into how I'm "reading" a situation penetrate deeper into and problematize my interpretations. When I've only captured part of the complexity in my representation, they'll say "you got to consider," or "that's true, but what about . . . ," or "yeah but there's also. . . . " Once I've validated my analysis through dialogic interaction, where they authorize what I'm thinking—then I set pen to paper. When the draft is in shape, they read the work (sometimes with me there) and add more information. I explain how the data works with a particular theory and they tell me if what I'm writing represents them with respect and decency.

Any authority Ellen's final text has, then, is due mostly to internal sources: internal to their shared histories, reciprocal relationships, and continual negotiation of their interdependencies. This becomes a social reflexivity, then, as opposed to a self reflexivity: a reflexivity based on relations as opposed to positions. Social reflexivity closes distances without erasing differences. In doing socially reflexive ethnographies, the knowledge we make emerges with the individuals we study. This means that the theories we use must come out of the rafters, must close the distances between the academy and the community. But too often, ethnographers and cultural studies theorists remain separate and above those they hope to understand; they embrace high theory as their source of authority.

FROM ON HIGH: SELF-CREATED AUTHORITY

Contemporary developments in cultural studies and composition scholarship have prompted many academics to move their work into the homes and communities of others. While these movements have great potential for building bridges and facilitating dialogue between and among diverse peoples, they also involve great risks: we may end up (re)producing distance between peoples, creating one-dimensional distinctions and categories that place us all within the same old hierarchies that we claim we're trying to change. When turning toward ethnography, we must continually grapple with questions of authority, the politics of representation, and the colonial history of anthropology. We cannot afford to forget that "anthropology first emerged in collaboration with colonialism and missionary activities, and [that] the traditional style of writing an ethnography supported the objectives of these endeavors: classification and control" (Traweek 1988, ix). Nor can we forget that classification and control were very *real* methods used to conquer, divide, assimilate, silence, and "enlighten" entire populations, tribes, and peoples. Filipino scholar Arnold Molina Azurin reminds us of the large role that ethnography played in the colonization of the Philippines. Azurin describes the complex ways in which colonial-era ethnographic descriptions and categories were used to "'document' the distinctions between colonizer and colonized," thereby "[legitimating] the right of the 'superior' races over the uncivilized peoples" (1995, 15). These colonial-era ethnographies were not only used to produce distance and distinction between the colonizer and the colonized, they were also used to create divisions within and among colonized Filipinos—by creating a hierarchy in which the colonizer always came out on top, while various groups and tribes of Filipinos were categorized according to "varying levels of primitiveness and degrees of savagery" (Azurin 1995, 24). With this colonial history in mind, we have reason to think critically about how we sometimes create or assume authority in representing the specific ways others speak, write, behave, live.

John Fiske's essay "Cultural Studies and the Culture of Everyday Life," is particularly illustrative of contemporary tensions and risks associated with ethnographic authority and representation. Identifying his work as consonant with cultural studies traditions and purposes, Fiske sets out "to examine critically and to restructure the relationship between dominant and subordinated cultures, . . . to interrogate the relationship between the academy and the rest of the social order" (1992, 164). Fiske interrogates this relationship through a cultural studies reading of several ethnographic texts, examining the everyday lives represented in these ethnographies.[3] For example, Fiske examines the everyday cultural practices of "a mainly black, working class culture" and "first generation urbanized Brazilian peasants" by juxtaposing descriptions of the material artifacts found in these people's homes, paying specific attention to the choice and arrangement of these material artifacts. Referring to material artifacts found in the homes of these Brazilian peasants, he writes:

> The plastic flowers are for Leal's newly suburbanized peasants deeply contradictory. They have a mystique because of the "mystery" of their production (unlike natural flowers)—they are fetishes, syntheses of symbolic meanings, of modernity; but they are also commodity fetishes. They require money, another fetish, and transform that money into an object of cultural display. Real money is not an appropriate decoration or cultural object, but transformed money is; its transformation occurs not just in its form, coin to plastic flower, but in the social formation, theirs to ours. (Fiske 1992, 157)

Based on these kinds of ethnographic descriptions and (re)interpretations, Fiske argues that (unlike the economically privileged), the economically oppressed use material artifacts to create richly textured living spaces in order to add "density" to their everyday lives. Fiske sees this creation of density as a strategy used by the oppressed to live within narrow material constraints, a strategy which allows them to compensate for "limits . . . [in] social experience" and mobility (1992, 157). Fiske's explanation may, in part, be true; some people may acquire material artifacts for the reasons that he says. One problem, however, is that Fiske neglects to consider the ways middle-class and wealthy people may also use material artifacts to add texture and density to their lives. In other words, Fiske neglects to consider the *range* of peoples and cultural practices he might find on the socio-economic ladder. Because he concentrates more closely on the habits, thoughts, and practices of those on the lower end of the ladder, working-class people and the poor, Fiske does not examine the *relationship* between "dominant and subordinate cultures" as much as he creates *distinctions* (sometimes false distinctions) between these (supposedly separate, non-overlapping) cultures.

Azurin's work on colonial-era ethnographies in the Philippines helps to explain why one-dimensional hierarchies create false dichotomies, distinctions, and superiority/authority over others. Because Fiske attempts to explain cultural practices in terms of a one-dimensional socio-economic hierarchy, he makes problematic assumptions about power and difference—assumptions that allow him to self-create his authority over the people he theorizes about. He does this even as he explains his scholarly mission:

> I intend to contribute to. . . . the development of ways of theorizing culture that grant the concrete practices of subordinated ways of living a degree of importance in theory which is the equivalent to that which they have in their own habitus, even though this *is distanced from, and socially subordinated to*, the [academic] habitus *whose discourses are necessary to produce theory*. (Fiske 1992, 165; my emphasis)

Employing a range of theories (Bourdieu, deCerteau, and Foucault), Fiske continually positions himself, and the entire academy, as distinct from and above the people he theorizes about. This distinction and distance is reinforced as Fiske associates secondary (false) distinctions with this primary one. For instance, Fiske distinguishes between the production of theory and everyday practice: producing theory is not an everyday practice; everyday practices are not informed by—do not produce—theory. Fiske not only associates practice solely with "subordinated" habituses and theory solely with academic habituses, he argues that academic habituses are *necessary* to produce theory.[4] By identifying himself as a member of the academy, Fiske not only grants himself the authority to re-represent these people's cultural practices, he also grants himself the authority to grant these practices *legitimacy*. Unreflexive about his own assumptions about power, he is only able to examine the relationship between the academy and the people he studies in a top-down manner, the end result a one-dimensional explanation of complicated, situated, cultural practices.

In the process of writing this essay, Terese has often asked herself: *How would a cultural studies theorist interpret the artifacts in my apartment? Would the photographs on my wall be interpreted as an attempt to bridge my distance with a culture that I may sometimes look upon with nostalgia? Would my artifacts be described as typical of a second-generation, American-born, Filipina (who is also half Irish), who grew up in the city (not in the rural areas of the Philippines), first-generation to graduate college, now middle-class . . . expression of cultural nostalgia? When I first read this essay by Fiske, I resented his reference to the "density" and "texture" of these people's lives—as if he didn't also have strategies for creating "density" and "texture" in his own life. I have thought about the kinds of oppression these Brazilian peasants may have experienced—dislocation, relocation, breaking of kinship ties, labor-intensive, low-paying jobs—yet, I resented Fiske's reduction of these Brazilian peasants' plastic flowers to mere "commodifications," monetary symbols of their resistance to an oppressive order. While I do not completely disagree with his explanation, I know his explanation leaves out a whole separate dimension. I think about my Lolo (grandfather), a man who relocated to the States at the age of 16 to make a better life for himself and for all those to follow him, a man who worked on the railroads, waited tables, and often swallowed his pride, a man who held a hand out to other Filipinos so they too could come to the States and make better lives for themselves, a man whose love and commitment I came to know through cultural practices that had complicated, multi-layered meanings.*

How would Fiske explain the loss these artifacts represent? Both of my grandparents are gone, and I sometimes feel so removed from our culture—geographically, linguistically, and socially. And if Fiske did acknowledge the loss, would he view my artifacts as an expression of nostalgia? Perhaps I am nostalgic, but how can such a complicated cultural practice be collapsed into the simple hanging of a picture, and further reduced into simple economic behavior? My cultural practices are nostalgic, not in a romantic way, but in an active way. I do not long to live in the past, but I do long to be connected to my past. My nostalgia is what Debbora Battaglia calls "active nostalgia" (1995, 78). In other words, my cultural practice of filling up my life with material artifacts (and theory) is a "transformative action with a connective purpose"; it continually reconnects me with my histories, my capabilities, my knowledge, and my heart—it repositions me in relationship to my present and my future.

Viewing cultural practices through a one-dimensional lens is risky: it limits our ability to be socially reflexive about our assumptions and our (always partial) explanations and claims. Because Fiske makes a distinction between theory and practice, he does not specifically consider the ways in which his own (academic) practice may be a creative strategy that allows him to compensate for his own limits in social experience or mobility—or one that justifies his virtual movement through these people's homes. Viewing cultural practices through a one-dimensional lens, he is unable to see himself as actively engaged in a cultural practice of scholarly activity, a practice through which he actively and continually re-positions himself in relation to other people. While he acknowledges that his academic habitus may be "at odds with those through which . . . the people live their everyday lives," he does not explore these differences in socially reflexive ways that would allow him to situate himself in *relation to* these people rather than in *distinction from* these people.

RE-POSITIONING AUTHORITY, RE-POSITIONING THE SELF

> To claim border crossing . . . as the deepest expression of a desired
> cultural practice within a multicultural democracy means that we
> must dare to envision ways such freedom of movement can be
> experienced by everyone.
>
> bell hooks, *Outlaw Culture*

In this quote, hooks speaks of a freedom of movement for everyone, particularly people who must cross the bridge of opportunity. We believe this freedom of movement can be facilitated when white middle and upper class people, particularly academics, reposition themselves in relation to others. We are all connected to others through our shared humanness; no matter how foreign someone's culture, class, gender may be to us, we can find ways to identify with others. Reflexive identification with other people often requires people to "dehegemonize their position and themselves and learn how to occupy the subject position of other" (Spivak 1990). In "Representations of Whiteness," hooks comments that "white people who shift locations . . . begin to see the world differently." She discusses the power this kind of repositioning has for deconstructing racism and reflecting on the ways our own cultural practices may reinscribe racism (1992a, 177). Although hooks doesn't pursue how this repositioning takes place, we believe it happens when we expand our social networks to include daily interactions with people from whom we typically distance ourselves. For many academics, this means establishing reciprocal, friendly relationships with people in the community where the university is located. This kind of identification requires effort and reciprocity between both self and others. We're arguing for social integration in all directions.

This repositioning is a complicated practice because those accustomed to the comfortable distance the academy often provides (in physical and intellectual locations) rarely seek to socialize with those outside their class and race. Academics need to subvert the ways in which universities isolate themselves from communities through physical isolation (fences, sprawling lawns, sometimes located miles away in the country or on hills) and intellectual isolation (claiming to maintain "objective distance" in social science research). These and other types of isolation not only make it possible for academics to shirk their civic duty while "making knowledge," but also make it that much more difficult for academics who wish to reposition themselves to do so.

Bourdieu's notion of habitus helps explain part of the difficulties in repositioning the self. The self, or "individual habitus" includes "durable and transposable" dispositions to act in certain ways that take shape in the "conditions associated with a particular class of conditions of existence" (Bourdieu 1991, 53-6). The habitus includes those actions and discourses that identify us as belonging to particular social and cultural groups. People feel more comfortable around those who act and speak in ways similar to theirs. Those who live within many types of conditions cross boundaries more than others who live within fewer types of class/status/race/gender conditions. When people initially come into contact with others, the habitus "structures new experiences in accordance with the structures produced by past experiences.. [and] tends to ensure its own constancy and its defiance against change through selection it makes with new information" (Bourdieu 1991, 60). This means the habitus remains rigid to new perspectives by rejecting "information capable of calling into question its accumulated information . . . and especially by avoiding exposure to such information [because] the habitus tends to favor experiences likely to reinforce it" (Bourdieu 1991, 61). We think this conception of a habitus rigid to alternative ways of constructing the world describes many academics (and upper-class whites) well. But those people who have many relationships with others from different cultures develop more flexible ways of behaving, understanding the world, and using language because they've been exposed to multiple cultures. They've had to cross borders and have often had to live with some discomforts when straddling multiple cultures.

Repositioning oneself means establishing reciprocal relationships with those outside one's "comfort zone." If a "contact zone" is a "social space where cultures meet, clash, and grapple with each other, often in contexts of highly asymmetrical relations of power" (Pratt 1991, 34), then a "comfort zone" is a context in which those with the luxury to do so can isolate themselves from contact zones.[5] A reflexive repositioning of academics lessens some of the social distance between races and classes of people. When we position ourselves in a variety of social networks, we're more likely to break down some of the prejudices and misconceptions we hold and begin to identify with people outside the "comfort zones" inequality produces. Instead of claiming our positions for the sake of locating ourselves in a power structure, we need to claim our positions for the sake of re-locating ourselves in ways that close social distances. One way to close distances might be to re-position ourselves through service learning or using our positions of comfort in order to approach communities (Cushman 1996).

Another way to close distances and forge connections is to continually reflect on our daily social practices, rethinking the historicity of these practices in order to reexamine how these practices work to maintain social distance and inequality, *and* to reposition ourselves in relation to those practices accordingly. In rethinking the historicity of our cultural practices, Battaglia reminds us that we cannot afford to be romantically nostalgic about our past(s). She argues that a longing for the past erases issues of social inequality and does not give us the power to reinvent our present. Active nostalgia, on the other hand, does have the power to reposition us in the present—in relation to our past, in relation to others, in relation to our futures. Rather than longing for the past, active nostalgia is "a nostalgia for a sense of future . . . [one that] enables or recalls to practice more meaningful patterns of relationship and self-action" (Battaglia 1995, 77 –78). In particular, active nostalgia occurs when specific cultural practices are used to reconnect us to our histories and future capabilities while offering us some disconnection and resistance to disempowering social inequities and realities. While Battaglia uses active nostalgia in discussing the cultural practices of displaced urban Trobrianders, we believe that all people can reconnect with their histories and resist the dominant ways various social structures guide our daily interactions and practices. Viewing academic work as a cultural practice allows us to question how we are positioning ourselves in relation to our histories and our present. What this means is that there is room and reason to reposition ourselves, to act and work through social reflection, and to negotiate our authority in all contexts. Otherwise, we risk reinforcing social distance, and, as hooks reminds us, it is through distance that stereotypes abound (hooks 1992a, 170).

While there will continue to be a need to question ethnographic authority, we are arguing for a more complicated definition of authority, one that acknowledges more complicated definitions of social identity, social reflexivity, and social positioning. Rather than viewing identity as one-dimensional, negotiated authority and reflexive identification see identity as a complicated web with multiple layers or dimensions that are not always visible or readily apparent. With this view, authority no longer arises de facto out of some one-dimension of our social position (academic, race, gender), but is carefully and actively negotiated through reflexive identification and social re-positioning. Rather than identifying ourselves against others, reflexive identification asks us to find and forge connections across boundaries—though not necessarily erasing all of them. We are not advocating an identification that erases difference. Rather than ignoring difference, reflexive identification asks that we use identification to discover the real differences, examine these differences in their historicity, and use our daily practices to reposition ourselves in relationship to these differences—in the present and in the future. While this process may be complicated, sometimes awkward, and sometimes messy, we see it as a way for composition researchers to venture out of their comfort zones to broaden their social networks. We need to question and obviate the social barriers between the university and the community—a dichotomy that is as socially problematic as it is self-destructive. Locating ourselves in communities, exercising author-ity, reflecting on our assumptions and actions—these are all cultural practices and social transactions through which we can either reproduce social distance or reposition/reconnect ourselves with new purposes and insights— purposes and insights that we have actively negotiated with others.

NOTES

1.   An analogy may help to illustrate how polyvocal texts often risk exoticizing the lives and voices of informants. In 1904, the United States engineered a massive ethnographic exhibit of Filipino people as part of the Louisiana Purchase Exposition in St. Louis, Missouri. According to Benito M. Vergara Jr., "the

Exposition's centerpiece [was] the Philippine reservation . . . [complete with] . . . 75,000 catalogued exhibits and 1,100 representatives" of different aboriginal tribes from the Philippines (1995, 112). Decontextualized from their homeland and indigenous ways of life, these Filipino peoples were recontextualized—put on display within a simulated environment created by U.S. colonial administrators and anthropologists. Against the larger backdrop of colonialism, these peoples and their cultures were not taken on their own terms. Vergara argues that this exhibit simultaneously legitimated America as worthy of imperial status and anthropology as worthy of disciplinary status (to document, record, and display these vanishing exotic others).

2.   The Cibecue Apache has a notion of privacy similar to the Cherokee. Unsolicited questions about a person's emotional state, physical appearance, or past experience "focuses attention on aspects of one's private person . . . [which] means that one has been the subject of a close but covert examination and that something . . . has been found wanting or out of the ordinary. As a result, the individual is forced to take notice of himself . . . a form of self-consciousness to which Apaches are keenly sensitive and therefore are anxious to avoid" (Basso 1979, 54). As a white Cherokee mixedblood, I too was socialized to be sensitive to the privacy of others to detract attention away from myself, to look down and away when someone singles me out. Yet, so many calls for self-reflexivity demand I compromise my own cultural beliefs at the same moment as I bring forward these beliefs.

3.   It is interesting to note that during the 19th century, anthropologists largely developed theories and analyses of other cultures through "armchair" methods. That is, ethnographic data was culled from travel diaries of missionaries and/or people employed in the colonies (Marcus and Fischer 1986; Stocking 1992). Like Fiske's approach in "Cultural Studies and the Culture of Everyday Life," academic anthropologists based their theories and analyses on data collected by others who had actually visited or worked in these foreign lands and experienced these cultures.

4.   For an excellent discussion of theory that happens outside of the academy, see bell hooks, "Out of the Academy and Into the Streets," 1992b.

5.   This isolation perpetuates the generalities we may hold about others. As bell hooks argues, we all tend to hold generalities about others because we don't experience the concrete specificities of those other(s); we all watch others "with a critical, 'ethnographic' gaze" (hooks 1992a, 167). Whether we like to admit it or not, we all hold some generalized theories about "the other(s)," whether written or oral, for it is the way we are taught to make sense of this world. Thus, academics are not the only ones who can distance themselves from "others" and they are not the only ones who can be reflexive about their socio-cultural positions as they make sense of their experiences.

CHAPTER THIRTEEN

Tracking Composition Research on the World Wide Web

Susan Romano

*T*HE RESEARCH NETWORK FORUM WEBSITE GREETS ITS VISITORS WITH AN olive-green image featuring two conference-style tables pulled together end to end and ringed with eight armless chairs. On each table rests a sheaf of plain white paper—one sewn at the spine, the other loose-leafed—suggesting work to be done, yet no writing implements are in sight. The nearest chair has been pushed back, inviting the visitor to stay awhile or perhaps signaling the abrupt and mysterious departure of some former researcher. "The Editors' Metaphoric Table/s," as website author Victor Vitanza calls them[1], have been supplied courtesy of another website and in the frame off to the right, Charles Bazerman, composition studies' research advocate, is called upon to articulate a purpose for this page: "the development of different approaches to the study of writing processes, written language, texts, and the teaching of writing has led to not-always-productive competition and mutual misunderstandings of each other's work" (1989, 223 –24).

In this essay I explore Bazerman's observation in the light of the new electronic technologies that are changing the ways we teach and research university writing.

I report my reading of the Research Network Forum website with uncommon reflexivity. A rudimentary but serviceable knowledge of HTML and a familiarity with NCTE/CCCC's political involvement in the national intellectual property debates have expanded my repertoire of reading protocols. So surprised was I, for example, at the aesthetic pleasure imparted by an olive-drab and ochre that, anticipating my use of these colors in my own web writing, I consulted a color chart and noted RGB values. Then, curious about the origins of the "borrowed" furniture, I followed the link supplied and found that the tables belong to a commercial, online furniture display. Furthermore, self-conscious about writing an adequate description of a table and a couple of chairs for this article, I note ruefully that for undergraduate writers in MU* spaces, creating visual impact in text and text only is but an elementary exercise. Bartholomae and Petrosky would say that the new technologies provide an array of new lenses through which to compose readings and writings.

The Research Network Forum website is the online instantiation of the face-to-face CCCC caucus established in 1987 enabling composition researchers to share work in progress in consultation with editors of our journals. Yet like the metaphoric tables, the website itself at the time of this reading is nearly empty. Several journal editors have used the site to introduce their online publications using the message forum provided for that purpose, but the conversation among writers and editors has yet to flourish[2]. I spot traces of composition research in the form of titles for papers presented at the 1997 CCCC Research Network Forum in Phoenix, yet on closer examination discover that although eleven of the sixty titles purport to be about computer-based composition, not a single title links to fuller representations of the research it stands for. Surely these false fronts mislead me, I tell myself, for absence of inquiry is unthinkable in this era of unprecedented transformation in literacy practices and literacy instruction. The labor of website author Vitanza, an active web writer and facilitator for those wishing to participate in the reshaping of writing in the digital age, goes without correspondence on the part of researchers, as do similar labors performed by others in our field.[3] My essay addresses the questions raised by this deceptively silent page: What research activities currently are underway among compositionists? What alterations in topic, procedure, and presentation are in progress? How does one go about locating on the World Wide Web a body of research on writing instruction?

A SHORT HISTORY

Over the past decade composition studies has incorporated into its repertoire of instructional practices an array of electronic applications pertinent to writing instruction. In the mid to late 1980s, when experimentation with locally networked classrooms and stand-alone hypertext applications was considered aberrational, those who taught writing in the new media called their work a revolution in educational practice, and indeed it was. Advocacy was necessarily central to the discourse on computer-based writing instruction in those days, for the historical, institutional separation of the liberal arts from technology had instilled in the general English professoriate a philosophical and practical antipathy for things mathematical, mechanical, and machine dependent. Although many English faculty in the late 1990s remain suspicious of electronic technologies and recalcitrant in their learning, others are now eager to gain proficiency in the uses of technology for teaching and scholarship, and their enthusiasm reflects a changing climate across academia. Paper tigers such as Sven Birkert's *The Gutenberg Elegies* raise hackles, but surely such arguments do not predict the future of computer technologies in education so aptly as do the numerous reports appearing in the *Chronicle of Higher Education* on its uses across the disciplines. Teaching writing with technology is no longer fragile and endangered, for in the eyes of many university administrators, virtual space has become a proper location for educational enterprise.

If at first writing teachers confined their experiments with computer-mediated communication to certain niches in the field—the written literacy of hearing-impaired students, for example, and the better implementation of social constructionist theories of learning[4]—soon they became stakeholders in larger issues of knowledge and its specialization, despecialization and dissemination. Now, in the middle stages of the revolution, compositionists working with digital media find themselves aligned with an expansive and multi-faceted literacy education movement that crosses disciplinary, institutional, and educational boundaries. Currently, for example, many university libraries offer near-daily instruction in HTML, online searching in the disciplines, evaluation and citation of sources, Boolean search techniques, netiquette, email, and java. Courses in web page construction, both its processes and purposes, are offered outside English departments as well as within, and student projects produced in such courses tend to look very much like those produced in humanities-sponsored courses.[5] Nor is online literacy the special province of post-secondary institutions, for incorporating literacy technologies into K through 12 curricula has become an important agenda item nationwide. Nor does level of education necessarily distinguish teacher from student, for teachers and students not infrequently find themselves co-learners in the classroom or occupy reversed roles.

NOT QUITE RESEARCH

Participation in this revolution in literacy instruction forces upon writing teachers a change of subject. Those mid-1980s teachers interested in teaching with technology broke ranks, turning away from the familiar tripartite relationship we honor—teachers, students, and texts—toward a fourth element, the writing tools and forms (or media) themselves. Whether considered tools (reputedly a reductive definition) or spaces (the preferred designation), the forms themselves exacted and continue to exact time and intellectual energy. Computer compositionists examine software critically, apply new applications to extant pedagogies, and develop alternatives to both. Acquisition of technical know-how is indispensable, for teachers must demystify the new writing applications before teaching their uses. Practice is scaffolded upon practice, as innovation succeeds innovation, and what only yesterday was current today is rendered obsolete. Indeed over the past decade, teachers of online writing have assembled an impressive portfolio of accomplishments. They have written software and developed pedagogies for local and wide-area networks, they have mastered applications for locating, viewing, and retrieving information stored on distant computers, they have developed sites housing retrievable information, they have learned high-end-user programming languages for World Wide Web publishing and MU* applications, they have become proficient in the creation and manipulation of images, video, and sound, and they have introduced design theory into rhetorical practice.

And yet if "technology" is difficult to recognize as a subject proper to academic inquiry in the humanities, and if collaborative authorship further obscures its identity, then finally, the forms of dissemination complete its disguise. Most frequently, the results of this extended inquiry into the uses of electronic technologies for writing instruction are disseminated quickly to an ever-expanding and eager community of like-minded teachers and researchers in oral and digital forms: local and national workshops, FAQs posted to mailgroups or housed on the World Wide Web, conference papers, electronic discussion groups, and web pages devoted to helping others master specific technologies. As a practical matter, news about teaching electronic literacy is best disseminated via electronic media to the already electronically literate. Yet even the rash of recent textbooks systematizing over a decade of inquiry into online writing instruction constitute a poor choice if their authors seek traditional, academic legitimation for this inquiry.[6]

What's more, electronic discussion forums and the proliferation of webbed syllabi partially obviate compositionists' felt need for access to each others' classroom. New electronic forms facilitate rich representations of classroom practices and ample opportunities for their discussion. And they do so in spades, for they furnish a volume of information that nearly defies mental processing. What was formerly available only in small doses via complicated publication processes has become available in altered but highly satisfying and inexpensive forms. Participants in electronic discussion lists exchange reports on teaching. They swap comparable or contradictory stories, and they provide careful readings and critiques of such reports. Populations of discussants vary from list to list and authority is established according to list population. WPA-L (Writing Program Administration), for example, often draws commentary from seasoned compositionists (e.g., Ed White, Louise Phelps, Theresa Enos) who bring to discussion their years of specialized and general experience in the field and, it should be well noted, an extended experience with traditional research. ACW-L (Alliance for Computer and Writing) on the other hand, features commentary by pioneering teachers experimenting with technology in the classroom who readily provide all comers with technical and pedagogical support, as well as offering reports on their own, perhaps unpublished, research.

On web pages, classroom practices typically are represented by syllabi, assignments, and course readings.[7] Collectively, these web representations, some of them elaborate and multifaceted (see, e.g., *Kairos* April 1997) comprise an archive of teaching materials. Typically, feedback mechanisms are provided, so that readers may engage the teacher-scholar authors of these pages one-on-one. The size of this online archive, its multiplicity, its "rhizomatic" character, its faint disdain for proper academic procedures, and its accessibility recommend it to many as an excellent method of teacher preparation. To others, discussion-produced knowledge and web representations may smack too strongly of lore (North 1987) or folklore (Hawisher and Pemberton 1991), for surely the teaching materials in this loose portfolio are not of equal value across institutional settings of varying technical support capabilities and differently prepared student and teacher populations.

My points here are several. First, while not replicating traditional teacher research, interactive discussion about pedagogy coupled with web representations of course materials weakens the impulse to conduct traditional studies, for as inquiry into a common concern is jointly undertaken, the purposes for research are partially satisfied. Second, the labor involved in supporting these new venues for pedagogical development goes unrecognized as academic work.[8]

RESEARCH: WHY? WHAT? WHERE?

According to our historians, writing instruction as currently practiced developed in response to substantive changes in higher education during the nineteenth century, when a formerly unified college curriculum fragmented and expanded into an array of independent disciplines, each legitimated by specialized research. Faculty interested in rhetoric and composition, so the story goes, missed the boat by "earn[ing] themselves a reputation as teachers, not scholars, a serious handicap in the new university" (Brereton 1995, 10). Conceiving writing instruction as pedagogical art, rather than scientific enterprise, composition theorists of the era failed to stake out territory in an epistemological commons privileging rigorous inquiry and the specialized production of knowledge. The insistent association of writing instruction with intensive labor only clinched its relegation to the margins of academic life.[9] Useful and necessary as intensive composition programs were to a late nineteenth-century university culture grappling with quadrupled admissions and new purposes for higher education, their developers styled a discourse on writing instruction that ignored the importance of research.

Although we may not argue from this history that research is key to composition studies' immediate future, certainly we can acknowledge the difficulty of forecasting from the midst of a rapidly changing order. Although compositionists at Harvard and Amherst in the nineteenth century appear to have espoused competing theories of writing instruction—Harvard scrutinizing student writing for error and Amherst teaching the craft of expression—neither theoretical perspective "won." Both institutions wound up contributing to the establishment of an unsatisfactory niche for composition studies in university hierarchies. In the introductory chapter of *The Orgins of Composition Studies in the American College, 1875 –1925,* John Brereton identifies three options available to late nineteenth-century composition and rhetoric faculty, each familiar to those of us going about our institutional business during the late twentieth century: First, attack the research model as inadequate; second, perform research recognizable as such by university peers; or third, break away from the English department entirely. Those rhetoric and composition faculty currently advocating teaching writing with technology utter similar calls to action, yet surely we must concede that the features proper to a strong discipline under a new order remain indiscernible to us. We do know that the university as a physical place is now being called into question by populations of students eager to consume education piecemeal by way of distance learning technologies, by legislators espousing virtual education as a cost cutting mechanism, and by corporate sponsors of commercialized education. Certainly we cannot, from our standpoint within history, make out the early twenty-first century practices equivalent to the research imperative of the late nineteenth century. Whether or not a web-visible body of research on current literacies and their teaching will prove important is not clear. Yet when the Western Governors Association advocates virtual education on grounds of cost-effectiveness and defines "actual competence" in opposition to "seat time" at traditional universities, certainly it is time to take stock of our professional expertise and plan for its development and effective public reception. Where, then, I ask in this essay, may I find a body of scholarship, that is, a body of research in the teaching of writing? How have we begun to imagine that twenty-first century equivalent of the nineteenth- and twentieth-century activity called research?

Stephen North, who but a decade ago composed our identity as scholarly writing instructors, holds that research as we know it is obsolete and, alongside it, the discipline itself. "Composition," he writes in "The Death of Paradigm Hope," "is a term that will disappear from college catalogues" (1997, 202). To the degree that disciplinary identity is bound up in a cumulative model of research (the century-old research model), argues North, composition studies is dying. Our new inquiries into literacy, its practices, and its instruction will come about instead as "breathless" responses to compelling literacy events.

I find North's prognosis for writing research powerful, particularly when considered in light of the interactive literacy events I am familiar with, where topics under discussion rise to fever pitch and then suddenly die off. I find his prognosis frightening as well for those of us owning up to a compositionist identity, precisely because his choice of metaphor is so very apt. Imagining research as "breathless" dialogue, as response to newly found or experienced literacies and as short-lived commentary exacted by situational practices may indeed account partially for what appears to be an absence on the World Wide Web of planned and sustained inquiry in traditional forms. The term "breathless" suggests to me that in searching for the sorts of research familiar to compositionists and other academics of a twentieth-century mindset, I seek an extinct form. Still, the three inquiries I document in the penultimate section of this essay quite possibly qualify as examples of "breathless" commentary on situations dropped into the laps of their authors by the grace of the new technologies *and* resemble traditional research as well. In the first research project I discuss below, author Laura Gurak examines how written language works during an episode of intense political interaction outside the academy; in the second, authors' Burgess and Mathis examine how students and their teachers rework their interpretive strategies when reading hypertext; and finally, an authors collective gathers virtually at the University of Illinois Chicago to plan the transmigration of English department work to a virtual environment.

Yet representing these three research-like projects on the World Wide Web does not appear to have been a simple procedure. North's prediction that "by the end of the decade . . . researchers of all kinds will simply post their studies directly through one or another network clearinghouse" (1997, 205) elides the evident difficulty of so doing. Indeed, by my estimate and recent inquiry, the rush is not on. In addition, although the examples I have selected are located in a region of cyberspace well trodden by compositionists, they bear no markers distinguishing themselves as research projects. I emphasize this point not because I wish to establish gatekeeping procedures but because I am not quite persuaded that we should discount the rhetorical effect of a highly visible and easily accessible complex of researched inquiries performed by writing teachers who have thought carefully not only about classroom-based activities such as drafts, peer review, and portfolios, but also about the role of literacy in human affairs. I would like to see writing teachers whose collective scholarship, practical knowledge, and institutional experience encompass both print and electronic technologies situated in policy-making positions. Although I am hesitant to argue that an aggressive, discipline-wide, writing research agenda translates unproblematically into influence, still I propose that when literacy education is conceived as a shared, interdisciplinary project, one properly commercial as well as academic, then bringing to the common table our scholar-practitioner, technology-rich wisdom in innovative, yet recognizable forms is certainly an idea to be carefully entertained.

North's proffered descriptor for the new research—"breathless"—is perhaps less common than another term bandied about without attribution to a single author: "Emergent," a term whose epideictic force and current cachet give good reason for its cautious usage, explains away estrangement from academic convention and argues tacitly for a deferral of judgment. "Emergent" implies a developmental cycle at whose end online scholarship comes into its own as a mature literacy practice. It implies a "natural" growth, divorced from human agency, guided by forces beyond human control. It may suggest that scholarship just happens and that the forms it takes are inevitable, and the lessons of composition history tend to support a view that human agency counts for little in such matters. Nevertheless, my observations while wandering across that sector of cyberspace where compositionists cross paths suggest a different scenario. I find composition scholars actively shaping the forms and procedures of scholarship, working at different locations within the off/online divide. I do not believe their sense of purpose contradicts, necessarily, the "breathlessness" that North invokes, yet their work suggests that breathlessness in research is as clear-eyed and hard-nosed as it is responsive, as much an instigator of adrenal exhaustion as the result of pituitary rush.

Setting out on my quest for representations of research on the World Wide Web, then, I turned to those sites known as gathering places for those of us interested in electronic discourse and its teaching: The Alliance for Computers and Writing (ACW) website, online journals *RhetNet, Kairos,* and *Computer*

Mediated Communication, and several university teaching and research web-sites. The folly of separating digital from print soon became apparent. Following my initial search, for example, *Computers and Composition,* the primary print venue for research in computer-based writing instruction, completed its Web archive of back issues and begun soliciting manuscripts designed for Web publication only.[10] Indeed, "off" and "on" line are best understood as interdependent conceptualizations, for like many web publications (MIT press and *The Atlantic Monthly* come to mind), not one of the three projects I have selected for close examination is published exclusively online. Settling on a broad, provisional definition of research that might stretch across the print-digital divide while remaining viable in both camps, I sought research activities represented as *planned and sustained inquiry.* My definition was deliberately overbroad. I ignored the classificatory schemes that over the years we have elaborated with some care, i.e., North's mid 1980s' and Kirsch and Sullivan's early 1990s' reports,[11] and I omitted the ethical dimensions of research developed by feminist scholars such as Porter and Sullivan.[12] I did so not because classification schemes are without value or because ethics can be set aside but because I wish to accommodate the "emergent" practices still under development by people yet unaccustomed to new formats, spaces, and tools for conducting and presenting this research. The two adjectives I proposed as constraints—"planned" and "sustained"—may prove to be important conditions that are well supported by new technologies requiring close attention to design (planning) and amenable to additions and revisions (sustaining).

PRE-RESEARCH?

Common to the discourses on electronic media both in and outside composition studies are motifs of excess and overload.[13] Attentive to these themes, founders of online journals have responded with organizational procedures intended to assist and promote recognizable scholarship. Working at the intersections of the traditional and the yet-to-be-defined, they corral excess and contain the breathless. The online journal *RhetNet,* for example, seeks and promotes episodes of breathless discursive action and preserves them for future analysis. "Think of *RhetNet,*" writes editor Eric Crump, as

> a mechanism for a community of teachers and scholars to exert some control over the gush of discourse it produces. That's why I like to portray the project as simultaneously radical and conservative. *RhetNet* is designed to provide rhetoric and internet students and scholars with the means of capturing, contextualizing, searching, and retrieving some of the intriguing and valuable conversations that occur on various parts of the Net, but which too often lie scattered and forgotten in dusty corners of the virtual world. It provides a repository of net scholarship on rhetoric and writing as generated on the net. . . . *RhetNet's* [purpose is to] act as an archive for Net conversations relating to rhetoric and writing. Few existing

places of discourse (mailing lists, newsgroups, chat systems, MU*s), make an effort to capture those conversations in a form that would allow them to be reviewed reflectively and commented upon in the future. They lack the archival intent that *RhetNet* provides. (Research Network Forum 1997)

Kairos, a journal that solicits publishable material in webbed form, responds not so much to the vastness of information and the capture of discursive treasures as to the mutability of online writing. Editor Dene Grigar grounds the mission of *Kairos* in the nature of hypertext as an ever fluctuating form inevitably subject to addition, modification, and deletion, as websites are removed or their content altered. Addressing the problem for researchers of disappearing data, Grigar writes a "defense of archiving":

> It is precisely these qualities—facilitation of change and resistance to stabilization—that have traditionally made the idea of archiving hypertextual writing problematic. Hypertext "blurs. . . conventional notions of completion" (Landow 59). Dynamic, it constantly changes in its form and content (52). Flexible, it defies ownership (Bolter 59). Thus, following pure theoretical notions of hypertext, we could argue that the potentiality of the text defies any attempt to capture it in any reclaimable form—that to do so undermines the integrity of its hypertextuality. . . . . (1997)

The material stakes for composition scholars working in the new forms appear to override theoretical considerations, however, and Grigar folds the constraints of hypertextual literacy into the politics of academic research:

> No one will deny the importance placed upon securing data for research— research that reinforces our relationship with the academy and the world around us. Tenure and promotion are predicated upon successful investigations that entail locating and documenting information and ideas. Likewise cultural change is fomented by substantive and innovative exploration. Research depends upon archived information. (1997)

Both journals play double roles as nurturers and preservers, instigators and archivers, promoting, providing, and preserving material and spaces for future researchers.

THREE RESEARCH PROJECTS: CLASSROOM READING, REALWORLD WRITING, AND ONLINE ENGLISH DEPARTMENTS

I began my inquiry at the Research Network Forum website, finding there unused opportunities for researchers to discuss web publication. I turned then to several online journals, finding there editors hard at work shoring up the structures to make online scholarship possible and presentable, even as they bend and challenge tradition. Then, persuaded by the sprawling nature of the internet that unaccounted for projects awaited my discovery, I began my search for web-published research anew at the Alliance for Computers and

Writing (ACW) website, a hub for online activity in computers and writing. Because the ACW site shelters all variety of computer-based literacy work, I did not expect to find my particular interest (research) supported with a dedicated link, and indeed it was not.[14] A chase across many promising pages finally yielded three projects that suit my intentions for this essay, each an inquiry firmly attached to the interests of composition studies scholars and each exemplifying what compositionists bring to the broader enterprise of online literacy education: Burgess and Mathis's "Scenarios for Computers in Composition," Laura Gurak's "Toward Broadening Our Research Agenda in Cyberspace," and the University of Illinois at Chicago TicToc Project.

Leaving a trail of links from the ACW website, I bookmarked university-sponsored computer research centers, finding these sites rich resources for both practical representations of teaching and more formal research. In fall, 1996, for example, The Ohio State University Computers in Composition and Literature (CCL) website featured a project developed by assistant directors Maureen Burgess and Lori Mathis in response to teachers' requests for training in web-based teaching. I tracked this research project as it shape-shifted from one presentational format to another. Originating in classroom research but first framed as a teacher workshop, the article features students' self-reported modifications in reading protocols as they moved between linear and hyper-textual reading. Thus the project approximates an old composition staple: observation of literacy behaviors and the solicitation of participant narratives. No synthesis was provided, no categories of analysis constructed, no sweeping conclusions reached, no cumulative research markers supplied. On my return to the CCL page the next spring, I found the project re-presented twice over: first, as advertisement for a 1997 CCCC workshop and second, as a link to its publication in *Computer Mediated Communication Magazine* (*CMC*), an online journal supporting hypertext articles (and linear articles converted to hypertext). The *CMC* version rallies around three familiar topoi: assignments, benefits for students, and anxieties for teachers[15] and retains a local flavor via repeated references to Ohio State facility and faculty.

Laura Gurak's research project, too, is familiar to writing teachers. Sharing Crump's penchant for combing the internet in search of high-interest sequences of discourse, Gurak selects two online literacy events—protests over Lotus MarketPlace and the Clipper chip—to examine the relationship between rhetorical practice and political outcome.[16] Her study taps into our longstanding anxieties about the separation of classroom teaching from "realworld" public discourse and is much in keeping with North's sense that contemporary research will provide commentary on literacy events, perhaps before it provides instruction on participation. North's and Gurak's arguments are aligned with assertions that language education is reactive and responds to existing social literacies rather than shaping them (Trimbur 1991; Street 1993; Marrou 1956).

Gurak publishes a full version of her study in book form but represents it online in *Computer Mediated Communication* by way of a short argument favoring anthropological and language-based methodologies for the study of online literacy. Arguing against the value of research conducted in the experimental vein (and hence aligning herself with North once more), Gurak writes:

> My hope, then, is that researchers in CMC will work to overcome the tendency toward technological determinism by situating their work between the sweeping and dichotomous yet interesting stories of the technological forecasters on the one hand and the somewhat narrow but more rigorous social science experiments in CMC. One way to approach this task is to analyze specific cases of life on the internet by the use of rhetorical, anthropological, cultural, and language-based criticism. Such studies have "real evidence" to support their claims but are often broader than a discrete experiment because when well done, these studies retain the critical and somewhat broader lens of a narrative or literary critic. (1996 "Toward Broadening our Research Agenda in Cyberspace")

Extending Gurak's argument beyond its particulars, we might surmise that scholars effectively using online materials not only will carve out relevant data from a morass of text and images, but will also provide their readers a careful rationale for their selections and methodology. The internet-supported practice of sampling or using "snapshots" as evidence for argument, for example, is an increasingly common response to the data excess and mutability crisis, yet this method supports only certain kinds of arguments and would not, perhaps, support studies such as Gurak's tracking of extended discursive events from impetus to outcome.[17]

Gurak's decision not to publish her primary research online and instead to present an argument—a species of editorial—about methodology provides a point of departure for considering what online publishing entails. What cultural and material pressures, we might ask (and Gurak herself will not be the source of definitive answers), drive publication decisions? Tenure considerations that make print publication the venue of choice? Lack of sufficient design expertise and/or technical support to publish full text online? Time constraints (for web design is indeed a time consuming endeavor)?

A third research project turns from Gurak's "realword" politics toward the institutional environments whose hierarchical disputes over the years have troubled compositionists over the past century. The website for the TicToc Project (Teaching In Cyberspace Through Online Courses) housed at the University of Illinois at Chicago presents a long-range plan to develop online curricula and promises analyses of the results of its implementation. The project is exemplary in its ethics, for its authors carefully accommodate differences among faculty members whose stakes in a virtual English department are not perfectly aligned, and it accommodates students and teachers of varying degrees of technical expertise. The site is exemplary in design, for its authors use a variety of electronic venues—email, MU*, web, electronic and print journals—and have employed multiple genres—summary statements of purpose, funding statements, graphical representations, logs of realtime brainstorming sessions, and theoretical articles addressing change. Turning the internet feature "mutability" to advantage, the authors have featured movement across time, from planning through execution to evaluation. Some of these authors are compositionists. Together they have envisioned an interactive, diverse community of scholars, modeled it, and presented it online for public examination.

RISKING RESEARCH

Most human beings today may reasonably expect to feel the effects of the digital revolution. The job of writing teachers may reasonably be construed as enabling students to participate in the new literacy practices. Because upcoming changes in higher education surely are as unsettling as those experienced a century ago during the rise of the research university, it seems naive to call for more research, better research, or even more carefully represented research. We may disagree among ourselves, as Bazerman worries, about which of the multiple activities now entailed in writing (from hand-written note taking to image "pinching") are properly taught in university classrooms; we may disagree about whether breathless discursive episodes are worth brief commentary or extended analysis. We may disagree about whether to construct our own websites or take advantage of those provided for us. We may foresee the alteration of research procedures and presentations and wonder which of these activities merits our attention. We may fearlessly entertain the notion that in the coming era, teaching will be a better candidate for reward than extended inquiry. This we cannot ascertain, for our vision is limited by our location at the center of the storm. However, because I would like readers of this essay to know where to go and what to expect when they are ready to take their research online, I close with self descriptions provided by three online journals and the Research Network Forum online site. Please note that *Computers and Composition* currently solicits manuscripts for online publication as well.

Computer Mediated Communication Magazine
<www.december.com/cmc/mag/masthead.html>
Computer-Mediated Communication Magazine. . . reports about people, events, technology, public policy, culture, practices, study, and applications related to human communication and interaction in online environments. CMC Magazine uses hypertext to layer and break up articles so that we can take advantage of hypertext links among the articles and their sections. . . . The editors [want] a chance to look for correspondences among the articles in an issue of the magazine—particularly if the article appears in a special focus or themed issue.

Kairos: A Journal for Teachers of Writing in Webbed Environments
<english.ttu.edu/kairos/current/index_nf.html>
Kairos represents more than just a publication containing information we need in order to do our jobs effectively or a place to publish ideas that will lead

to tenure and promotion. Instead, like any electronic text produced in this "late age of print," to borrow Jay David Bolter's term for our time (2), it holds historical significance. For contained in our web texts are views and visions of thinkers representing this early age of technology.

RhetNet: Cyberjournal for Rhetoric and Writing
<www.missouri.edu/~rhetnet/>
RhetNet's Purpose:

1. To act as an archive for Net conversations relating to rhetoric and writing. . . .

2. To offer a place for original publication of articles and essays. We're interested in retaining some aspects of traditional scholarly publishing, or at least exploring the possibilities for the co-existence of network and print-oriented forms and sensibilities.

3. To offer opportunities for community participation in new forms of old functions (like peer review, editing, production, etc.).

4. To serve as an opportunity to try out ideas for new forms of publishing the academic conversations of the rhetoric and writing community.

Research Network Forum: Editors' Metaphoric Table/s
<www.uta.edu/english/V/rnftable.html>

If you are a researcher in the field of Rhetoric and Composition, please Click On! our hypernews site, where our discussions are taking place, ask questions or respond to what's being or not being said. (And please . . . stay with us, for we have plans to establish new "metaphoric tables" on a variety of other issues. Below you will find some useful links.)

NOTES

1. Vitanza writes, "About the table and chairs, I cannot lie . . . I borrowed . . . appropriated them from Bent Krogh: Trans-It Tables and Chairs."

2. *CMC Magazine; CWRL-Computers; Writing, Rhetoric, and Literature; Eastgate Systems; Journal of Advanced Composition; Kairos; Media Ecology; Pre/Text; Readerly/Writerly Texts;* and *RhetNet* are represented by their respective editors.

3. Victor Vitanza is editor of the alternative scholarly journal *Pre/Text*, host of infamous and well-attended electronic discussion lists, maintainer of a personal website with valuable links to rhetoric resources and courses, developer of the Spoon Collective, and author of the several textbooks about online writing, e.g., *Cyberreader* and *Writing for the World Wide Web*.

4. In the mid 1980s, Gallaudet University pioneered classroom use of computer-networked conversation with deaf students, and the University of Texas at Austin's Computer Research Lab developed online social constructionist pedagogies.

5. At this writing, one might compare student projects for the University of California at Berkeley Interdisciplinary Studies courses (e.g., Rosie Hsueh's project

at <www.OCF.Berkeley.EDU/~roseying/ids110/> with student projects at the West Virginia University Center for Literary Computing (e.g., <www.as.wvu.edu/~swarshau/96/eng2/>.

6. Anderson, et al., *Teaching Online;* Condon and Butler, *Writing the Information Superhighway;* Crump and Carbone, *English Online;* Rodriguez, *The Research Paper and the World Wide Web.*

7. Many web pages additionally support message forums, and some feature student work as well.

8. Fred Kemp, for example, established Megabyte U, the first online discussion group for teachers of writing, and has been instrumental in developing and sustaining many Alliance for Computers and Writing projects.

9. See Brereton, "Introduction," for a cogent account of this era in our disciplinary history.

10. *Computers and Composition* may be accessed online at <www.cwrl.utexas.edu/~ccjrnl/>.

11. Stephen North, in the 1980s, and Gesa Kirsch and Patricia Sullivan, in the 1990s, provided classification schemes for established research practices. North's divisions bear a somewhat Whitean stamp, as the predisposition of the researcher rather than the design or practice is foregrounded: experimentalists, clinicians, formalists, and ethnographers. Kirsch and Sullivan, on the other hand, focus on epistemological differences. Essayists in this collection examine the premises, procedures, and limitations peculiar to historical, feminist, ethnographic, experimental, and descriptive research and address as well the case study, discourse analysis, and the movement we know as teacher research.

12. I note certain ethical conventions that circulate in compositon studies (e.g., Kirsch and Sullivan; Porter and Sullivan): that researchers determine questions based on their familiarity with the needs of a proposed readership, that they consider the human populations having stakes in the question, that they locate, evaluate, and analyze evidence in light of both question and stakes, that they consider the limitations of their methods, methodologies, and conclusions, and that they synthesize findings for purposes of presentation and dissemination.

13. See, for example, Nicholas Negroponte (and Condon and Butler) on the personal agent (a softbot) as data organizer; for an ethical/rhetorical argument, see Gesa Kirsch's recent examination of the rhetorical effects of poly-vocal texts.

14. The website description foregrounds its evolving and practical character; it has been designed as an "immediate and continuing source of practical information."

15. The introduction to the *CMC Magazine* version reads as follows: "Maureen Burgess describes a workshop which CCL ran in the Spring 1996 Quarter for instructors interested in incorporating Web writing and reading strategies into their English classrooms. She then focuses on one website analysis assignment that she taught to a second-level writing class. Lori Mathis focuses on a workshop that CCL provided on HTML authoring for instructors, and her section provides specific Web-authoring handouts and templates which have proven helpful to CCL instructors. She discusses the benefits HTML authoring can bring to English instructors, as well as the anxiety that learning HTML code can produce in those not experienced with computer languages."

16.   "In 1990, Lotus Development Corporation announced the forthcoming production of a direct-mail marketing database that would contain the names, addresses, and spending habits of 120 million American consumers. . . . .In 1994, the U.S. government proposed a new encryption standard called the Clipper chip, which, for the purposes of national security, could decrypt any message on any telephone in which it was installed" (Yale University Press description, <www.yale.edu/yup/F97/gurakF97.html> (7 July 1997).

17.   From October 1 to October 10, 1995, for example, the Massachusetts Institute of Technology sponsored a global snapshot project, soliciting sample texts from diverse on-line locations and venues with the objective of freeze-framing and archiving scenes from the internet as material evidence for future historians. Snapshots of student web projects, for example, would serve a researcher much as lists of Harvard dissertation defense topics have served historian S. Michael Halloran—as a means for determining how broader social and political concerns inform the teaching of rhetoric and composition in a given era.

CHAPTER FOURTEEN

Farther Afield
Rethinking the Contributions of Research

Ruth Ray and Ellen Barton

INTRODUCTION

O VER THE PAST SEVERAL YEARS, COMPOSITION RESEARCHERS HAVE BROAD- ened their inquiry to investigate sites outside of schools and universities. The impetus behind this move is a desire to understand the various forms of language and literacy in the workplace and the world, as well as the ways in which particular cultural contexts shape and define acts of reading, writing, and speaking (see, for example, Bazerman and Paradis 1991; Doheny-Farina 1991; Herndl 1993; Lunsford, Moglen, and Slevin 1990; Moss 1994; Schaafsma 1993). Implicit in many of these studies is the assumption that to study "afield" is, ultimately, to come to a better understanding of life back home. Indeed, some composition theorists have argued explicitly that we must conduct field research in non-academic sites in order to understand our own situatedness in terms of research, theory-making, and practice. In "Kitchen Tables and Rented Rooms: The Extracurriculum of Composition," for example, Anne Ruggles Gere (1994) calls for literacy research that is generated outside the "textual car- nivals" (Miller 1991) that operate in academe. She argues that by studying the writing and rhetoric initiated by the general public in women's groups, com- munity centers, nursing homes, support groups—anywhere texts are gener- ated from within the group by a desire to put into language the lived experience of its members—compositionists will learn more about how liter- acy functions culturally, as well as intellectually. For Gere, researchers inter- ested in shaping a composition theory sophisticated enough to address the issues of 21st century literacy "need to uncouple composition and schooling, to consider the situatedness of composition practices, to focus on the experi- ences of writers not always visible to us inside the walls of the academy" (80).

As composition scholars have entered field sites, however, they have made a number of assumptions about their presence and effects. Following principles of feminist research articulated by Sandra Harding (1989), Deborah Cameron et al. (1992), Michelle Fine (1992), and other scholars, many composition researchers increasingly have sought to establish collaborative connections with the subjects they study and to make contributions to their communities. As Joanne Addison (1997) argues, it is important to conduct "research *on, for,* and *with* the participants" (113, author's emphasis); the goal of such research is "empowerment through knowledge sharing and action," and "[addressing] the agendas of subjects" (115). Similarly, Ellen Cushman (1996) has argued strongly for the position that "in doing our scholarly work, we should take a social responsibility for the people from and with whom we come to understand a topic" (11).

In most composition research, these responsibilities have been defined generally in terms of enhancing literacy skills through various forms of pedagogy. For example, in arguing that Glynda Hull and Mike Rose's essay "Rethinking Remediation" stands as an example of research that reflects such ethical principles, Gesa Kirsch (1992) notes, "Hull and Rose got an intimate look at basic writers in a remedial English course, and the students received valuable tutoring lessons and a deeper understanding of their writing processes" (263). Ethnographers and other researchers entering communities and classrooms have offered English lessons (Weinstein-Shr 1994), translation services (Farr 1994), computer services (Dautermann 1996), teaching techniques (Dale 1996), literacy tutoring (Peck, Flower, and Higgins 1995) and other volunteer services such as basketball coaching (Mahiri). Even Cushman, although she points to her support in helping people negotiate the maze of social services and providing them with transportation and driving lessons, contributes mostly the activities of a literacy volunteer. In sum, a growing consensus among compositionists is that researchers who enter the field should expect to establish collaborative relationships with subjects and design research projects that reciprocally benefit both researcher and community (cf. the collection of essays edited by Peter Mortenson and Gesa Kirsch entitled *Ethics and Representation in Qualitative Studies of Literacy*).

We suggest that when composition research is uncoupled from schooling, these assumptions about contributions to communities need to be examined. Compositionsts have assumed non-problematically that participants and institutions will support a reciprocal collaboration. More specifically, compositionists have assumed that communities will understand and value the research in the same ways the researcher does and that participants will see the researcher's role—and their own—in the same ways the researcher has conceptualized them. While these assumptions may apply when research takes place in schools, classrooms, and literacy centers (where the practical goals for language and literacy development are similar to the research goals of literacy research), they are challenged in field sites where literacy is neither foregrounded nor valued in the same way it is in composition studies.

In this chapter, we argue that the experience of conducting field research in non-academic sites challenges compositionists' blithe assumptions about their contributions (or their lack of contributions) to such communities. We describe research we have conducted independently in two types of institutions—nursing homes and medical clinics—in order to discuss the issues that field research raises about the relative value of composition studies within those communities. We show how our research was ultimately re-shaped by the values and interests of the people in these settings; indeed, we found that our studies took on a life of their own outside the theoretical paradigms from which we had conceived them. Our presence as researchers was valued within those settings, but not in the ways we expected, and not in ways that we could always control. Our overall purpose in this chapter is to consider the limits and possibilities of research conducted in the field by addressing two broad questions: What can composition researchers learn from studying how spoken and written texts function in communities that do not share our scholarly interests? And what challenges do compositionists face when we operate on assumptions about the value of our research within these communities?

TWO PROJECTS IN THE FIELD

Project 1: Self-Representation Among the Elderly: A Study of Writing Groups in Senior Centers and Nursing Homes (Ruth Ray)

For the past three years, I have been investigating the functions of autobiographical writing in nursing homes. I have conducted ethnographic observations and interviews around writing groups facilitated in six different nursing homes by the same geriatric social worker, as well as writing groups in two other sites which I developed and facilitated myself. The segment of the research I describe in this chapter was initially presented to the Brookdale Foundation—the funding agency which has supported the project since its inception—as an inquiry into subjectivity and self-representation in the institutional context of the nursing home. The project was conceived as a means to determine how the elderly, particularly elderly women, construct the "self" when writing and talking about their lives and to determine whether these self-representations change over time as a result of writing group interactions with other elders.

Two working hypotheses structured the inquiry. The first hypothesis, informed by feminist theories of autobiography and social constructionist theories in composition, was that through the act of writing about themselves, sharing this work with their peers, and responding to the self-representations of other group members, elderly women would come to see their lives in different ways and to articulate new aspects of their identities. The second hypothesis was that an enhanced ability to create and re-create the "self" or, more accurately, to recognize multiple "selves" in the "languaging" of lived experiences would have beneficial effects on elderly women's mood and perceived quality of life. The second hypothesis was informed by research conducted in geriatric social work which determined that participation in writing groups promotes positive change in nursing home residents, particularly in terms of reduced depression and ability to communicate feelings and ideas to others (Supiano et al. 1989). Significantly, Supiano et al. concluded that the elderly who benefited most from writing groups were those for whom such activity would typically be considered inappropriate—people with no previous writing experience, the severely depressed, and the cognitively impaired (Alzheimer's and stroke patients, for example).

The six writing groups I observed under the supervision of a geriatric social worker were directed specifically to the clinically depressed and/or cognitively impaired. Joyce, the social worker, has a master's degree and provides consultation and services through the auspices of a University-sponsored geriatric center. She received a grant from Community Mental Health Services to conduct writing groups in nursing homes for people with mental health diagnoses. Most of her group members had a dementing illness or thought disorder (such as schizophrenia) and had been diagnosed with some level of depression. The two groups I facilitated myself were directed to the non-depressed or mildly depressed and the cognitively intact or mildly impaired, as determined by nursing home staff. Group members were predominantly white females ranging in age from 58 to 98, with the majority in their eighties, reflecting the demographics of most nursing homes nationwide. All groups consisted of six to ten members who met once a week for an hour to write about their lives with the assistance of volunteer scribes. Since the majority of group members used wheelchairs and were physically unable to write, most composed aloud and dictated to the volunteers, who wrote down verbatim what was said and, when necessary, prompted the "writers" with questions designed to encourage exemplification and elaboration of the text.

My initial thought about this study was that the primary audience would be feminist scholars of autobiography and composition researchers. Within feminist studies, I considered the research a contribution to narrative studies of the female self. In this case, my research would analyze narratives of older women in the process of discursively "constructing the self" within an institutional setting which, in large part, socially constructs their identities *for* them. Specifically, the medical chart is the primary text of a person's life in a nursing home. Through the discourses of bio-medicine, governmental regulation, and law, the medical chart documents all "salient" information about the nursing home resident, including medical diagnoses, medications administered, changes in health and mental status, assisted daily living activities performed by staff, Medicare/Medicaid coverage, existence of living wills and advance directives. These institutional discourses focus on levels of able-bodiedness and construct a subject stripped of the distinguishing features of family and cultural history, race, ethnicity, class, gender relations, and sexuality. Within composition studies, I considered the research important in terms of what it would reveal about the functions of writing groups and the motivations of writers in a context far removed from schools and universities. I was interested in documenting who among the frail elderly join writing groups, for what purposes, and to what effect, as well as how the writing group itself functions within the social context of the nursing home. I wondered if these groups might function the way women's study groups have functioned historically—to provide a forum and audience for practicing literacy skills, as well as trying alternative forms of self-definition and expression (Gere 1987).

In order to secure funding for the project from a foundation which supports gerontological research exclusively, I developed a discourse around the value of the research to the interdisciplinary field of gerontology, which consists primarily of medical and social science inquiry. I presented the project as relevant to at least three areas of existing research: life-course studies informed by psychological theories of adult development (Erikson, Maslow, Levinson et al. 1978; Levinson 1996); research in social work on the uses of groups in institutional settings (Burnside 1978); and general inquiry into "quality of life" in long-term care facilities, especially in terms of the connections between self-image, self-concept, and presence of others to affirm one's sense of self (Atchley 1991; Birren et al. 1991). More directly, I saw my project as a contribution to the developing area of humanistic gerontology, which interprets the meanings of old age through the lenses of philosophy, history, and literary studies (Cole et al. 1992). To this body of literature, I would bring the perspective and methodology of the textual critic and feminist scholar. My rationale at the time of funding was based entirely on "theory hope" (Fish 1989): theoretically, it seemed logical that the research would prove relevant to gerontologists; however, never having conducted research in nursing homes and operating on an extremely superficial knowledge of institutional life and the effects of various disabilities on language, memory, and textual construction, I couldn't be sure if the study would actually pan out in terms of its contributions to gerontologists, either academic or practitioner.

In terms of the relevance of the research to the nursing home communities in which the investigations were conducted, I saw it as limited to the provision of my weekly service in the writing groups while I collected my data. I would function as a volunteer scribe in the groups facilitated by the social worker and as an outside "activities volunteer" for the two groups I facilitated myself. Clearly, data collection and interpretation were primary, with my volunteer services an added bonus.

Project 2: Discourses of Disability: Interactional and Textual Practices in the
Social Construction of Disability (Ellen Barton)

For the past four years, I have been investigating the rhetorical nature of the abundance of language that surrounds and shapes the experience of disability in contemporary American society. I designed a large interdisciplinary project to collect and analyze oral and written language within linguistic and rhetorical frameworks. To collect instances of the actual social experience of disability in naturally-occurring oral language, I observed and recorded 125 encounters between medical professionals and families who have a child with a disability in order to see how the prevailing medical discourse of disability is presented and received. I also conducted and recorded 50 home interviews with families, primarily mothers, in order to see how the experience of disability was interpreted in narratives and conversations, and I attended and recorded 20 group meetings, both support group meetings and advocacy trainings, in order to see how the experience of disability was interpreted in more public settings and in settings with a more directed agenda. To collect representations of disability in written language, I embarked upon three studies: a study of the changing traditions of representing disability in the popular media, with the specific project of analyzing articles about disability in *The Reader's Digest*; a study of the enduring practices of representing disability in fund-raising, with the specific project of charity advertising during the founding years of the United Way in the 1950s; and a study of the textual strategies representing disability in activist criticism, with the specific project of analyzing argumentation in the activist newsletter/magazine *The Disability Rag*.

The theoretical and methodological frameworks for the project combined linguistics, rhetoric, and disability studies in a discourse analysis of the interactional and textual practices in the social construction of disability. Disability studies is an emerging interdisciplinary field growing out of work in medical anthropology, sociology, social work, public policy, and feminist studies (Albrecht 1992; Ferguson, Ferguson, and Taylor 1992; Fine and Asch 1988; Goffman 1963; Hillyer 1995; Ingstad and Whyte 1995; Nagler 1993; the journal of this field is the *Disability Studies Quarterly*). These critics and researchers see disability in counterpoint to prevailing biomedical models of disability as physical and/or mental impairment(s). In this field, disability is seen primarily as a social construction: as Robert Murphy (1987) notes in his classic work *The Body Silent*, "Disability is defined by society and given meaning by culture; it is a social malady" (4), and as Jenny Morris (1991) sums up in her activist and feminist criticism, "[I]t is environmental barriers and social attitudes which disable us. To put it very simply, it is not the inability to walk which disables someone but the steps into the building" (10).

My study, I hoped, would have value and significance to these scholarly discussions of disability in several disciplines. By collecting and analyzing the ways different groups talk and write about disability, I would offer a discursive approach to understanding the ways individuals with disabilities are objectified, categorized, valorized, and ignored in American society as we all participate in the social construction of disability. In the early stages of the project, I had high interdisciplinary hopes for the development and dissemination of the research to its intersecting fields of disability studies, linguistics, and rhetoric, but I had no specific plans to return to the sites of inquiry with the research findings.

Perhaps because the design of this research was interdisciplinary and the field component was informed more by linguistics than composition, the project was not conceived primarily as a study of literacy activities, although, ironically, one of the first articles to emerge from the research was a study of literacy practices in medical encounters (see my "Literacy in (Inter)Action"). It is important to note, though, that none of the field sites initially seemed to be an obvious match for the typical contributions of literacy researcher. However, the literacy practices of participants in medical encounters and parents in private and public conversations are complex and subtle and of great interest to researchers in the community of literacy studies. But the pedagogical activities I might have to offer in return were not of obvious interest or value to the participants in the research. I could document many of the literacy practices within the discourse of medicine—the creation of a medical chart as an authoritative literacy product, for example, or the elimination of certain kinds of detail in the dictation of notes, or the use of forms and reports to communicate results and recommendations.

Similarly, I could describe many of the rhetorical practices within the discourse of support groups—the valorization of personal experience over professional expertise, for example, or the summary of laws and rights pertaining to disability, or the construction of advocacy discourse. Finally I could describe many of the common themes of disability narratives, including themes of stigma, normalization, experience, and growing expertise. But I had no obvious pedagogical contributions to make to the community. I didn't feel well-qualified to teach medical professionals how to improve their summary skills. I didn't feel well-trained to facilitate therapeutic discussions of personal experience. I didn't feel well-versed in the details of contemporary federal law and state regulations with respect to the rights of persons with disabilities. And I certainly did not feel presumptuous enough to show parents how to change or improve their narrative tellings. In sum, even if I had been looking for ways to contribute to the communities I studied in the field, I didn't see the relevance of my interest and training in composition.

My relationship with the sites of research, I thought, was bounded and uncomplicated. The field, as traditionally defined by sociolinguists, linguistic anthropologists, and discourse analysts, is simply the place to get oral language data; I assumed that my role entailed identifying interesting sites and assuring that I left those sites with material to be transcribed and analyzed. Similarly, I had no particular plans to maintain the relationships I established with informants and subjects in the field; in fact, I was reluctant to sustain relationships with medical professionals, since the theoretical frameworks of disability studies and medicine are in some degree of conflict, and the most predictable direction for the analysis would be a critique of the interactional practices within the discourse of medicine. Further, I had no desire to explore my situated relationship within the field site: the fact that the entire project was conceived out of my experience as the mother of a child with a disability played no role, I thought, in the actual research once I had intellectualized it in terms of the project's scholarly disciplines.

Ultimately, I did not envision the project as a contribution to the community, even to the community of parents, within which I am a more or less active member. Although I was aware of calls for close relationships with researchers and subjects and even for contributions from researcher to community, I considered the establishment of such relationships part of feminist research in case study and/or ethnographic design, which were not the theoretical or methodological framework of my project. I simply did not see how linguistic and rhetorical analyses would provide any contributions of interest to the field sites. I considered the audience for the project to be scholars in linguistics, composition/rhetoric, and disability studies, and perhaps medicine. I deliberately eliminated other audiences, especially non-scholarly ones such as parents and families, professionals who work with them, and the general public, having discarded the possibility of writing a trade publication that would speak to a broader audience. (Although I read and admired many such publications, such as Kathryn Black's *In the Shadow of Polio: A Personal and Social History*, as a classically trained linguist, I recoiled from the idea of foregrounding my personal experiences in scholarly research.) I did not consider my decision to distance myself unethical, just typical of a scholar doing disciplinary and interdisciplinary research. What I did not understand about the field sites, however, was that the representation of the project by participants would prove to be a significant challenge to my own.

Project 1: The Question of Relevance

It became clear almost immediately that the nursing home communities I studied had no particular interest in my scholarly pursuit of self-representation through writing. They allowed me to conduct research on site because of the personal benefits they believed would accrue to residents, not because of any interest in my theories of methodologies, or even my pedagogical contributions as a writing teacher. Nurses, activities directors and social workers most valued the therapeutic potential of the writing groups for individual members. Writing as therapy, particularly psychotherapy (or "reminiscence therapy," as social workers call it) was an area about which I knew nothing and initially had little interest in exploring. However, the staff I interviewed talked about the writing groups solely in terms of their social and emotional effects, as indicated in the following excerpt from an interview with the activities director (Carol) and assistant director (Sue) at a facility where Joyce (the geriatric social worker) had conducted groups for several consecutive years:

Ruth: So, then, overall, what would you say is the purpose of the writing group?
Carol: I think mainly just to bring up the emotions. I mean, you can see it in their stories, and just the longing to share and—
Sue: I would say on one level the stimulation, just basic stimulation, feeling good about who they are, and they're not just . . . .
Carol: And what was good with [Joyce] is that when (they wrote) and it didn't even pertain to the topic . . . I mean, she made it seem like the most important story, as she was reading it. And I think that made the person feel umm . . . .

Sue: She's got great voice inflection and things like that. Just her character, her body language.

These staff members saw the writing group as providing a type and level of interpersonal exchange that did not typically occur in the residents' daily lives. A large part of the success of the group, as they saw it, was the presence of several outside volunteers who came with Joyce to provide constant stimuli during the sessions.

In the following excerpt, I have just asked why residents who could not see and did not have the physical capability to write agreed to attend the writing groups:

Sue: Probably 'cause they had somebody to listen to 'em. They [the volunteers] let you talk—

Carol: Mmmhmm. They like to talk to someone.

Sue: Yeah, right. Yeah, that's a big thing. Just have them tell about their past. I think what really helped this time was, you know, when we tried to do [our own writing group] before, we tried to do it alone . . . . and with eight people [in the group], there's no way [we could handle it].

Carol: And you had three more, like five [volunteers] in there sometimes helping. So [residents] weren't just sitting there.

Sue: It got busy. They like to be busy. They like things to (have) action. They don't like to have to wait for fifteen minutes before somebody gets to them.

Carol: And we just don't have the staff to do that, to have that many people.

In a half-hour interview, these activities directors barely mention the written texts or the activity of writing. Clearly, from their perspective, the writing groups are valuable as a means to provide stimulation and sustained attention to residents—the main goals of activities programming in nursing homes.

The comments of a social worker at another nursing home suggest that staff value emotional and social stimulation in terms of its physical as well as psychological effects. In the following excerpt, I am talking with Alice, the Director of Social Work, about the effects of Joyce's writing group on individual members, in this case, Mr. Fox:

I'm glad he was able to attend. He is diagnosed with depression . . . . I think he's been able to make it to a lot of 'em [writing group sessions]. You know. But umm prior to that he was starting to spend more time in his room again. And we were kinda scared about that because we were hoping he wasn't ((whispers)) going to die. ((speaks softly)) Because we did go through that and his condition started dropping. He wasn't eating. . . . And not wanting to take medications there for a little while. But umm, I was really glad that we could see that, the change, and then he started attending these writing classes and umm he's not a real sociable person because he's more quiet, but he can offer information, and I think that made him feel important to participate in the class.

In our interview, this social worker focused primarily on the dynamics of the writing group and the value of one-on-one attention provided by outside volunteers. In the hectic world of the nursing home where a social worker's time is consumed by paper work and "intake procedures," she most keenly felt her own lack of ability to interact with residents on anything more than a quick and superficial level.

Nursing home staff defined Joyce's role as group facilitator largely in terms of her ability to create a therapeutic environment through interactional style. Many described her as pleasant and hospitable, encouraging, inclusive, and above all, highly personalized. In fact, Joyce modeled these behaviors and encouraged volunteers working with the writing groups to behave similarly. Volunteer scribes were told to visit group members in their rooms, remind them of the time, encourage them to attend, and assist them to the meeting room. Each group member received a name tag and was greeted individually when entering the room. The sessions typically began with a comment on the value of the residents' presence, followed by a short oral reading on the topic of the day (an early childhood memory, school days, love and romance, a seasonal memory, etc.); a brief discussion; and a 15–20 minute period of writing with assistance from the scribes. Sessions concluded with Joyce reading aloud what each member had written. Volunteers would sit next to a group member, repeat the topic of the day, and write down what the member said, trying to retain as many individual expressions and speech patterns as possible. Joyce's stated goal was to get at least one written line from each group member—a challenging task for the severely impaired—and to acknowledge each of the writer's efforts through the oral readings. She would precede each reading by mention of the writer's name ("All right, Louise, this is your story") and would usually follow it with an encouraging comment ("Louise, that's a wonderful, wonderful story.") or a comment to stimulate further response ("How many of the rest of you grew up on farms or had a country childhood?").

Joyce exercised primary control over the function of the group within each nursing home. She suggested which residents should be included in the group and took sole responsibility for the functioning of the sessions; when she was ill, the group did not meet. She determined when the sessions began and ended, what topics would be addressed and in what order, oversaw the typing of the final products, and handled distribution of the texts. (Writings were handed out to group members each week and posted on bulletin boards in the nursing homes.)

Although many residents verbally expressed interest and pleasure in the writing group meetings, neither the act of writing nor the final written texts was the highest priority. In the context of the nursing home, the meetings of the writing group took a distinct second place to a variety of other activities, planned or unplanned: family visits, outings, trips to the doctor, physical therapy sessions, and hair appointments always took priority. If the resident had had a fitful night or was feeling upset about something, she/he might decline to attend the writing group session. Some came and chose to listen only. Some agreed to come, then changed their minds halfway through and requested to be taken back to their rooms. Some came and fell asleep. When the typed writings were distributed at the beginning of each session, few chose to edit or revise them, even though they sometimes contained obvious errors. This resident behavior is consistent with the beliefs of the nursing home staff and on-site social workers, indicating that what is valued overall is social activity and cognitive/emotional stimulation over the writing process or the actual written text.

In my interview with Joyce, she emphasized the social and emotional value of the writing groups and provided some insight into why these elements are so important within the context of a nursing home:

Ruth: What do you expect to happen in the course of a six-week writing group?
Joyce: Well, I have some goals. I have some goals for individuals. First, that they become comfortable just expressing themselves in this sort of verbal form of writing. And that they feel the respect of the [scribe] for what they've written and this—for me the most important dynamic is that volunteer-individual [connection] . . . and that over time they become more self-expressive. And by that I mean comfortable sharing personal feelings and ideas.

In order to facilitate such expressivist goals, certain aspects of the nursing home environment must be taken into account:

Joyce: The nursing home population and institution—it's hard to separate these out—require a more active form of facilitation. And you just can't compare them with writing groups [in other settings], but even in comparison with other treatment groups, say a group for community-dwelling depressed older adults [where] the facilitator takes a diminishing leadership role. And over time the goal is that the group becomes more self-governing and develops sort of a peer leadership style. In the nursing home, you're dealing with people who are more frail to begin with, who are more dependent, and who are in a setting which validates, rightly or wrongly, their dependence. There's a recognition of this being reality. But the other thing is, it's much easier to give care to people than to help them perform self-care. And so it's a cyclical process. And so the facilitator is much more directive in a nursing home group. And in a community group, there's just no way that the leader would be the reader, for example. And in the nursing home group, between the dependency issues that I already addressed and sensory loss, instances of that, it has to happen. Now, hearing loss I think is another factor because in groups with a high proportion of people with hearing loss, not only does the leader have to read everything, but the leader has to repeat the statements of other people, which already makes it seem less like their statement because it's being filtered through a switchboard operator.

The effect on me of observing and volunteering in these groups, as well as interviewing activities directors and social workers, was significant. In fact, when I finally facilitated two groups of my own, I ran them exactly the way Joyce did, deferring to her expertise, even though I am an experienced writer and composition teacher who has taught college-level autobiographical writing for years. I was just as directive as she had been, despite my long-held reputation as a non-directive facilitator in the college classroom. I did try to encourage group members to revise, but most made only minimal changes in their texts (corrections of spellings, particularly of people and places, were most prevalent). In one group, I attempted to elevate the prominence of the written texts by putting together a booklet of the writings and distributing copies to group members and nursing home administrators as well as placing one at the main reception desk. Residents were pleased with their books and showed them to other residents and family members, but in their final evaluations, most still focused on the group activity itself as most valuable. As one resident said in his final assessment of the writing group, "You learn quite a bit of what's going on with other people." Of particular value were my oral readings at the end of each session. During this time, group members said they had a chance to hear the thoughts, feelings, and memories of people whom they often didn't know well and had barely conversed with beyond polite exchanges in the hallway or dining room. Sometimes they were surprised that a seemingly unresponsive resident had produced such an interesting piece of writing.

My role as university researcher, beyond the initial representation of the project to solicit informed consent from all participants, was largely ignored in the context of the writing groups. I became, for the most part, just another of Joyce's volunteers. Joyce supported this role definition with her occasional references to me as one of the assistants ("Ruth and Judy and I are going to be sitting next to you and asking you to respond to this question"). As a volunteer, my value to the community was seen primarily in terms of personal characteristics—"an attractive young woman" who pushed wheelchairs to and fro, got people out of their rooms once a week for an hour, and engaged reluctant residents in conversations about their lives. In short, my disciplinary interests and values (textual production of the "self" and analysis of spoken and written texts in terms of discursive conventions of self-representation) were inconsequential in terms of the values of the community (importance of the nursing home residents' feelings and the health-value of group interactions).

After three years of researching in nursing homes, I now find it easier to speak of the relevance of this project in the community's terms and to value my role as volunteer. This shift in my own perception occurred in increments, but I remember one particular exchange with a writing group member that clarified my role. Mary was a developmentally disabled woman who could neither read, write, nor speak beyond "yeah" and "uh." On the day that I worked with her, I was doubtful about her abilities. When I said "hello," she squinted her eyes and tilted her head up, peering out from eyelids crusted with matter.

She had no teeth, and her tongue, covered with food particles, filled her mouth. Because her mouth was always open, she gave the appearance of wearing a constant grin. I wondered what I could possibly write down for her. In the following excerpt from my interview with Joyce, which occurs several months into the project after I have volunteered in four different writing groups, I am struggling to explain my attempts to "write" with Mary:

> *Ruth:*   I had an interchange with Mary. Now, I always had a hard time interacting with her and getting anything. This is the day you were doing the romance topic.
>
> *Joyce:* Oh, gosh, yes.
>
> *Ruth:*   And she was, the book [you had read from] was there sitting in front of her and we pulled, she pulled the book over. And we just looked at the book. And I pointed to pictures and she laughed at pictures. And it was clear that there were certain pictures she liked a lot, the ones about animals, and—we didn't get anything written, but it was a very pleasant interchange, for me anyway. And I kind of felt like we had a little bond after that.
>
> *Joyce:* Good.
>
> *Ruth:*   You know, 'cause she'd point to me and smile and laugh. And it just occurred to me that there were a lot more important things happening there than creating a piece of writing.

Naive as my comments sound to me in retrospect, it was a revelation at the time that a writing group in a nursing home was *not* primarily about writing and that group members could benefit regardless of their literacy levels and physical disabilities. As a result of such field research, then, I have come to examine more critically the nature and purpose of my inquiry into "discursive identity." I have also come to elevate my role as a person over my role as an academic within the communities I have studied.

Project 2: The Question of Representation

When I entered the field sites, I thought my role was that of a researcher, more specifically a linguist collecting oral language data. I thought my role was summed up perfectly in the introduction to my informed consent document, supposedly written in plain language:

> I am a linguist, a person who studies language, and I am studying the language of disability. To study the language of disability, I am tape recording many different events—clinic appointments people have with doctors and nurses, conversations and stories that people have about their experiences with disability, and so on. After I collect and transcribe all of this taped material, I will analyze the language for themes which describe the experiences of people and families who are living with disabilities. I hope one day to write a book about the relationships between language, disability, and American society.

As required by informed consent regulations, I conscientiously pointed out to parents that "This is a research project and it may not be of any direct benefit to [your] child." (For information on informed consent, see Anderson 1996).

In my first few observations at the Pediatric Hospital's Child Evaluation Unit, a clinic which specializes in the diagnosis of new or suspected disabilities, and the Child Care Clinic, a large health and welfare organization specializing in the care of children with disabilities, I pretty much stuck to my script. I introduced myself as an English professor at Wayne State University and tried to describe my interests in research on language. To some of my participants, mostly medical professionals, I made a few bumbling attempts to explain the importance of social construction to my thinking about disability, but I soon reverted to using the vague combination of "language and disability." I soon noted, however, that participants—both medical professionals and parents—turned my scholarly project into an applied project that could make a contribution to the community as they defined it.

During my observations at the Pediatric Evaluation Unit, the developmental pediatrician who ran the clinic took upon herself the task of introducing the project to her patients. She gave the project a practical focus and value:

> I have a question to ask. I am now involved in a research study. And they're looking at communications between professionals and families with children who have problems. And one of the university professors from down at Wayne, who is studying linguistics, how people talk to one another, would like to sit in and tape the session and talk to you.

This was typically the way that clinic workers talked about the project. For example, during my observations at the Child Care Clinic, the clinic nurse once had occasion to introduce me to a new nurse in the middle of a medical encounter, and she described me and my project as follows:

> This is Ellen, and she's a researcher, and she is in here listening to what we say, how we say it, what we say, the terminology we use with the parents . . . how well we communicate.

What is interesting to me is that both representations of the project were simplifications. My own simplification of the theoretical framework of disability studies was to describe a set of discursive practices opaquely as "the language of disability." The medical professionals' simplification was to describe the research as the study of communication. In their descriptions, the medical professionals retained my designated role as a researcher, and even the definition of a linguist as a person who studies language. However, in contrast to my coded reference to social construction as the "language of disability," the pediatrician and the nurse represented the project more concretely as one which studies talk between professionals and families. In medicine, in parents' groups, and even in the general public, the complicated communication between patients and families on the one hand and doctors and other medical professionals on the other is a familiar issue. What I want to point out here, though, is that it was not *my* issue, at least as I defined the project. When the project was defined for me, however, it was described in terms of an issue of direct relevance to the community.

The first few times I entered the field to observe and record medical encounters, I introduced myself to participants solely as an English professor or a linguist. I thought this was the only salient aspect of my identity. I quickly learned, however, that what was interesting about me to the medical professionals and families I wanted to observe was not my researcher role but my role as parent of a child with a disability. The way that others represented me illustrated that my credibility as a researcher was best achieved in personal rather than academic terms. In the encounters I observed, the medical professionals almost never referred to me overtly during the course of business. When they did bring me into the conversation, however, it was always in terms of my common identity with the families. In the Pediatric Evaluation Unit, for example, when the developmental pediatrician referred to me for the first time, she used my case as an example of the need to be patient during the sometimes lengthy process of discovering whether, in fact, a disability might be diagnosed:

Dr. Harris: Um I think the problem—((to me)) May I use an example?
Ellen: Mine? Sure.
Dr. Harris: Um I think the classic example is when—Dr. Barton has a daughter who has cerebral palsy. And when they first came to see me we knew that something was wrong in terms of what she was able to do motorically but we weren't sure what was going on—And um—
               And the first time I saw her I said yes I agree with you something's wrong. And the second time I came back I said yes, things were still not right but they're looking better now. And the third time I came back it became very apparent—We'd waited out the time—[We knew?] exactly which way we were going. We were going back into a new phase that showed something totally different than what we were originally looking at, and made it very clear by the third or fourth time that we were dealing with a child that was going to have significant motor problems.
               But it was only through going through that—Because some of the kids that will have early motor problems will work them through.

I remember this occasion well. I almost jumped out of my chair when the physician brought me into the conversation, making me a participant rather than an observer. It was not that I felt exploited or violated in any way but I was astonished the physician would bring up my experience as potentially useful in her discussions with families. After this initial occasion, the physician in the Pediatric Evaluation Unit talked about my daughter or my family occasionally, any time she felt that a point in my case was somehow interesting or useful for the case at hand. Just as she had re-defined my project in terms of the issue of communication, which was potentially relevant for participants in an ongoing medical relationship, she similarly re-defined my identity in terms of issues relevant to her ongoing communication with patients. What was relevant about me, though, was my personal experience, not my professional status as researcher as an English professor, a linguist, or even a generic researcher.

At the Child Care Clinic, the process of revealing a fuller version of my identity arose out of my own concerns about being an ethical researcher in the field, especially in terms of the informed consent process. The Child Care Clinic was a busy, bustling institution, one in which the medical staff routinely assumed a fair degree of authority during the typical course of encounters. One of the ways in which this kind of asymmetrical and authoritative relationship would be played out was in the collection of signatures. Parents often needed to provide a signature for different reasons in the Child Care Clinic, and signatures were typically gathered without much sharing of authority. Usually, a form was presented and signed without much discussion:

Dietitian: I need you to fill something out for me.
Mother: Oh, for WIC.
Dietitian: Yes.
(WIC—Women, Infants, and Children—is a supplemental food program for low-income families.)

Often forms were presented for signatures without any explanations from the staff or any comments from the families:

Nurse: I need you to sign this.

I, too, was in the process of collecting signatures as part of the informed consent procedure, but during my first few observations I was acutely aware that parents often signed my form without paying much attention to my elaborate explanation that this was a research project and that a signature signaled their informed consent to voluntary participation. I was concerned that parents were signing my form based on a perception that I came in with full authority of the institution, that my presence and my clipboard meant that they *had* to sign. I then began introducing myself not only as a researcher but also as a parent, trying to separate myself from official staff in the Child Care Clinic:

I'll take this minute to start showing you this consent form. It looks more cumbersome than it is, but it's required for any university study. It simply says that this is a research project, you need informed consent, you need to know what the research is about so that you can make a judgment about participation. Um, this says that I'm a linguist, I'm a person who studies language. I'm studying language [and] disability, and I got interested in this project because I have a four-year-old girl with a disability.

When I identified myself as another parent, I did so to distinguish myself from medical professionals with authority over the participants in the encounter. I thought of this disclosure simply as a device to ensure ethical consent to participation in my study. I did not realize at the time, however, that while I had successfully moved the proffered reasons for participation away from the authority of the clinic, I had shifted the reasons for participation to a personal connection based on shared identity as fellow parents. The reason for participation was not automatic submission to institutional authority, but it was also not participation for the sake of contributing to research alone. The terms of consent were shifted to the connection between me and the parents as fellow members of the parents' community, and members of this community thus may legitimately have a different claim on the research—an interest, for example, in issues directly relevant to families and advocacy groups.

Making matters even more complicated was the fact that my data reflects this shared identity as well. When I conducted my field interviews, I used a similar procedure for informed consent, explaining that my interests in this research project arose in part out of my experience as a parent. On one occasion, a mother must have missed this statement initially and identified me solely as a university researcher. During the middle of the interview, however, our shared identity became clear to her:

> I can kind of relate more to other people that's in my situation more than I can people's that not in my situation. You know. Just from you just telling me that you have [a] child—I feel more comfortable with you now. I really do.

The rest of the interview was markedly different. The mother became much more animated, interested, and engaged in the whole process, telling anecdotes rather than giving minimal answers, asking questions as well as answering them, and seemingly enjoying the chance to talk about her experiences rather than simply replying to a set of questions about her child. This particular interview forced me to think about the whole set of interviews not as material any field researcher could have gathered but as material that only I could have gathered, material that was inextricably linked to my identity as the mother of a child with a disability. I had been planning to ignore as extraneous any material based on personal sharing between my participants and me, but I found that this particular data was powerfully heuristic: it exposed my assumptions about the project and my role as researcher, as well as my participants' challenges to those assumptions.

More and more, review of my field materials reveals what seems like a conspiracy to shift my project away from its academic and scholarly contributions toward its applied value and significance. My relationship with others in the field did not remain clearly bounded but expanded to take into account the familiar refrain that many parents gave as their reason for participating: "Anything to help the children." When my data collection ended, I thought I was "leaving the field" to go back to the academy, but the field came with me and seemed to ask for a return, in the sense of reconceptualizing the project in terms of its theoretical concerns and applied significance. In spite of my initial assumptions and unconscious resistance, I was forced to explore my personal connections with and ethical commitments to the communities I had entered.

CONCLUSIONS AND IMPLICATIONS

Even with ethical commitments to reconceptualizing research issues and exploring the applied value of research within communities, matters related to the field are not easily resolved. There remains the question of what to contribute when neither the theoretical nor pedagogical goals of literacy studies seem particularly relevant in a field site. In both of our projects, theoretical descriptions of the nature and practice of literacy activities did not seem to be of interest to participants. More specifically, the typical theoretical product of literacy research—critique—would not have been appropriate in either of these settings. Critiquing the literacy practices of professionals, particularly if this critique incorporates an oppositional dimension, runs a considerable risk of being seriously uninformed. Critiquing the literacy practices of patients and families—written texts or narrative tellings—seems churlish. Further, the typical pedagogical goals of literacy research—assisting and improving reading and writing—also were not of interest or relevance to participants. Professionals did not ask us for suggestions to improve their facilitation of writing groups or their summary skills. Patients and families did not ask us to correct their errors or improve their narrative skills. Our interests in literacy and expertise in teaching were simply not of primary value to our field sites.

We both thus faced a number of dilemmas in our attempts to understand and articulate the contributions we had to offer communities. Consistent with earlier assumptions of composition researchers, we could continue to foreground our own disciplinary perspectives, trying to make our traditional theoretical and applied perspectives on literacy relevant, but in doing so, we would run the risks of providing uninvited critiques and unsolicited services. In response to our experiences in the field, however, we have determined that it is important to foreground the communities' representations of our research and to pursue the areas of interest to them. We now recognize the relevance of community contributions to the *theoretical* aspects of our research and no longer *assume* the relevance of our theoretical or pedagogical contributions to the community. For the nursing home project, this means engaging in new research on writing as therapy and considering the ways writing groups are constructed as therapeutic environments within the larger context of the nursing home. For the disability project, this means engaging in new research on communication in medical discourse. For both projects, the new research directions allow the opportunity for community-sponsored forums which present findings that are actually of interest to members—in training volunteers, for example, or in presenting workshops to support groups, or in developing in-services for professionals and other staff. For neither project, though, will "community contribution" mean teaching literacy skills in the traditional sense of composition studies.

What we have learned from our work in the field is that communities are mainly invested in meeting their own goals. They therefore construct and represent research projects in ways that are consistent with those goals. What we had to learn was how to discard our disciplinary-based assumptions about "giving back" via literacy services alone. We had to re-define our ethical commitments to these communities not in our terms but in theirs. Both of us began our research with very traditional assumptions about "the field" and our potential (or lack of potential) to contribute to it. Both of us left the field with troubling questions about our roles and responsibilities. Both of us now have to work through our responses to these questions, both in terms of reconceptualizing the theoretical nature of the research and redefining its applied significance. In the end, these reconceptualizations—and the interests they make visible outside the walls of academe—provide the best reason for uncoupling research and schooling.

PART FOUR

Remaking Knowledge and Rewriting Practice

CHAPTER FIFTEEN

A Rhetoric of Teacher-Talk
Or How To Make
More Out of Lore

Wendy Bishop

S OME TIME AGO, I PROMISED TO DO QUITE A FEW THINGS IN THIS CHAPTER
space. I would "create a preliminary rhetoric of teacher talk—lore, story,
narrative research, testimony, literacy autobiography, and so on." I would begin
by refusing to argue about whether "teachers' experiences create knowledge for
the field" and focus on the issue of "*how do* teachers do this?" In my chapter, I
would "claim value for teacher-talk as an important contributor to knowledge-
making in composition by defining and illustrating some genres of teacher-
talk and then by examining the political and social ramifications involved in
insisting that we value making knowledge in this manner." Among my more
traditional promises, I included an assurance that I would "suggest ways to
read such talk more critically and to produce it more effectively."

So here we are, you and I, reading my chapter together. I want to do those
things but I want to do them in an exploratory, experimental, generative way
instead of a predictably academic way;[1] I want to enact my claims because it is
action in writing and teaching and in thinking about both that keep me—and
I would argue you, readers whom I imagine, whom I imagine as fellow teachers—engaged in the profession.

BEING MULTI-DIALECTAL—HAVING STYLES FOR OUR STORIES

As a composition specialist in English studies, I feel a need to be tri-lingual.
I attempt to speak literature, creative writing, and composition and rhetoric.
As a rhetorician-in-training, I had to develop dialectal fluency—becoming
slowly more confident at reading empirical research, historical scholarship,
theoretical discourses. However, the ur-language for me across these territories
was and remains narrative. In each dialect, as in each educational language, I
strive to make meaning through storytelling; analogy building; choice of
metaphors; descriptions of thoughts, practices, and insights that will resonate
from my experience to your experience.

The icing on this textual cake is style—I have become (sometimes have
been forced to become) interested in the strategic results of word choice, subtle

modulations of textual voice(s), refinements of my writer's audience (and editor) awareness. I have had to learn to read better, to analyze rhetorical choices, ploys, effects, and actions. This ur-affiliation is a result of my self-labeling—of seeing myself as a writer teacher, one who writes and teaches writing. The dual affiliation allows me to ply the territories between individuality and community, authors and readers, lore and learning, research and practice. Scholarship is always, for me, in service of these goals.

In fact, such movement seems like a matter of inhabitation rather than of passage between locations. As my friend Alys Culhane, who is visiting this week, observed yesterday during a writing break—about her first attempt at going down-hill on rollerblades—she has learned that she doesn't have to go downhill fast, fall, stand (and hide the pain of sudden dislocation) and then pretend she can handle the course (as she did yesterday). Sleeping on the problem (as writers sleep on writing problems), she woke up (sore) realizing she could learn by slaloming down the road, going from side to side, braking her speed. She'll do this until she learns how to integrate starting with stopping, speeding with slowing. She's out there right now, making accommodations and connections. Just as I am in here at the computer making connections between theory and praxis, through narrative.

CALL ME A ROMANTIC

Once some reviewer of something I submitted to a composition journal called me to task for using the terms *narrative* and *story* interchangeably just as more recently an anonymous reviewer of a poetry textbook I am finishing was textually incensed when I referred to the narrator of a poem when I should have been speaking it seems of the speaker "First of all, each poem has a *speaker*, technically, not a *narrator*" he/she wrote to my publisher and over the publisher's shoulder, to me.

I could respond by showing that my friendly dictionary (as opposed to my unfriendly anonymous reviewer) claims that narrative and story are synonymous. You can call me romantic, but I don't have any trouble with foregoing literary discourse concerning narration (narratology?) in order to make a teaching point and to alternate my terms (it becomes boring to me and to you when I say story over and over so I choose to vary this word with the synonym *narration* and substitute *storyteller* for *narrator*, and vice versa).

Nor am I as concerned these days as my poetry textbook reviewer is with genre-based terminological precision. I suppose I grab-bag my poetics from other genres because the students in my poetic technique classes are quite often writing majors who specialize in fiction but are required by my department to take a class in another technique (poetic or dramatic) before graduating. It is obviously functional, then, to import the term narrator and to discuss narrative in my poetry classes.

This is not to say I don't like, value, and advocate precision of language; I appreciate the reviewer's correction and will change my terms since by contracting to write a textbook on poetic form, I've accepted the responsibility of accuracy. Readers also have a right to expect that I'll know where I'm coming from (even when I might be trying to go somewhere different). Still (and obviously), I don't like the tone or the spirit of the correction regarding narrator/speaker that I received.

I ask my students to be precise themselves though I have no intention of shaking the master-teacher's stick at them. For instance, I gave a mini-talk last Wednesday on why poets in my class might choose to distinguish more carefully between homonyms—"soar/sore" made a real difference in a poem (perhaps even productively), but "to/too" didn't make as much, except to my hyper-literate eye. I do realize that to simplify the connections between story/narration is strategic for *this* chapter whereas it would represent professional provincialism if I were to attend a conference on narrative theory and do the same. While I have harmed no beginning poet by talking in a language they could understand about the speaker of their poem, it behooves me to learn to use the more generally accepted—because generically accurate—term. I conform for clarity's sake and to enter the discourses of academic poetry circles. Clarity is a historic strategy of teacher talk but it does not represent—as is sometimes assumed—an intellectual deficiency. It is an example of dialect switching and audience accessing that I think is crucial for writer teachers in our profession to undertake.

Call me a romantic, then, for I'm still most interested in considering what the mis-use of "soar/sore" might do to a line in a poem than what it says about my students' previous interactions with or indifference to usage instruction. This doesn't mean I won't teach such distinctions or that I don't try to please you with my prose; it simply means that I've experienced a shift in the value I attach to such rule-making and rule-enforcing and to making such reader accommodations—each matters, but not at all (or no longer) wholly.

And I prefer to read writers for whom this also seems true—friends and current fave writers (actually friends because they are fave writers and this appreciation of their writing led me to seek them out and make friends) include Libby Rankin and Lad Tobin. I value their teacher-talk (as I do that of Peter Elbow, Toby Fulwiler, Donald Murray, Tom Newkirk, Stephen North [particularly in live conference presentations when his 1987 *The Making of Knowledge in Composition* "lore" doom-saying can be forgotten and his wry, ironic writer teacher persona blossoms via anecdotes and stories], Mary Rose O'Reilley, Mike Rose, Nancy Sommers, Peter Stillman, Jane Tompkins, Victor Villanueva, Winston Weathers, Art Young, and others who should be listed but whose names I forget for a moment right now). In fact, teacher talk may appear "simple"—a type of academic primer-prose—less as a result of romance with the solitary ideal of the individual writer than as a desire for direct communication, and a love of language that is used precisely, with a solid side-dish of humor or irony.

Intellect, humor, irony, clarity, sincerity, generosity—I find these in the prose of the writers who move me, from whom I learn about their teaching.

Lest you say—but of course, these are "famous" people in composition, let me remind you that those I now know as friends, I did not know ten years ago, except in print where they are accessible to us all. I've seen many of these lore experts enter new conversation after new conversation—in a friendly, informative manner—at conferences around the country. Teacher talk is, after all, about teaching and talk.

IF I COUNT THE WAYS, DO YOU LIKE ME BETTER (AND TRUST ME MORE?)

Research is a useful, learned skill. Once I learn it, I can "research" any topic and report it quantitatively and/or qualitatively. Numbers are not better than words nor vice versa. Nor should one dominate the other. Still, in some circles, numbers have more power, authority, cachet, charisma. The rhetoric of science is structured to convince us of its disinterested inevitability. But by parody, I think I can show you that any research project can be given the number turn. It goes something like this:

Research sample:

Six issues of the journal *College Composition and Communication*. 1.5 years: February 1996 through May 1997. I chose *CCC* because it is our representative journal—used to support tenure-reviews, urged on new affiliates to the National Council of Teachers of English who declare college memberships, vehicle of central discussions.

Sample selection:

This study focuses on recent strategies of teacher-talk. I chose to review one year (four issues) of the journal under discussion but decided to combine academic and calendar years, hence the calendar year 1996 and the academic year 1996–1997. In making this decision, I broaden my research agenda from a doable review of four issues to a manageable review of six issues.

The research question:

What's going on in terms of (scholarly) teacher-talk? (Is scholarly teacher-talk an oxymoron?) My strategy is to profile the general contents—who is writing—and then to look at opening gambits. How do these writer teacher scholars begin their works, engaging the reader by what rhetorical strategies?

Initial results:

Six issues. Twenty-nine main articles. Six "Interchanges" (which replace earlier "Classroom Samplers"; that is, talk and dialogue replaces how-to). Of 29 articles by 36 authors (or author-functions), 23 are women, 13 are men, 4 articles are co-authored.

Rhetorical strategies of opening paragraphs in these issues:

After a first reading and category development (initially I created five main categories with several sub-categories), I refined my categories of rhetorical openings to three: Authors chose to open essays using a personal/teaching story (8 articles), by citing or alluding to historical precedent or urgent/ongoing professional concerns (10 articles), or by focusing on thesis development (in this category some historical/professional allusions were also included but the thrust was toward orienting the reader to the upcoming essay focus) (11 articles).

Let me prepare a chart. Should you care to argue with me and my numbers, you'll easily find you might have categorized the following writers differently.

Table
Opening Gambits of Articles in *CCC* Feb 1996-May 1997

Story (8)	*Historical/Professional (10)*	*Thesis Development (11)*
Kurlioff	Minock	Charney
Faigley	Grimm	Bizzell
Schreiner	Huot	Lynch, George, and Cooper
Smith	Sirc	Canagarajah
Royster	Leonard	Anderson
Welch	Soliday	Marshall
Spooner and Yancey	Marback	Cushman
Wells	Straub	Greg and Thompson
	Fishman and McCarthy	Lunsford and Ede
	Lunsford and West	Homer
		McAndrew

Observations and discussion:

There was a 2:1 ratio of scholarly/historical/theoretical openings to narrative openings for the essays reviewed. Further researchers will need to see if opening gambits predict an author's commitment to teacher-talk. For example (see further discussion below), at least two authors reversed their commitment after the first paragraph. This may be true and may also indicate a third strategy—the reversed opening promise/teaser/tickler.

WHICH OF MY/YOUR STORIES COUNT(S), TOLD HOW? WHY?

Each of us could read through these *CCC* articles, and we would do so for different reasons.

I could read:

> On February 24, 1991, Arthur Colbert, a Temple University criminal justice major, was stopped by two Philadelphia police officers as he looked for his date's address. They accused Colbert of running a crack house under the name "Hakim" and took him to a deserted building. (Wells 325).

Wells's opening engages as a newspaper article would engage. Reading this dramatic beginning, I'm inclined to move on, although I wonder (since this essay is in a composition journal) how (if) the author will connect this to classrooms (my—perhaps not your—major interest). As always when I read— overly busy and tired as a parent, teacher, writer—I scan ahead, looking to see if engagement will be worth my while, relieved when I hear the connection: "I was fascinated by this story. . . As a citizen, I was angry; as a teacher, I was upset that a student had been brutalized. But as a writing teacher, I was triumphant." While this first person voice might stop other readers, it calls to me to continue and, incidentally, along the way, I admire the balanced sentences that I just quoted. I continue, expecting to appreciate what this writer wrote—or should I say "how" this writer wrote. Whether I need information on the topic, though, of course, will also influence my further engagement.

Or I could read:

> A new preoccupation with research methodology and its implications has overtaken composition studies, particularly in the area of technical and profes- sional communication. As in previous visits to this topic, the major concerns are whether empirical methods have any legitimate place in composition stud- ies, and, if not, how we are to achieve intellectual authority without them. (Charney 567)

This essay engages me because the title "Empiricism Is Not a Four-Letter Word" is provocative—promising some humor and irony on a seemingly humorless topic (empirical research). However, the essay quickly ceases to invite me—despite it being an essay I "should" read. Perhaps this is because I rebel against duty (I'm writing a methods textbook on ethnographic writing research and should "know" what's going on in research discussions) and the author-evacuated (empirical report echoing) prose, leads me to leave the jour- nal on the nearby kitchen counter because constructions like "As in previous visits to this topic, the major concerns are whether . . . " signal an overdressed, overstuffed prose style that may be far less humorous and human than the title promises. I resist disappointment. I stop reading. I feel both a little guilty (lazy) and a little taken advantage of.

Or I could read:

> I was talking with a novelist recently about various kinds of writing—nothing special, just happy-hour talk—and I found my earnest self assuring him that, oh yes, academic writing nowadays will tolerate a number of different styles and voices. (I should know, right? I'm in academic publishing.) He choked; he

slapped my arm; he laughed out loud. I don't remember if he spit his drink back in the glass. Silly me, I was serious. (Spooner and Yancey 252).

Perhaps too eagerly, I have moved on to Spooner and Yancey. But, having seen various incarnations of this essay in draft form, since it was composed, before journal publication, for a collection I co-edited, I have trouble reading it again. That is, I have been too familiar for too long with its alternate style format to settle down and read it. Until today, a year later, when I look at it again with my researcher's eye and find the opening surprisingly informal. I'm also engaged because the essay is immediately useful—about my topic at hand—why some teacher talk (style) is being allowed and some not. Spooner and Yancey perform their thesis by writing in an alternate style—narrative and informal ("just happy-hour talk") and parenthetical ("I should know, right?") and slangy ("he choked" and "silly me") to develop an argument, support a thesis.
Or I could read this:

After the first meeting of Composition and Literature 102, a student, Sydney, lingers and says to me breathlessly, "I had such a wonderful class last semester with Jim, and he told me that you're an even more wonderful teacher than he is, and so I'm so glad to be in your class." (Welch 41).

Okay. In order to play fair I move from an essay I know (Spooner and Yancey) to one I don't know (Welch). Welch opens her essay with a teacher story and I browse on expecting more—only to find the essay veers into a more deeply theoretical discourse: "In this essay, I want to pick up on that perspective and add that the classroom's tense, charged, and sometimes erotic and antagonistic attachments are central to revision—revision as a strategy for intervening in the meanings and identifications of a text, revision as a strategy for intervening in the meanings and identifications of one's life" (42).
Here—in these finely tuned and balanced sentences—repetition is used to focus and develop a thesis. At this switch—I start to feel that the opening story was a come-on, an advertisement, a gambit, intended to draw me in but leaving me unsatisfied at the way the essay neglects to deliver on its teacher talk promises. I start to skim, to fly like a hovercraft over story-turned-professional-text and I never find myself dipping into the stream again—because no further classroom tales reach up to reengage me. Unfortunately, it's back to the bookshelf.
Or finally, I could read this:

In his "Afterthoughts on Rhetoric and Public Discourse," S. Michael Halloran finds that "the efforts of citizens to shape the fate of their community . . . would surely have been of interest to American neoclassical rhetoricians of the late eighteenth and early nineteenth centuries." Unfortunately, he sees an "apparent lack of interest in such 'Public Discourse' among new rhetoricians of late twentieth-century English departments" (2). One way to increase our participation in public discourse is to bridge the university and community through activism. (Cushman 7).

Cushman's essay performs the opposite turn. I'm put off by the opening strategy. Where Welch's story invited me in (I might say "trapped me" into reading on), Cushman's opening citation of an authority led me to predict the same old tale—one of academic correctness—until I turn the page and see a half-page footnote on the left and a photograph on the right. I immediately page through the essay and decide that the humor of the sub-titles: "Red Robin Hoods," "Much Obliged," and "No Mother Teresas Here," alone will lead me to re-read both for content and because I want to speculate about how this author passed the gatekeepers referred to in the Spooner/Yancey quote—the ones who laughed out loud at the assertion that we now tolerate different styles and voices for teacher-talk.

Of course, you could read these also. Your ways, for your purposes.

We do, but how do we? Why should we? How are we/are we making more out of lore?

WHAT'S REALLY ON MY/YOUR BEDSIDE TABLE (REALLY?)

The Rand McNally road atlas—for a car camping trip I'm taking at the end of June. This is a prewriting aid, both for the trip and for a nonfiction essay I've been invited to write about the trip.

Six *CCC*s for this chapter: Feb, May, Oct, Dec 1996, plus Feb and May 1997.

A Long Rainy Season, haiku and tanka by Japanese women—because I'm interested and in order to refute a second reviewer of the poetry textbook who argued that because the haiku was traditionally composed by men (as I duly noted) I was foolish to speculate on what haiku Japanese women did write or might have written (and to encourage my students to do so in a writing exercise).

The June 12, 1997 *Rolling Stone* with Jakob Dylan on the cover. Like my whole generation, probably, I can't help looking at his father in him and in so doing at my own past.

The May 26, 1997 *New Yorker*. I immediately got lost in Don DeLillo's nonfiction Comment essay "The Artist Naked in a Cage" about the imprisonment of the Chinese writer Wei Jingsheng, both for its humanitarian content and its alternate style. The piece is written in associative crots—eleven numbered sections. Something that wouldn't have flown in academic or art writing ten years ago but now does often enough to encourage other writers to push against the style restrictions since readers are being educated to read such work.

A book on hummingbirds, their life and behavior. For a poem I'm planning to write as I find the hummingbird is becoming a totemic animal for me.

Why am I asking you and me to do this? Because it is a way of analyzing our own rhetorical practices and preferences. Because I believe we write in response to what we have read and in order to compose, in part, what we want to read. The strategy of reading my own reading has been pointed out previously. Toby Fulwiler's 1988 essay in *Writers on Writing*, Vol. II refers to Harry Brent's 1985 essay in the original volume which does this. Fulwiler explains he wishes he had written Brent's essay. Brent lists his bedside reading to show how reading creates other writing: argument enough to push us to develop rhetoric(s) of teacher talk which will in turn encourage us to read more. And Rick Moody constructed a literacy autobiography for *The New Yorker* from a long list of books he has retained on his shelves (1995).

I am asking you to do this, too, to suggest that you might think of the strategies you might steal from the books you read to make your own writing about teaching more appealing to your readers, whoever they may be (just as you might analyze your own writing to discover your own rhetorical strategies as Alys Culhane and I do with my how-to essay in the Appendix). Seeing what we do in our teacher talk is a way to see what more we might do next.

I admire DeLillo's crots because I have been experimenting with the same technique since being offered the term in Winston Weathers' *An Alternate Style* (1980) (which friends and I followed up on in *Elements of Alternate Style* 1997c). I use crots to construct this essay. And, like Cushman, humorous subtitles. And I'm aware of a developing tradition in composition of referring to one's own literacy autobiography (as, for example, when I discuss my own training in the strands of English studies). This chapter—-that you are reading right now if you are reading these words—also performs intentionally and *implicitly* as a how-to chapter while I share an *explicitly* how-to essay in the appendix. In that essay, by narrating the way a teaching exercise developed and matured, I try to both share and suggest its use and to show how I think the act of reflective practice works: i.e., to provide a meta-how-to to my main text here (for more advocacy of the how-to essay, see my collection, *Teaching Lives*).

Back to reading. These are just today's books on today's night stand. But there is another trend developing in the field of rhetoric and composition that I'd like to mention—evidence for this trend can be found on my coffee table.

WHY ARE BOOKS ON FEELING AND SAYING RISING TO THE SURFACE (OR IS IT ONLY IN MY HOUSE)?

Ten years ago, there were few books in composition in which teachers asserted their authority through story (see O'Reilley 1993), or engaged their audience with the humorous anecdote (see Tobin's *Writing Relationships*, 1993, for a fine twice-told tale of grading). Cognition seemed to take place in the clean well-lighted rooms of the talk-aloud protocol researcher. In general, empirical researchers agreed that affect was swampy territory, better left alone because it was impossible to "accurately" explore.

New, narrative-based collections show why storytelling is a strong suit of the teacher *and* researcher (Trimmer 1997; Roen et al. 1998). And there are more books on feeling and saying. Some of this work was pioneered by Alice Brand (1985) who drew on her mixed cognitive and creative writing credentials, some by Robert Brooke (1987) who called our attention to psychological theory, and some by powerful literacy essayists like Mike Rose, Nancy Sommers, and James Moffett, who tell stories of coming into language and literacy in words that couldn't be ignored and by writing research ethnographers who report the literacy learning/life of others (Atwell 1987; Bissex 1980; Brooke 1991; Chiseri-Strater 1991; Perl and Wilson 1986; Rankin 1984; and others). More recently I've acquired (or participated in) collections that honored students' voices (see Hunter and Fontaine 1993) and feeling (Brand and Graves1994; McLeod 1997) and spirituality (Foehr and Schiller 1996). I suggest writer teachers can examine these for useful encouragement and support for their talk.

RESISTING (OR AMPLIFYING) YOUR OWN RHETORIC—OR THE LESSON OF THE LOAVES AND FISHES

More and more of this stuff is being written and published. Lore creates more lore. There's some that's good, some that's bad. There's some that's a joy to read and some that's slow going. I do know this: 1) You have to train yourself as a reader and writer of teacher talk. Collect samples you like, analyze them, imitate them. 2) Some teachers are allowed to talk more because of their reputations and some because of their skill and sometimes these combine into a powerful double-whammy. But less known teachers are doing so also—often in the exciting journals that aren't touted as central to our profession, that aren't driven by the (very real) need to act as our conservative center. Informally, I'd say *CCC* is currently most responsive to professionalization market-forces. Other journals offer sites for more Bakhtinian, stylistic, carnivalistic experimentation. On the creative writing side—try *Writing on the Edge*. On the theory-play side—try *Pre/text*. On the collaborative side—try *Dialogue*. To create your own style sampler of teacher talk, you might do as I did (see below) a couple of years ago. What follows is a much shortened version of a rhetoric of alternate style I compiled for an essay "Preaching What We Practice as Professionals in Writing" (1997b). Since my interest was and remains teaching—the writers I recommend are primarily writer teachers who write/talk/participate via:

Literacy Autobiographies
Imitations
Symposia/Forums/Dialogic Writings
Collaborative and Alternate Research
Meta-analysis and Institutional Critiques

Literacy Autobiographies. Include books by Henry Louis Gates Jr., Nancy Mairs, Richard Rodriguez, Mike Rose, and Victor Villanueva. Stretch the genre to include portions of Peter Elbow's *What Is English?* (1990) or Trinh Min-ha's

Woman, Native, Other (1989). It is a rare CCCC Chair's address of the last few years that hasn't relied on personal testimony (see Bridwell-Bowles (1995), Gere (1994), and McQuade (1992).

Imitations. Word-play asserts our double-consciousness as members of the writing *and* the literary community. Look at the number of literary puns made in conference titles. Jane Tompkin's often cited "Postcards from the Edge" (1993) borrows title and form from Carrie Fischer's novel of the same name. Lynn Bloom's "I Want a Writing Director" (1992) intentionally parodies Judy Syfer's "I Want a Wife" that was a mainstay for some years of freshman anthologies while Nancy Sommers' "I Stand Here Writing" (1993) plays off of another equally anthologized work, Tillie Olsen's short story "I Stand Here Ironing."

Symposia/Forums/Dialogic Writings. CCC now hosts symposia, grouping essayists together, with room for reply and rebuttal. Examples include the "Symposium on The Professional Standards Committee 'Progress Report'" (see Merrill et al. 1992) and newly labeled "In Focus" sections like the one on "Feminist Experiences" (see Eichorn et al. 1992). The Erika Lindemann and Gary Tate (1993, 1995) debate about the purposes of first-year writing has taken place across several years and engendered a number of readers' responses as has the David Bartholomae ("Writing with Teachers" 1995) and Peter Elbow ("Being a Writer" 1995) essays and response essays (Bartholomae et al 1995). See also *Rhetoric Review*'s "Burkean Parlor" section, that allows for initialed only or anonymous comment and response. Journals continue to highlight the interview format *(Journal of Advanced Composition, Writing on the Edge* and more recently *Composition Studies*). And one journal developed in response to its editors' desire to change the review process itself (see Hunter and Wallace's introduction to the journal *Dialogue*).

Collaborative and Alternate Research. The teacher-research movement has led to introspective and collaborative projects in which students and teachers research and write together (see Anderson et. al. 1990; Bishop and Teichman 1992). Co-authored research like that of Lisa Ede and Andrea Lunsford's in *Singular Texts/Plural Authors* (1990) can produce writing voices that are so clearly intertwined that the scholarly traditions of listing first and second authors has to be problematized.

Alternate research can require alternate styles of formats. Robert Connors and Andrea Lunsford "become" Ma and Pa Kettle (1993). Beverly Lyon Clark and Sonja Wiedenhaupt's essay, "On Blocking and Unblocking Sonja: A Case Study in Two Voices" (1992) required two different typographies. Janis Haswell and Richard H. Haswell's research report "Gendership and the Miswriting of Students" (1995) includes student texts as well as photographs of students. More recently, Ellen Cushman in her "Rhetorician as Agent of Social Change" (1996) provides three archival photographs.

Meta-analysis and Institutional Critiques. For feminist critique, we have essays by Lillian Bridwell-Bowles (1992, 1995); Sara Farris Eichorn and colleagues (1992); Elizabeth Flynn (1988, 1990), Olivia Frey (1990), Jane Tompkins (1993) and Lynn Bloom (1992). When a Donald Murray essay was rejected from a journal for being too much like an essay by Donald Murray various authors commented on this issue, including Murray (see Hult 1994; Murray 1994; Rankin 1994).

Bob Mayberry's account of life in one English department in the Spring 1995 issue of *Composition Studies* testifies to disturbing working conditions on personal grounds. Ellen Strenski looks at writing program metaphors (1989), and Sheryl Fontaine and Susan Hunter examine the "voices" of composition, using a collage technique (1993). Our institutional critiques, then, run the gamut of scholarly collections like Richard Bullock and John Trimbur's *The Politics of Writing Instruction* (1991), to literacy autobiographies like Rose's (1989), to essayist calls for change like Mayberry's (1995), to rhetorical analyses like those of Fontaine and Hunter (1992).

Alternative Style Explorations.

The imitations and critiques often register a sense of author's pleasure, of writer's breakthrough and play. Carl Leggo's essay on voice in *Rhetoric Review* offers teachers a list of 100 questions to ask students before demanding they compose in "their own" voices (1991). Toby Fulwiler's "Propositions of a Personal Nature" is a literacy autobiography composed in an alternately styled, numbered list (1988). Kathleen Blake Yancey and Michael Spooner continue their multi-voiced, diversely formatted conversations with their 1998 article "A Single Good Mind."

Lillian Bridwell-Bowles (1992) argues that we need to allow students the same diverse discourses that we as teachers are beginning to use for presenting our ideas. Elizabeth Anne Leonard in "Assignment #9" asks for a writing space that is neither just experimental nor only typical: "I want a writing that is everything" (1997); and she asks for it in a text that samples many styles, including collage and montage. And indeed, the informal essay is becoming more widespread and varied (see Auslander 1993, 1994; Herron 1992, among many others) and the academic poem (formerly published in *CCC* and occasionally still found in *WOE, EJ, RR*) could be considered an alternate form for commenting on the academic experience.

As my writing students might say: Check it out.

I say, we can and should make more out of lore in these ways, in yet undiscovered ways.

CONCLUSIONS OF SORTS

When we stroll through the house of teaching lore, we might well ask who it is we're dressed for. Or put it this way: We know the bell tolls for us. We know that even if we won't stop for death, death will stop for us. We know that, really, we have choices as writers with voices just as we have choices when we dress each morning. We can dress as we imagine teachers should dress (we've all done this) or as is most comfortable for us when we teach. We can respect or disrespect our teaching, we can fluff our feathers up so we appear more than we are, or we can get too shabby from absent-minded or unself-confident or overly-frugal neglect. We can—often (and, of course, not always)—but still I assert—often—choose. When we choose how we will be read and how we read others, we should and could begin to build our own (profession-wide?) categories of value or at least know why some categories are valued over others. We have and will make more out of lore than Steve ever imagined, back then.

NOTES

1.   My brutal distinction between teacher talk and academic talk follows on the heels of the 1995 Bartholomae and Elbow debate, and I certainly expect to add no new refinements to that discussion. For my purposes here, when considering teacher talk, I am looking at author-present prose which celebrates the first-person voice, incorporates many storytelling/narrative strategies, and invites readers into the story—often by including classroom narratives and student voices. For my purposes here, when considering scholarly or academic writing, I am looking at author-evacuated prose[2] that eschews the metaphoric or story potential for the specialized discourse/jargon of the area under discussion. In so doing, the prose sets up barbed wire fences that separate the inner and outer territories and distinguishes sharply between those who know and speak the dialect and those who don't, those who have passes to enter and exit through the gates and checkpoints and those who are not allowed through and in. Here is a sample of each voice, taken from the same essay (as is often the case, writers shift dialects midstream, sometimes in effective, sometimes in schizophrenic ways). I leave it to you, dear reader, to decide which example is which.

> Using subject position as a terministic screen in cross-boundary discourse permits analysis to operate kaleidoscopically, thereby permitting interpretation to be richly informed by the converging of dialectical perspectives. (Royster 1996, 29)

> What comes to mind for me is another saying that I heard constantly when I was growing up, "Do unto others as you would have them do unto you." In this case, we would be implored to draw conclusions about others with care and, when we do draw conclusions, to use the same type of sense and sensibility that we would ideally like for others to use in drawing conclusions about us. (Royster 1996, 33)

> Anyway, for the purposes of this chapter, think perhaps about the difference between generalist and specialist—someone who can teacher talk to anyone and someone who talks to a select few teachers just (or very) like him and/or her.

2.   See Clifford Geertz who introduces the idea of author-evacuated and author-present prose in *Works and Lives* (1988).

APPENDIX:

A HOW-TO ESSAY FOR TEACHERS (OR: A RHETORIC
OF MY RHETORIC)

As I mentioned above, Alys Culhane was visiting while I wrote this chapter and the essay you find here. In discussing it, we decided to examine the way the how-to essay performs by adding our reader's annotations to the text, thinking we would then invite you to add your own. My thanks to Alys for her usual thoughtful response to writing about writing.

Key

My annotations:	"I'M READING TO ANALYZE MY OWN RHETORICAL CHOICES"
Alys's annotations:	*"I'm reading to see how this teacher-essayist constructs her essay [my interest is in personal pedagogical essays]"*
Any other writing:	your annotations (we invite you to add them)

What I learned this Week and How I Might Say So (Today Only) About The Fat Draft and Memory Draft Revision Exercise

I have been developing a revision exercise for about three years now. It started in rough draft frustration. I had carefully developed a scheme to ask for drafting levels from students for their workshop papers—my version of zero drafting to final drafting, rough to finished, early to late. In this scheme, I tried to encourage attention to early work but not total commitment to it—something along the lines of "draft your heart out" but then be willing, still, to revise. I called my levels, for probably obvious reasons, 1) rough (unfinished but complete initial conception), 2) professional (any draft in progress shared with small or large groups or me for take-home response), and 3) portfolio—the last draft of the class (see also "Designing").

The writer lets me in on what she is doing. How essayistic; she completes her own reading.

I ALLUDE TO ZERO DRAFT TO SHOW I'VE READ ESSAYS ON REVISION, ASSUMING YOU'VE DONE THE SAME.

ordering . . .

REFERRING TO PREVIOUS TEACHING ESSAY TO 1) SAVE TIME, 2) ASSERT AUTHORITY

Immediately, I had trouble with students' rough drafts. While rough drafts could be hand-written—I didn't want them that rough—as rough as they seemed to be, as rough as conjured by the word—with shoe tracks and strange teeth marks, with stains of undisclosed liquids on paper scraps. Not all rough drafts arrived in class

problem..
detail; writing isn't formulaic

MY CREATIVE WRITER'S VOICE SNEAKING IN

looking this rough, but enough of them did to make me feel a little off center as I moved from paired responders to paired responders. So, one year, I added the concept of "full breath" rough draft—asking that the writer try to rough-out (a new improved meaning of rough, I hoped, taken from the artist's sketch) the full draft even if there were holes in it, for instance, parenthetical notes to the self to add this or that. "There should be enough 'stuff' there, text, words, ideas," I explained, "that you don't have to apologize to readers and tell them what you had *hoped* would be there; readers have the right to focus on what is there." This helped some.

solution . . .

Another year (these are teacher-talk years, of course—I'm not sure how many classes worked through this with me), and I added the fat draft. From frustration at the "how-many pages-should this draft be?" questions and the still regularly appearing overly rough rough drafts. One particularly dismal professional draft day—the time this class had moved from rough to professional but most writers still came in with only a page or two on their self-chosen topics in an elective writing class, I said, arbitrarily—"Everyone double your draft by next class. It doesn't have to be good (though it certainly may be) but it does have to be double. If you eked out one page—get to a minimum of two. If you wrote for ten pages, take the challenge of composing twenty." Doubling, I figured, was an equal opportunity challenge. And doubling would give revisers something to eliminate, alter, and shape (at this point, no one could revise by shaping, because they were still trying so hard to go forward at all).

INTENTIONAL STYLE-PLAY TO BRING READER IN (ASSUMES A COMMON SENSE OF HUMOR/POSITION)

COMPLICATION NOTED (ATTEMPT TO SHOW PROPOSED SOLUTIONS AREN'T SURE-FIRE)

MORE DIALOGUE— ASSERTING THE CLASSROOM BASE FOR THIS ESSAY

Fat draft revision had benefits—many students liked it, they said. And I saw that they needed the push; often they could obey a doubling directive although they hadn't been able to live up to an imagined page estimate (not that I give these but they do ask for them: should it be five pages, and so on?). Doubling five to ten as any writer knows is less threatening than "sit down and write ten pages."

What the teacher and student writer learn points to the unpredictability of writing!

While doubling, one student lost her draft. She panicked when the disk came up blank, and wrote a new draft. The next morning she found the old draft, combined it with the new and wrote this up in her process cover sheet. The memory draft was born—another way to double, to revise for length in order to revise for new focus.

This week, when revising my classroom handouts on fat and memory drafting, I sat at home thinking about the new advanced essay writing class I was preparing. Twenty eager-to-graduate seniors who were many of them taking the class as a final graduation assignment. Though they are friendly people and most are writing majors, they're eager to get on the road, not inclined to draft more than in response to class requirements. I considered how best to present fat and memory drafting options, whether I should have them do one and then the other as the handout suggested might be useful, wondering how I know the assignment does work (it does), how I would know/learn if a sequence of fat then memory, or memory and then fat, or memory for certain types of writers and fat for other types of writers was preferable?

As I wondered this, I began to see the history of composition research unfold before me—treatment groups to case studies to an observation of another teacher's class composing. Then, as a writer, as a teacher of writers, as a devisor of these exercises and a practitioner at times of them, I achieved teaching insight—understanding that these drafting exercises must and should function differently for each writer. Certainly the exercise solved an initial problem—allowing students to achieve more length, more text to work with—but solutions always raise further questions. In this case, was it useless to ask for a fat draft for a student with only one page? Equally, was it really useful to take a fluent drafter of ten pages and drag him or her to twenty? Classroom intuition and a need for handout efficiency caused me to group the two exercises together as "related" but I hadn't *understood* the relationship previously—memory drafts (generally) for full initial drafts would encourage the writer to choose/focus on "best of": salient points, memorable rhetorical turns, crucial stories. They could elaborate on those and re-evaluate the matrix. Fat drafts were probably more productive for those who didn't yet know where they were going. If writing-is-an-act-of-thinking theorists and writing research is right—these writers did need more words available to think through.

On Monday, I presented the assignment in this new-to-me light. Today, I'll ask the class about the choices they made and why they made them. Next week, I'll look for further confirmation or confusion of my theory in the papers they turn in.

self/reader reflexivity

This is how (maybe, I think so today at least) to use fat and memory drafts in your writing classrooms.

uncertainty—this is real

CHAPTER SIXTEEN

Theory, Practice, and the Bridge Between
The Methods Course and Reflective Rhetoric

Kathleen Blake Yancey

There is little need for pedagogy; she is finding her own truths with metaphor.

Spencer Nadler

We are what we imagine.

N. Scott Momaday

H OW HAVE I TAUGHT? HOW DO I UNDERSTAND MY OWN TEACHING? WHAT have my students learned? When I say that a methods class—a class in teaching prospective teachers—went well, that the students did learn, that I think they'll be good teachers, what do I mean? And how would I know that such assertions were true? Could I theorize more generally about my course; and more, could I theorize about how such a course-qua-type fosters the development of the student-becoming-teacher?

Short of treating students like rats in a lab or plants in a rooting medium, we can't know the answers to these questions—if by the word know, we mean the product of a monological process characterized by a scientific, technical rigor that is predictive in nature. I take it as axiomatic that since students aren't rats or plants, we can't know in that way. More precisely, I take it as axiomatic that when we work with human beings, such knowing is impossible: such knowing is too singular, too reductive, ultimately too inhuman. Life and the people who populate it are too rich and too complex for such a knowing.

Which (alas) doesn't get us off the hook: we do have a need to know what works, especially when we are working with people, perhaps more especially when we are working with people-who-are-our-students. We need to be able to identify causes of desired effects so that we can repeat them deliberately and purposefully. Given the diverse populations we serve, we need to learn how plural (perhaps even how contradictory) those effects are. And speaking very specifically as a teacher working with college students who think they too want to be English teachers—that is, as a very real teacher with very real students—I need to know what "works," what in my curriculum helps students develop the identity of teacher and how and why it "works," and for whom it works. Likewise, I need to know what gets in the way of that goal, and if that obstacle blocks only all students or just some. Ideally, I would take this knowing and weave it into something larger, a theory of how such a course achieves its goals and not: first, for this term's students-who-want-to-be-teachers; second, for the general group of students-who-want-to-be-teachers.

This chapter hopes to demonstrate how to theorize in this way—from practice and by means of reflection—as it weaves such a theory.

✳✳✳

One way to know how a student, a class, and a curriculum work—is it together?—is to see our own teaching and learning *practices* as a source of knowledge, metaphorically as a text that can be systematically observed, questioned, understood, generalized about, and refuted—in a phrase, *reflected upon*. In defining our our practice this way, as a source of knowledge, we also define ourselves as causal inquirers. According to Donald Schön, a causal inquirer focuses on a particular situation in a single organization in order to understand the problems and discords and even successes produced. Such understanding, such knowledge, is produced not by means of scientific laws, but rather through models of behavior that are generated from specific situations. As Schön puts it,

> when it [reflection] is successful, it yields not covering laws but prototypical models of causal patterns that may guide inquiry in other . . . situations—prototypes that depend, for their validity, on modification and testing in "the next situation." "Reflective transfer" seems to me a good label for this kind of generalization. (97)

Reflective transfer, the procedure that enables us to learn from and theorize our practice requires four steps: that we (1) observe and examine our own practice; (2) make hypotheses about successes and failures, as well as the reasons for each; and (3) shape the next iteration of similar experience according to what we have learned; when we (4) begin the cycle again. In the methods course, such reflective transfer has a specific application: to help us understand the *processes* by which students learn, the *assignments* that motivate and structure such learning, the responses to assignments that invite both insight and continuing engagement, and the *tasks* that resemble "real" teaching enough that to complete them one acts as (in the process of becoming) a teacher.

As defined here, reflection is necessarily collaborative: I might plan and "deliver" the curriculum, but my students will "experience" it. The points of intersection among both—the *delivered* and the *experienced* curricula—locate the place where learning and teaching occurs. In its location-as-intersection, the curriculum might also be seen as a kind of contact zone where students and the teacher negotiate their teaching and learning. To understand curriculum-as-negotitiation, of course, we rely on students' articulation of it—that is, not so much on their articulation of what they've learned that we planned, but rather their articulation of what they learned that we might not have expected. When such articulation is written, it is made visible and thus subject to review. It is, then, through their articulation of experience and a teacher's review of that articulation in light of her intent—in this case, my own—that she begins to understand the phenomenon that we are calling the methods class.

As I have discussed elsewhere (Yancey 1998), I began thinking about these issues several years ago when I determined either to teach this course in a more productive way, or to give it up. Basically, what I did was to re-design the course, replacing texts, devising new assignments, and building in reflection throughout—in bi-weekly letters, in a closed email listserver discussion, in informal texts that asked students to record and comment upon their own learning, and in formal texts that made the same demands but that called for more definitive conclusions.

Both the structures and the timing of these places for reflection vary, as the list above suggests; seen collectively, these *forms of reflection* provide multiple contexts which themselves encourage insight, both individually and together. Because they work in different genres and because they require different kinds of intellectual work, they provide multiple frames through which to understand the same experience, and it is often, as Arthur Koestler reminds us, through the crossing of such frames that insight is generated. The letters, for instance, are unstructured; they favor the writer who prefers the open page and a personal approach. Other textual places, like the formal assignments, are highly structured and highly conventionalized.

Throughout the term, I read student texts three ways. First, I collect each assignment, I respond to individual texts, and in my response, I invite additional dialogue. Second, I read the responses to each assignment in the aggregate, as a set that helps me see if my expectations are met and to determine if mid-course corrections are required. Third, at the end of the term, I read the texts in a way I am calling "reflective" (Yancey 98). To engage in this reading, I make the two steps that Lee Shulman suggests we teachers must initiate to make knowledge from our practice: (1) occlude the flow of work, and (2) present what we find to a public audience. Given that it's the end of the term, the flow of work does cease; it's a convenient stopping place. But before I can present what I may have learned, there is yet another, intermediate step: I have to read the data. In my methods course, that is a lot of material: in addition to a standard midterm, a fairly conventional paper, multiple reflective letters and emails, and about 15 in-class writing exercises, I also ask for a collaboratively produced curriculum unit and a final portfolio. Which data, then, to read? And as important, how to read?

Reading the data isn't an unusual or unlikely task, not for an English teacher. We don't call them data, but texts in fact are one kind of data, and English teachers are experienced aplenty in the reading of texts. That's what this intermediate step requires, that we *read, plot, interpret* and *evaluate* as we do for any fine text. These data are simply fine classroom texts, a set of them that we read in the aggregate as well as individually so that patterns are discerned, absences and presences made real, theory-from-practice made. Which data to read is another question, one that can take different answers. In earlier work with the methods class, for example, I've focused on reading a set of portfolios from quite different students, almost as case studies (Yancey 97). That reading has reminded me how different my students can be, taught me that the course I experience as a unified phenomenon is pluralized in student experience. Reading through selected portfolios, however, is only one means of seeing the course. Another way to see the course is to focus on particular assignments, not so much to see if the students learned what I had planned for them to learn, but rather (or perhaps also) to discern what students did learn. To do this, I put carefully designed questions to these texts. Do these texts, for instance, share common themes? If so, what does that tell us about a theory of development for prospective teachers? If not, how might that observation alter our theory? This semester, as we'll see, I've been especially interested in two aspects of teacher development.

- First, how can we help prospective teachers see their prospective students as both like them and as unlike them?
- Second, how can we help prospective teachers articulate their own learning as they learn so that they can "teach" this way, so that they can see how to direct their own—and their students'—learning?

***

It's a Monday evening early in the term, cool by Charlotte standards. We've been focusing on writing and rhetoric, taking up concepts like writing process and rhetorical situation and invention—concepts and processes that I hope these students will take into their classrooms eventually. Unfortunately, concepts such as these are new to these students, regardless of age or gender or ethnicity, and we do have a mix.[1] English majors, they've written many texts, but they haven't studied the writing or the rhetoric of texts at all.

Working at state-of-the-art PCs, students are responding to a set of sequenced categories designed to accomplish two goals. The first of the goals is to help further students' understanding of invention by giving them practice in cubing, the technique through which one investigates a subject by viewing it from multiple perspectives. I specify the first category, description, allowing five minutes for writing. The students compose at the keyboard, Leslie moving fast, her fingers barely catching her swirling thoughts, Sharon thinking for a full three minutes before putting the first finger to key. Another two minutes, and I move us to the second category, comparison; another five minutes, and I move us to contrast; then in their turn to analysis, critique, and evaluation. I'm hoping that students will learn about the power of cubing, about the insight that can be generated by explicitly moving around and through and within and without a subject.

This lesson is about more than inventional process, however; it's also about the subject under investigation, their ideal class, populated by particularized students. My goal in choosing this topic is no doubt obvious. My students have the opportunity—indeed, the task—of articulating what may only be tacit—their dream situation. At the same time, because cubing is multi-perspectival, the task requires that they see this ideal as less-than, as one that brings with it a set of students whose needs and aspirations, even when those students are good ones, can be at odds with those of the teacher. Put in the form of questions: Who are the students in this (ideal) class? How will they cooperate? How will they resist?

Leslie responds with a perspective that I have found to be all too typical: she's becoming a teacher so that she can *become her own high school teacher.* "This classroom," she says, "is almost identical to my own 11th grade honors class. There were three or four students who knew it all, and three or four who never participated. . . . I find that this classroom is unequal, just as my own." What's unusual about Leslie's response is that even as she articulates this vision, she begins its revision:

> This classroom is different mainly because it is going to be filled with energy. . . . No boring rows for a small class of 15. This class will introduce a balance between the previous literature and up and coming literature. More discussion, less standardized book report tests, and more "thinking" and "communicating" skills. More group work and more individualized thought. Definitely some sort of free writing whether in journal form or not.

Of course, I don't know which came first, the chicken or the egg: did Leslie understand tacitly that some changes to her model of the good teacher had to be made, or did the cubing exercise itself "force" such an insight? What I do know is that the cubing exercise—and this is the first time I've used it—is producing a kind of process in which *as the model is articulated, it undergoes revision.* Not that the model itself is the problem. Many of these students did have fine high school teachers, as did Leslie; it's to be expected (and hoped) that they will work from this model, and by now I've come to expect this kind of identification. But the identification wants to be a point of departure, not the terminus: that's what the cubing offers, a chance to see that identification from multiple perspectives, to contextualize it so as to understand and perhaps modify it; to develop a teacherly identity, rather than assume one already formed. Of course not all students want to replicate previous teachers: at the other end of the spectrum are those students whose schooling was troubled, who want to change school, who seem to want to *become the teacher they wish they'd had.* We see this in Jill, the second prototype.

> In contrast, my ideal class is nothing like my real experiences in school. It was like climbing a mountain with many people situated on peeks above me, ready

to knock me off and send me hurdling back to the beginning. My gear and backpack were like my wits and they kept me on the mountain despite my foes.

Given this sense of her own experience, perhaps it's not surprising that Jill focuses on her class not from a curricular perspective, but from a social one. She talks exclusively about the students, about their transition from elementary school:

All of my students have just left the security of the elementary school and feel overwhelmed by having so many classes and teachers to keep up with. They also feel threatened by the older ninth graders in the school. Many would like to go back to their smaller elementary world where they were top dog. Now, they are on the bottom of the totem pole and feel vulnerable in their new surroundings.

Jill sees the students as "insecure," as a "challenge" and even "paranoid," as she puts it, "as to how they look to everyone else in the class." And then Jill does something that I am learning to take as a developmental mark of teacher identity formation. Asked to compare her ideal classroom, Jill works as she did before, from a metaphor that provides a frame through which she can connect the old with the new, in this case a familiar race track as frame for her new, imagined class.

Teaching this group of students is like driving a race car around a crowded track. I have to have a lot of competent skills to maneuver in and out of the students working in groups, I have to have the ability to know where each child is and what I can do to help them and still stay one step ahead so I will not be run out of the room or off the track.

Several observations are worth noting here. First, while the category did ask for comparison, it didn't specify metaphor. Jill supplies comparison by means of metaphor, and we see her rely on this form of conceptualization throughout. Second, the metaphor here makes sense: I can see how teaching is related to the direction and speed and chaos and safety issues we associate with a racetrack. How important might it be that the metaphor make sense? Is there a problem if it doesn't? Third, while I think faculty in general are aware of the power of metaphor to help students grasp the unknown in many different kinds of classes (eg, see Allen), I'm also beginning to think that such metaphorical understanding is a key component of teacher identity formation. I've noted it more and more frequently now in student work in this course, not because it was invited, but because it was seized on as a means for students to express relationships they were struggling to articulate. Perhaps as important, I've observed that it's the better students who make this move. If I'm correct about this, then other questions arise:

how is it important;
what does it contribute:

shouldn't we therefore be inviting such metaphorical work;
when might we invite it;
are some metaphors better than others;
how should we respond to it?

***

A second task I use this term asks for another kind of identification: of these prospective teachers with students. That may seem obvious—that teachers teach students—but many of the prospective teachers I've encountered are like Leslie: the students they expect to teach will, they think, be just like the ones they knew in high school, *3 or 4 students who knew it all, and 3 or 4 who never participated.* What they need to understand, first, is that the students they will teach may be—probably will be—quite different than the ones they knew: more diverse, interested in different activities (and even music), challenging in ways they can only begin to appreciate. Second, the role that they as teachers will play with regard to students, of course, will be completely different. The classmate who amused them-as-student is the one who disrupts them-as-teacher. Third, and in some ways more to the point, our students are not like us: they do not necessarily love to read and write, they do not want to participate in class, they do not want to go to college. Despite those differences, however, we need to be able to identify with them, perhaps most especially with the students who seem so foreign to us. Identification is the point at which learning and teaching can begin.[2]

To accomplish this aim of helping students identify with students, I've created a focused exercise that comes in two parts. In the first, we look in class at a student text written by a high school student named Ryan: a literary analysis. I ask the members of the class to read the text and to respond to it as a high school teacher. After they do this, we share perceptions and responses. The text itself is read almost universally by the entire class, though given the text I've chosen, that's no surprise. As one student put it,

> Looking . . . at Ryan's Vietnam paper, a paper flawed by grammatical errors, by poor transitions from paragraph to paragraph and by incomplete development of ideas, the reader would deduce that Ryan . . . is an unskilled writer who is trying to complete an assignment but does not have the linguistic skills to do so.

The responses to Ryan's text are first efforts: i.e., critical, not necessarily because the prospective teachers want to be critical, but because they too read out of their experience, so they think being critical is a mark of a good teacher, the smart teacher. (This in itself tells us something else about our own practice, but this is a story for another day.) We talk about the rhetorical stance of respondent; we talk about the role of praise in developing text and writer; we link the two. What genuine praise can we offer to Ryan?

But more importantly, after this first exercise in reading and responding to student texts, I offer a surprise: an entire portfolio that Ryan has composed. It opens with a résumé, includes a letter based on a piece of literature, includes the paper we just looked at as well as some inventional work and an earlier draft that preceded it. Take the portfolio home, I say, and read it. Think about it. And write:

- Who is this student?
- What can he do well?
- What kind of writing would suit his interests?
- What kind of curriculum might suit him?
- What recommendations will you make?

What my students make of Ryan could fill the course. They do exactly what it is that I do here: *read the data, reflect upon it, make meaning.* So while we read Ryan similarly, we posit alternative theories about what might work with him.

In answer to who Ryan is: a student who isn't very academic. "His résumé," Lynn notes, "doesn't include the academic courses he has taken . . . but does list his electives [Horticulture I and II, Landscaping, Woodworking, and Drafting]. Judging by these classes . . . I tend to think that his interests are more vocational than scholastic." Ryan has held restaurant and landscaping jobs, and "he is Vice President of the Future Farmers of America; he's not only a hard worker, but someone who is capable of assuming a responsible leadership position. His résumé indicates that he is looking for another landscaping position but doesn't mention his plans (if any) to continue on to college to further his education."

As to what he can do well, we see the beginnings of disagreement. Some of the students think he can write well—he "seems to have a good grasp on the writing process" and "he is a very good student"—while others think he "appears to be doing just enough to get by." As to what kinds of writing we might ask of him and what curriculum would suit him and what recommendations we would make, we have many options to consider. Given Ryan's blue-collar work interests, Karen suggests "Perhaps something with a socialistic ring . . . . I believe leaning it more toward socialistic novels might get more in touch with Ryan's life. Books such as *The Grapes of Wrath, The Jungle,* or *The Good Earth* might be more of an inspiration than *Fallen Angels.*" Alternatively, Sharon suggests a rhetorically informed, work-based approach more congruent with what she understands as his interests:

Ryan's efforts at writing about a Vietnam movie and book were not successful, but if he had been asked to write a different type of paper on a different topic, the results might have been different. Ryan is interested in horticulture. If he were asked to write directions for a specific task such as planting azaleas, he might produce a document which would be useful to his customers at the Flower Mill. Ryan has also been employed for several years. He might be able to write a list of suggestions that teenage jobseekers could use to get and keep jobs. If he saw a reason for writing something, a job application essay for example, he would work hard to produce an acceptable document. His writing and editing efforts would have purpose to them. He would be motivated to learn from his mistakes.

Without my introducing a tech-prep model, Sharon's response sounds the arguments for it, a curriculum that draws from and also informs the work-related experiences of students preparing to enter the world of work after high school.

Jill begins by *identifying Ryan as one of us.* "Overall," she says, "Ryan would probably do better writing about a topic he liked, but then so would all of us." Of course. But Jill wants the best of both worlds, the tech-prep orientation that extends beyond. Put as a question, is there a way to bridge the gap from what we like to what else we might learn to like? Jill suggests how we might in the language of her philosophy of teaching:

> Being an expressivist teacher, I would encourage Ryan to write about a topic . . . which he really cared about. This would help him to develop his writing skills with a topic that he would put a lot of effort into. Once he was confident in his skills, I would lead him into other areas of writing such as the Vietnam paper he worked on for his teacher. At least, maybe it would bridge a gap for him and let him see how all writing is interconnected, and that he could do well writing on any subject.

Ryan's portfolio was intended to show that while different from us, he is at the same time very like us. By reading Ryan through his own texts, we can see—and value—the kid that our curriculum is supposed to help, we can see the debates about curriculum and how they develop, we can take those up ourselves in the language of the profession—as applied to a real student.

Ryan begins to make the curriculum real. The students begin to work as reflective practitioners.

***

Undergraduate students talk about becoming teachers with an implied sense (almost urgent) that as one migrates to the position of teacher, she or he leaves—abandons or abdicates?—the position of student. But good teachers are always students: learning about their own learning processes, about their teaching, about curricula, about students. And increasingly, teachers are working not alone, but together to undertake this learning, whether they do this within a school, as part of a National Council of Teachers of English (NCTE)-sponsored research group, as participants in an advanced institute of the National Writing Project, or as members of an American Association of Higher Education (AAHE) teaching circle. The kind of inquiry, then, characteristic of faculty is what the next assignment seeks to foster.

All the students are assigned to a group that is to design a very short, non-graded curriculum unit. The activity is what I call a "finger exercise," a piano-based term for rehearsal, in this case a rehearsal for the team-based formal curriculum unit the students will create later in the term. Given that they have never completed a unit before, there is much to be learned, about themselves as learners, about processes and strategies that work (or don't), about how the pieces of a unit should fit, about thinking like a teacher.

Halfway through the exercise, the students are asked to reflect on it, in a variation of what Schön calls reflection-in-action: "We think critically about the thinking that got us into this fix or opportunity; and we may in the process, restructure strategies of action, understandings of phenomena, or ways of framing problems." (28) To reflect in this way, students are asked to address three questions:

- How's it going?
- What's left to do?
- What are you learning?

The first question, of course, requires a kind of judgment-in-process, the kind of judgment that informs formative assessment. Based on such an evaluation, we continue with our plans, or we rewrite them. The second question calls for both projection and planning: given our understandings—of a project in-progress and of what the final product should look like—what else do we need to do? The third question goes to what it is that the students can take with them. It's here that I focus.

A talented soccer player, Shayna still wants to teach alone:

I would like to say that I am learning how to play nice with my group mates. I am definitely opposed to some of the ideas, but I guess I have to learn to compromise. I know that I would do things differently, more creatively. I am learning that I might not be too bad at this stuff. I have a lot of ideas that are interesting to me, at least. I have learned and I am trying to learn to implement the idea of fit between assessment and class instruction. This is one of the things I am struggling with in my group.

Regardless of task, students always can learn about themselves; the self presents a starting place for learning about material and about students and about how to make those match in useful ways. What happens, however, when what is intended as a starting place marks only stasis?

Wendy has learned both about herself and about how to proceed. "I have learned to speak up and to not be intimidated by the rush to get finished . . . . I also should back up my thoughts and support what I am saying to add validity while not sounding like a 'know-it-all.'" Wendy's learning about herself is thus relativized to working with others successfully, and to do this, she sees the need to communicate in qualified ways, with *support* and *thought* for the sake of *validity*. And she is learning about sequence as well:

I think that as we developed the unit, we made a mistake by choosing the text and the activity before we stated the goal. I feel that most of our work has been an attempt to create and structure our unit so that it fits the text and activity instead of working from our goal and then choosing the text and activity.

How we structure what we do matters: for teachers as well as for students, which is what Lynn discovered as well:

> Although I am not in an actual classroom, I think this lesson is forcing me to learn about the flow of knowledge. There must be an obvious flow to the information students receive and the assignments you ask them to do. This is also helping me understand the length of time needed for specific activities and the importance of the directions you as the teacher provide. If you don't give good directions, you don't have much of a right to complain if you get shoddy work in return.

According to Lynn, the *flow of knowledge* is created through *information* and *assignments* and timing and *directions*. In an ideal world, Lynn could take this unit into a real school and see how it fares as *flow of knowledge*. Even in our world, however, she understands a multi-faceted way to approach curriculum planning.

Perhaps Leslie says it best: "I'm learning to think like a teacher. That's a lot."

***

The end of the term: students have brought in all their texts, informal, formal and those in-between. Somehow they need to select from these a set that will show that they know what it means to be a teacher, can do some of what that requires, understand some of what else needs to be learned. I set a list of questions to help them frame these tasks:

- Describe the student who came through the door in January.
- Describe the teacher to be who is leaving in May.
- What has this person learned about theory?
- How does this theory connect to/extend what you have learned/experienced previously?
- What are the relationships among theory, practice, and reflection?

The intent of the questions is to help the students move, retrospectively, from the student to the prospective teacher, from a knowledge of theory in the abstract to an awareness of practice theorized through the lens of reflection. As I read these finger exercises, I again see the different forms that the course took, the diverse curricula that these students *experienced*.

Karen plays back to me a clean, reductive version of these inter-relationships: "Via reflection, you tie together the loose strings of your starting theory and the practice you have encountered to create a custom theory that suits you as a teacher and your students to a 'T.'" Well, yes. But no: somehow it doesn't seem quite so simple to me.

Naila, a returning student, represents a population that is increasing in size. Surprisingly, the curriculum that was, admittedly, geared to the novice seems to provide what she needs as well, and it is now that she sorts through it all, reflectively.

With knowledge of the various theories of English (such as the social construct, expressive, and the uncommon sense approaches to teaching), I have come to the place where I can at least consider those views rather than ignore them because they do not fit in with my own view of teaching. Ignorance of these approaches only brought fear of these approaches. Now that I have come to understand them better, I am more free to implement them as I see fit.

Leslie, the most typical of the students in this course, talks about who she was, who she is, and how they are still linked.

I would have to say that the person who came into the class in January was very ideal. I had dreams of a perfect class with awesome students. . . . Perhaps, but not entirely, the individual thought more about her future job as "the teacher" and not her job to educate "the students." I say not entirely because I know that she emphasized students' needs but did not know the proper avenues to take to prioritize them.

As important, Leslie sees a less tidy, but more accurate way for theory, practice and reflection to work:

Theory, practice and reflection relate in one simple word: *teacher*. The teacher has to correlate them. He/she has to decide who, how, why, etc. The theory may not always fit the practice, but the reflection will show that mismatch. Basically, I find in practice a theory may have to be readjusted, worked identically, or discarded. A reflection, however, should be constant in order to see what fits, works and needs tossing and revising.

***

I'm reading the portfolios that these students have composed: more than half of them use metaphor as a means of expressing what they've learned and who they've become.

***

I began this reflective quest by looking at two questions:

- First, how can we help prospective teachers see their prospective students as both like them and unlike them?
- Second, how can we help prospective teachers articulate their own learning as they learn so that they understand how we make knowledge from experience and use that to help them direct their own—and their students'—learning?

I think the tasks I set—the cubing and the work with Ryan's portfolio—began to help these prospective teachers see their prospective students as something more than replications of themselves (people who love to read and write already). I also think the mix—between the imagined students created through the cubing and the textually embodied real students—was serendipitous. Should I modify the sequence so as to make the mix, and the textually embodied students particuarly, more integral to the course, possibly by introducing the portfolio very early and returning to it periodically; or using a set of portfolios, perhaps from different kinds of students, at predictable points during the term; or asking that the students that we construct through reading the portfolios be put into dialectic with the imagined ones?

I think the reflection in action worked fairly well for all the students. Some of them saw how their learning will benefit them as teachers; some saw how it could work for them as students: all them learned. Again, though, I need to make more of an explicit link from this reflection in action to *reflective teaching:* so, how to do that, and when?

***

My claim has also been that teaching this course reflectively is a knowledge-making enterprise. If that's so, what have I learned?

That prospective teachers often bring with them a model of a teacher they want to be, their favorite teacher or the one they wished they'd had. Identifying which model they are working from, asking them if it's appropriate given the other information, and providing opportunities for model revision is a primary objective of a methods course. Question: Do "better" students tend to favor a particular kind of model? Do all models require revision?

That better students tend to focus on the curriculum and the students; weaker ones tend to focus on themselves. Like Leslie and Lynn, the better student, by which I mean the student who has developed some readiness to teach, can move to think about teaching rhetorically—as a subject matter having an audience as well as a rhetor. Weaker students, like Karen, still learn, but that learning is focused more on self, less on the rhetoric of teaching. Question: what activities, what questions can help weaker students move outside the self? Or is there, in fact, a way to accelerate such readiness?

That seeing a high school student through multiple texts exerts a profound influence on prospective teachers. Through such a rich portrait, they see a human being even when he or she seems quite different from them. They then begin to take up important curricular matters, to articulate their own sense of fit between kid and school, to begin to develop their own theory about curriculum and teaching. Question: Is this an activity that we should perhaps start with? Can I be more specific about the kind of influence I think it exerts?

That in many ways this course is an exercise in identity and identification. Now I've made this claim before, and it seems pretty obvious (Yancey 1997). What I didn't appreciate then and am only coming to appreciate now, however, is twofold: (1) the multiple kinds of identity; and (2) the ways they interact and can even be at cross-purposes. For instance:

- We have a student identity: the product of what I've called the lived curriculum, including learning styles, work habits, and so on; this is what the prospective teachers bring into the classroom with them;

- We have identity qua invention: inventing an identity, in this case the identity of teacher (and such an identity is multi-selved); this is perhaps the overall purpose of the course, to start the processes that will continue throughout a teaching life;
- We have identification with the teacher: the link between a prospective teacher and a teacher from the past, and the link between a prospective teacher and the group of teachers that she or he will become a part of;
- We have identification with the prospective students: seeing in those students oneself so that the students are not positioned as alien, especially when their linguistic virtuosity seems at odds with the values that tend to inculcate college English departments; appreciating what that student brings to the class;
- We have over-identification with both students and teachers (Yancey, forthcoming): this takes the form of wanting to replicate another teacher, or seeing a student so much as a version of an earlier self of ours that we can't see the student in any other way, despite what such a frame masks; such an identification needs revision.

Negotiating among these is the life-long act of inventing oneself as a teacher.

That prospective teachers can reflect—can read the data, interpret it, and make sense of it—when they walk in the door. The students in this course experienced no difficulty in reading Ryan's texts, in talking about his strengths, in using the understanding so gleaned to think about learning and teaching. Such reflection should be a primary activity of the course, particularly of a methods course that does not have a practicum attached to it. These texts provide one means of making several abstract issues real. Question: What other kinds of reflection should we include? Toward what end?

That all students are ready to deal with theory-practice relationships, but the weaker students will tend to understand them more mechanistically. Question: how can we avoid this?

That I am developing here a profile of weaker/stronger student. The weaker student is focused on self, sees relationships mechanistically, tends to want to replicate a model rather then develop her/his own. The stronger student isn't necessarily more flexible, but is able to manage the multiple variables in a teaching situation in a theorized way; s/he is able to see how something works for students quite apart from how it server his or her interests. S/he also has a stronger sense of the model of teacher s/he seeks to embody.

That if such a profile is accurate, it would have implications for the methods course; what might those be?

That the methods course in some sense isn't really about methods or materials or goals—about the information on the syllabus—at all, or it's about much more than that. It's a rhetorical activity through which students begin to invent themselves as teachers, through which they navigate between and among various kinds of identity and identifications, through which through their own reflections they learn how to articulate these issues.

***

The term concluded, I'm reading the student evaluations of the course. The resistance to much of this pedagogy and philosophy hasn't (I'm afraid) disappeared yet. I get high marks for what I know, and high marks for the challenges I pose, but the students also say that it's too much, too fast, too different. I've heard this before.

Again, I think about why.

One book the students read is Mayher's *Uncommon Sense*, and what they say is true: I advocate Mayher's approach; I see it as mine. Many of them do not share my enthusiasm, those who do grow into it slowly, and (I remind myself) it's easy to see why. They embody common sense, these students: common sense is how they have both succeeded and won praise. *It's not surprising—indeed, it's predictable—that they would want to be common sense teachers themselves.* I've known this, I've seen this before, but I'm appreciating it anew. I'm finding another way to articulate it.

As I think about and express this observation, however, I have to do what it is that I have asked them to do, with Ryan: first, read the data; second, read the data from their perspective, not mine, so that I can devise a better curriculum *for them*. I've read the data, and I begin to think about it in the Perry's terms of dualism, more specifically as applied by Anson to faculty development.

In talking about teaching styles, Anson sketches what he calls a "continuum of development, from the rigidly dualistic style to the balanced, mature, reflective style." Unsure of "their own expertise and authority," novice teachers particularly, Anson speculates,

> may be especially vulnerable to this dualism. Threatened by the prospect of admitting to students that they can't say with certainty what makes writing 'good'—that 'good' and 'bad' are actually relative and often subjective concepts—these teachers cling desperately to what they do know and can impose objectively as standards for assessment: the rules of punctuation . . . . For the dualistic teacher, response is teacher-based and egocentric, a way of displaying intellectual prowess, a way of asserting authority. (356) In other words, Anson is suggesting a kind of developmental process, and although he is profiling the teacher of writing, it seems to fit for the developing teacher of English more generally as well. He speaks about moving from the right/wrong stance of dualism, to a kind of relativism, then to a "reflective" teaching "related to the depth of a teacher's explorations into the practice and teaching of composition" (356).

This makes sense to me, but it raises several questions. If teachers and prospective teachers follow such a developmental process, is it stage-bound? In other words, do prospective teachers proceed in these three steps as outlined, in sequence? If so, shouldn't I beginning with the first stage, a dualistic one? Worse, have I been short-circuiting a necessary developmental process when I ask students to leap ahead: to practice the stance of a reflective teacher? Or, assuming a stage-bound model: is there a way of preparing for students for it, even accelerating it? Or: is it the case that the developmental process as outlined here isn't stage-bound at all, but rather cyclic? I mention this because in working with some graduate tutors to try and determine how it is that they think they learned to tutor—and I take tutoring to be a form of teaching—we decided on "cycling" as the metaphor. There were, these tutors say, various experiences that they as tutors shared, but *the progress of those experiences differed from individual to individual.* Overall, the progress was recursive. Thus, the metaphor of the cycle. Perhaps that's what I sense here as well, especially since some of the prospective teachers described herein moved very quickly to relative and reflective stances. In fact, in some cases, I think they *started* with the more mature stances. That's what I think I saw in some of the responses, in the cubing, for instance, and in the work with Ryan. But how can I be certain of this? And if there is development of this sort, and if it is cyclic, how else might I change the course to accommodate that? I wonder, even offhandedly, if trying to develop this metaphor and then using it with the prospective teachers would help us all create a new language that we could use to talk about this development, a frame against which we could plot it, a(nother) means for inventing themselves as teachers.

I find myself, you see, like my students: looking for metaphors that help me understand.

***

When reflection "works," it raises as many questions as it answers, perhaps more. It works from the particular to the general without ever leaving the particular. It works by asking that we articulate the tacit, that we frame our observations multiply, that we look for a coherence that patterns without disguising or discoloring or misrepresenting.

Through a systematic, coherent, and often-analytical reflection, we learn—what we know now, and what we need to learn next.

NOTES

1. This observation, that future English teachers know a fair amount about literature and relatively little about rhetoric, is not news: see, for instance, Beth Burch, "Finding Out What's in Their Heads."
2. Although it's beyond the scope of this paper, there seems to be a clear connection between the sense of identity invoked here and Kenneth Burke's notion of identification.

CHAPTER SEVENTEEN

Rewriting Praxis (and Redefining Texts) in Composition Research

Nancy Maloney Grimm
Anne Frances Wysocki
Marilyn M. Cooper

THE GENERAL CALL

"We were simply in a mess, not in research…"
Shaughnessy, quoted in Maher, 234

*I*N 1994, I RECEIVED A CALL FOR CONTRIBUTIONS TO A WRITING CENTER collection that would feature multivoiced perspectives on writing center issues. I approached two other graduate students, Marsha Penti and Suhail Islam, about joining me in composing a chapter for the book. The call for proposals stipulated that chapters had to be written by at least three authors: a faculty member and/or writing center director, a writing center tutor, and a student-user of a writing center.

The call for proposals came at a time when the three of us had too much on our plates already. All three of us were people in midlife with professional, family, and graduate school responsibilities; we each qualified in all three roles: we were faculty, we were writing center tutors, and we used writing centers. One potential collaborator—Marsha Penti—was my colleague, friend, or employee, depending on which room or which conversation we were engaged in at the time. Together we shared a passion for writing center work rooted in family histories of immigrant and working-class experience, and we shared a strong commitment to bringing revisionist literacy theory to bear on daily practice. The other potential collaborator, Suhail Islam, a native of Bangladesh, combines an interest in postcolonial studies with an affinity for writing center work.

The three of us longed for ways to merge critically the understandings we gained from working with writing center students, the theories we discussed in graduate seminars and writing center meetings, and the habits and practices of many years of composition teaching. Aware of the gaps we discovered regularly in the writing center between what teachers intended and students understood, we sought for ways to achieve a similar perspective on our own teaching efforts. Aware of the ways our reading of revisionist theories offered new perspectives on writing center work, we looked for ways to bring these to bear on writing center practice.

The ways we "just normally" do things—like writing an academic article—come into question when they no longer seem useful. To many scholars now—in cultural studies, education, anthropology, as well as composition studies—an epistemology that requires a unified perspective no longer seems useful in making sense of situations structured by multiple perspectives, and thus, too, representing this research in an article that takes up a unified perspective and unified conclusions becomes frustrating... if not a misrepresentation. Lucille McCarthy and Stephen Fishman (for example) note that:

> *the single-voiced, monologic style of academic discourse makes it a difficult form in which to present the multivoiced situations the naturalistic investigator seeks to represent. Although the impersonal voice of academic writing can describe various interpretations or opinions, it is not well designed to capture the diverse ways informants go at the world and their diverse discourses, exactly what naturalistic inquiry aims to construct. (156)*

Similarly, the breakdown between public and private spaces and public and private areas of life—along with the realization that an individual's rational thinking, once believed to be essentially separate from the local circumstances of the individual's life, is ineluctably influenced by autobiographical factors—has led to frustration with dispassionate, impersonal ways of representing research. Looking for ways to include the multiple voices and perspectives that construct rich representations of phenomena and for new ways to relate the general and particular, theory and practice, these scholars have rejected the straitjacket of the well-made academic article with its unified perspective and coherent argument; they have turned instead to biographical, autobiographical, and personal narratives and to collaborative multi-voiced texts, and to disjunctive, hypertextual, or poetic forms. These experiments offer us an occasion to redefine not only knowledge but also how we represent knowledge in texts.

On a Web page, Michael Spooner and Kathleen Yancey (writing as Myka Vielstimmig) argue, quickly, for these new textual representations and what they might bring:

> *This, then is not an argument *against* The Essay or print or conventional logic. It is an argument *toward* another kind of essay: a text whose logic is*

intuitive, associative, emergent,
dialogic, multiple.

It admits

narrative

and

exposition

and

pattern.

It allows, as Susan Miller
says of the collaborative
essay, for

differentiation

without exclusion, such that
it resists becoming unified in
a community of shared final
ends. It is an essay of
radically different identity
politics, of radically different
mentality.

It is an essay the academy is learning
to write.

(Vielstimmig)

Spooner and Yancey's enthusiasm for such experiments comes out of the context of the paratactic writing they have learned to value in electronic exchanges, where multiple voices and multiple perspectives intertwine. Similarly, in a book-piece that takes its form from hypertext, Carole Maso addresses directly those who are "afraid.... that the novel is dying." She equates the "traditional" forms of book-writing with business as usual, with exclusion and hegemony, the Rolling Stones, the Oklahoma City bombing, Nazism... and she says:

> *The future is all the people who've ever been kept out, singing.... May we learn something from each other. Electronic writing will help us to think about impermanence, facility, fragility and freedom, spatial intensities, irreverences, experimentation, new worlds, clean slates.... (56, 59)*

Maso says that she has a dream:

> *....that this new tolerance might set a tone, give an example. This openness in acceptance of texts, of forms, this freedom, this embrace will serve as models for how to live. Will be the model for a new world order—in my dream. A way to live better—in my dream. (60)*

But the call for new texts that mix voices and perspectives comes as well from those whose writing appears primarily on paper. Ruth Behar, in writing her book *Translated Woman*, discovered that to represent different voices and perspectives she needed to also mix genres, and she calls her book a *historia*, a Spanish word used by her subject/comadre that does not distinguish between history and story. Behar notes:

> *The texts we write today partake of the same crisscrossed genealogy and fluctuating value that characterizes all of our other commodities; they are as polyglot as the automobile part stamped "Made in Brazil" that are commissioned for a factory in Detroit but produced in a sweatshop in Los Angeles employing Latino and Asian migrants. (17)*

Closer to our own fields, Richard Miller, echoing Lester Faigley's remark that ethics "is finding the spaces to listen" (239), muses that :

> *...whether one is constructing a self or studying a culture, one must confront the sheer necessity of acquiring a kind of multi-vocal fluency, an ability to hear things previously shut out or ignored, to attend to matters that might otherwise be overlooked or dismissed as irrelevant, to accept, in effect, the fact that learning to speak in such a way that one gets heard is a lifelong project that involves, perhaps paradoxically, first learning how to listen better to others. (285)*

These calls for new ways of writing and new ways of listening that emphasize paying attention to the multiple voices and polyglot texts that structure our lives assume not only a new definition of knowledge as essentially collaborative, complex, and often contradictory, but also assume a new purpose for knowledge. As Maso suggests, they are implicit calls for "a new world order .... a way to live better." In this same vein, Patricia Sullivan makes clear that the motivation for finding ways to include the voices of others in research writing is not just epistemological but also ethical, that scholars can no longer think of knowledge as a product they construct in isolation from those others they study but rather as powerful practices that affect others who must be included if we are to develop ethical and effective practices. Sullivan concludes, "If we consider at the outset where our speech is going and what it will do there, and if we enlist the voices of others to guide us along the way, trusting the other to teach us what we need to know, we will be less likely to fall prey to the temptation ever before us as academics to view research as an end in itself and the knowledge we produce as its own justification" (112).

What these calls for new writing recognize is that if theory changes—if theory recognizes the need for opening our work to voices expressing what has hitherto gone unheard—then practice too must change... as well as, then, the fluctuating relations between theory and practice. In what follows, we consider several of the strategies that allow written representations of research to respond to these calls; we also pause over some of the discomforts that meet these attempts to bridge theory and practice.

RE-WRITING: REPRESENTATIONS OF OTHERS AND SELVES

Composition scholars such as Susan Miller, Lester Faigley, and Marguerite Helmers have challenged us to revise our negative representations of students as others whose lack of agency, skill, knowledge, and motivation make our ministrations necessary. Similarly, in arguing for new forms of designing and representing ethnographic work in composition, Patricia Sullivan points out:

> *A central question, then, for those who write ethnographies about writing communities is: How can we conceive and reflect the "other," the not-us, in the process of inquiry such that we convey otherness in its own terms? How can we adequately transcribe and represent the lived experiences of others—inscribe an other's reality—in a text that is marked through and through by our own discursive presence? (97)*

She advocates new strategies of representation of research, such as self-reflexivity, dialogue, and collaborative writing (the latter two of which she finds exemplified in Denny Taylor and Catherine Dorsey-Gaines' *Growing Up Literate*, Elizabeth Chiseri-Strater's *Academic Literacies*, and Danling Fu's *My Trouble Is My English*). And she argues that it is essential for us to find effective ways to acknowledge in our writing "not only our own agency but our responsibility to effect what change we can when we encounter social inequities" (112).

At the time of that paper call, I was in a full-time professional staff position as the director of the writing center, and Marsha and Suhail were graduate teaching assistants who taught in the composition program and worked in the writing center. Although I was responsible for supervising and training them in the writing center, I was also their colleague in graduate seminars. Having gotten into the habit of regarding composition practices from students' perspectives before I began graduate study, I was attracted to research that risks calling attention to the gaps that are visible from underneath the social fabric of teaching, a perspective that reveals tangled threads and skipped stitches. My interest in literacy theory intersected with Suhail's and Marsha's theoretical interests. Together we admired and discussed the work of scholars like Elizabeth Ellsworth, Anne DiPardo, Carol Severino, Linda Brodkey, Lester Faigley, Glynda Hull, and Mike Rose who showed how in spite of the best individual and institutional intentions, we composition specialists often miss the mark, especially with students whose experience falls outside the white middle class subjectivity typically invoked by composition practices.

The three of us were convinced that writing centers had much to gain from a reformulation of subjectivity that would enable students to do more than accept the positions offered to them. We also knew from experience that writing centers had much to contribute to the field's discussion of how students negotiate their personal histories with institutional expectations and how students exceed the normalized subjectivity. Both writing center workers and composition scholars had much to learn from richer contextualizations of student performances. The primary issue that concerned us was the extent to which the writing center was implicated, along with composition, in the cultural work of regulating student subjectivity. We had witnessed many students trying to write the paper the teacher wanted them to write, adjusting what they wanted to say in response to hints they collected about what teachers were "looking for." Many of the students at our technological university, although not particularly interested in writing, were motivated enough by concern about their grade point averages to do what they were expected to do. They had learned to use the writing center to improve their performance. Because they are predominantly a white, urban, middle-class population, they are pretty good at "psyching out" their teachers. They had learned what Brodkey calls the fluency trick—"write a thesis statement simple enough that it can *appear* to be adequately elaborated and naturally resolved in the requisite number of words" (137). "Good" student writers who master the fluency trick learn to ignore the complexity of topics.

The students who had the most difficulty learning the fluency trick were those whose backgrounds were not white, middle-class, urban; these were the students who frequently were told their papers were undeveloped. We wanted to learn more from those students, to have access to their thinking about their work in a composition course in order to better understand the degree to which the tacit expectations of composition practices were regulating access and subjectivity. As writing center workers, we wanted to think about ways we might suggest that such students could both recognize and intervene in the subjectivity constructed by an assignment. We suspected that "writing that matters" might be different for such students. We hoped that in our multiple roles as writing center and composition specialists we might begin to design courses that created more space and more support for students to negotiate their conflicts with the cultural work of composition.

James Clifford opens the collection *Writing Culture* by considering a photograph of Stephen Tyler in the field writing notes with his back turned to his informant and argues that this collection "undermines overly transparent modes of authority, and it draws attention to the historical predicament of ethnography, the fact that it is always caught up in the invention, not the representation of cultures" (2). This problematizing of the relationship between the anthropologist in the field and his or her informants and therefore of the ability—and the goal—of impersonal, univocal anthropological discourse to represent cultures accurately led many of the collection's contributors to "enthusiastically advocate experimental forms of writing" and to fuse approaches from a variety of disciplines (3). Ruth Behar acknowledges the impact on anthropology of the idea of ethnography as writing proposed in this collection but traces her own experimental *historia* instead to earlier critiques of anthropology by Chicanos and Chicanas and especially Chicana creative writers who had taken up the question of who has the right to represent cultures "by writing their culture in highly innovative forms that combined personal ethnographies with critique, poetry, and storytelling" (15). Behar notes especially as influences on her work the novels of Sandra Cisneros and Gloria Anzaldúa's *Borderlands/La Frontera*, a book that has also been influential in composition and literacy studies.

> Marsha, Suhail, and I entered into the project in the spirit of bridging the gap between theory and practice and in the desire to bring differently situated voices into theoretical discussions of subjectivity and agency. Not only did the exigencies of daily life make it difficult to merge our understandings, but also our acceptance of our institutional roles kept these understandings separated. Those of us who are moving about among the various sites of knowledge production often have the strongest sense of the connections and the contradictions and yet at the same time we have the least amount of time to reflect on them.
>
> Although all three of us simultaneously held all three of the subject positions called for in the proposal, we wanted undergraduate writing center students to be part of our discussions. We worried that the students we most wanted to join us—those students who frequently earned C+s in spite of what they thought were their best efforts—were not likely to be eager coauthors on a faculty research project. We had little time to reflect on how to sort out our responsibilities as collaborators, and for a while it looked as though another good idea would die for want of time to implement it.
>
> That is, until one day during the first week of a new term when Marsha popped into my office. She had two students in her cultural studies based composition class whom her intuition told her would make good collaborators. Serendipity ruled: both students had already signed up for weekly appointments in the writing center with Suhail. Marsha approached Rebecca Townsend and Jeff Barrett about whether they would be interested in working with us and after a meeting to learn further details, they surprised us by readily agreeing to be partners in what, for want of a better term to put on a file folder, I began calling the "Agency Project."

At the time, we did not think of ourselves as researchers, but instead as collaborators preparing to write a multi-voiced paper. We weren't worried about data collection or methodology or triangulation because we were representing this project to ourselves as writing an interpretive essay that would bring theoretical discussions of subjectivity and agency to bear on the experience of two students enrolled in a cultural studies based composition course. We made only a few deliberate decisions. Suhail didn't have time to be a full participant, so Marsha and I agreed to draw him in later in the project. Jeff and Rebecca were interested in talking about the issues we presented to them, but reluctant to assume the role of writers, so we agreed that I would meet with them individually several times during the progress of the course and tape our conversations for later retrieval. In order to not influence Marsha's judgment of Rebecca's or Jeff's work nor to give Rebecca and Jeff reason to feel they had to embellish their sense of what they were learning (or not learning), we agreed that Marsha would not have access to details of the conversations until final grades were submitted. Rebecca and Jeff knew they could share details of their discussions with Marsha or Suhail if they chose, but as much as possible we wanted Rebecca and Jeff's experiences in the course to be as they would have been had they not participated in the project. We did not want to treat them as "subjects" of a study we were conducting but instead as reflective partners in a collaborative project.

Aside from these deliberate decisions, the preparations assumed other forms by default, influenced by our scholarly interests, our previous research experience in ethnography and case study, our varied personal and political histories. We made no attempt to achieve an objective stance; we were writing together because of intersections and intuitions. Marsha, Suhail, and I articulated questions about the degree to which students of working class backgrounds—students who fall outside the "preeconomic, presexual, prepolitical" subjectivity that composition assignments generally offer them (S. Miller 87)— were able to claim agency in a curriculum influenced by a cultural studies model. We drew on our memories of literacy experiences that attempted to impose a neutralized dominant culture on imaginations that had been formed by nonmainstream experiences. Our reading of theory, our personal backgrounds, our writing center experience had raised our concerns about the whole regulatory project of composition, and we wondered if any approach to teaching composition allowed students to fashion positions that allowed them to negotiate the cultural expectations of composition with their personal histories. We were articulating questions that couldn't be answered but certainly questions that needed to be explored; we wanted to hear from Jeff and

Rebecca about the ways their literacy histories intersected with their efforts in composition. Would a cultural studies approach allow students of difference increased opportunities to claim a critical edge from (or on) their experience or was this intent of cultural studies subsumed in composition's overall conservative function of recruiting students into middle class attitudes, values, ways of thinking, speaking, and writing? And so our work began—not as ethnographic or case study research—but instead as conversations and explorations that would lead to a collaborative essay of interest to writing center people.

Scheduling and facilitating individual conversations with Jeff and Rebecca was the easy part. Rapport was also easy to achieve with two students so strongly unaffected by all the middle-class routines of polite conversation. Jeff was taciturn and his wry humor about institutional work (either his experience in the Navy or in school) frequently made me laugh. Rebecca was emotionally honest and totally disregarded conversational barriers normally in place between student and teacher. I grew attached to both students, and respect for their efforts in the face of institutional barriers and frustration brought tears to my eyes as snatches of their remarks returned to me as I drove home from work.

No, there was no researcher's objectivity here.

During a frantic term in which I traveled on job interviews, completed and defended my dissertation, and maintained my full-time responsibilities as director of the writing center and campus learning centers, I luxuriated in the pleasure of closing my office door, turning down the answering machine, and sitting down to talk with Rebecca or Jeff about what I came to understand as their conflicted relationship with school and with literacy. Our one hour scheduled appointments stretched into two as I listened to their stories, and they offered more details. On the other hand, I had no problem maintaining the agreement to not discuss details with Marsha or Suhail as life outside those rare quiet conversations was so hectic.

These struggles with how to include the undergraduate students, how to manage relationships with collaborators, and how to think about what kind of research is being undertaken show how closely intermingled are the questions of what research is and what it is supposed to achieve and what practices—both collecting "data" or stories and writing articles—can enact that theory. In anthropology, the stimulus to think concurrently about what kind of knowledge anthropologists were constructing and how they were interacting with their subjects came not only from *Writing Culture* but also from feminist social theory. Feminists too were concerned with questions of how to listen better to others, to represent their perspectives, and to represent the knowledge that comes out of the encounter between ethnographer and other, but they also wanted to find a way to make room in academic discourse for their own multiple voices traditionally relegated to other genres such as autobiography, the personal essay, and fiction.

> Though Margery Wolf's <u>A Thrice Told Tale</u> is written as a critique of experimental writing in ethnography, paradoxically it can be read as a model multivocal text, one that demonstrates the richness and complexity of understanding that multivocal texts can create as well as some of the practices that are being developed to convey partial and ambiguous truths. Wolf offers three different representations of the same event: a short story written near the time of the event, a set of fieldnotes taken during the event, and an article published in <u>American Ethnologist</u> thirty years after the event—and she frames these three "quite different versions" (2) with commentaries on their relative validity and usefulness to anthropologists and other probable audiences. In weaving together accounts from different times and different perspectives written in different genres, it opens a broader field of possibilities for interpretation of the event than Wolf is able to suggest in her journal article alone, and in its representation of the relationship between Wolf and her Taiwanese research assistant Wu Chieh, it allows a more contextualized understanding of the interpretations Wolf offers.
>
> The event that is the focus of Wolf's study involved a woman in a Taiwanese village (identified as Mrs. Tan or subject 48 in alternate versions) who fell or jumped into a rice paddy and who subsequently behaved in bizarre ways. The question for all concerned (villagers and anthropologists) was why she was behaving this way. Here's a conversation from the short story between the narrator anthropologist and her research assistant:
>
>> Wu Chieh was having trouble meeting my eyes. There was a squirminess in her manner that I had seen before when a subject of our research touched on a belief or custom she wished to avoid, either from delicacy or from personal uncertainty. To give her time, I launched into a brief lecture on the nature of mental illness and its relationship to other illnesses. She politely ignored me and peeled an orange.
>>
>> "Some say she isn't crazy. Maybe it's something else..."
>>
>> "Something else?"
>>
>> "Mmmmm."

"What else? What do you mean?"

"I don't know." When Wu Chieh uses the phrase, "I don't know," she uses it as a direct translation from the Mandarin pu hsiao te. Sometimes she doesn't even bother to translate it into English. What it means is either "I know nothing about this subject and I don't care to learn anything about it," or "There is nothing more I wish to say about the subject." When she says it, in Chinese or English, I know I have reached the end of that particular path.

"How did she get into the rice paddy?"

"She jumped in."

"Ugh."

"Well, she made mistake. She was trying to get into the river."

"Oh." A river is a traditional site for suicides or suicide attempts, particularly among Taiwanese women. Wu Chieh understood the significance of my "oh."

"She wasn't trying to do that. She..." Her eyes dropped again. I tried to find another question that couldn't be answered with pu hsiao te.

"How do you know she wasn't trying to do that?"

"She said so. She said she had to go there to meet someone, something" To my amazement, Wu Chieh burst into tears and rushed from the room." (20-21)

Later, the narrator of the short story tells how she manipulated Wu Chieh into telling her what the people who didn't think the woman was crazy thought, which leads to the following conversation:

"Well, they think a god is calling her."

"Calling her for what? Do you mean a god wants her to kill herself?"

"No. Why do you always think that? She wasn't trying to commit suicide that day. The god was calling her and she just got confused..."

"Well, I am confused too. Why is a god calling Mrs. Tan?"

"Nobody knows that. They just choose some people."

"Choose them for what?"

"To speak for them... you know, to be their tang-ki." (29)

The narrator comments:

As I listened to Wu Chieh, who had been my daily companion, fellow researcher, English student, and

> employee for fully a year, speaking about gods calling
> people to be tang-ki as if it were a not uncommon expe-
> rience, I realized once again that we were separated by
> more than age, education, and status. (29-30)

Later, in a commentary, Wolf notes that the set of fieldnotes
on this event comes directly from Wu Chieh who was much
engaged by it—unlike Wolf and her husband who were at
the time pursuing another research topic. Wolf remarks,
"ever since I began this project I have wondered about the
extent to which Wu Chieh lived a double life during this
time, reporting one set of interviews and observations for
the foreign anthropologists and collecting another set for
herself, an unsophisticated nineteen-year-old Taiwanese
woman who was trying to make sense out of her own
world" (84).

Wolf compares her situation to that of Renato Rosaldo, who
similarly collected data that seemed inconsequential to him
at the time: "Only after he had left the field did he
recognize the significance of what his informants had
insisted that he record" (85). The fieldnotes do indeed show
Wu Chieh actively pursuing the question of whether people
thought Mrs. Tan was a tang-ki, and they show her
reporting her inquiries to the foreign anthropologists,
whether or not the foreign anthropologists were interested
in the question:

> March 10, 1960
>
> ...
>
> Tonight Wu Chieh heard 479 (F 37) and 487 (F 50)
> talking about the events of the day, and they agreed
> that she couldn't be a real tang-ki because she seemed
> to be talking aimlessly at times.
>
> ...
>
> 83 (F 64), 439 (F 57), 366 (F 43), 128 (F 34), 395 (M
> 51) seem to believe that 48 is a real tang-ki. Most of
> the other women are still doubtful. During the
> afternoon events reported above, only 84 (M 39) and
> 330 (M 59) among the people in the crowd we talked
> with doubted that a god was somehow involved.
>
> ...
>
> March 14, 1960
>
> Present: 31 (F 30), 113 (F 25), & 9 (F 84)
>
> Wu Chieh asked: "Is 48 really a tang-ki?" At first they
> all answered, "Who knows?" (75-77)

When I read <u>A Thrice Told Tale</u> with my students in a
graduate seminar on qualitative methods, we talked a lot
about the perspective of the Chinese subjects of the research,
probably because two Chinese students were in the class. I
said that because of the depiction of the cultural clash
between the anthropologist and Wu Chieh, the short story
gave me the clearest sense of Taiwanese village culture.
(Interestingly, Wolf notes that "the fiction I created.... seemed
to me when I came upon it again after all these years to be
an accurate rendering of what had happened." (85) The
Chinese students in my class preferred the fieldnotes, clearly
the only direct representation of the villagers' perspective,
and they pointed out how Wolf never for a moment gave any
serious consideration to the villagers' belief that a god was
somehow involved in causing Mrs. Tan's behavior.

In the journal article "The Woman Who Didn't Become a
Shaman" that takes this event as its basis, Wolf does not
give Wu Chieh credit for choosing "the topic <u>she</u> thought we
should be attending to" (85), commenting only that because
Mrs. Tan was not successful in becoming a <u>tang-ki</u> she
naturally did not recognize the event as meaningful and as
a result has had to rely on "the randomly recorded voices
of villagers" (109). Using this incomplete data and
referring to the scholarship on shamanism in Taiwan, Wolf
argues in the article mainly for a structural interpretation
of why Mrs. Tan did not become a <u>tang-ki</u>: Wolf argues only
that Mrs. Tan "was an outsider—socially and
genealogically" (113). But in her conclusion, drawing on
feminist psychology that she admits is dangerous to apply
to Chinese culture, Wolf interestingly returns to the first
interpretation her narrator offered in the short story:

> I continue to wonder whether or not Mrs. Tan, on that
> fateful day when she threw herself into the rice paddy,
> was not, as some claimed, trying to get to the river.
> Suicide (often by drowning) is a solution for many
> (younger) Chinese women who have trouble creating
> a new self in a strange place. Perhaps when she was
> pulled out of the muck of the paddy, she made one final
> attempt to join the social world of the village by way of
> a god who had more reality for her than the people
> among whom she lived. Unfortunately, her self was so
> poorly established that she could not carry it off. The
> self that spoke with the gods could not be used to
> construct a self capable of surviving in a social world
> constructed by strangers. (115-16)

A Thrice Told Tale thus offers many alternate and, if not
mutually exclusive, clearly contradictory interpretations of
the reasons for Mrs. Tan's behavior: perhaps she was
crazy, perhaps she was called by a god, perhaps she was
tormented by a god, perhaps she was constructed as an outsider, perhaps she was unable to construct a self, perhaps
she was confused. In contrast, "The Woman Who Didn't
Become a Shaman" offers only two interpretations, neither
of which entered into the villagers' discussions (as reported
in the field notes) and one of which (suicide) is explicitly
rejected by Wu Chieh (as reported in the short story). The
villagers' dominant explanation, that gods were somehow
involved, either in tormenting Mrs. Tan (so that she went
crazy) or in choosing her to be a tang-ki, is entertained by
Wolf only in terms of the function shamans serve in
Taiwanese culture in offering medical advice and social
problem-solving. That Mrs. Tan might have been suffering
from mental illness, or might simply have been unhappy or
"confused," as Wu Chieh says, is also not considered in the
article despite fieldnotes that indicate that "something like
this had happened to 48 once before" (62) when she was a
girl, and her mother believed that it was "because someone
did something to hurt her" (63).

I am not suggesting that the explanations Wolf argues for
in her article are not good explanations or that she should
have discussed more thoroughly in her article other
promising explanations that arose in the fieldwork. I simply
want to point out how the genre of the "realist"
ethnography requires her to offer a univocal explanation of
the phenomenon she observes (for as she presents it Mrs.
Tan's inability to construct a self really just adds a new
twist to the structural explanation) and leaves her no way
to consider in any detail the understanding of Taiwanese
culture that comes out of the conflict between the foreign
anthropologist's ways of making sense of Mrs. Tan's behavior and Wu Chieh's and the villager's ways of making sense
of it, a conflict that the several versions and the
commentaries in the book highlight.

In her article, Wolf mentions almost in passing that "What
Western observers might classify as mental illness is not
necessarily so classified in Taiwan or China" (108). The
book makes me wonder what insights on this question
might have arisen if Wolf had, instead of lecturing Wu

Chieh on mental illness, discussed with her the varying interpretations the two were developing of Mrs. Tan's behavior, and if she had considered answering Wu Chieh's question of why she immediately concluded that Mrs. Tan had been trying to commit suicide, an interpretation that, like her first written version of the event in the short story, she continued to find more compelling than the explanation in the journal article warranted by anthropological theory. Wolf does note that "unfortunately" this was not one of the times that she and Wu Chieh "talked a lot about 'life'" and that "nothing in my personal journal tells me what, if anything, she was thinking about the Tan affair other than what she reported to us and I recorded in the fieldnotes" (84-85), but nothing in her representations of her interaction with Wu Chieh shows a hint of a shared inquiry into their different views. It makes me wonder whether now, considering her reading in feminist social science subsequent to the fieldwork, she might regard Wu Chieh as more of a collaborative researcher than the naive assistant she is portrayed as in the short story and whether she might have considered representing in her journal article (if the journal were open to a more flexible form), as she does in the commentary on the fieldnotes, the extent to which Wu Chieh's interests shaped her own research question.

The complexities of the representations in such kinds of multiple/multiplied writings are not thus limited to the representations of others. Those who set out to write such pieces necessarily give some representation of themselves as well: the ruse of the neutral observer cannot be maintained for readers whose sense of the participants is enriched and enlivened by writing that allows differing perspectives (whether they are the perspectives of people or genres). Perhaps, as we become more accustomed to what these new written representations can make possible, writers will see the necessity of more openly accounting for their decision-making in the process of creating these representations.

Would some consider it a ruse that Marsha, Suhail, and I claimed that we were not conducting qualitative research? Would they think we were avoiding our professional responsibility to think through the implications of our work with Rebecca and Jeff? Thomas Newkirk might ask, as he does of other literacy researchers, including Brodkey and Hull, Rose, et al., if we had taken advantage of Marsha's students by asking them to participate in the project. Did we allow them ample opportunity to speak for themselves? Did I consider how I would convey potential "bad news" to Marsha or Suhail? Would I have been willing to intervene in her or Suhail's practices if I had discovered either Rebecca or Jeff were being harmed by their approaches? The ethical issues that Newkirk raises cannot be dismissed.

On the other hand, these ethical concerns are based on bad faith assumptions about teachers' and tutors' interactions with students and about colleagues' interactions with one another. The three of us had observed one another's interactions with students in the open environment of the writing center and had established relationships based on mutual respect. We hoped that engaging in this project with Rebecca and Jeff would offer them opportunities to locate the cultural work of literacy in something outside themselves. Yes, I struggled with ethical qualms about my responsibilities to students who have shared intimate details of their lives with us, details that we planned to publish. Accepting their position as collaborators rather than subjects, Rebecca and Jeff refused the option of using pseudonyms, and I regularly worried about my responsibility to their parents and their former teachers who were all implicated in discussions of individual literacy histories. To write, Marsha and Suhail and I had to negotiate complex interpersonal and professional relationships, along with feelings made more touchy by dissertation deadlines, job searches, health problems, family tensions. Marsha admitted that my having "secret" access to her students' thinking about their work in her course made her feel as though I was "having an affair" with her students. Rebecca's and Jeff's comments, such as Rebecca's reference to the "experiment" we were "conducting," caused us to reencounter regularly our concerns about how successful we were in positioning them as research partners rather than subjects of a study. We worked to respect their busy schedules, their reluctance to write and their eagerness to talk, while still urging them to read and write with us.

The effort to write across our differences forced us into awareness of all that structures what we do: social codes, personal histories, classroom practices, philosophies of composition, institutional histories, past performances, weekly priorities, and time commitments. In addition, we were mindful of the need to take our interpretive responsibility seriously, so as writers Marsha and I worked to set up the theoretical frame that motivated the questions we asked ourselves. We cited the work of subjectivity theorists who had offered us rethinkings of the ways we conceptualized identity and agency, and we referred to literacy theorists who have challenged autonomous notions of literacy. By the time we had negotiated the complexities of collaboratively writing up a project involving five differently situated people, we had seventy pages, three times what the editors called for. We encountered frustration trying to bring together voices we had kept separate to protect the integrity of the project, trying to do it under deadline, and trying to coax Rebecca and Jeff into critical roles when they wanted to be appreciative readers. We worried about the theoretical language shutting them out. That we produced a text at all was something we wanted to celebrate rather than critique.

But the editors did critique and they insisted that we must reduce the length, a job that we had to negotiate when we were no longer all on the same campus. Marsha and I wrestled with our complicated mix of literacy and subjectivity theory juxtaposed with composition and pruned the twelve pages of theoretical discussion down to seven.

*T*he writings we have been discussing thus far have placed themselves outside the expected "forms" of academic writing by using multiple voices or genres to represent their work. But, as we began work on this project, it became clear to us that such writings, together with other writings that prioritize the autobiographical or the formal or the narrative, not only offer to us strategies for holding onto differing particularities as we generalize in our research; they also—overtly or not—help us think around another concern of our profession, that of the sticky Theory-Practice dance.

As is evident from reviewers' responses to manuscripts, articles in composition studies are expected to treat theory and practice as separate categories and to contain the mix or articulation of theory and practice proper to the particular subfield they take up. Articles about composition pedagogy, for example, must contain theory that clearly underpins the practices discussed, but must not contain only theory. Articles about writing center practices, in contrast, are often criticized for containing explanations of theory, which are considered to be irrelevant or exclusionary for the audience of writing center tutors. But at the same time there has also been a lot of questioning in composition studies of the traditional ways of conceiving of the relationship between theory and practice.

Joseph Harris complains that we have used theory "constatively as an attempt to ground practice in a disinterested account of the processes of language or learning or composing" (145), and he argues that, "Instead of coming before practice, then, theory comes out of practice—theory helps us explain what we are already doing" (147). Although his agenda seems mainly to reverse the priority of theory over practice, his comments hint at a more complicated relation, one that Louise Phelps develops further. Citing the notion of praxis (which recognizes the intimate back-and-forth relation of theory and practice in action), she suggests that "the formal counterpart or 'antistrophe' to Theory is informal reasoning—the reflective processes of hypothesizing, questioning, testing, connecting, and so forth, that characterize everyday life and generate the theories that people live by" (208). Phelps' notion of informal reasoning is much like what Patricia Harkin has called lore, a postdisciplinary, nonfoundational mode of producing knowledge: "Unlike the linear, cause-and-effect relations that are represented by disciplinary techniques, lore arranges its data serially, spatially, paratactically, like a rhizome" (134).

How then to write so that we don't schizophrenically alternate between theory and practice or so that we don't, instead, tilt towards one side or the other? How can we write so that theory and practice are held in tension?

> .... but the complexities of human behavior defeated my every attempt at making generalizations. (134)

That statement comes within the last ten pages of Vivian Gussin Paley's White Teacher, and—in spite of these words—Paley certainly has made generalizations throughout the book, generalizations about the necessity of discussing skin color and cultural practices and other differences in classrooms. How could she not make generalizations? After all, as she herself writes in her Preface, "You do not share your experiences without the belief that there are lessons that have been learned" (xv).

White Teacher, like Paley's other books, is built narratively and written in the first-person, almost as though it were Paley's day-to-day journal. The book contains nothing that is overtly or formally theoretic; there are no references to any other writers, and there is at the end no formal conclusion with particular recommendations. Instead, the book opens with Paley's description of how she, over years of teaching, comes to realize that acting color-blind in class might be a problem and then proceeds through her changing thoughts and various actions (and adjustments and corrections) as she works with children and parents to make her classes more openly comfortable with difference. Instead of "theory," there are detailed and close observations of particular children and their play and arguments and costume-construction:

> The next day Ayana was not in school. Sylvia looked all over for her.
>
> "Where's that black girl with the brown dress?"
>
> "You mean Ayana?"
>
> "I mean the black girl in the brown dress with the French braids and white knee socks and the dot on her cheek."

> "Oh, you must mean Ayana. She's not here today. She has a cold."
>
> "She's my friend. She's my first friend."
>
> Sylvia continued to have problems all year. But it is fair to say that the doll corner episode with Ayana made a profound change in her. She began to act as if this classroom might be a safe place. (74)

It is difficult for me to pull examples from the book to quote, because Paley's descriptions are so detailed; the above passage is preceded by a lengthy passage about Sylvia's first destructive days in class, a passage through which we learn about Sylvia's intelligences, boisterousness, and desires. And because the descriptions of what happens between children are so detailed, the book is also thick with emotion, both the children's, as they scuffle and cry about slights and problems at home, and Paley's, as she responds to actions that anger or sadden her. Paley also keeps the book anchored in her own particular ways of thinking, writing about how she tries to understand the actions and reactions of the non-white children in her class by thinking back to her experiences as a Jewish child in overtly gentile classrooms—and about how she is sometimes tripped up by this connection.

What methods and practices can I then take from a book that is so relentlessly particular? What "theory" comes from this writing?

The questions raised by Harris, Phelps, and Harkin, among others, suggest to us that praxis, informal reasoning, and lore are not mere additional (and subordinate) ways of producing knowledge; instead they undermine the traditional split between theory and practice. Theory and Practice (the formalization in publication of everyday practices of writing teachers) have been separated through the operations of disciplinary discourse, which produces them as alternate codified forms of representing thinking and acting. Theory (as opposed to theorizing) has been the province of philosophy (though the province has been invaded by literary studies and cultural studies, among others), which established itself, and its valuing of abstract universals, as the dominant discipline (over rhetoric) long ago, and has never quite lost its cache as the epitome of academic work. Practice, with its valuing of reflective action in particular circumstances, is an upstart category in comparison (though some trace its tenets to the discredited Rhetoric of the Sophists), the province of disciplines with much less academic status (education, applied linguistics, etc.). Though the kind of generalizing thinking that characterizes theorizing and the particularized thinking that characterizes everyday practices are easily related, and indeed difficult to separate as thinkers work back and forth between the immediacies that confront them and contextualizing reflection on what they know, formalized Theory and Practice are schizophrenic, difficult to relate; they are, it turns out, alternate representations (in accord with different conventions and values) of very much the same kind of thinking.

The kind of thinking in acting that Harkin calls lore and Phelps calls informal reasoning—and that Miller figures as the play of the personal against the theoretical/academic—is part of everyone's working life to the extent that they are reflective practitioners; as Gramsci says, "all men are philosophers" (323) in this sense. Finding ways to represent this kind of thinking in action, and to uncover the everyday praxis that relates theory and practice, is one goal of the current experiments in academic discourse.

> Before anything else, however, what stays with me from Paley's particular writing is a sense of an imperfect classroom. Paley describes her stumbles and mistakes, along with the tensions between children and parents and teachers. There is no happy ending to this book, either really or theoretically; instead, there is for me the sense of ongoing work and thought and slow uneven movement towards (perhaps) something better: there are young people learning with a teacher about the complexities of living together. Paley's book—along with other, similar, first-person narrative books about classrooms (Sylvia Ashton-Warner's Teacher, for example, or Marilyn Burns and Bonnie Tank's A Collection of Math Lessons series)—encourage my desire for classes that are ethical and that support the particularities of the people within them, but they do not encourage me to think I can simply bring the writers' strategies and methods wholesale into my class in order to make this happen. And this is one of their particular values, I think, and it is the result of their authors' ways of writing.

> Formal scientific research requires that one's results be repeatable (theoretically) anywhere, by anyone, under similar conditions—and this requirement has led, not only within the sciences but within composition, to styles (and arguments for styles) of writing that strive for the impersonal and objective. In Knowledge and Power: Towards a Political Philosophy of Science, Joseph Rouse argues that our attempts to have such scientific practice have led us to make a world that is more standardized than it had been:

> Science sometimes "works" only if we change the world
> to suit it. These changes are less evident within science,
> because much of what is involved comprises general
> features of the construction of laboratories. They are
> also partially concealed in the case of technological
> extensions by the massive general effort within
> industrialized societies to make widely applicable the
> standardized units of measurement, the common
> techniques of observing, counting, measuring, and moni-
> toring things, and the purified substances and
> specialized equipment that give science within
> laboratories rigorous control over the microworlds they
> construct....
> Too much of scientific knowledge involves preparing the
> situation to make laws applicable to it and learning how
> to describe it in terms to which laws can attach. (118-
> 119)

I am not trying to slide in an argument here that any scientific (or scientifically-based) research is somehow wrong;
rather, I want to understand Paley's writing, like that of the
other authors I have mentioned, as a necessary
counterweight to any suggestion that one's research in a
composition classroom—and one's writing about that
research—should lead others to desire the re-creation of
one's methods. In trying to keep what I think is a
necessary tension between our needs to learn generally and
our desires not to efface "the complexities of human behavior" (as I wrote above, quoting Paley), Paley's writing keeps
me aware of those complexities at the same time she
encourages me to think about how (in this particular
instance) we discuss race in <u>my</u> classrooms.

When I think, then, about how I might have practices similar
to Paley's within my classes, I cannot overlook the
particularities of Paley's class: she has made those
particularities too much a part of her writing for me to imagine my class is enough like hers that I could simply import
her methods wholesale. There is, it is too obvious to mention,
the unavoidable difference of ages between the people in her
classes and in mine. But, as I read Paley, I cannot help but
think closely of particular people in my classes, spurred by
Paley's lively descriptions of the people in her classes. I
cannot help but see the differences between her methods and
mine, and I cannot help but think about how her strategies
grow out of and back into where and when she is, and with
whom. Her writing, when I want to make use of it,

encourages me then to think about the particularities of my classes, and how I must modify and shift her methods for my own use. As well, her continual references to herself and her background encourage me to question why I desire what I do in my classes. Because of her way of writing, then, I do not think I can read her book without being very aware of the complexities of the classroom.

And, finally, I think that there is a certain approach to theory that I gain from Paley's writing. I wrote above that Paley's book contains nothing that is formally theoretic, but there is certainly a kind of practical theory at work in what she does. Because she observes her students (and herself) so closely, she is able to construct specific responses to specific problems—as when she notices that the girls playing in the doll corner have been consistently "combative" over a period of time, whereas the boys, involved in making all the necessary costumes for their superhero play, have been playing "together on a higher level than is usually the case in kindergarten" (97); she figures out how to get the girls more involved in making the costumes for their play (rather than using ready-made dressups), and is eventually able to conclude that

> I could see that the operation involved in creating the materials for play often led to more mature social behavior. It is as if the establishment of self-identity that accompanies the role of craftsman makes it less necessary to use the social arena for combat. (99-100).

And so Paley does generalize about what happens in her classroom, and so her work depends on a level of theoretic understanding of human behavior, but her writing allows us to see how that theory changes in response to the situations of her class—and her generalizations are always confined: she never allows me to believe that her generalities define any child in her kindergarten classes. She may make generalizations about the needs of children of kindergarten age—but those generalizations are continually broken open by her observations about how particular children express or satisfy those needs:

> Marcia and Eddy were both early readers, a skill that seemed out of context; they were more like nursery school children. They had not got to the point where they wondered what other children thought of them or where they fit in the various social arrangements in the class. Marcia knew she was a girl and that she was

black, but this information did not have social meaning
for her. She saw no reason to be part of a group and
there was no attempt to identify with group goals. If
Eddie had not been in the class, she would have played
alone. Kindergarten is, for most children, the time of
awakening to the society of the peer group, but there
are always children who have not yet reached this
point. (134-135)

What builds in my mind as I read her writing, then, are
classrooms of particular children with a particular teacher,
a teacher who is continually observing and considering and
searching for patterns of both behavior and understanding,
and passing those skills on to the people in her class. It is a
use of theory that, I believe, holds the tension between
what is common in our classrooms and what is ours alone.

RE-READING

*Does it matter—do you need to know—that we talked about
this chapter and then two of us went out kayaking on Lake
Superior? Is that a self-indulgent way to begin, writer-based
prose, something that matters only to us? Or does it signify
something important to you, something about local context
that affects how you make sense of what we write? Does it
help you to know that one of us said to the other—pointing at
how a giant white pine had wrapped its roots around smooth
rocks, clinging to the cliff over the lake—"that, that's the
metaphor for our structure"? The roots are the twisted strands
of conversations in the fields of composition studies, education,
literary studies, and anthropology, branching off, rejoining,
multiplying; the rocks our smoothly shaped (we hope)
considerations of moments that touch on the question of new
forms of academic writing.*

When we compose multivocal texts for academic readers or when we
compose texts that attempt to incorporate the perspectives of
groups generally excluded from the discourse of the academy or when we
write autobiographical narratives, we inevitably jar readers. Though we
intend our texts to complicate knowledge that we previously took for
granted, they also present problems for readers who have been trained to
value a unified perspective, clear conclusions, unequivocal evidence, and
explicit structural signals. How can writers help readers learn how to read

differently, not to be jarred, for example, by that abrupt entry of the white pine on Lake Superior? To what extent must readers learn to be open to new forms and to finding new ways to read texts? How can writers learn to make these new texts valid representations of research; how can readers learn to assess these new texts critically?

> It bears reiterating that the reader consults an ethnographic text for news of the world conveyed to him by an accredited reporter.
> (Graham Watson, quoted in Wolf 56)

Wolf, while agreeing with the postmodernists of Writing Culture that ethnographies represent only partial truths and that ethnographers must carefully weigh their responsibilities to those others they represent in their texts, argues strongly for traditional "realist" ethnographic texts and against the reflexive, multivocal texts advocated by postmodernist anthropologists. As she says, "like most anthropologists, I remain more interested in why Chinese peasants do what they do, and, as Graham Watson (1987: 36) puts it, in 'getting the news out'" (1). Her concern that content not be eclipsed by formal experiments follows Watson in being framed as a concern for what readers want from ethnographic texts; Gesa Kirsch, who cites Wolf in her own critique of experimental texts, sums up many of the limitations Wolf discusses for readers of such texts when they move outside the expected forms:

> They can disguise writers' continuing authorial control, they can fail to provide the theoretical framework and cultural context necessary for understanding the multiple voices emerging in a single text, they make new and difficult demands on readers, they require tolerance for ambiguity and contradictory claims, and they easily become elitist and exclusionary. (Kirsch 193-94)

Both avowedly feminist scholars, Wolf and Kirsch embrace the goal of including multiple voices and subjectivities in academic research, but they point out another tension between theory and practice that we too share, that, as Kirsch puts it, "the rush to celebrate these new textual practices leaves little room for critical analysis of their potential effects on readers, writers, and public discourse." (191)

In theory, feminist and postmodern scholars (among others) believe that knowledge is socially constructed and thus that all truths are partial, that contradictory perspectives may all be true, and that as a consequence the inclusion of multiple voices is not only ethically but epistemologically necessary in valid research, but they have difficulties in bringing their practices of writing and reading in line with these beliefs. Even when strongly motivated by changes in fundamental beliefs, new practices are hard to develop. Narrative texts like Paley's <u>White Teacher</u> that blur traditional boundaries between theory and practice, generalizations and particular descriptions, impersonal research and personally felt experiences raise anew questions about the validity of knowledge that relies on praxis and emotion. As Wolf notes, "There was a time—and not so long ago—that publishing [the short story that relates the events she analyzed in her journal article] would have cast a shadow of doubt, a questioning of legitimacy, over my mainstream anthropological publications" (50).

Multivocal texts—those that mix sections written in genres like fiction, poetry, interviews, letters, and autobiography with sections written in academic discourse and that sometimes also experiment with form to represent these different voices and genres—raise the same questions of validity along with the additional questions of interpretive responsibility (Kirsch); not only are writers and readers reluctant to credit multivocal and experimental texts, they must also develop new practices to help them create useful interpretations in multivocal texts.

The written representations we have been discussing (and attempting) are not free variations in form, but ask to be read (we think) with the same patience, the same open ear and eye, that we hope to have when we meet strangers and others. Aligned with how our theories are pushing us towards new kinds of research, our work is also pushing us to consider not only how we represent others, but also how we represent our selves, our arguments, and even our words on paper or screen. All of these written representations—the ones we have discussed earlier, as well as this piece you are now reading, or the Spooner and Yancey piece we cited earlier—ask us to step out of the reading practices we have learned, to move away (but not to give up) the generalities of our practice in order better to attend to the specific.

Each piece can thus approach us as though we were learning to read all over again. Each piece asks effort, if we are to substantiate the hopes expressed in the calls at the beginning of our writing.

How would I proceed in my own writing if I were to entangle myself in questions like these: How do other people see me when they see me as a mother with my child? What are the cultural models through which others will see me? How do I see myself? How do I keep myself from being swallowed up totally by the words and models of others?

These are the questions that helped me re-read Julia Kristeva's Stabat Mater. In Stabat Mater Kristeva considers the Virgin Mary being shown in representations with particular, historically- and culturally-bound theological and psychoanalytical weight, representations that have (evidently) been satisfactory for others, at other times, but that now she argues can only give us "a motherhood that today remains, after the Virgin, without a discourse"; Kristeva's writing thus closes with an opening, a suggestion that there is now a "need of an ethics for this 'second' sex, which, as one asserts it, is reawakening" (379-380). In order to get to this opening, however, she has had to argue that discourse about motherhood—when it is completely bound up with the discourse surrounding Mary—isn't satisfying for her, that she exists in excess of that discourse.

How does one argue that excess?

One could do it politely and "by the Law," with a text that stayed within bounds... but the problem is precisely that the bounds are what Kristeva believes herself already to be outside. So, I think, the "form" she gives to her text shows the problem of those bounds and so serves as an argument against them.

There are thus two texts that make up Stabat Mater: there is one text that is full of precise academic and religious references, tracing the dates and decisions and hymns that delimit the Virgin as a certain kind of virgin and as a certain kind of body and psychology, and then there is a text of sensuality, mostly, a text written outside the other text, in a different typeface, a text that breaks out as a child breaks out, a text that pulls us into Kristeva's own particular experience of having a child. I can see no way, given our sense of what makes an academic text, for Kristeva to integrate the two texts into one linearly-argued, disembodied, text; to do so would be showing that there is no need for a new ethics, to show that the general discourse of Mary can contain the particular discourse of Kristeva and her child. The form of the text is thus inseparable from its content, from its argument. To accept this arrangement of text, then, this split, non-linear, sensual and academic text, one must accept—or at least accept the possibility—of its argument, that particular women live in excess of general representations of woman.

In *Stabat Mater,* Kristeva is working to hold on, we think, precisely to that tension between the general and the specific, the personal and the cultural, that we have been circling in our writing. Her strategy is a visually tense piece.

Academic readers are trained to use texts, to make them into bricks for the foundations of their own arguments, to turn them into straw houses, to use them in creating or resolving problems. One reviewer in particular read us as he/she had been trained to do. He/she sniffed at our methodology, disputed the need for our complicated theoretical apparatus, questioned the relevance of a focus on teaching issues for a writing center audience, complained about our "longwindedness," pointed to occasions where our tone was self-promoting. He/she looked for coherence and interrogated its lack, read our narratives as case studies and doubted their "validity." He/she interpreted our student collaborators as "teacher-pleasers" in ways that made it easy to dismiss the ways their stories implicated all teachers in the project of reproducing social class. He/she claimed we were advertising MTU's cultural studies program and worried that we were drawing conclusions from positions of intimacy/empathy. Overall, the more univocal and more narratively based chapters in the collection we were contributing to were reviewed more favorably than those that did not seek a unified perspective or voice.

How could we have expected otherwise? Busy readers are in the same position we writers were in: with little time to read, they default to familiar practices, reading for what they can use, looking for our point, for our evidence, for our focus. A multivocal text frustrates entrenched reading habits. As writers we had failed to provide reading lessons for our unwieldy text.

How do we write to prepare readers for such writing? How do we judge whether such writing is worth our time when we are asked to read it?

How would I proceed in my writing if I were to entangle myself in questions like these: How do I call attention to an in-use-daily communication-technology, to show just how strange it is and the odd history and psychology bound up with it, to show just how much we have made it an invisible and unquestioned extension of our selves and bodies?

The book built out of that question has the usual scholarly apparatus of extensive citations (and citations of not-easily-dismissed writers (Nietzsche, Freud, Heidegger, Einstein, Lacan, Derrida, among others)) and is clearly a product of careful and extensive thought... but Avital Ronell's <u>The Telephone Book</u> is also an odd size for an academic book, much taller than we have come to expect, and its internal visual presentation is... well, also unexpected, with pages of blurred or many-sized type, pages with unusual devices for showing paragraph divisions, pages of split columns, pages of crossed-out words. Why? Because of what Ronell believes a telephone (as we have received it) does: "Already heterogeneous, the self that speaks into the phone or receives the call splits off from its worldly complexity, relocating partial selves to transmitting voices" (351). The phone is something (we tell ourselves) that makes our lives easier and in so doing it becomes something in which we can forget our selves, and whose construction by Bell and Watson we can forget, along with its being shaped by and helping to shape the stories we tell ourselves about ourselves in philosophy and psychology and technology. The telephone is something we don't question, even if it might be (as Ronell argues) intricately tied into our cultural circuits of racism and sexism and...

And so the book presents the specific historical and material development of the telephone-as-we-know-it, but in so doing Ronell wants to make the materiality of the phone present and not just something perhaps called to mind by the "meaning" of the words; it is as though, instead, she is embodying different voices on the page, making visible specific choices that took place at specific times for specific purposes. What happens for me, then, as I read is that not just my telephone communications become odd but also the other methods I use for exchanging my words with others. <u>The Telephone Book</u>, then, if I am open to Ronell's questions and arguments, makes both the Telephone and the Book odd; as Ronell writes at the beginning,

> At first you may find the way the book runs to be disturbing, but we have had to break up its logic typographically. Like the electronic impulse, it is flooded with signals. To crack open the closural sovereignty of the Book, we have feigned silence and disconnection, suspending the tranquil cadencing of paragraphs and conventional divisions.... Our problem was how to

> maintain an open switchboard, one that disrupts a
> normally functioning text equipped with proper shock
> absorbers. (unpaged, from "A User's Manual" section of
> the book)

> If I am open to Ronell's arguments (including the visual
> ones), then I am left asking why we take the telephone and
> the book as they are, unquestioned in their structures and
> connections to what might usually seem completely other
> parts of our lives.

Writers can set up a text (or texts) that calls our usual expectations into
question and, like Kristeva, provide only implicit hints for reading, or, like
Ronell, provide direct explanation for their decisions. Experimental
writing—because it does work in that area where writers try to pull the
particular out of our general reading habits—must be a place of give-and-
take between writers and readers.

> As writers Marsha and I had failed to provide reading lessons for our
> unwieldy text. We had written from the moon, offering our theory
> without explaining our stake in it, particularly our stake as writing cen-
> ter people, offering our voices without explaining what had drawn us to
> the project (Harris 1994a). Marsha and I had hoped that readers would
> simply listen to the student stories and allow their words and histories
> to penetrate the protective varnish that separates teachers from stu-
> dents. We had hoped that by witnessing the students' efforts to come to
> terms with literacy, that teachers and writing center workers might
> rethink the naive subjectivity constructed for students. But we had not
> explicitly invited them to do that. We had pretended we were not doing
> research when in fact we were redefining what research might look like.
> We had moved the practice of writing center conversations into an area
> called research, but we had reported more than we explained. We had
> failed to consider how we wanted our new discourse to be evaluated.

Because of the way they encourage alternate explanations and allow the
inclusion of more contexts, experimental texts open a possibility we speak
of elsewhere in this chapter, the possibility that the texts can betray things
about the writer. In these negotiated sites, neither writers nor readers are
fully in control of the interpretations that can be constructed. But readers
still expect writers to demonstrate some sort of control over their material,
to orient readers somehow to what is being presented.

> If Wolf reveals more than she says about her reasons for
> her attachment to the suicide explanation and the
> development of her understanding of her relationships with
> informants, she still also remains enough in control of her
> text that readers do not struggle with how to make use of

it; as a whole A Thrice Told Tale has as much to say about why Chinese peasants do what they do as it does about why ethnographers do what they do. Wolf does not disguise her "continuing authorial control" (Kirsch); she provides much theoretical and cultural context necessary for understanding both the anthropologists' and the Taiwanese voices represented; and though reading her text as an ethnography may make new demands on readers to consider the contradictory claims presented in the various versions of the event and in the commentaries, A Thrice Told Tale can hardly be accused of being "elitist and exclusionary" (Kirsch), or as Wolf worries, "so obscure that native speakers of English with a Ph.D. in anthropology find it difficult to understand" (138).

Two strategies she uses to achieve this control are also evident in other successful multivocal academic books, like Ruth Behar's Translated Woman: Crossing the Border with Esperanza's Story and David Schaafsma's Eating on the Street: Teaching Literacy in a Multicultural Society. Like A Thrice Told Tale, both these books contain sections written in different genres framed by or interspersed with sections of academic discourse, and both, like A Thrice Told Tale, focus narrowly on a single incident (a conflict in a teachers' meeting in Eating on the Street) or a single person's experience (Esperanza in Translated Woman) which is contextualized and interpreted from a variety of perspectives. Connecting or framing sections written in more traditional academic discourse, like Wolf's commentaries or Behar's introduction and reflections, allows writers of multivocal texts to explore how the interpretations that the text represents have been constructed, which in turn allows readers to critically assess the interpretations the writer proposes.

The use of multiple genres allows writers to better represent the differences among possible interpretations of a single incident and allows readers to more completely consider those interpretations on their own terms than does the description of different interpretations within the unified perspective of traditional academic discourse. Thus, instead of describing the various perspectives of the participants in the teacher's meeting, Schaafsma transcribes interviews with the different teachers in which he explores with each of them what they felt was at stake and why they took the positions they did. And instead of combining her translations of Esperanza's stories into the academic contexts of feminist theory and Mexican history with her representations of Esperanza's <u>historias</u> in a single unified account, Behar allows each a separate section and a separate genre that fits the different beliefs and values of each.

Experimental texts can be serious attempts to join practice and theory, to align the ways we represent knowledge in texts with our redefinition of knowledge as collaborative, complex, and often contradictory. As Harris says about academic writing that includes the personal, the new written representations "are invoked not for [their] own sake but to define and further articulate a critical position, to locate the writer in an ongoing exchange of views and ideas about a subject" (162). Experimental texts can mystify and exclude readers, but they can also be attempts to balance the inherent tensions Bakhtin noted in language between the centripetal forces of the traditional forms of communicating, which we inherit and on which we rely, and the centrifugal forces of the new understandings that develop as we interact with each other and the world.

Did it help you to know how to read this text from what we wrote at the beginning of this section? Or do we have to explain more explicitly what we alluded to there, that these new experiments in academic discourse that mix theory and practice, generalizations and particular experience, different genres and different voices, autobiography and argument may be easier for some people than for others to embrace, more natural to their ways of thinking because they are more natural to their lives and work? We work in an interdisciplinary department in a Research II Institution, which means that we teach and advise and meet as much as we write. We live in a small town, where public and private lives, work and play, and the various roles we play in our community comingle on a daily basis. We spend a lot of time, all three of us, gazing at Lake Superior where two of us have summer residences, locally known as camps. (The one of us without a camp also teaches (and works with) graphic design and multimedia development.) For us, then, all things most naturally flow together: the most satisfying patterns are always the most complex, the best roads are always not the straightest, the best ideas combine thoughts from various realms, and any *patterns we impose, like the wind on the lake, can only be temporary, incomplete symptoms, however real.*

TO CONCLUDE...

We take to heart Harris's advice that writers "work to make themselves present in their texts not only through their prose style but through also trying to state what draws them to the subject or issue at hand, to be as clear as possible about the sort of role, if any, that they have played in the events they are discussing, and to define what they see as being at stake for both themselves and others in that discussion" (Harris 1994a,161). Those of us engaged in rewriting praxis need to invoke the playful postmodern reader that lies within. We need to articulate our theoretical standpoints not in abstract, long-winded terms but in more condensed forms, perhaps in soundbites, in pattern, in poetry. As much as we might write to invite empathic recognition or to invoke an emotional response that challenges rather than ratifies the status quo, we need to allow for the possibilities that our stories can betray us, that our readers are as likely to poke at our ethos as they previously poked at our evidence and rationales. We write differently not to encourage voyeurism, not to evoke sympathy, not to create victim roles for students, but to involve multiple voices, to make theory/practice connections, to create space for students to enter educational discourse, to critically examine our practices, and to make visible our ethical commitments.

Experimenting with various written representations allows us to take more critical positions, to increase the perspectives we bring to our work, to revise our theories in the crucible of practice, to write in ways that matter. Such writing moves us into richer understandings of the interpersonal, cultural, and political dimensions of our work, but also complicates our relations with ourselves and with our readers. Our efforts to produce knowledge differently will necessarily be received differently. Although these approaches to representing our research may emerge more naturally from our workplaces, although they may come from natural sources carrying no pretense of scholarly neutrality, it does not mean they are any more intellectually honest or valid than more traditional scholarship. With Sullivan, we have argued that these approaches assume that research is not a product, but is rather a set of practices, whose evaluation must include their effects on those we study. For composition studies, then, a final evaluation of these writings, necessarily delayed, might ride on whether students like Rebecca and Jeff come to know us as responding to and making room for their voices, rather than speaking for them or representing them as others.

CHAPTER EIGHTEEN

Coming (in)to Consciousness
One Asian American Teacher's Journey into Activist Teaching and Research

Gail Y. Okawa

O VER TEN YEARS AGO, C. H. KNOBLAUCH AND LIL BRANNON (1984) REMINDED us how essential it is for teachers to "become conscious of the philosophical dimensions of their work because nothing short of that consciousness will make instruction sensible and deliberate, the result of knowledge, not folklore, and of design, not just custom or accident" (2). In his term *conscientizacao*, Paulo Freire (1970, 19) had embodied this concept even earlier as he challenged teachers to question our own complicity in banking models of education. For Freire (1970), teachers, the traditional oppressors, can be of the oppressed as well; coming to critical consciousness becomes a liberatory alternative, involving reflective reconsidering and the discovery of a dialectical relationship between theory and practice, between human beings and the world. His lessons became more imperative and poignant as I was notified of his death on the morning of May 3, 1997, and felt the magnitude of the loss even while composing this essay.

In culturally diverse teaching and learning settings where cultural assumptions cannot be taken for granted, the importance of critical consciousness is further magnified. In a teacher's developing such an awareness, personal identity and professional credibility are continually challenged; thus, the meaning of activist teaching and research expands in value and dimension. In this essay, I explore a growing awareness of critically conscious learning, teaching, and research, narratively and autobiographically. Much current interdisciplinary research on narrative acknowledges its value in the construction of meaning, the significance of autobiography in reflective thought (e.g., Rosen, Riessman, White, Bruner, Chafe, Graham). I will risk the medium of autobiographical narrative also because I believe such writing provides a means of resistance to the isolation and objectification typical of the academy. As a way of accessing subjective knowledge and experience while simultaneously becoming the representation of that knowledge and experience[1], teacher narrative has the potential for both personal and social value, as Antonio Gramsci's (1985) view of autobiography reveals:

> Autobiography can be conceived "politically." One knows that one's life is similar to that of a thousand others, but through "chance" it has had opportunities that the thousand others in reality could not or did not have. By narrating it, one creates this possibility, suggests the process, indicates the opening (132).

For the teacher of color, this process can also serve an autoethnographic purpose, what Mary Louise Pratt (1991) defines as one in which a subordinated or marginalized writer engages in a representation of herself in response to representations by the dominant group (35). It adds an historical dimension and complicates political implications. Though the present narrative represents the perspective of one teacher, it may be a shared journey of many.

"ONCE MORE AGAIN": RECONSIDERATIONS

One summer in Kyoto, Japan, when I was a transient student of Japanese Noh theatre, my sensei (teacher), a well-known Noh actor, commanded me to practice my dance movements over and over again. I would follow his lead and he would adjust my stance, the tilt of my fan, the turn of my head; and he would instruct me to perform this once more—"mo ikai"—and once more—"mo ikai" again in his gruff voice. We didn't communicate much beyond that, given that he didn't speak English and I spoke only minimal Japanese at the time. Now I see that his was not so much a pedagogy of imitation (as some would ascribe to the Japanese), but rather one of internalization—of internalizing a rhythm of the process. As a student of Japanese culture, I had been drawn to the study of this esoteric theatre form—beyond the reading of plays to the viewing of them and to the actual experience of its movements. I studied Noh briefly but intensively that summer, not with aspirations of becoming an actor myself, but with being able to convey an experience of learning to my students at some future time.[2]

When Donna Yamada Bolima first ventured into the writing center where I worked one day in the mid-1980s, neither she nor I realized that in applying for a tutoring job there she would be inheriting that recursive rhythm—in translation—and participating in a transformative period in both our lives. Following a six-year hiatus from teaching in a conventional educational setting, I had found myself in Seattle, in this writing center at the University of Washington. The writing center was a part of the university's Educational Opportunity Program (EOP) Instructional Center, and I had been hired as a writing instructor for a federally funded TRIO project called Student Support Services, housed within the same university office. Being in this setting would influence my career and my life in significant ways[3]; I couldn't have predicted its challenges and rewards.

Past composition experience had given me little basis for this new enterprise. While completing a master's degree in English at Duke University years earlier, I had begun my first full-time teaching position at a women's liberal arts college amid the tobacco fields of the Virginia Piedmont. We were not trained to teach writing in those days when composition was only beginning to problematize itself. I taught three sections of composition both semesters my first year, following in the foot paths of my own teachers who were equally untrained although some were nonetheless inspiring. The college used McCrimmon's *Writing with a Purpose*, Perrine's *Sound and Sense*, and other collections and works of literary prose. For composition students, mine and, I suspect, many others', writing was in a vacuum and often vacuous as a result. I am not proud of my early composition instruction; teaching writing was for me only imitative and product-oriented.

After some time using the prescribed literary texts to teach composition, I sought to respond to prevailing societal demands for "relevance" and to bring the widespread questioning of the *status quo* into the classroom by experimenting with R. D. Laing's (1968) *The Politics of Experience* and a book on the civil disobedience of the Berrigans, two activist Catholic priests among the Catonsville Nine, timely choices that challenged students to interrogate their own views. Despite the absence of a theoretical foundation, to the extent that I stepped outside prescribed models, my choices situated me slightly to the left of a "current traditional" ideological center.

Once again, now years later in Seattle, I was a new writing instructor and, as a "practitioner," had to become familiar with aspects of the composition field and its characters through a side door. I sought advice from William Irmscher, the Director of Composition, before his retirement and became aware of his venerated place in the profession, although I was as yet unaware of what constituted that profession. By the early 1980s writing and language studies had produced a significant cohort of scholars/researchers like Irmscher, Janet Emig, Geneva Smitherman, Peter Elbow, Mina Shaughnessy, Richard Lloyd-Jones, Shirley Brice Heath, Miriam Chaplin, Donald Graves, Ann Berthoff, Charles Cooper, and others—from differing paradigms and perspectives to be sure. Difficulty with writing had become problematized; no longer was there a simple dichotomy of those who could and those who couldn't in the research—but a sense of greater complexity in the process, the relationships of writer to task, of writer to teacher, of teacher and student to learning. Reconsiderations.

When I joined the writing center staff, it served the less than ten percent of the university's 33,000 students who were admitted through the Educational Opportunity Program. Of culturally and linguistically diverse origins, EOP students entered under the rubric "African American, American Indian, Asian and Pacific Islander, Chicano/Latino, or economically disadvantaged White." But "beyond these bureaucratic descriptions, each student, of course, [came] from complex and unique circumstances quite hidden from those who would teach him or her" (Okawa 1993, 169). They identified themselves as Quinault, Vietnamese, Panamanian, African American, Makah, Mexican, Taiwanese, Tlingit, Pakistani, Anglo, Japanese American, Chicano. They spoke a variety of languages, many of them bilingual or bidialectal, some of them multilingual, and spanned a range of ages, socioeconomic and scholastic backgrounds. Coming from the traditional classroom where teachers and students often have been socialized to play roles, I found that working closely with students as a writing center instructor opened up a new world of relationships for me while I came to serve as tutor, advisor, advocate and, in some cases, mentor, confidant, and friend. I began to hear the stories. There among these students and professional staff, many of whom represented a spectrum of cultural and linguistic backgrounds themselves, I witnessed many selves developing, mine among them, as I experienced a different context for my own ethnic identity. From these students and colleagues I could learn about ethnicity, share my own, and feel comfortable being my "ethnic self." While I had come to understand and define my Japanese American heritage in the course of my studies in Japan, I began to identify myself also as an Asian American in the U.S. and to see my location and affinities among other ethnic groups of color. Reconsiderations once more again.

Working with novice writers of these different ethnic and linguistic backgrounds on their writing in the writing center and workshops, I also saw the composing process from their points of view—through their eyes, struggles, and successes—without the complicating role of teacher/grader. At the beginning of one Fall Quarter not long after I began my job, I met James, a freshman who hoped to become a doctor. "Non-traditional" because he was an African American in his mid-twenties, James had entered the university through the EOP and was enrolled in the first quarter of the two-quarter EOP English composition sequence for "basic writers." When he first came into the writing center, he was a bit cocky but eager to learn. His composition instructor was a Puerto Rican doctoral student from New York City who established a good working relationship with James and encouraged him to write, to develop his own voice, as he never had before. Working closely with him as well, I, too, saw his writing evolve. In a personal narrative, he described the complex experience of returning to a childhood home, how as he approached the neighborhood where he grew up, his heart started "beating like a tom-tom." I still remember the metaphor. His images were rich with feeling and memory. In the second quarter of the basic writing course, he ended up in another teacher's class. She was neither sensitive to James as a person nor understanding of his strengths in writing. I watched him grow increasingly more frustrated and discouraged in the class. By the end of the second quarter, any interest or confidence he had developed as a writer had been squelched.

Experiences like these began to raise social and political questions at the juncture of learning and teaching for me, particularly on issues of authority, ethnicity, culture, and class. I hadn't thought about teaching and learning to write in quite these terms before—even in relation to myself and my own writing: who the student was, who the teacher was, their positions and interrelationships. In James' experience, it seemed that his teachers' understanding of him and ability or choice to empathize with him had something to do with his learning and his emotions about writing. Although my classmates and I as students had talked often about "good" teachers and "bad" teachers and I had tried to model my own teaching after those I admired with relative success, I had not reflected on the assumptions underlying my choices.

Equally important, in working first as a writing center instructor with James and other students and later as a classroom teacher with English as a Second Language (ESL) students at the university, I began to realize that, outside of literature classes where the narratives read are primarily canonized fiction, narratives in composition classes—especially the personal narratives of students—are often viewed as the less favored mode of discourse. In classrooms where English teaching is still governed by what Richard E. Young (1978) calls "current-traditional rhetoric" or remnants of the modes, an implicit hierarchy exists. My repeated experience with teachers and textbooks since I worked with James has revealed that narrative, especially personal narrative, is assumed to be on the "simple" end of the evolutionary scale of discourse, while forms like exposition and argumentation are on the "complex" end. Such binary oppositional values extend to judgments about cognition when narrative is associated with a "writer-based" stage of development (Flower 1979; but see DiPardo 1990, and Rosen 1984).

In considering James and others, I have found these assumptions to be highly problematic: the teachers who see the writing—and by extension the writers—of personal narrative to be simplistic or cognitively arrested have a limited, culturally biased view. Courtney Cazden & Dell Hymes acknowledged this cultural bias in 1978. Anne DiPardo (1990), who has since provided a careful analysis of the opposition between narrative and exposition in the Western rhetorical tradition, maintains that the dichotomy and the privileging of exposition are culturally-based and artificial. What's more, this privileging of discourse places already inexperienced writers at further disadvantage. At the time that I worked with James, I intuitively valued narrative but had yet to develop a theoretical understanding of the importance of autobiographical narrative writing to critical reflection and the analysis and formation of identity. Nonetheless, as writing instructors teaching under the Office of Minority Affairs, my colleagues and I regularly participated in the training of TAs assigned to teach "EOP English" and frequently met and consulted with them to discuss the progress and problems of EOP students. In such roles and relationships, I developed a greater understanding of critical issues in multicultural education—how social and political factors figure into the educational equation, particularly with regard to literacy and language. This awareness became the foundation for the next phase in my journey.

MAKING THE UNCONSCIOUS CONSCIOUS

In 1984, I took on the responsibility of coordinating the tutor training program at the EOP Writing Center. A change in administration at the Instructional Center had provided the opportunity and it seemed to others like a good fit. I had always enjoyed working closely with students and had become aware of various problems with budget cuts and personnel in the center—the need to reenvision the existing tutor recruitment and training program "to realize more fully the writing center's potential" in working with EOP students (Okawa 1993, 171).

Having neither a formal theoretical background in composition or writing center administration nor experience in recruiting and training writing tutors, I was free to dig deeply into learned as well as intuitive knowledge in my own life and to draw from those around me. At first, much of the content for such training seemed obvious: the literature on composition theory and research, of which there was a growing amount; on composition teaching, of which there was less; on writing center theory and practice, of which there was relatively little at the time, especially regarding settings such as ours with a complex multicultural clientele. Thom Hawkins' writing center at UC-Berkeley came close and I heavily consulted his article on the social dimension of peer tutoring (1980), as well as Stephen North's (1984) "The Idea of a Writing Center" and Thomas Reigstad & Donald McAndrew's (1984) *Training Tutors for Writing Conferences.*

Ultimately, however, we at our center had to plumb the depths of our own experience and creativity; the program became a joint venture, especially among the tutors and me.[4] To begin with, I believed that

> at a writing center like the EOP, which serves multicultural and multilingual students, peers or other tutors who mirror the students' diversity and who are themselves learning to take on challenges in the academic world can become important role models for less experienced writers. (Okawa1993, 171)

Staffing the center with a multicultural cohort of writing tutors reflected a significant change in philosophy and practice and was no small feat—the concerted effort of EOP English teachers, counselors, and tutors. Donna Yamada Bolima came to apply for a tutoring position at the encouragement of another tutor. She was an EOP student and single parent of two children, and I was still in the early stages of reorganizing and revising the program's curriculum and structure. Of Anglo/Japanese American heritage, she readily tapped into my experience as a Japanese American woman as she explored issues of her own identity and history; at the same time, Donna, together with other tutors, worked with me to build a program that became for many, in George Hunter's (1993) words, both nurturing and communal.

As our program evolved, beyond piecing together training materials on tutoring, I learned most from the tutors. I developed a healthy respect for their stories, their questions, and perspectives—on conferencing, on articles regarding theory and research that I often brought to the table, on the connections between their work and their lives. At our weekly training meetings, discussions of relationships between theory and practice—their insights and mine—became dialogical, cyclical, and critically reflective as they raised issues and described experiences, we jointly shared our perceptions, and they went back—once more again—to the writing center to practice. Theory emerged out of or was critiqued from our experience. On one occasion, we read Patricia Bizzell's (1986) "What Happens When Basic Writers Come to College?" and could appreciate her taxonomy of different conflicts encountered by students. But to her concluding assertion regarding basic writers having "more to lose in modifying their earlier world views"—that "precisely because of the hegemonic power of the academic world view, my hypothesis is that they will also find its acquisition well worth the risks" (301), one tutor asked, "Is it?" This caused us to reconsider Bizzell's assumptions in light of our own experience and that of the writers we served.

In the context of the academy's hegemony and its traditional exclusionary stance with reference to students of color and other nontraditional students, one issue that continued to loom large for us was the complex question of the writer's identity and authority: not only *who* has ownership of a written text, but perhaps more important, who has the *right* to control ownership of a text? Who has the *right* to write in the academy? In addressing this question, I learned through experience that "the training of tutors is a political act, as is the tutoring and teaching of writing. What I call 'self-discovering' had to begin with the trainer and the tutors and our views of learners and learning" (Okawa 1993, 175). This process involved tutors' developing

> an understanding of and respect for the culturally based experience and the expectations that they and their students brought to each tutoring session. Developing such sensitivities required that the tutors be critically reflective. For example, they needed to explore and critique their own attitudes toward language, their cultural and socioeconomic values, and their worldviews . . . .In this way, tutors could respond not according to prescribed rules of writing center behavior ("when this happens, do this"), but according to their own sense of social responsibility based on their own informed decisions . . . . (Okawa 1993, 176 –177)

I was beginning to understand the concept of "pedagogy," although not the word itself. Then in 1987, I learned about Paulo Freire. What I read in *Pedagogy of the Oppressed* influenced me profoundly, validated and gave clarity to my existing thoughts, and shaped new perspectives and practices. That spring, I coincidentally heard about a week-long summer workshop focusing on Freire and his work. Held in southern California, it included as principal speakers Freire himself, Henry Giroux, and Michael Apple, who espoused a social critique and pedagogy that gave me renewed hope in education and educators. The session was very well-attended and people of color made up a fairly good contingent. At some point, however, I remember that some of us began to feel a familiar discomfort and powerlessness in relation to the dominant group. We formed a People of Color Caucus—a pan-ethnic group—and asked Freire to meet with us. We sat together with him, educators of African

American, Latino/a, Asian American, and American Indian backgrounds, to discuss matters of race, class, and social and political oppression that we had experienced and observed. To the questions, "What can be done? What are we to do?," Freire gave us advice that I have never forgotten: "Find the spaces," he replied. "Invade the spaces" (n.p.). More than anything else that he could have said, these words have continued to empower me and give me hope in moments of despair, even as I write a decade later. In the fall, I excitedly related this experience to the tutors at the writing center and our reading of Freire's writing gave a revitalized direction to our work.

For some EOP Writing Center tutors, the experience of tutoring became life-changing—more than a job. Having grown up on the Yakima Indian Reservation, Shana Windsor (1991), an EOP student like Donna at the time, writes about losing her identity in her writing and in school until she encounters an alternative view:

> I figured out through our tutor-training seminars exactly what part of myself was missing in my writing. . . . I had in essence succeeded in doing exactly what Indian elders fear their young people will do when we go to college: I was not allowing my home culture to exist in hopes of gaining academic validation . . . .When I came to the writing center, I was amazed and shocked that others found my culture a valuable asset instead of a hindrance. . . . And in recognizing my culture's right to exist within academia, I have not only developed a pride for who I am but a strength to express—and encourage others to express—their own cultural ideals, beliefs, and values. (19 –20)

Likewise, Lucy Chang (1991) describes how "working at the writing center with many "students like me" gave her "the power of cultural confidence" (17) as a Korean American in encounters with stereotyping at the university. George Hunter, who identified himself as "African American, American Indian, and Asian," writes that the writing center and his associations there

> literally brought me in from the cold of feelings of racial isolation . . . . Because of my academic pursuits as an English major, I have often (almost always) found myself to be the only minority in a classroom. . . . Though I love the English language and its literature, strangely enough, I have never had the occasion to discuss in depth the very human issues of racism, I think partly because of the discipline itself. (quoted in Okawa 1993, 189)

For some like Donna, this experience became a kind of inheritance and an opportunity to cultivate her sense of self and values as she became a high school Upward Bound teacher:

> The biggest motivator . . . that I've found for some of [my] students has been my willingness to validate them by giving them the authority for their learning, in much the same way that I was given that opportunity through the Peer Tutor Training. Not only have I seen how collaborative learning and respect for

diverse learning styles can empower students and other tutors, but I have found value in striving to be an educator who is willing to be a learner. (Bolima)

For me, the theories and research on writing had to find their way into the internalized and unconscious rhythm of what we practiced as individuals and as a community, just as our unconscious knowledge and practice became a part of what we could consciously know through our stories.

TIME FOR SYNTHESIS

Seasoned by a newfound awareness of the institutional and human politics in education, especially regarding race, ethnicity, and gender, and upon the urging and support of many EOP Writing Center tutors, I entered a doctoral program in English at Indiana University of Pennsylvania. I needed time to think and theorize. Early on in my coursework, my interest in people's life stories—demonstrated academically in my master's thesis research on Nathanael West's life and work, then in a study of folk toy artisans in Japan and of an anthropologist named Frederick Starr, and finally in glimpses into the lives of tutors like Donna, Shana, Lucy, and George[5]—began to shape what was to become my dissertation project. Through a preliminary study conducted in the summer of 1991,[6] I discovered both the richness of teacher narratives and the feasibility of such research.

Reading Stories, Reading Ourselves

The project actually had its origins earlier that year. I was in the throes of doctoral coursework when I attended the 1991 CCCC Annual Convention in Boston. At the time, I had an idea for my dissertation, very much in its infancy, and tossed it around over Boston clam chowder with a fellow graduate student, whom I will call Miguel. I barely knew him then, but he was very supportive of my idea—at the time, to learn something about people of color who become writing/language arts teachers and to create a forum for the voices of composition teachers of color through their life-narratives. He volunteered to write his.

In conducting this preliminary study, I sketched out the initial purpose and structure of what became my dissertation project, making my way over various institutional hurdles in the process. More importantly, I gained the valuable experience of locating and working with preliminary study participants, negotiating my relationship with the writers and their texts, analyzing their narratives, learning about imprecision in aspects of my design, and realizing my personal responsibility and limitations as a researcher working cross culturally with other teachers of color. My experience with Miguel and his narrative, in particular, profoundly shaped my perception of and commitment to the project and, I believe now, epitomizes the process of critical reflection in research.

Born and reared in Texas, Miguel identifies himself as a Chicano, a "Valley Tejano," a Texas Mexican. He was 36 when we started this project, old enough to be more than scorched by segregation and bussing in Texas, young enough to experience the complexities and contradictions of affirmative action programs as a graduate student. After volunteering to participate, what Miguel finally produced was a rich 30-page narrative; what was most important was what happened to both of us in the process.

The day after the submission "deadline" Miguel called me. He was printing his narrative as we spoke and promised to send it out in a couple of days. In a letter of a week earlier, he had written about the value of the process for him: "So far, it's been an enlightening project, as I think I've arrived at some insights that I'd not [had] before" (Letter, July 24, 1991). Now in this phone call, he said that it had also been quite "a pathological process," "painful," but that it "helped a lot" in his writing and other things: "writing the piece has helped me to deal with my demons, to recuperate my past, recuperate my self" (Field notes, August 2, 1991). The complexity of the process was profound to me. In a letter accompanying the narrative he finally sent, he writes about the dimensions of his experience with this narrative, a kind of meta-commentary about its content, about the relationship between his personal life and his own experience with literacy, past and present:

> I will perhaps be perceived as digressing too much into my past, but many of these things are *important for the context* that I felt needed to be set up. . . . [T]he piece is not . . . as much about learning to write and teaching composition as it is about me and the *circumstances surrounding my education*. . . . For me, there were too many things happening outside the proverbial classroom that affected what was going on within it. . . . [B]efore one can be expected to perform well within a classroom, as both a student and a teacher, one has to take care of business outside the classroom. For people like me, taking care of business outside the classroom affected me in ways that I feel adversely affected my performance in the classroom. . . . There was a constant struggle to keep things straight. [emphasis mine] (letter, August 4, 1991)

His comments illustrate, as Ramón Saldívar (1990) points out, that "the social world represented in the writings of Chicano men and women is an emphatically political one" (4), that their "narratives . . . are predominantly critical and ideological" (6).

In this letter Miguel is frank, insightful, gripping in his honesty and emotion. He situates his experience solidly in a social process of discovery—of a search for a familial and communal past and present—what W. A. Nericcio (1988), in discussing Chicano literary autobiography, calls a struggle with "self-definition on an individual and collective basis" (166). In doing so he had to relive his pain:

> The "Great Books" classes—if they taught me anything, it was the importance of history to a person's understanding of his or her place in this thing called time. Much of my folks' past has been lost or erased because of the ideologically

turbulent times that pervaded their places of origin. It's been my task to try and find out as much as I possibly can about those forces which have shaped their—our—lives. I don't want to die until my understanding of this past is rich and full. My cup does not as yet run over.

And because it does not run over, this cup of my ill-fated understanding of my past, I have had an emotionally difficult—very difficult—time writing what I've written for you in this piece. The difficulty lay not in the actual composition of the piece; the difficulty came from waking up the next morning hungover from the drinking I had to subject myself to after sitting down and writing about my past. I wanted to forget rather than remember what happened to me and my family, as well as to people like me. (letter, August 4, 1991)

I could feel his anguish, an anguish greater than his own, a communal anguish. I shed my own tears as I read of his and I came to realize with overwhelming emotion what I had started, my responsibility in such a project: the "carving of the face" that Gloria Anzaldúa (1987, 22) writes of is Miguel finding words for his experience, drinking in despair over the past that he chose to recall. I realized that it was I who served as catalyst without knowing the manifold repercussions of my request.

In spite of my idealistic and theoretical intentions to be open and flexible as a reader, however, I found myself having some specific expectations about narrativity (Prince 1982) as I read Miguel's piece, bemoaning its lack of specificity of time and place, the absence of narrative detail. I felt uneasy about the criticism but plunged on. Both in a phone conversation and in a letter, I asked him to consider this:

As I told you [on the phone], I see this piece to be more a narrative essay than a narrative per se, mainly because the sense of time and place often remains unspecified (e.g., details about where you were—the Valley vs. A- as places, how you felt physically and spiritually packing pineapples, etc.).* Though the general chronological/spatial context is evident, the absence of specificity/descriptive and narrative detail* left me feeling kind of hungry. As a reader, I wanted more, feeling teased where you gave only so much, then held back.

*Prince (1982) refers to these points as characteristic of narrative, providing lower-higher degrees of narrativity (a "good story"). (letter, September 20, 1991)

Yet despite the promised candidness of my comments I found that I felt uncomfortable with the "teacherly" response: To what purpose? What was the critique for? I wasn't asking him to revise, to write a "better" narrative for me; the comment wasn't so much teacherly as the habitual nature of the critique. Partly because of this experience, I realized that I had unknowingly set up this preliminary study to emphasize the written discourse, the text over the teacher. In writing my dissertation proposal, in deciding to study teachers and their lives rather than their texts alone, I added the interview/conversation component which would allow me to shift my focus from texts to lives and which would make my responses to the written narrative not an academic exercise but a part of a real dialogue between the teachers and me.

In understanding Miguel's narrative, I had to suspend my expectations as much as possible, to learn to read again. I based this initial reading on what I call "meta-metaphorical analysis," a method drawn from the study of metaphor as a cultural phenomenon (Lakoff & Johnson1980; Munby 1986). Moving one step beyond the explicit, I attempted to identify and understand the "meta-metaphors" in the teacher's text, how Miguel subconsciously or unconsciously conceptualized his experiences. These metaphors provided me with heuristic lenses, implicit thematic vantage points from which to view this teacher's experience and images. My later reading of Miguel's manuscript, however, provided a significantly different experience from my readings in Fall 1991 and informed my receptiveness to and perception of the teacher narratives in the dissertation itself. It gave me a still more complex and dynamic picture of Miguel's experience with literacy, culture, and the academy.

For example, beginning with his title "My Experience with Writing and the Teaching of Writing in College: A Life from the Boundary," Miguel appropriates Mike Rose's (1989) title as the teller of his own tale, Rose having told not only his own story but those of his students. Equally important, Miguel situates himself with respect to "college," using the topographical and political boundary metaphor not uncommon in Chicano/a literature (e.g., see Anzaldúa 1987; Mora 1986; Gomez-Peña 1988) where locational images of borders, borderlands, terrain, and outsiders abound. In the early pages of his narrative, the phrase "a life from the boundary" seems to reflect some sense of longing to move from the margin into the mainstream—his aspirations to become a writer and an attorney, majoring in philosophy and pre-law.

One dominant theme in Miguel's narrative emerges as an extension of the locational boundary metaphor. In his reflections, Miguel seems to conceptualize the course of his life as a writer and writing teacher in terms of travel, as a journey outward—forays away from his familial and geographical center. The boundary shifts and expands in larger and larger concentric circles: to school (when he enters the fourth grade, he is bussed from his home in A—, Texas to East A—"where the schools for Mexican Americans were located, even though there was a school much closer that I could have attended," 13), to work, to navy boot camp, to college, to graduate school elsewhere in Texas and then in the north, and finally a returning home to teach in Texas. This geographical movement corresponds to a developing sense of identity, ethnic and professional.

In the course of the narrative itself, Miguel portrays a dramatic change in his sense of self as a person and as a teacher, in ethnic identification vis-a-vis the academic establishment. Although the narrator early on assumes a tone and rhetorical stance of a passive, naive, almost fatalistic persona, he develops an increasingly critical perspective as only a life *at* the boundary, not *within* the boundary, can. Nericcio (1988) observes that

Chicano autobiography and novels utilizing the autobiographical mode render into words the collective Mexican-American quest for identity. More often than not this narrative follows our development through education. Time and time again one encounters figures developing through and against their 'own' culture within education. (173)

Miguel's telling of his life experience is in itself a critique of his social and educational environment.

In completing the preliminary study, I also learned the consequences of imprecision—how my limited understanding of research in general and the field of narrative research in particular led me originally to ask for a narrative about the teacher's "experience with writing and with the teaching of writing as a teacher/writer of color." Realizing the vagueness of the prompt helped me to be more specific and explicit in conceptualizing the final project, focusing on teachers' personal life histories rather than on their classroom experience.

More importantly, I came face to face with the difficulty and the profound responsibility involved in conducting such auto/biographical research. For example, in the following brief section of his narrative, Miguel describes an early experience he had with teaching writing:

Standing in front of my students for [the] very first time had an incredible effect on me, as I saw in their eyes the same look of hunger—a hunger for . . . a better way of living. But something was still very much amiss . . . .I didn't have the skills to give my students what they needed, which was some minimal amount of literacy. At the end of that first semester of teaching, I remember sitting in a Pizza Hut with some other TAs and the head of the lower division writing courses. . . . I remember crying and [feeling] emotionally distraught because I felt that I had failed at teaching my students what they needed. I had failed my own people, and had allowed myself to be placed in the position, not of helping them, but of actually acting as a gatekeeper barring them from entering . . . the . . . realms of higher learning. The oil of truth, it seemed, would not be flowing down their way, and I had found myself with my hand on the valve that controlled the flow of this oil. (13)

I could see, among other things, his strong identification with his students' lives as well as his fierce commitment to helping them toward a different and better life. I could also see the inadequacy and despair that he felt in his conflicted roles as teacher-gatekeeper, a critique of himself and the system that caused and continues to cause the hunger. After my first reading of Miguel's narrative, I wrote:

I have found that revising my point of departure has been more challenging than I had expected: I am not looking at published texts, relatively static, distant and safe; I am looking at evolving people and their evolving texts, both constantly in flux, sometimes frighteningly close and fragile. (Okawa 1991, 20)

I realize daily that this is a serious proposition, that I must reexamine and revise basic assumptions. Beginning with a small sampling of teachers' stories has been invaluable in informing and sensitizing me to problems and procedures to consider in an extended study. . . . I find myself constantly reflecting and reshaping and redefining—a healthy though often confusing and frustrating creative process. (Okawa 1991, 29)

Despite the conflict that this awareness caused in me, Miguel's words spurred me to believe that stories such as his would give us insights into the issues and odds that teachers of color may face in entering the language and literacy field. Becoming aware of how readily we may objectify another, I believe that in conducting such studies we must pay equally close attention to how and what *we* (as researchers and readers) see, how, as Richard J. Murphy (1990) asserts, through story "we come to understand ourselves" (59).

Auto/biography: Weaving Ikat, Weaving Lives

The dissertation study that emerged from these thoughts and encounters was itself an act of resistance against the isolation that I have felt and that many teachers of color feel in the academic world,[7] a move towards community-building, Freire's (1987) "invasion of spaces." From my experience with Miguel, I became convinced that life-narratives of other teachers of color in language and literacy education would indirectly address the increasingly serious problem of "minority underrepresentation" in education by providing the English teaching field with critical materials that would allow us to learn *from* teachers' lives as well as *about* them. The narratives themselves, written and told by English teachers of color like Miguel, through their own eyes and in their own voices, would provide different perspectives on learning and teaching writing—views shaped by events, persons, environments, choices, and issues in the teachers' lives; role models for prospective teachers of color; and access to new knowledge regarding teacher recruitment and development. At the same time, the autobiographical narratives would give teachers of color an avenue for understanding and validating their own knowledge and experience (Newkirk 1991), as well as a significant forum, a means of cultivating their voices in the history and lore of the field (cf., Goodson 1992). Finally, these stories could provide a dialogic bridge between our idiosyncratic monocultural world views, based on what Maxine Greene (1991) calls "the likelihood of inclusion, the inclusion of those of us who read" (x).

Thus, I asked teachers from African American, Asian American, American Indian and Latino/Latina backgrounds, who were then teaching in English/language arts, to write their narratives about how they came to English teaching. Focusing on the teachers and their personal experience with literacy, ethnicity, and becoming writing teachers, I was intent on exploring persons, not texts, personal lives, not classrooms, seeing the teachers' narrative re-presentations of themselves in their own voices about their paths to literacy and teaching.

Following a close reading and analysis of each narrative and always mindful of the advantages and limits of my position as an insider researcher, I held extensive in-person conversations about the written pieces with the individual teachers. These were taped, transcribed, and analyzed as well. The process of analysis and synthesis proved both fascinating and frustrating. Each teacher's life story became a way of accessing the teacher's knowledge and experience at the same time that it became the representation of that knowledge and experience. However, since I was again treading on new ground in this study rather than replicating an existing model, I found myself in a constant state of reflection and reconsideration:

> No matter what the slant of our eyes, we see our lives from the inside out and outside in, in a continuous process: as the teachers look within their experience and see out through their eyes and in again as I may see them, so do I see them from the outside in while glimpsing myself from the inside out and the outside in as they may see me. (field notes, April, 1994)

To do this kind of seeing, a process that I call "bifocality of difference," and to share an aspect of this experience in turn with the reader, I found myself creating a second level of field text, mid-way between the field texts that D. Jean Clandinin & F. Michael Connelly (1994) describe—the "raw" written narratives and transcribed conversations—and the research text. As I discovered both the need for this text and the form of the text in studying the experiences of Julia, the first teacher, I made the following notes:

> I need to write this intermediate field text portrait in such a way that I bring the teacher's portrayal of her life experience to light, preferably in her own words— I need the particularity, the detail, to bring the texture of the fabric of her life to the reader. For this reason, summary (Butt et al. 1992) is, in many ways, inadequate to the task.
>
> For now, I will call this a "research/biographical portrait." This portrait reflects my interpretation and recasting of the teacher's experiences along chronological lines, a composite of the "raw" descriptions of experience in the field texts. The composite becomes a re-presentation of the teacher's life story *viz.* her developing literacy and identity as a writing teacher. In this way, I as researcher can begin to capture the particulars of her experience as well as to portray/suggest the complex way we have worked to reconstruct it—the particulars essential to this research. Kind of like a warp-weft ikat, the previously dyed threads of her story and of my retelling of it overlap for the most part but at the edges the design is not clear-cut and distinct, leaving space for multi-dimensional interpretations in our on-going conversation. (n.d.)

After many fits and starts with terminology, I finally felt comfortable with "auto/biographical portrait" because "auto/biography" acknowledged our collaborative roles and voices—our joint agency—and resolved some of the conflict in what Clandinin & Connelly (1994) describe as the struggle for a research voice [which] is captured by the analogy of living on a knife edge as one struggles to express one's own voice in the midst of an inquiry designed to capture the participants' experience and represent their voices, all the while attempting to create a research text. (423)

In this study, each teacher was naturally quite individual in ethnic background, gender, age, socioeconomic and political orientations, and writing/teaching experience. To convey the uniqueness of each person's life experience, I had to exploit the case study approach fully in the sense that "the power of this method is its capacity for particularization, for the creating of portraits of individual writers" (Newkirk 1991, 129).

Through particularity, the word-portrait provided the texture of the life as I attempted to capture the rhythm and spirit of the teacher's experience and language. As I grappled with this process, I read how Sarah Lawrence Lightfoot sees portraiture based on her personal experience: "portraits capture essence . . . . portraits make the subjects feel 'seen' in a way they have never felt seen before, fully attended to, wrapped up in an empathetic gaze" (in Ayers, 1989 19). In my field notes I recalled my own past and present experience with the process of portraiture:

> This supports what I want to do in an exciting way: I had thought of writing portraits and used the term in my projected table of contents last fall. This concept of "portraiture," which I have since read about in Ayers (1989), helps to crystallize what I want to do with the portraits—to capture the essence of each teacher as I have seen her/him and experienced it through their writing and talking. I am not trying to arrive at truth in any objective way, but am finding the essence of their selves and lives as they have portrayed it and as I have filtered it through my lenses, not a camera lens this time where the camera would record a physical reality, but a painter's eye that I had forgotten I had, for my painter's hand has remained dormant for decades (since my "portrait" of [my father] and my studio classes in college). Like Manuel [one of the participant teachers], I always liked to draw and paint more than write as a child; this, not the written word, was my favored medium, which somehow got overlaid with the tasks of growing up . . . . (field notes, July 12, 1993)

The "empathetic gaze" described by Lightfoot recalls the value of empathy—the importance of "developing the capacity for empathy" affirmed by Patricia Hill Collins' (216) Black feminist epistemology. Empathy became critical to the process of building relationships as well as to the substance of the relationship itself, as the portraits in the study illustrated.

In writing the auto/biographies, I felt like a weaver—with a painter's eye but a weaver's hand—as the words, pre-dyed threads of the individual teacher's stories, and of my re-presenting of them maintained their own color, pattern, and integrity as I wove them together. As a writer exploring the teachers' life experiences in this intensely recursive reading and writing process, I consciously chose not to privilege their written over their spoken words but rather to let the power of the narrator's discourse determine its use.

Learning Coherence
or What Do Teachers Learn from Self-Reflection and Writing?

In retrospect, one of the most important results of the study was that the methodology allowed both participants and researcher to see some coherence in our lives, the kind of benefit to the teachers that I had hoped would result from the research process, but that I had not anticipated for myself. Elliot Mishler (1986) refers to "themal coherence," that is, "how utterances express a speaker's recurrent assumptions, beliefs, and goals" (89), drawing on the taxonomy of Agar and Hobbs. For these teachers of color, writing their stories and talking with me involved finding such themal coherence—new relationships and thus new dimensions of meaning in their life experiences, insights into how ethnicity, race, class, and other social factors have figured in. Jeff became aware of the strong relationship between his present attitudes and his past experience, finding

> that there's a stronger relationship to the history that I have to writing, in terms of resistance I had to traditional forms of English . . . .I hadn't thought about it and I think your questions helped me to think through and make those connections. That was really important for me today to see that relationship. (Okawa 1995, 340)

His references to relationships and connections, his history and resistance, were thematic in his auto/biography. Susan observed that reflecting on her learning experience gave her a new grounding for future action:

> It gave me a certain sense of solidness—looking back on my own writing process . . . gave me a solid understanding of what I've gone through in my learning process and what steps I've taken to solidify myself—my own voice. It's kind of made it more concrete . . . . it gave a lot of insight—solid insight—and that helps with my teaching now. (Okawa 1995, 340)

Her images of "solidness," "a solid understanding," and solidifying herself stand in direct contrast to earlier images of chaos and "the abyss" in her life-narrative, reflecting a new-found secure and sound presence in terms of both her identity and voice. Julia contemplated the pervasiveness of writing and teaching in her life—how much a part of the process of living it has been for her:

> I think the one thing I learned is that it's been a pretty on-going thing—that writing and teaching and teaching of writing has been very much a part of my experience for many, many years . . . . to look back at it was to see that it [was] a part of my life and a part of my thought system. (Okawa 1995, 340)

From a different angle, Manuel commented on the value of seeing himself through someone else's perspective, reinforcing my metaphor of "seeing from the inside out and the outside in" in a recursive process:

I got to see myself like somebody else sees me which is really hard for me to do .... It's very hard for me to see myself and sometimes, 'cause you're living in it, it's really hard for you to put your life into perspective .... That's one of the things I gained from this, and while I was writing the narrative I was thinking . . . things were just coming up that I'd never thought about in years. They'd just been put away. (Okawa 1995, 341)

In recalling "things" that had "just been put away," Manuel, as others, was able to reconstruct and re-present his life in different dimensions.

For Miguel and all participants in this dissertation project—teachers and researcher—this process seemed to expand perspectives of our knowledge as persons and teachers and, as such, was mutually empowering. As a researcher, I not only found meaning in the teacher's stories by reading, studying, and discussing them, but learned more about teaching from them and found additional coherence in my own experience, seeing my life in relation to their lives. Because voices were "released" (McCracken, 1995) through this study in this way, the methodology provided a means for empathy, a much needed exchange in troubled times like ours.

COMING FULL CIRCLE

Henry Giroux & Paulo Freire (1987) assert that oppression is made more possible with the loss of historical memory. In the face of colonization, physical or mental, we do well to record, reclaim, and reconsider our stories. Individually, as we discover our own coherence, like Miguel, like the tutors in the writing center and teachers in my study, we may develop our personal identity and strength; socially and communally as educators of color, "we make the revolutionary history" (3), as bell hooks (1989) advises. For this reason, a major purpose in such explictly or implicitly collaborative projects among educators of color is autoethnographic; we re-present ourselves in person and in words, write or co-write our own histories in the context of statistics of absence and underrepresentation.

In my reflections for this essay, I see now that my models for teaching, learning, and research were, in part, unconscious:

Several years prior to my arrival in Seattle in 1980, I had spent some time working at a pottery amid rice fields in rural Japan, serving as an apprentice to the master potter. It was an opportunity that had quite serendipitously fallen into my lap and though I did learn something about making things of clay, I learned more of traditional Japanese educational and work relationships. Though unplanned, this was in a sense a reencounter with my brief experience with Noh performance a few years earlier. Over months rather than weeks, I was "once more again" a novice, this time entering into a pottery community with its own discourse and expectations. It was here that I really learned the Japanese language while also learning what it meant to observe and to listen and to be the last apprentice in—sweeping, cleaning, cooking, kneading clay, firing the kama (kiln) during all night vigils, and throwing pots "mo ikai" until the rhythm finally came. Humbling. We worked together and ate together, the sensei, other apprentices, and I, always building the community. Later, studying traditional folk toy artisans and other craftspeople, I found these same kinds of relationships and rhythms—now a study in pedagogy.

Now as I write, I have become aware that I integrated these images and relationships years later into both the writing center tutor training and my research. As at the pottery, despite an implicit hierarchy, we—tutors and trainer, teachers and researcher—worked along side each other in the educative process. The reality of tutor training required that I become more aware of my internalized experience and, after the fact, I observed that "the tutor training process evolved along a community/family-building model" (1993, 181). Yet even at the time of that writing, I failed to make a connection with a significant part of my own past, only to become conscious of it now years later through these reflections. My past has not been set aside by my present; my life has more coherence than I had previously thought. Now I see mirrored images of communities, of stories of teaching and learning.

Another image returns: in one of my wanderings in the vicinity of the pottery in Japan, I discovered a single large rock in the middle of a pond. The creatures beneath the surface must have stirred, creating expanding concentric circles around the rock. Ripples and reverberations. It was like a zen garden. A recovery of such memories can be liberatory; liberation is the gift of critical research.

NOTES

1.   Michael Connelly and D. Jean Clandinin (1990) refer to narrative as "phenomenon and method" (2).

2.   In a sense, the experience and not merely the introduction was a gift of my own *sensei* (teacher/mentor) Richard N. McKinnon in Seattle, Washington, one that I recognize in its depth and entirety only now.

3.   I have written quite extensively about the tutors and tutor training program, as well as the context and background, of the EOP Writing Center in Okawa (1993), "Redefining Authority: Multicultural Students and Tutors at the Educational Opportunity Program Writing Center at the University of Washington," *Writing Centers in Context*; and in Okawa, Fox, Chang, Windsor, Chavez, & Hayes (1991), "Multi-Cultural Voices: Peer Tutoring and Critical Reflection in the Writing Center," *Writing Center Journal*.

4.   See above Okawa, 1993; Okawa, Fox, Chang, Windsor, Chavez, and Hayes, 1991.

5.   These tutors, together with Nadine Fabbi Shushan, presented their narratives at the Pacific Coast Writing Centers Association Annual Conference in Tacoma, WA, October, 1989.

6.   This account is derived from chapter one of my dissertation, *Expanding Perspectives of Teacher Knowledge: A Descriptive Study of Autobiographical*

Narratives of Writing Teachers of Color, 1995. Other references to this study and subsequent dissertation research are derived from different chapters of the same work.

7.   See, for example, González, 1995; Holloway, 1993; hooks, 1989; Ling, 1987; Villanueva, 1993, and others who problematize this experience.

WORKS CITED

Adams, H. 1995. A Grassroots Think Tank: Linking Writing and Community-Building. *Democracy & Education: The Magazine for Classroom Teachers*. Athens, OH: Ohio University College of Education. Winter: 9–16.

Addison, J. 1997. Data Analysis and Subject Representation in Empowering Composition Research. *Written Communication* 14: 106-128.

Albrecht, G. 1992. *The Disability Business: Rehabilitation in America*. Newbury Park, CA: Sage.

Allen, Michael. 1995. Valuing Differences: Portnet's First Year. *Assessing Writing* 2: 67-90.

———, et al. 1997. Portfolios, WAC, Email and Assessment: An Inquiry on Portnet. Yancey and Weiser: 370–384.

The Alliance for Computers and Writing. (7 July 1998) http://english.ttu.edu/acw

American Psychological Association, American Educational Research Association, and National Council on Measurement in Education. 1974. Standards for Educational and Psychological Tests. Washington, DC: American Psychological Association.

Anastasi, Anne. 1986. Evolving Concepts of Test Validation. *Annual Review of Psychology* 37:1-15.

Anderson, P. 1996. Ethics, Institutional Review Boards, and the Involvement of Human Participants in Composition Research. Mortensen and Kirsch: 260-286.

Anderson, Richard C. and P. David Pearson. 1984. A Schema-Theoretic View of Basic Processes in Reading Comprehension. *Handbook of Reading Research*. ed. P. David Pearson. New York: Longman.

Anderson, Worth, Cynthia Best, Alycia Black, John Hurst, Brandt Miller and Susan Miller. 1990. Cross-Curricular Underlife: A Collaborative Report on Ways with Academic Worlds. *CCC* 41: 11-36.

Anson, Chris. 1989. Response Styles and Ways of Knowing. *Writing and Response: Theory, Practice, Research*, ed Chris Anson. Urbana: NCTE. 332-367.

Anstendig, Linda, and David Hicks. 1996. *Writing Through Literature*. Upper Saddle River, NJ: Prentice Hall.

Anzaldúa, Gloria. 1987. La Conciencia De La Mestiza: Towards a New Consciousness. *Borderlands/la Frontera: The New Mestiza*. San Francisco, CA: Spinsters/Aunt Lute Book Company.

Ashton-Warnewr, Sylvia. 1963. *Teacher* NY: Simon and Schuster.

Atchley, R. C. 1991. The Influence of Aging or Frailty on Perceptions and Expressions of the Self: Theoretical and Methodological Issues. In J. E. Birren et al. 207-225.

Atwell, Nancie.1987. *In the Middle: Writing, Reading and Learning with Adolescents*. Portsmouth, NH: Boynton/Cook Heinemann.

Auslander, Bonnie. 1993. In Search of Mr. Write. Editor's Choice. *College English* 55: 531-532.

———. 1994. Lip-Synching with Your Dog. *Writing on the Edge* 5: 53-54.

Axelrod, Rise B., and Charles R. Cooper. 1997. *The St. Martin's Guide to Writing.* 5th ed. NY:St. Martin's.

Ayers, W. C. 1989. *The Good Preschool Teacher: Six Teachers Reflect on Their Lives.* NY: Teachers College Press.

Azurin, Arnold Molina. 1995. *Reinventing the Filipino Sense of Being and Becoming: Critical Analyses of the Orthodox Views in Anthropology, History, Folklore and Letters.* 2nd ed. Diliman, Quezon City: U of Philippines P.

Baker, Sheridan. 1998. *The Practical Stylist with Readings and Handbook.* 8th ed. NY: Longman.

Balester, Valerie. 1993. *Cultural Divide: A Study of African-American College Level Writers.* Portsmouth, NH: Boynton-Cook.

Barthes, Roland.1995. The Death of the Author. In *Authorship: From Plato to the Postmodern*, ed. Stan Burke. Edinburgh: Edinburgh UP. 142-148. First published in *Image–Music–Text*, ed. and trans. by Stephen Heath. NY: Hill, 1977.

———. 1968. *Writing Degree Zero.* Trans. by A. Lavers and C. Smith. NY: Hill and Wang.

Bartholomae, D. 1995. Writing With Teachers: A Conversation with Peter Elbow. *CCC* 46: 62-71.

———. 1993. The Tidy House: Basic Writing and the American Curriculum. *Journal of Basic Writing* 12: 4-21.

Barton, E. 1997. Literacy in (Inter)action. *College English* 59: 408-437.

Basso, Keith. 1979. Portraits of the Whiteman: Linguistic Play and Cultural Symbols Among the Western Apache. Cambridge: Cambridge UP.

Bateman, Donald. 1996. Collected Writings, ed. James Zebroski. Unpublished manuscript.

Battaglia, Debbora, ed. 1995. On Practical Nostalgia: Self-Prospecting Among Urban Trobianders. In *Rhetorics of Self-Making.* Berkeley: U of California P.

Bazerman, Charles. 1989. What are We Doing as a Research Community? *Rhetoric Review* 7: 223–24.

———. 1988. *Shaping Written Knowledge: The Genre and Activity of the Experimental Article in Science.* Madison: U of Wisconsin P.

———. and J. Paradis, ed. 1991. *Textual Dynamics of the Profession.* Madison: U of Wisconsin.

Behar, Ruth. 1993. *Translated Woman: Crossing the Border with Esperenza's Story.* Boston: Beacon Press.

——— and Deborah A. Gordon, ed. 1995. *Women Writing Culture.* Berkeley: U of California P.

Berlin, James A. 1996. *Rhetorics, Poetics, and Cultures: Refiguring College English Studies.* Urbana: NCTE.

———. 1988. Rhetoric and Ideology in the Writing Class. *College English.* 50: 477-493.

———. 1987. *Rhetoric and Reality.* Carbondale: So. IL UP.

———. 1982. Contemporary Composition: The Major Pedagogical Theories. *College English* 44: 765-77.

Bernstein, Richard. 1990. When Parentheses are Transgressive. *New York Times Magazine*, 29 July: 16.

Berthoff, Ann E. 1996. Problem Dissolving by Triadic Means. *College English* 58:9-21.

———. 1991. Semiotics and Edward Sapir. In *Recent Developments in Theory and History: The Semiotic Web*, eds. T. Sebeok, et al. NY: Mouton. 47-60.

———. 1990. Killer Dichotomies: Reading In/ Reading Out. In *Farther Along: Transforming Dichotomies in Rhetoric and Composition*, ed. H. Roskelly and K. Ronald. Portsmouth, NH: Boynton/Cook Heinemann. 12-24.

———. 1981. *The Making of Meaning: Metaphors, Models, and Maxims for Writing Teachers*. Portsmouth, NH: Boynton/Cook Heinemann.

———. 1971. The Problem of Problem Solving. *CCC*. 21:237-242.

Bialostosky, Don H., Wendy Bishop, Susan Welsh. 1995. Interchanges: Responses to Bartholomae and Elbow. *CCC* 46: 184-103.

Birren, J. E., J. E. Lubben, J. C. Rowe, and D. E. Deutchman, eds. 1991. *The Concept and Measurement of Quality of Life in the Frail Elderly*. San Diego: Academic Press.

Bishop, Wendy. Forthcoming. *Thirteen Ways of Looking for a Poem: A Guide to Writing Poetry*. NY: Longman.

———. 1997a. *Teaching Lives: Essays and Stories*. Logan, UT: Utah State UP.

———. 1992. I-Witnessing in Composition: Turning Ethnographic Data into Narratives. *Rhetoric Review* 11: 147-157.

——— and Hans Ostrom, eds. 1997a. *Genre and Writing: Issues, Arguments, Alternatives*. Portsmouth, NH: Boynton/Cook Heinemann. 3-16.

——— and Hans Ostrom, eds. 1997b. *Elements of Alternate Style: Essays on Writing and Revision*. Portsmouth, NH: Boynton/Cook, Heinemann.

——— and Sandra Teichman. 1993. Tales of Two Teachers: Writing Together in Writing Classrooms. *English Leadership Quarterly* 15: 2–5.

Bissex, Glenda. 1980. *GNYS AT WRK: A Child Learns to Write and Read*. Cambridge: Harvard UP.

Bizzell, Patricia. 1992. *Academic Discourse and Critical Consciousness*. Pittsburgh: U of Pittsburgh P.

———. 1986. What Happens When Basic Writers Come to College? *CCC* 37: 294-301.

———. Marxist Ideas in Composition Studies. Harkin and Schilb. 52-68.

——— and B. Herzberg. 1986. Revision of What Makes Writing Good. *CCC* 37: 244-247.

Black, K. 1996. *In the Shadow of Polio: a Personal and Social History*. Reading, MA: Addison-Wesley.

Blakeslee, Ann M., Caroline M. Cole, and Theresa Conefrey. 1996. Constructing Voices in Writing Research: Developing Participatory Approaches to Situated Inquiry. Mortensen and Kirsch. 134-154.

Bledstein, B. J. 1976. *The Culture of Professionalism: The Middle Class and the Development of Higher Education in America*. NY: Norton.

Bleich, D. 1993. Ethnography and the Study of Literacy: Prospects for Socially Generous Research. Gere. 176-102.

Bloom, Lynn Z. 1996. Freshman Composition as a Middle-Class Enterprise. *College English* 58: 654-675.

———. 1992. I Want a Writing Director. *CCC* 43: 176-178.

———, Donald A. Daiker, and Edward M. White, eds. 1996. *Composition in the Twenty-First Century: Crisis and Change*. Carbondale: So. IL UP.

Bolima, Donna Y. 1989. Speaking from Silence. Paper presented at the Pacific Coast Writing Centers Association Annual Conference, Tacoma, WA.

Borland, Katherine. 1991. "That's Not What I Said": Interpretive Conflict in Oral Narrative Research, in *Women's Words*, ed. Sherna Berger Gluck and Daphne Patai. NY: Routledge. 63-75.

Bourdieu, Pierre. 1991. *Language and Symbolic Power.* Cambridge: Harvard UP.

———. 1990. The Scholastic Point of View. *Cultural Anthropology* 5: 380–391.

———. 1988. *The Predicament of Culture: Twentieth Century Ethnography, Literature, and Art.* Cambridge: Harvard UP.

——— and Jean-Claude Passeron. 1990. *Reproduction in Education, Society and Culture.* Newbury Park, CA: Sage.

Boyer, Ernest. 1990. *Scholarship Reconsidered: Priorities of the Professoriate.* Princeton: The Carnegie Foundation.

Braddock, Richard, Richard Lloyd-Jones, and Lowell Schoer. 1963. *Research in Written Composition.* Urbana: NCTE.

Brady, Jeanne, and Adrianna Hernandez. 1993. Feminist Literacies: Toward Emancipatory Possibilities of Solidarity. In *Critical Literacy: Politics, Praxis, and the Postmodern*, ed. Colin Lankshear and Peter L. McLaren, 323-334. Albany: SUNY P.

Brand, Alice. 1985. Hot Cognition: Emotions and Writing Behavior. *JAC* 6: 5-15.

——— and Richard L. Graves, ed. 1994. *Presence of Mind: Writing and the Domain Beyond the Cognitive.* Portsmouth, NH: Boynton/Cook Heinemann.

Brent, Harry. 1985. Epistemological Presumptions in the Writing Process: The Importance of Content to Writing. Waldrep. 45-62.

Brereton, John. 1995. *The Origins of Composition Studies in the American College, 1875–1925: A Documentary History.* Pittsburgh: U of Pittsburgh P.

Bridwell-Bowles, Lillian. 1995. Freedom, Form, Function: Varieties of Academic Discourse. *CCC* 46: 46-62.

———. 1992. Discourse and Diversity: Experimental Writing within the Academy. *CCC* 43: 349-368.

Britton, James. 1970. *Language and Learning.* NY: Penguin.

Broadhead, Glenn J. and Richard C. Freed. 1986. The Variables of Composition: Process and Product in a Business Setting. *Studies in Writing and Rhetoric.* Carbondale: So. IL UP.

Brodkey, Linda. 1996. *Writing Permitted in Designated Areas Only.* Minneapolis: U of Minnesota P.

———. 1994. Writing on the Bias. *College English* 56: 527–547.

Bronfebrenner, Urie. 1976. The Experimental Ecology of Education. *Educational Researcher* 5: 5-15.

Brooke, Robert. 1991. *Writing and Sense of Self: Identity Negotiation in Writing Workshops.* Urbana: NCTE.

———. 1987. Lacan, Transference, and Writing Instruction. *College English* 49: 679-691.

Brown, Stuart, Paul R. Meyer, and Theresa Enos. 1994. Doctoral Programs in Rhetoric and Composition: A Catalog of the Profession. *Rhetoric Review* 12: 240–251.

Bruffee, Kenneth A. 1984. Collaborative Learning and the "Conversation of Mankind". *College English* 46: 635-652.

Bruner, J. 1986. *Actual Minds, Possible Worlds.* Cambridge: Harvard UP.

Bullock, Richard and John Trimbur, eds. 1991. *The Politics of Writing Instruction: Postsecondary.* Portsmouth, NH: Boynton/Cook Heinemann.

Burch. Beth. 1997. Finding Out What's in Their Heads: Using Teaching Portfolios to Assess English Education Students—and Programs. Yancey and Weiser. 263-278.

Burgess, Maureen and Lori Mathis. 1996. Scenarios for Computers in Composition. *Computer Mediated Communication Magazine.* http://www.december.com/cmc/mag/1996/sep/burmat.html

Burke, Stan, ed. 1995. *Authorship: From Plato to the Postmodern.* Edinburgh: Edinburgh UP.

Burnett, Rebecca E., and Helen Rothschild Ewald. 1994. Rabbit Trails, Ephemera, and Other Stories: Feminist Methodology and Collaborative Research. *JAC* 14: 21-51.

Burns, Marilyn and Bonnie Tank. 1988. A Collection of Math Lessons. New Rochelle, NY: Math Solution Pubs.

Burnside, I. M., ed. 1978. *Working with the Elderly: Group Processes and Techniques.* North Scituate, MA: Duxbury Press.

Butt, R., Raymond, D., McCue, G., & Yamagishi, L. 1992. Collaborative Autobiography and the Teacher's Voice. I. F. Goodson. 51-98.

Cameron, D., E. Frazer, P. Harvey, M. Rampton, and K. Richardson. 1992. *Researching Language: Issues of Power and Method.* NY: Routledge.

Cazden, Courtney, and Hymes, Dell. 1978. Narrative Thinking and Story-telling Rights: a Folklorist's Clue to a Critique of Education. *Keystone Folklore* 22: 22-35.

Chafe, W. L. 1990. Some Things That Narratives Tell Us about the Mind. In *Narrative Thought and Narrative Language*, ed. B. K. Britton and A. D. Pellegrini. Hillsdale, NJ: Erlbaum. 79-97.

Chang, Lucy J. Y. 1991. The Spirit of Vision: Writing from the Inside/Outside. *Writing Center Journal* 12: 15-18.

Charney, Davida. 1996. Empiricism Is Not a Four-Letter Word. *CCC* 47: 567-593.

Chatman, S. 1978. *Story and Discourse: Narrative Structure in Fiction and Film.* Ithaca: Cornell UP.

Chiang, Yuet-Sim D. Forthcoming. Inside Out: English Literacy and Cultural Identity Among Asian Americans. In *Language Minority Students, English as a Second Language, and College Composition*, ed. Linda Harklau, Kay Losey and Meryl Siegel. Mahwah, NJ: Erlbaum.

————. 1998. English—Yours, Mine, or Ours: Language Teaching and the Needs of "Non-native" Speakers of English. In *Situated Stories: Valuing Diversity in Composition Research*, ed. Emily Decker and Kathleen Geissler. Portsmouth, NH: Boynton/Cook Heinemann. 128-141

————. 1992. The Process-Oriented Writing Workshop and "Non-Native" Speakers of English: A Teacher-Researcher Study. Dissertation. Lincoln: U of Nebraska P.

————. 1991. A Voice of One's Own: Reconsidering the Needs of Non-Native Speakers of English. ED340014.

Chiseri-Strater, Elizabeth. 1996. Turning in Upon Ourselves: Positionality, Subjectivity, and Reflexivity in Case Study and Ethnographic Research. Mortensen and Kirsch. 115-133.

————.1991. *Academic Literacies: The Public and Private Discourse of University Students.* Portsmouth, NH: Boynton/Cook Heinemann.

Clandinin, D. J., and Connelly, F. M. 1994. Personal Experience Methods. Denzin and Lincoln 413-427.

Clark, Beverly, Lyon Clark and Sonja. 1992. On Blocking and Unblocking Sonja: A Case Study in Two Voices. *CCC* 43: 55-74.

Cliff, M. 1988. A Journey into Speech. *The Graywolf Annual Five: Multicultural Literacy: Opening the American Mind*, ed. R. Simonson and S. Walker. Saint Paul: Graywolf Press. 57-62.

Clifford, James. 1988. *The Predicament of Culture: Twentieth Century Ethnography, Literature, and Art*. Cambridge: Harvard University P.

———. 1986. Introduction: Partial Truths. In *Writing Culture: The Poetics and Politics of Ethnography*, ed. James Clifford and George E. Marcus. Berkeley: U of California P. 1-26.

——— and George E. Marcus, ed. 1986. *Writing Culture: The Poetics and Politics of Ethnography*. Berkeley: U of California P.

Clifford, John. 1992. Responses to the Essays: Toward an Ethical Community of Writers. Forman, 95–103.

Cole, R., D. VanTassel, and R. Kastenbaum, ed. 1992. *Handbook of the Humanities and Aging*. NY: Springer.

Collins, P. H. 1991. *Black Feminist Thought: Knowledge, Consciousness, and the Politics of Empowerment*. NY: Routledge.

Commonwealth Partnership, The. 1996. What you Should Know: An Open Letter to New PhDs. *Profession 96*: 79–81.

Computers and Composition. www.cwrl.utexas.edu/~ccjrnl/

Computer Mediated Communication Magazine. http://www.december.com/cmc/mag/

Connelly, F. M., & Clandinin, D. J. 1990. Stories of Experience and Narrative Inquiry. *Educational Researcher* 19: 2-14.

Connors, Robert J. 1996. The Abolition Debate in Composition: A Short History. Lynn Z. Bloom, et al. 47-63.

———. 1995. The New Abolitionism: Toward a Historical Background. In *Reconceiving Writing, Rethinking Writing Instruction*, ed. J. Petraglia. Mahwah, NJ: Erlbaum. 3–26.

———. 1991. Rhetoric in the Modern University: The Creation of an Underclass. In *The Politics of Writing Instruction: Postsecondary*, ed. R. Bullock and J. Trimbur. Portsmouth, NH: Boynton/Cook Heinemann. 55–84.

———. 1984. Journals in Composition Studies. *College English* 46: 348–365.

——— and Andrea Lunsford. 1993. Teachers' Rhetorical Comments on Student Papers. *CCC* 44: 200-223.

Cooper, Peter. 1984. The Assessment of Writing Ability: A Review of Research. Princeton: Educational Testing Service: *GREB*, No. 82-15R.

Corbett, Edward P.J. 1971. The Theory and Practice of Imitation in Classical Rhetoric. *CCC* 22: 243-250.

Covino, William A., and David A. Jolliffe. 1995. An Introduction to Rhetoric. In *Rhetoric: Concepts, Definitions, Boundaries*. Boston: Allyn and Bacon. 1-26.

Cronbach, Lee J. 1988. Five Perspectives on Validity Argument. *Test Validity*, ed. Harold Wainer. Hillside, NJ: Erlbaum.

———. 1971. Test Validation. *Educational Measurement* 2nd Edition. ed. Robert L. Thorndike. Washington, DC: American Council on Education.

——— and Paul E. Meehl. 1955. Construct Validity in Psychological Tests. *Psychological Bulletin* 52: 281-302.

Crowley, Sharon. 1996. Around 1971: Current-Traditional Rhetoric and Process Models of Composing. Bloom et al. 64-74.

———. 1994. Ancient Rhetorics for Contemporary Students. NY: Macmillan.

———. 1984. Neo-Romanticism and the History of Rhetoric. *PRE/TEXT* 5: 19-38.

Crump, Eric. 25 May 1997. Rhetnet: http://www.missouri.edu/~rhetnet/

Cushman, Donald P., and Gerard A. Hauser. 1973. Weaver's Rhetorical Theory: Axiology and the Adjustment of Belief, Invention, and Judgment. *Quarterly Journal of Speech* 59: 319–329.

Cushman, Ellen. 1996. The Rhetorician as an Agent of Social Change. *CCC* 47:7-28.

Dale, H. 1996. Dilemmas of Fidelity: Qualitative Research in the Classroom. Mortensen and Kirsch. 77-94.

Damrosch, David. 1995. *We Scholars: Changing the Culture of the University*. Cambridge: Harvard UP.

Danette, Paul and Davida Charney.1995. Introducing Chaos (Theory) into Science and Engineering: Effects of Rhetorical Strategies on Scientific Readers. *Written Communication* 12: 396-438.

D'Angelo, Frank. 1975. *A Conceptual Theory of Rhetoric*. Cambridge, MA: Winthrop.

Daniell, Beth. 1994. Theory, Theory Talk, and Composition. In *Writing Theory and Critical Theory*, ed. John Clifford and John Schilb. New York: MLA. 127-140.

Daniels, G. H. 1967. The Process of Professionalization in American Science: The Emergent Period, 1820–1860. *Isis* 58: 151–166.

Dautermann, J. 1996. Social and Institutional Power Relationships in Studies of Workplace Writing. Mortensen and Kirsch. 241-259.

Denzin, Norman K. and Yvonna S. Lincoln, ed. 1994. *Handbook of Qualitative Research*. Thousand Oaks, CA: Sage.

Derrida, Jacques. 1990. Signature Event Context. *The Rhetorical Tradition: From Classical Times to the Present*, ed. Patricia Bizzell and Bruce Herzberg. Boston: Bedford Books: 1168-1184.

———. *Of Grammatology*. 1974. Trans. Spivak. Baltimore: Johns Hopkins UP.

Diehl, C. 1978. *Americans and German Scholarship*, 1779–1870. New Haven: Yale UP.

DiPardo, Anne. 1990. Narrative Knowers, Expository Knowledge. *Written Communication* 7: 59-95.

Dobrin, Sidney I. 1997. *Constructing Knowledges:The Politics of Theory-Building and Pedagogy in Composition*. Albany: SUNY P.

Doheny-Farina, S. 1991. Creating a Text/Creating a Company: the Role of a Text in the Rise and Decline of a New Organization. In *Textual Dynamics of the Profession*, ed. C. Bazerman and J. Paradis. Madison: U of Wisconsin P. 306-335.

Du Bois, W.E.B. 1982 *The Souls of Black Folk*. NY: Penguin.

Durst, Russel. 1990. The Mongoose and the Rat in Composition Research: Insights from the *RTE* Annotated Bibliography. *CCC* 41: 393–408.

———, Marjorie Roemer, and Lucille Schultz. 1994. Portfolio Negotiation: Acts in Speech. *New Directions in Portfolio Assessment*. ed. Laurel Black, Donald A. Daiker, Jeffrey Sommers, and Gail Stygall. Portsmouth, NH: Boynton/Cook Heinemann.

Eckert, Penelope. 1989. *Jocks and Burnouts: Social Categories and Identity in the High School*. NY: Teachers College Press.

Ede, Lisa and Andrea Lunsford. 1990. *Singular Texts/Plural Authors: Perspectives on Collaborative Writing*. Carbondale: So. IL UP.

Eichhorn, Jill, Sara Farris, Karen Hayes, Adriana Hernandez, Susan C. Jarratt, Karen Powers-Stubbs, and Marian M. Sciachitano. 1992. A Symposium on Feminist Experiences in the Composition Classroom. *CCC* 43: 297-322.

Elbow, Peter. 1995. Being a Writer vs. Being an Academic: A Conflict in Goals. *CCC* 46: 72-83.

————. *What Is English?*. 1990. NY and Urbana: MLA and NCTE.

Emerson, Ralph Waldo. Nature.1950. *Selected Writings of Emerson*, ed. Brooks Atkinson. NY: Modern Library.

Englehard, George Jr., Belita Gordon and Stephen Gabrielson. 1992. The Influences of Mode of Discourse, Experiential Demand, and Gender on the Quality of Student Writing. *Research in the Teaching of English* 26: 315-336.

Erikson, E. 1951. *Childhood and Society*. NY: Norton.

Faigley, Lester. 1992. *Fragments of Rationality: Postmodernity and the Subject of Composition*. Pittsburgh: U of Pittsburgh P.

———— Roger Cherry, David A. Jolliffe, and Anna M. Skinner. 1985. *Assessing Writers' Knowledge and Processes of Composing*. Norwood: Ablex.

Farr, Marcia. 1994. En Los Dos Idiomas: Literacy Practices among Chicano Mexicanos. In *Literacy Across Communities*, ed. B. Moss. Cresskill, NJ: Hampton Press. 9-48.

Ferguson, P., D. Ferguson, and S. Taylor, ed. 1992. *Interpreting Disability: a Qualitative Reader*. NY: Teacher's College Press.

Fine, Michelle. 1992. *Disruptive Voices: The Possibilities of Feminist Research*. Ann Arbor: U of Michigan P.

———— and A. Asch, ed. 1988. *Women with Disabilities: Essays in Psychology, Culture, and Politics*. Philadelphia: Temple UP.

Fischer, M.M.J. 1994. Autobiographical Voices (1, 2, 3) and Mosaic Memory: Experimental Sondages in the (Post)modern World. In *Autobiography & Postmodernism*, ed. K. Ashley, L. Gilmore, and G. Peters. Amherst: U of Massachusetts P. 79-129.

Fish, Stanley. 1989. *Doing What Comes Naturally: Change, Rhetoric, and the Practice of Theory in Literary and Legal Studies*. Durham, NC: Duke UP.

————. "Anti- Foundationalism: Theory-Hope and the Teaching of Writing". Keynote, Penn State Conference on Rhetoric and Composition. 1987.

————. 1980. *Is There a Text in This Class: The Authority of Interpretive Communities*. Cambridge, MA: Harvard UP.

Fiske, John. 1992. Cultural Studies and the Culture of Everyday Life. In *Cultural Studies*, ed. Lawrence Grossberg, Cary Nelson, and Paula A. Treichler. NY: Routledge. 154-173.

Flower, Linda. 1979. Writer-based prose: A cognitive basis for problems in writing. *College English* 41: 19-37.

Flynn, Elizabeth. 1990. Composing "Composing as a Woman": A Perspective on Research. *CCC* 41: 83-89.

————. 1988. Composing as a Woman. *CCC* 39: 423-435.

Foehr, Regina, and Susan Schiller, ed. 1997. *Spiritual Empowerment in Pedagogy*. Portsmouth, NH: Boynton/Cook Heinemann.

Fontaine, Sheryl and Susan Hunter. 1992. Rendering the "Text" of Composition. *JAC* 12: 395-406.

Forman, Janis, ed. *New Visions of Collaborative Writing*. Portsmouth NH: Boynton/Cook Heinemann.

Foucault, Michel. 1977. What Is an Author? In *Language, Countermemory, Practice: Selected Essays and Interviews*, ed. Donald F. Bouchard. Trans. Donald F. Bouchard and Sherry Simon. Ithaca: Cornell UP.

Fox, Thomas. 1990. *The Social Uses of Writing: Politics and Pedagogy*. Norwood NJ: Ablex.

Frederiksen, John and Allan Collins. 1989. A Systems Approach to Educational Testing. *Educational Researcher*. 18: 27-32.

Freedman, Sara W. 1984. The Registers of Student and Professional Expository Writing: Influences on Teachers' Responses. *New Directions in Composition Research*, ed. Richard Beach and Lillian Bridwell. NY: Guilford Books.

Freire, Paulo. 1993. *Pedagogy of the Oppressed*. 20th Anniversary ed. Trans. Myra Bergman Ramos. NY: Continuum.

———. 1987. Conversations with People of Color Caucus. *Dialogue with Paulo Freire Conference*. Irvine, CA: U of California-Irvine.

———. 1985. *Education, Liberation, and the Church. In The Politics of Education: Culture, Power, and Liberation*. Trans. Donaldo Macedo. NY: Bergin & Garvey.

———. 1974. Conscientization. *Cross Currents* 21:23-31.

Frey, Olivia. 1990. Beyond Literary Darwinism: Women's Voices and Critical Discourse. *College English* 52: 507-526.

Frost, Robert. 1963. Home Burial. In *Selected Poems of Robert Frost*. NY: Rinehart. 41–45.

———. 1970 There Are Roughly Zones. In *Chief Modern Poets of Britain and America*. 5th edition., ed. G. Sanders, J. Nelson, M. Rosenthal. Toronto: Macmillan . II:92-93.

Fu, Danling. 1995. "My Trouble is My English": Asian Students and the American Dream. Portsmouth, NH: Boynton/Cook Heinemann.

Fulkerson, Richard. 1990. Composition Theory in the Eighties: Axiological Consensus and Paradigmatic Diversity. *CCC* 41: 409-429.

Fulwiler, Toby. 1988. Propositions of a Personal Nature. Waldrep. Vol. II:85-88.

Galeano, E. 1988. In Defense of the Word. Simonson and Walker. 113-125.

Gamble, Henry Y. 1995. *Books and Readers in the Early Church: A History of Early Christian Texts*. New Haven: Yale UP.

Geertz, Clifford. 1988. *Works and Lives: The Anthropologist as Author*. Stanford: Stanford UP.

———. 1983. *Local Knowledge: Further Essays in Interpretive Anthropology*. NY: Basic Books.

———. 1973. *The Interpretation of Cultures*. NY: Basic Books.

Geisler, C. 1994. *Academic Literacy and the Nature of Expertise: Reading, Writing, and Knowing in Academic Philosophy*. Hillsdale, NJ: Erlbaum.

Gere, Anne Ruggles. 1994. Kitchen Tables and Rented Rooms: The Extracurriculum of Composition. *CCC* 45: 75-92.

———. 1993. *Into the Field: Sites of Composition Studies*. NY: MLA.

———. 1987. *Writing Groups: History, Theory, and Implications*. Carbondale: So. IL UP.

———. 1980. Written Composition: Toward a Theory of Evaluation. *College English* 42:44-58.

Gibson, Margaret and John Ogbu, ed. 1991. Minority Status and Schooling: A Comparative Study of Immigrant and Involuntary Minorities. *Garland Reference Library of Social Science*. NY: Garland.

Giroux, H. A., and Freire, P. 1987. Introduction.*Critical Pedagogy and Cultural Power*, D. W. Livingstone & Contributors. South Hadley, MA: Bergin & Garvey.

Glaser, Barney G. and Anselm L. Strauss. 1967. *The Discovery of Grounded Theory: Strategies for Qualitative Research*. Chicago: Aldine.

Goffman, E. 1963. *Stigma: Notes on the Management of Spoiled Identity*. Englewood Cliffs, NJ: Prentice Hall.

Goggin, Maureen Daly. 1997. Composing a Discipline: The Role of Scholarly Journals in the Disciplinary Emergence of Rhetoric and Composition Since 1950. *Rhetoric Review* 15: 322-349.

————. 1995. The Disciplinary Instability of Composition. In *Reconceiving Writing: Rethinking Writing Instruction*, ed. Joseph Petraglia. Mahwah, NJ: Erlbaum.

Goldman, A.E. 1996. *Take My Word: Autobiographical Innovations of Ethnic American Working Women*. Berkeley: U of CA P.

Gómez-Peña, G. 1988. Documented/Undocumented. Simonson and Walker. 127-134.

González, María Christina. 1995. In Search of the Voice I Always Had. In *The Leaning Ivory Tower: Latino Proffessors in American Universities*, ed. Raymond V. Padilla and Rudolfo Chavez Chavez. Albany: SUNY P. 77–90.

Goodson, I. F., ed. 1992. *Studying Teachers' Lives*. NY: Teachers College P.

Gould, Janice. 1996. Literacy as a Tool of Displacement: Evidence from the 19th Century Indian Boarding Schools. Paper presented at the CCCC annual convention. Phoenix, Arizona.

Graham, R. J. 1991. *Reading and Writing the Self: Autobiography in Education and the Curriculum*. NY: Teachers College P.

Gramsci, Antonio. 1985. *Selections from Cultural Writings*. D. Frogacs & G. Nowell-Smith, ed. W. Boelhower, trans. Cambridge: Harvard UP.

————. 1971. *Selections from the Prison Notebooks*, ed. and trans. by Quinton Hoare and Geoffrey Nowell Smith. New York: International.

Greene, M. 1991. Foreword. *Stories Li:es Tell: Narrative and Dialogue in Education*, ed. C. Witherell and N. Noddings. NY: Teachers College P.

Gregory, Marshall. 1998. Marshall Gregory Responds. *College English* 60: 89-93.

————. 1997. The Many-Headed Hydra of Theory vs. the Unifying Mission of Teaching. *College English* 59: 41-58.

Grigar, Dene. 1997. Defensio Tabularum: A Defense of Archiving Writing Created for Webbed Environments. Kairos: http://english.ttu.edu/kairos/2.1

Grimm, Nancy, et.al. 1998. "Rethinking Agency." In *Weaving Knowledge Together: Writing Centers and Collaboration*, ed. Carol Peterson Haviland, Maria Notarangelo, Lene Whitley-Putz, and Thia Wolf. National Writing Centers Press.

Gross, Patricia A. 1992. Shared Meaning: Whole Language Reader Response at the Secondary Level. Paper presented at the annual meeting of the National Reading Conference. ED359491.

Guice, Sherry. 1992. Readers, Texts, And Contexts in a Sixth-Grade Community of Readers. Paper presented at the Annual Meeting of the National Reading Conference. ED369071.

Guilford, J. P. 1946. New Standards for Test Validation. *Educational and Psychological Measurement* 6: 427-439.

Gurak, Laura. 1996. Toward Broadening Our Research Agenda in Cyberspace. *Computer Mediated Communications Magazine*: February.

————. 1997. *Persuasion and Privacy in Cyberspace: The Online Protests Over Lotus Marketplace and the Clipper Chip*. New Haven: Yale University P.

Gutierrez, Gustavo. 1973. *A Theology of Liberation*. Trans. Sister Caridad Inda and John Eagleson. Maryknoll, NY: Orbis Press.

Hairston, Maxine. 1982. The Winds of Change: Thomas Kuhn and the Revolution in the Teaching of Writing. *CCC* 33: 76–88.

Halliday, Michael A. K. 1978. *Language as Social Semiotic*. Baltimore: Edward Arnold.

Harding Sandra. 1989. Is There a Feminist Methodology? *Feminism and Science*, ed. N. Tuana. Bloomington: Indiana UP.

————. 1987. Is There a Feminist Method? *Feminism and Methodology*, ed. Sandra Harding. Bloomington: Indiana UP.

Harkin, Patricia and John Schilb, ed. 1991. *Contending With Words: Composition and Rhetoric in a Postmodern Age*. NY: MLA.

Harris, Joseph. 1997. *A Teaching Subject: Composition Since 1996*.Upper Saddle River, NJ: Prentice-Hall.

———. 1997. Person, Position, Style. *Publishing in Rhetoric and Composition*, ed. G.A. Olson and T.W. Taylor. Albany, NY: SUNY P.

———. 1995. Renegotiating the Contact Zone. *Journal of Basic Writing* 14:27-42.

———. 1994a From the Editor. Writing from the Moon.*CCC* 45: 161–163.

———. 1994b. The Rhetoric of Theory. In *Writing Theory and Critical Theory*, ed. John Clifford and John Schilb. New York: MLA.

———. 1992. The Other Reader. *JAC* 12: 27-37.

———. 1991. After Dartmouth: Growth and Conflict in English. *College English* 53: 631-646.

Hashimoto, I. 1983. Toward a Taxonomy of Scholarly Publication. *College English* 45: 500–505.

Haswell, Janis and Richard H. Haswell. 1995. Gendership and the Miswriting of Students. *CCC* 46: 223-254.

Haswell, Richard. 1998. Multiple Inquiry in the Validation of Writing Tests. *Assessing Writing* 5: 89-109.

Haswell, Richard and Susan Wyche-Smith. 1994. A Two-Tiered Rating Procedure for Placement Essays. *Assessment in Practice*, ed. Trudy Banta. San Francisco: Jossey Bass.

Hawisher, Gail and Michael A. Pemberton. 1991. The Case for Teacher as Researcher in Computers and Composition Studies. *The Writing Instructor* 10: 77–86.

Hawkins, Hugh. 1979. University Identity: The Teaching and Research Functions. *The Organization of Knowledge in Modern America, 1860–1920*, ed. A. Oleson and John Voss. Baltimore: Johns Hopkins UP. 285–312.

Hawkins, Thom. 1980. Intimacy and Audience: the Relationship Between Revision and the Social Dimension of Peer Tutoring. *College English* 42: 64-68.

Heath, Shirley Brice, and Milbrey W. McLaughlin. 1993. *Identity and Inner-City Youth: Beyond Ethnicity and Gender*. NY: Teachers College Press.

Heilker, Paul and Peter Vandenberg. 1996. *Keywords in Composition Studies*. Portsmouth, NH: Boynton/Cook Heinemann.

Herndl, C. 1993. Teaching Discourse and Reproducing Culture: a Critique of Research and Pedagogy in Professional and Non-academic Writing. *CCC* 44: 349-63.

Herron, Jerry. 1992. Writing for My Father. *College English* 54: 928-937.

———. 1988. Universities and the Myth of Cultural Decline. Detroit: Wayne State UP.

Hillyer, B. 1995. *Feminism and Disability*. Norman: U of OK P.

Holloway, K. F. C. 1993. Cultural Politics in the Academic Community: Masking the Color Line. *College English* 55: 610-617.

hooks, bell. 1994. *Outlaw Culture: Resisting Representations*. NY: Routledge.

———. 1992a. *Black Looks: Race and Representation*. Boston: South End Press.

———. 1992b. *Out of the Academy and Into the Streets*. Ms. III:1: 80-82.

———. 1989. *Talking Back: Thinking Feminist, Thinking Black*. Boston: South End Press.

Horner, Bruce. 1997. Students, Authorship, and the Work of Composition. *College English* 59: 505-529.

———. 1996. Discoursing Basic Writing. *CCC* 47: 199-222.

Horner, Winifred Bryan. Forthcoming. The New Abolitionism Comes to Plagiarism. *Perspectives on Plagiarism and Intellectual Property in a Postmodern World*, ed. Alice Roy and Lise Buranen. Albany NY: SUNY P.

———, ed. 1983. *Composition and Literature: Bridging the Gap*. Chicago: U of Chicago P.

Howard, Rebecca Moore. 1995. Plagiarisms, Authorships, and the Academic Death Penalty. *College English* 57: 708-36.

———. 1993. A Plagiarism Pentimento. *Journal of Teaching Writing* 11: 233-246.

Huberman, A. Michael and Matthew B. Miles. 1994. Data Management and Analysis Methods. Denzin and Lincoln. 428-444.

Hull, Glynda, and Mike Rose. 1989. Rethinking Remediation: Toward a Social-Cognitive Understanding of Problematic Reading and Writing. *Written Communication* 6: 139-154.

Hult, Christine A. 1994. Over the Edge: When Reviewers Collide. *Writing on the Edge* 5: 24-28.

Hunter, Susan and Sheryl Fontaine, ed. 1993. *Writing Ourselves into the Story: Unheard Voices from Composition Studies*. Carbondale: So. IL UP.

Huot, Brian. 1996. Toward a New Theory for Writing Assessment. *CCC* 47: 549-566.

———. 1993. The Influence of Holistic Scoring Procedures on Reading and Rating Student Essays. Williamson and Huot.

Ingstad, B. and S. Whyte. 1995. *Disability and Culture*. Berkeley: U of California P.

Iser, Wolfgang. 1978. *The Act of Reading*. Baltimore: John Hopkins UP.

Jarratt, Susan C. Feminism and Composition Studies: The Case for Conflict. Harkin and Schilb. 105-123.

Jaszi, Peter, and Martha Woodmansee. 1996. The Ethical Reaches of Authorship. *South Atlantic Quarterly* 95: 947-977.

Kairos: A Journal for Teachers of Writing in Webbed Environments. http://english. ttu.edu./kairos

Kennedy, Mary Lynch, William J. Kennedy, and Hadley M. Smith. 1996. *Writing in the Disciplines: A Reader for Writers*. 3rd ed. Upper Saddle River, NJ: Prentice Hall.

Kent, Thomas. 1993. Language Philosophy, Writing, and Reading: A Conversation With Donald Davidson. *JAC*. 13: 1-20.

Kerr, T. 1996. Research. Heilker and Vandenberg. 201–205.

Kinneavy, James. 1971. *A Theory of Discourse*. NY: Norton.

KIRIS Writing Portfolio Assessment Guide. 1994. Frankfort, KY: Kentucky State Department of Education.

Kirsch, Gesa E. 1997. Multi-Vocal Texts and Interpretive Responsibility. *College English* 59: 191-202.

——— and Joy S. Ritchie. 1995. Beyond the Personal: Theorizing a Politics of Location in Composition Research. *CCC* 46: 7-29.

——— and Patricia A. Sullivan. 1992. *Methods and Methodology in Composition Research*. Carbondale: So. IL UP.

Kitzhaber, Albert. 1953. *Rhetoric in American Colleges, 1850–1900*. Dissertation. U of WA.

Klein, J. 1990. Across the Boundaries. *Social Epistemology* 4: 267-80.

Knoblauch, C. H., and Brannon, Lil. 1984. *Rhetorical Traditions and the Teaching of Writing*. Upper Montclair, NJ: Boynton/Cook Heinemann.

Kristeva, Julia. 1985. Stabat Mater. *Poetics Today* 6: 135–152.

Laing, R. D. 1968. *The Politics of Experience*. NY: Ballantine.

Lakoff, G., and Johnson, M. 1980. *Metaphors We Live by*. Chicago: U of Chicago P.

Lather, Patti. 1991. *Getting Smart: Feminist Research and Pedagogy with/in the Postmodern*. NY: Routledge.

———. 1986. Research as Praxis. *Harvard Educational Review* 56: 257-277.

Lauer, Janice M. 1993. A Response to 'The History of Composition: Reclaiming Our Lost Generations. *JAC* 13: 252-254.

———. 1992. Rhetoric and Composition Studies: A Multimodal Discipline. In *Defining the New Rhetorics*, ed. Theresa Enos and Stuart Brown. Newbury Park, CA: Sage Publications. 44-54.

———. 1984. Composition Studies: Dappled Discipline. *Rhetoric Review* 3: 20–29.

———. 1972. Response to Ann Berthoff, "The Problem of Problem Solving" *CCC* 23: 208-210.

———. 1970. Heuristics and Composition. *CCC* 21:396-404.

——— and J.W. Asher. 1988. *Composition Research: Empirical Designs*. NY: Oxford UP.

Lee, Frances. 1995. The Power of Language. *Bay Area Writing Project Newsletter*. Winter: 6.

Leggo, Carl. 1991. Questions I Need to Ask Before I Advise My Students To Write in Their Own Voices. *Rhetoric Review* 10: 143-152.

LeJeune, P. 1989. *On Autobiography*. Trans. K. Leary. Minneapolis: U of MN P.

Lentricchia, Frank. 1996. Last Will and Testament of an Ex-Literary Critic. *Lingua Franca* September/October: 59-67.

Leonard, Elizabeth Anne. 1997. Assignment #9: A Text which Engages the Socially Constructed Identity of Its Writer. *CCC* 48: 215-230.

Levinson, D. J. et al. 1996. *The Seasons of a Woman's Life*. NY: Knopf.

———. et al. 1978. *The Seasons of a Man's Life*. NY: Knopf.

Lévi-Strauss, Claude. 1966. *The Savage Mind*. Trans. George Weidenfeld and Nicolson, Chicago: U of Chicago P.

Lim, Geok-Lin, Shirley. 1990. Semiotics, Experience and the Material Self: An Inquiry into the Subject of the Contemporary Asian Woman Writer. *World Englishes* 9: 175-191.

Lincoln, Yvonna and E.G. Guba. 1985. *Naturalistic Inquiry*. Beverly Hills: Sage.

Lindemann, Erika. 1995. Three Views of English 101. *College English* 57: 287-302.

———. 1993. Freshman Composition: No Place for Literature. *College English* 55: 311-316.

Lindquist, Julie. 1995. Bullshit on "What If": An Ethnographic Rhetoric of Political Argument in a Working Class Bar. Dissertation. U of IL at Chicago.

Ling, A. 1987. I'm Here: an Asian Woman's Response. *New Literary History* 19: 151-160.

Lionnet, F. 1989. *Autobiographical Voices: Race, Gender, Self-Portraiture*. Ithaca: Cornell UP.

Little, Sherry Burgus, and Shirley K. Rose. 1994. A Home of Our Own: Establishing a Department of Rhetoric and Writing Studies at San Diego State University. *WPA* 18: 16-28.

Lloyd-Jones, Richard. 1977. Primary Trait Scoring. In *Evaluating Writing: Describing, Measuring, Judging*. ed. Charles R. Cooper and Lee Odell. Urbana: NCTE.

Lord, Frederick M. and Melvyn R. Novick. 1968. *Statistical Theories of Mental Test Scores*. Reading, MA: Addison-Wesley.

Lorde, Audre. 1984. *Sister Outsider: Essays and Speeches*. CA: Closing Press.

Lowe, Teresa J. and Brian Huot. 1997. Using KIRIS Portfolios to Place Students in First-Year Composition at the University of Louisville. *Kentucky English Bulletin* 46: 46-64.

Lu, Min-Zhan. 1992. Conflict and Struggle: The Enemies or Preconditions of Basic Writing. *College English* 54: 887-913.

Lunsford, Andrea. 1992. *Rhetoric and Composition. An Introduction to Scholarship in Modern Languages and Literatures*, 2nd Ed. ed. J. Gibaldi. NY: MLA.

———, H. Moglen, and J. Slevin, ed. 1990. *The Right to Literacy*. NY: MLA.

MacDonald, Susan Peck . 1994. *Professional Academic Writing in the Humanities and Social Sciences* Carbondale: So. IL UP.

Mack, Nancy. 1996. From Practice to Praxis: How Teaching Develops the Field. Watson Conference, U of Louisville.

Magnotto, Joyce Neff. 1996. Writing from a Distance: Virtual and Material Reality in a Televised Composition Course. Report to the Office of Research, Economic Development, and Graduate Studies, Old Dominion University.

———. 1995. Literacy Among Undergraduates: How We Represent Students as Writers and What It Means When We Don't. In *Rhetoric, Cultural Studies, and Literacy*, ed. J. F. Reynolds. Hillsdale, NJ: Erlbaum.

———. 1991. The Construction of College Writing in a Cross-Disciplinary Community College Writing Center: An Analysis of Student, Tutor, and Faculty Representations. Dissertation. U of PA.

Mahala, Daniel and Jody Swilky. 1996. Telling Stories, Speaking Personally: Reconsidering the Place of Lived Experience in Composition. *JAC* 16: 363-388.

Maher, Jane. 1997. *Mina P. Shughnessy: Her Life and Work.* Urbana: NCTE.

Mailloux, Steven. 1989. *Rhetorical Power.* Ithaca, NY: Cornell UP.

Marcus, George E. and Michael Fischer. 1986. *Anthropology as Cultural Critique: An Experimental Moment in the Human Sciences.* Chicago: U of Chicago P.

Markley, Robert. 1988. Discussion. Conference Transcript. *The Eighteenth Century* 29: 81–92.

Marrou, H. I. 1956. *A History of Education in Antiquity.* Madison: U of WI P.

Marx, Karl. 1990. *Capital: A Critique of Political Economy.* NY: Penguin.

Mascia-Lees, Frances E, Patricia Sharpe, and Colleen Ballerino Cohen. 1989. The Postmodernist Turn in Anthropology: Cautions from a Feminist Perspective. *Signs: Journal of Women in Culture and Society* 15:305-437.

Maslow, A. H. 1971. *The Farther Reaches of Human Nature.* NY: Penguin.

Maso, Carole. 1996. Rupture, Verge, and Precipe/Precipe, Verge, and Hurt Not. In *Tolstoy's Dictaphone: Technology and the Muse*, ed. Sven Birkets. Saint Paul: Graywolf Press.

Mayberry, Bob. 1995. Opening Doors. *Composition Studies/Freshman English News* 23: 678-693.

Mayher, John. 1990. *Uncommon Sense.* Portsmouth, NH: Boynton/Cook Heinemann.

McCarthy, Thomas. 1992. Doing the Right Thing in Cross-cultural Representations. *Ethics* 102:635-649.

McCarthy, Lucille Parkinson, and Stephen M. Fishman. 1996. A Text for Too Many Voices: Representing Diversity in Reports of Naturalistic Research. Mortensen and Kirsch. A

McCracken, Ellen. 1991. Metaplagiarism and the Critic's Role as Detective: Ricardo Piglia's Reinvention of Roberto Arlt. *PMLA* 106: 1071-1082.

McCracken, H. Thomas. 1995. *Conversation.* Youngstown, OH: Youngstown State University.

McLeod, Susan. 1997. *Notes on the Heart: Affective Issues in the Writing Classroom.* Carbondale: So. IL UP.

McQuade, Donald. 1992. Living In—and On—the Margins. *CCC* 43: 11-22.

Merrill, Robert, et al. 1992. Symposium on the 1991 Progress Report from the CCCC Committee on Professional Standards. *CCC* 43: 154-175.

Messick, Samuel. 1989. Validity. *Educational Measurement* Third Edition. ed. Robert R. Linn. NY: American Council on Education. 13–103.

Miles, Matthew B. and A. Michael Huberman. 1994. *Qualitative Data Analysis: An Expanded Sourcebook*. 2nd ed. London: Sage.

Miller, Carolyn. Kairos in the Rhetoric of Science. In A *Rhetoric of Doing*, ed. Stephen P. Witte, N. Nakadate, and Roger Cherry. Carbondale: So. IL UP. 309-327.

Miller, Richard E. 1996. The Nervous System. *College English* 58: 265–86.

———. 1994. Fault Lines in the Contact Zone. *College English* 56: 389-408.

Miller, Susan. 1991a. The Feminization of Composition. In *The Politics of Writing Instruction: Postsecondary*, ed. R. Bullock and J. Trimbur. Portsmouth, NH: Boynton/Cook Heinemann. 39–54.

———. 1991b. *Textual Carnivals: The Politics of Composition*. Carbondale: So. IL UP.

Minh-ha, Trinh T. 1989. *Woman, Native, Other: Writing Postcoloniality and Feminism*. Bloomington: Indiana UP.

Minock, Mary. 1995. Toward a Postmodern Pedagogy of Imitation. *JAC* 15: 489-510.

Mishler, E. G. 1986. *Research Interviewing: Narrative and Context*. Cambridge, MA: Harvard UP.

Moffett, James. 1968. *Teaching the Universe of Discourse*. Boston: Houghton Mifflin.

Mohanty, Chandra. 1991. Cartographies of Struggle: Third World Women and the Politics of Feminism in *Third World Women and the Politics of Feminism*. Chandra Mohanty, Ann Russo, and Lourdes Torres, ed. Bloomington: Indiana UP. 1–47.

———, Ann Russo, and Lourdes Torres. 1991. *Third World Women and the Politics of Feminism*. Bloomington: Indiana UP.

Moneyhun, Clyde. 1994. All Dressed Up and OTM: One ABD's View of the Profession. *Rhetoric Review* 12: 406–412.

Moody, Rick. 1995. Primary Sources. *The New Yorker* June 5: 80-82.

Mora, P. 1986. *Borders*. Houston: Arte Publico Press.

Morris, J. 1991. *Pride Against Prejudice: Transforming Attitudes to Disability*. Philadelphia: New Society Press.

Morrison, Toni. 1992. *Playing in the Dark: Whiteness and the Literary Imagination*. NY: Vintage Books.

Mortensen, Peter and Gesa E. Kirsch. 1996. *Ethics and Representation in Qualitative Studies of Literacy*. Urbana: NCTE.

Moss, Beverly., ed. 1994. *Literacy Across Communities*. Cresskill, NJ: Hampton Press.

———. 1992. Ethnography and Composition: Study Language at Home. Kirsch and Sullivan. 153-171.

Moss, Pamela A. 1998. Testing the Test of Test: A Response to Multiple Inquiry in the Validation of Writing Tests. *Assessing Writing* 5: 111-122.

Munby, H. 1986. Metaphor in the Thinking of Teachers: an Exploratory Study. *Journal of Curriculum Studies*, 18: 197-209.

Murphy, Michael. 1995. *Camp Happens: Modernity, Postmodernity, and Recycled Culture*. Dissertation. Syracuse University.

Murphy, R. J., Jr. 1990. On Stories and Scholarship. In *Rhetoric and Composition*, R. Graves ed. Portsmouth, NH: Heinemann.

Murphy, Robert. 1987. *The Body Silent*. NY: Henry Holt.

Murray, Donald.. 1994a. A Preface on Rejection. *Writing on the Edge* 5: 29-30.

————. 1994b. Pushing the Edge. *Writing on the Edge* 5: 31-41.

Myers, Greg. 1986. Reality, Consensus, and Reform in the Rhetoric of Composition Teaching. *College English* 48: 154-174.

————. 1985. The Social Construction of Two Biologists' Proposals. *Written Communication* 2 : 219-245.

Nagler, M., ed. 1993. *Perspectives on Disability*. 2nd ed. Palo Alto, CA: Health Markets Research.

Nericcio, W. A. 1988. Autobiographies at La Frontera: the Quest for Mexican-American Narrative. *The Americas Review* 16: 165-187.

Newkirk, Thomas. 1996. Seduction and Betrayal in Qualitative Research. Mortensen and Kirsch.

————. 1991. The Politics of Composition Research: The Conspiracy Against Experience. *In The Politics of Writing Instruction: Postsecondary*, ed. R. Bullock and J. Trimbur. Portsmouth, NH: Boynton/Cook Heinemann. 119–135.

North, Stephen M. 1996. The Death of Paradigm Hope, the End of Paradigm Guilt, and the Future of (Research in) Composition. Bloom, Daiker, and White, 194–207.

————. 1987. *The Making of Knowledge in Composition: Portrait of an Emerging Field*. Portsmouth, NH: Boynton/Cook Heinemann.

————. 1984. The Idea of a Writing Center. *College English* 46: 433-36.

Okawa, G. Y. 1995. Expanding Perspectives of Teacher Knowledge: a Descriptive Study of Autobiographical Narratives of Writing Teachers of Color. Dissertation. IU of PA.

————. 1993. Redefining Authority: Multicultural Students and Tutors at the Educational Opportunity Program Writing Center at the U of Washington. In *Writing Centers in Context: Twelve Case Studies*, ed. J. Harris & J. Kinkead. Urbana: NCTE. 166-191.

————. 1991. Constructing Borders and Identities: Personal Narratives of Writing Teachers of Color. Unpublished Manuscript. Indiana University of Pennsylvania.

———— Fox, T., Chang, L. J. Y., Windsor, S. R., Chavez, Jr., F. B., & Hayes, L. 1991. Multi-cultural Voices: Peer Tutoring and Critical Reflection in the Writing Center. *Writing Center Journal* 12: 11-32.

Oleson, A., and J. Voss, ed. 1979. Introduction. *The Organization of Knowledge in Modern America, 1860–1920*. Baltimore: Johns Hopkins UP. vii–xxiii.

Ollman, Bertell. 1976. *Alienation: Marx's Conception of Man in Capitalist Society*. NY: Cambridge UP.

Olson, D. R. 1977. *The Languages of Instruction: The Literate Bias of Schooling. In Schooling and the Acquisition of Knowledge*, ed. R. C. Anderson, R. J. Spiro, and W. E. Montague, Hillsdale, NJ: Erlbaum. 65–89.

O'Reilley, Mary Rose. 1993. *The Peaceable Classroom*. Portsmouth, NH: Boynton/Cook Heinemann.

Paley, Vivian Gussin. 1979. *White Teacher*. Cambridge: Harvard UP.

Parker, William Riley. 1953. *The MLA, 1883-1953*. Publication of the Modern Language Association 68: 3–39.

Peck, W., L. Flower, and L. Higgins. 1995. *Community Literacy*. CCC 46: 199-222.

Penfield, E. 1992. Freshman English/Advanced Writing: How Do We Distinguish the Two? In *Teaching Advanced Composition: Why and How*. Portsmouth, NH: Boynton/Cook Heinemann.

Pennycook, Alastair. 1994. *The Cultural Politics of English as an International Language*. NY: Longman.

Penticoff, Richard and Linda Brodkey. 1992. Writing About Difference: Hard Cases for Cultural Studies. In *Cultural Studies in the English Classroom*, ed. James A. Berlin and Michael J. Vivion. Portsmouth NH: Boynton/Cook Heinemann. 123-144.

Perelman, Chaim. 1982. *The Realm of Rhetoric*. Notre Dame, IN: Notre Dame UP.

Perl, Sondra and Nancy Wilson. 1986. *Through Teachers' Eyes*. Portsmouth, NH: Boynton/Cook Heinemann.

Petraglia, Joseph, editor. 1995. *Reconceiving Writing: Rethinking Writing Instruction*. Mahwah, NJ: Erlbaum.

Phelps, Louise Wetherbee. 1991. Practical Wisdom and the Geography of Knowledge in Composition. *College English* 53:863-885.

———. 1988. *Composition as a Human Science: Contributions to the Self-Understanding of a Discipline*. NY: Oxford UP.

Pippen, Carol L. 1991. A Social Scene of Writing: The Peer Group Talk of Three Women English-Education Majors Enrolled in an Advanced Composition Class. Dissertation. U of PA.

Porter, James and Patricia Sullivan. 1997. *Opening Spaces: Writing Technologies and Critical Research Practices*. Norwood, NJ: Ablex.

Powell, Malea. 1996. Listening for the Ghosts that Remain: A Mixed Blood Reimagines Rhetoric. Paper presented at the CCCC annual convention. Phoenix, Arizona.

———. n.d. Custer's Very Last Stand: Rhetoric, the Academy, and the Un-Seeing of the American Indian. Unpublished essay.

Pratt, Mary Louise. 1991. Arts of the Contact Zone. *Profession* 1991. NY: MLA. 33-40.

Prince, G. 1982. *Narratology: the Form and Function of Narrative*. NY: Mouton Publishers.

Pula, Judith J. and Brian Huot. 1993. A Model of Background Influences on Holistic Raters. Williamson and Huot.

Qualley, Donna J. 1994. Being Two Places at Once: Feminism and the Development of Both/And Perspectives. *Pedagogy in the Age of Politics: Writing and Reading in the Academy*, ed. Patricia A. Sullivan and Donna J. Qualley. Urbana: NCTE. 25-42.

Radway, Janice A. 1989. The Book of the Month Club and the General Reader: The Uses of Serious Fiction. *Reading in America: Literature and Social History*, ed. Cathy N. Davidson. Baltimore: John Hopkins UP.

Ramage, John D., and John C. Bean. 1997. *The Allyn and Bacon Guide to Writing*. Boston: Allyn and Bacon.

Randall, Marilyn. 1991 Appropriate(d) Discourse: Plagiarism and Decolonization. *New Literary History* 22: 525-541.

Rankin, Elizabeth. 1994a. *Seeing Yourself as a Teacher: Conversations with Five New Teachers in a University Writing Program*. Urbana: NCTE.

———. 1994b. The Second Motion of the Mind: Reviewing, Mentoring, Judgment, and Generosity. *Writing on the Edge* 5: 42-52.

———. 1990. Taking Practitioner Inquiry Seriously: An Argument with Stephen North. *Rhetoric Review* 8: 260–267.

Razack, Sherene H. 1998. *Looking White People in the Eye: Gender, Race, and Culture in Courtrooms and Classrooms*. Toronto: U of Toronto P.

Reigstad, Thomas, and McAndrew, Donald. 1984. *Training Tutors for Writing Conferences*. Urbana: NCTE.

Reinharz, Shulamit. 1992. *Feminist Methods in Social Research*. NY: Oxford UP.

Research Network Forum: Editors' Metaphoric Table/s. http://www.uta.edu/english/ v/rnftable.html

RhetNet: A Cyberjournal for Rhetoric nd Writing. http://www.missouri.edu/~rhetnet/

Rich, Adrienne. 1979. *On Lies, Secrets, and Silence: Selected Prose.* London: W. W. Norton.

Richards, Thomas J. and Lyn Richards. 1994. Using Computers in Qualitative Research. In Denzin and Lincoln. 445-462.

Riessman, C. K. 1993. *Narrative Analysis.* Newbury Park, CA: Sage.

Roen, Duane, Stuart C. Brown, Theresa Enos, ed. 1998. *Living Rhetoric and Composition: Stories of the Discipline.* Hillsdale, NJ: Erlbaum.

Ronell, Avital.1989. *The Telephone Book: Technology, Schizophrenia, Electric Speech.* Lincoln: U of Nebraska P.

Rose, Mike. 1989. *Lives on the Boundary.* NY: Penguin Books.

Rosen, H. 1985. *Stories and Meanings.* London: National Association for the Teaching of English.

Rouse, Joseph. 1987. *Knowledge and Power: Towards a Political Philosophy of Science.* Ithaca: Connell UP.

Royster, Jacqueline Jones. 1996. When the First Voice You Hear is Not Your Own. *CCC* 47: 29-40.

Saldívar, Ramón. 1990. *Chicano Narrative: the Dialects of Difference.* Wisconsin: U of Wisconsin P.

Schaafsma, D. 1993. *Eating on the Street: Teaching Literacy in a Multicultural Society.* Pittsburgh: U of Pittsburgh P.

Scharton, Maurice. 1996. *The Politics of Validity. Assessment of Writing: Politics, Policies, Practices.* ed. Edward M. White, William D. Lutz and Sandra Kamuskiri. NY: MLA.

Schilb, John. Cultural Studies, Postmodernism, and Composition. In Harkin, Patricia and John Schilb. 173-188.

———. 1994. Getting Disciplined. *Rhetoric Review* 12: 398–405.

———. 1992. The Sociological Imagination and the Ethics of Collaboration. Forman.

Schneider, Alison. 1998. Bad Blood in the English Department: the Rift Between Composition and Literature. *The Chronicle of Higher Education.* 13 Feb.

Schön, Donald A. 1995. Causality and Causal Inference in the Study of Organizations. *Rethinking Knowledge: Reflections across the Disciplines,* ed. Robert F. Goodman and Walter R. Fisher. Albany: SUNY P. 69-103.

———. 1987. *Educating the Reflective Practitioner.* San Francisco: Jossey-Bass.

———. 1983. *The Reflective Practitioner: How Professionals Think in Action.* New York: Basic Books.

Selfe, Cynthia. 1996. Theme of the 1997 Convention. In *Call for Program Proposals,* 1997 *CCC* Annual Convention, Urbana: NCTE.

Shamoon, Linda and Beverly Wall. 1995. The Things That Go Without Saying in Composition Studies: A Colloquy including Robert Schwegler, Nedra Reynolds, Linda Shamoon, Marjorie Roemer, Beverly Wall, Linda Petersen, Lynn Z. Bloom, Roxanne Mountford, John Trimbur, Judith Goleman, Robert Connors. *JAC.* 15: 281-320.

Shepard, Lorrie. 1993. *Evaluating Test Validity. Review of Research in Education* 19: 405-450.

Shulman, Lee. 1996. Course Anatomy: The Dissection and Transformation of Knowledge. *American Association of Higher Education Conference on Faculty Roles and Rewards,* Atlanta.

Silverman, David and Brian Torode. 1980. *The Material Word: Some Theories of Language and Its Limits.* London: Routledge & Kegan Paul.

Simonson, R and S. Walker, ed. 1988. *The Graywolf Annual 5: Multicultural Literacy: Opening the American Mind.* Saint Paul: Graywolf Press.

Slevin, James F. 1994. Leading the Way. *Rhetoric Review* 12: 416–421.

Smagorinsky, Peter, and Melissa E. Whiting. 1995. *How English Teachers Get Taught: Methods of Teaching the Methods Class.* Urbana: NCTE.

Smith, Frank. 1982. *Understanding Reading,* Third Edition. NY: Holt, Rhinehart and Winston.

Smith, Louise M. 1982. Teaching Tales and Theories: An Ethnographic Next Step? Paper Presented at the annual meeting of the AERA. ED225227.

Smith, William L. 1993. Assessing the Reliability and Adequacy of Using Holistic Scoring of Essays as a College Composition Placement Program Technique. Williamson and Huot.

Sommers, Nancy. 1993. I Stand Here Writing. *College English* 55: 420-428.

Sosnoski, James. 1994. *Token Professionals and Master Critics: A Critique of Orthodoxy in Literary Studies.* Albany, NY: SUNY P.

Spatt, Brenda. 1996. *Writing from Sources.* 4th ed. NY: St. Martin's.

Spellmeyer, Kurt. 1996. After Theory: From Textuality to Attunement with the World. *College English* 58: 893-913.

Spigelman, Candace. 1996. The Dialectics of Ownership in Peer Writing Groups. Dissertation. Temple U.

Spivak, Gayatri Chakravorty. 1990. The Post-Colonial Critic: *Interviews, Strategies and Dialogues,* ed. Sarah Harasym. NY: Routledge.

Spooner, Michael and Kathleen Yancey. 1996. Postings on a Genre of Email. *CCC* 47: 252-278.

Spradley, J.P. 1979. *The Ethnographic Interview.* Fort Worth: Harcourt Brace Jovanovich College Publishers.

Squires, G., S. Helen, M. Parlett, and T. Becher. 1979. *Interdisciplinarity.* London: Nuffield Foundation.

Stallybrass, Peter, and Allon White. 1986. *The Politics and Poetics of Transgression.* Ithaca, NY: Cornell UP.

Stanley, Liz, ed. 1990. *Feminist Praxis: Research, Theory and Epistemology in Feminist Sociology.* NY: Routledge.

———— and Sue Wise. 1990. *Method, Methodology and Epistemology in Feminist Research Processes.* 20-60.

Steinitz, Victoria Anne and Ellen Rachel Solomon. 1986. *Starting Out: Class and Community in the Lives of Working-Class Youth.* Philadelphia: Temple UP.

Stewart, Susan. 1991. *Crimes of Writing: Problems in the Containment of Representation.* NY: Oxford UP.

Stocking, George W. 1992. In *The Ethnographer's Magic and Other Essays in the History of Anthropology.* Madison: U of WI P.

Strauss, Anselm L. 1987. *Qualitative Analysis for Social Scientists.* NY: Cambridge UP.

Strauss, Anselm and Juliet Corbin. 1994. Grounded Theory Methodology: An Overview. Denzin and Lincoln. 273-285.

————. 1990. *Basics of Qualitative Research: Grounded Theory Procedures and Techniques.* Newbury Park, CA: Sage.

Strenski, Ellen. 1989. Disciplines and Communities, "Armies" and "Monasteries," and the Teaching of Composition. *Rhetoric Review* 8: 137-145.

Stuckey, J. Elspeth. 1991. *The Violence of Literacy*. Portsmouth, NH: Boynton/Cook Heinemann.

Sullivan, Patricia A. 1996. Ethnography and the Problem of the "Other." Mortensen and Kirsch. 97-114.

———. 1992. Feminism and Methodology in Composition Studies. Kirsch and Sullivan . 37-61.

Supiano, K. P., R. J. Ozminkowski, R. Campbell, and C. Lapidos. 1989. Effectiveness of Writing Groups in Nursing Homes. *Journal of Applied Gerontology* 8: 382-400.

Swales, John. 1984. Research into the Structures of Introductions to Journal Articles and Its Application to the Teaching of Academic Writing, in *Common Ground: Shared Interests in English for Special Purposes and Communication Studies*, ed. R. Williams, John Swales, and J. Kirkman. Oxford: Pergamon. 77-86.

Tate, Gary. 1995. Notes on the Dying of A Conversation. *College English* 57: 303-309.

———. 1993. A Place for Literature in Freshman English. *College English* 55: 317-321.

Taylor, Dennie. 1996. *Toxic Literacies: Exposing the Injustice of Bureaucratic Texts*. Portsmouth, NH: Heinemann.

——— and Catherine Dorsey-Gaines. 1988. *Growing Up Literate: Learning From Inner-City Families*. Portsmouth, NH: Heinemann.

Thralls, Charlotte. 1992. Bakhtin, Collaborative Partners, and Published Discourse: A Collaborative View of Composing. Forman 59–71.

Thwing, C. F. 1906. *A History of Higher Education in America*. NY: Appleton.

Tictoc Project. 19 May 1997. http://www.uic.edu/depts/engl/projects/tictoc/main.htm

Tobin, Lad. 1993. *Writing Relationships: What Really Happens in the Composition Class*. Portsmouth, NH: Boynton/Cook Heinemann.

Tompkins, Jane. 1993. Postcards from the Edge. *JAC* 13: 449-457.

———. 1989. Me and My Shadow. In *Gender and Theory: Dialogues on Feminist Criticism*, ed. Linda Kauffman. Oxford: Blackwell.

Torgovnick, Marianna. 1990. Experimental Critical Writing. *Profession 90*:25-27.

Touraine, Alain. 1974. *The Academic System in American Society. The Carnegie Commission on Higher Education* 3. NY: McGraw.

Trachsel, Mary. 1992. *Institutionalizing Literacy: The Historical Role of College Entrance Examinations*. Carbondale: So. IL UP.

Traweek, Sharon. 1988. *Beamtimes and Lifetimes: The World of High Energy Physicists*. Cambridge: Harvard UP.

Trimbur, J. 1994. Taking the Social Turn: Teaching Writing Post-Process. *CCC* 45: 108-118.

———. 1991. Literacy and the Discourse of Crisis. Bullock and Trimbur.

———. 1989. Consensus and Difference in Collaborative Learning *College English* 51: 602-616.

Trimmer, Joseph, ed. 1997. *Narrative as Knowledge: Tales of the Teaching Life*. Portsmouth, NH: Boynton/Cook Heinemann.

Tsing, Anna Lowenhaupt. 1993. *In the Realm of the Diamond Queen: Marginality in an Out-of-the-Way Place*. Princeton: Princeton UP.

Turner, R. S. 1983. The Prussian Universities and the Research Imperative, 1806–1848. Dissertation. Princeton U. 1972. Ann Arbor: UMI.

Vandenberg, Peter. 1993. The Politics of Knowledge Dissemination: Academic Journals in Composition Studies. Dissertation. Texas Christian University. Ann Arbor: UMI.

Varnum, Robin. 1993. Reply. *JAC* 13: 254-256.

———. 1992. The History of Composition: Reclaiming Our Lost Generations. *JAC* 12: 39-56.

Veal, Ramon L. and Sally A. Hudson. 1983. Direct and Indirect Measures for the Large-Scale Evaluation of Writing. *Research in the Teaching of English* 17: 290-296.

Veeser, H.A. ed. 1996. *Confessions of the Critics.* NY: Routledge.

Vergara, Benito M., Jr. 1995. *Displaying Filipinos: Photography and Colonialism in Early 20th Century Philippines.* Quezon City: U of Philippines P.

Veysey, Laurence R. 1979. The Plural Organized Worlds of the Humanities. In *The Organization of Knowledge in Modern America, 1860–1920*, ed. A. Oleson and J. Voss. 51–106. Baltimore: Johns Hopkins UP.

———. 1965. *The Emergence of the American University.* Chicago: U of Chicago P.

Vielstimmig, Myka. 1997. (Michael Spooner and Kathleen Blake Yancey). In a Station of the Metro. http://www.usu.edu/~usupress/myka/myka.htm.

Villanueva, Victor Jr. 1993. *Bootstraps: From an American Academic of Color.* Urbana: NCTE.

Villenas, S. 1996. The Colonizer/Colonized Chicana Ethnographer: Identity, Marginalization, and Co-optation in the Field. *Harvard Educational Review* 66: 711-731.

Waldrep, Tom, ed. 1988. *Writers on Writing.* Vol. II. NY: Random House.

——— ed. 1985. *Writers on Writing.* NY: Random House.

Weathers, Winston. 1980. *An Alternate Style: Options in Composition.* Rochelle Park, NJ: Hayden.

Weaver, Richard. 1964. *Visions of Order.* Baton Rouge: LSUP.

Weinstein-Shr, G. 1994. From Mountaintops to City Streets: Literacy in Philadelphia's Hmong Community. *In Literacy Across Communities*, ed. B. Moss. Cresskill, NJ: Hampton.

Weitz, Andrew L. 1995. Agents of Meaning: A Study of College Writers and Their Representations of Self. Dissertation. NY U.

Welch, Nancy. 1996. Revising a Writer's Identity. *CCC* 47: 40-6l.

Wells, Susan. 1996. What Do We Want from Public Writing? *CCC* 47: 325-341.

Western Governors University. www.wgu.edu/wgu/

White, Edward M. 1995. *Assigning, Responding, Evaluating: A Writing Teacher's Guide.* 3rd ed. NY: St. Martin's.

———. 1995. *Teaching and Assessing Writing* Second Edition. San Francisco: Jossey Bass.

———. 1994. The Worship of Efficiency: Untangling Theoretical and Practical Considerations in Writing Assessment. *Assessing Writing* 1: 147-174.

———. 1994. Writing Assessment Beyond the Classroom: Will Writing Teachers Play a Role. Bloom, Daiker, and White. 101–111.

———. 1993. Holistic Scoring: Past Triumphs and Future Challenges. Williamson and Huot.

White, H. 1981. The Value of Narrativity in the Representation of Reality. In W.J.T. Mitchell, ed., *On Narrative.* Chicago: U of Chicago P.

White, Kimberly. 1992. Themes to Theory: A Data Analysis Process. ED352167.

Williamson, Michael M. and Brian Huot, ed. 1993. *Validating Holistic Scoring for Writing Assessment: Theoretical and Empirical Foundations.* Cresskill, NJ: Hampton.

Wimsatt, William K., Jr., and Monroe C. Beardsley. 1954. *The Verbal Icon: Studies in the Meaning of Poetry.* Lexington: U of Kentucky P.

Windsor, Shana R. 1991. Writing and Tutoring with Bi-cultural Awareness. In *Multicultural Voices: Peer Tutoring and Critical Reflection in the Writing Center. The Writing Center Journal* 12: 18-20.

Wolf, Margery. 1992. *A Thrice Told Tale: Feminism, Postmodernism and Ethnographic Responsibility.* Stanford: Stanford UP.

Wolfe, Edward M. 1997. The Relationship Between Essay Reading Style and Scoring Proficiency in a Psychometric Scoring System. *Assessing Writing* 4: 83-106.

Woodmansee, Martha. 1994. *The Author, Art, and the Market: Rereading the History of Aesthetics.* NY: Columbia UP.

———— and Peter Jaszi. 1995. The Law of Texts: Copyright in the Academy. *College English* 57: 769-787.

Yancey, Kathleen Blake. 1998. *Reflection in the Writing Classroom.* Logan: Utah State UP.

———— and Michael Spooner. 1998. A Single Good Mind: Collaboration, Cooperation, and the Writing Self. *CCC* 49: 45-62.

———— and Irwin Weiser, eds. 1997. *Situating Portfolios: Four Reflections.* Logan, UT: Utah State UP.

Yee, Marian. 1991. Are You the Teacher? In *Composition and Resistance*, ed. C. Mark Hurlbert and Michael Blitz. Portsmouth: Boynton/Cook Heinemann. 25-30.

Young, Richard E. 1978. Paradigms and Problems: Needed Research in Rhetorical Invention. In C. R. Cooper & L. Odell, *Research on Composing: Points of Departure.* Urbana: NCTE. 29-47.

Young, Richard, Alton Becker, and Kenneth Pike. 1970. *Rhetoric: Discovery and Change.* NY: Harcourt, Brace Jovanovich.

Zebroski James. 1996. Zones oi Development: Identity and Social Formation in Composition Studies 1970-1995: The Expressivist Menace—Retrojected Histories, Mythic Origins. Paper presented at the Watson Conference on Reflection, History, and Narrative: The Professionalization of Composition 1963-1983. U of Louisville.

————. 1994. *Thinking Through Theory: Vygotskian Perspectives on the Teaching of Writing.* Portsmouth, NH: Boynton/Cook Heinemann.

CONTRIBUTORS

CHRIS M. ANSON is Morse-Alumni Distinguished Teaching Professor of English at the University of Minnesota. Among his authored, co-authored, and edited books are *Writing in Context* (Holt, Rinehart & Winston, 1988), *Writing and Response: Theory, Practice and Research* (NCTE, 1989), *A Field Guide to Writing* (HarperCollins, 1991), *Writing Across the Curriculum* (Greenwood, 1993), *Scenarios for Teaching Writing* (NCTE, 1993), *Using Journals in the Classroom* (Christopher-Gordon, 1995), and *The Longman Handbook for Writers and Readers* (Longman, 1996). His articles have appeared in numerous journals and edited collections. His research interests include writing to learn, response to writing, and the nature of literacy in and out of schools.

ELLEN BARTON is an Associate Professor in the Department of English at Wayne State University where she teaches in the Linguistics Program and the Composition Program. This paper is drawn from a larger study entitled "Discourses of Disability," an investigation of the interactional and textual practices in the social construction of disability in contemporary America. Papers from the project have been published in *College English*, *TEXT*, and several edited volumes. Other research interests in composition include discourse analysis, empirical research methods, and journal histories.

WENDY BISHOP teaches writing at Florida State University. Her most recent book is *Teaching Lives: Essays and Stories* (Utah State University Press 1997). Forthcoming work includes nonfiction in *When We Say We're Home* (University of Utah Press, 1999), and poetry chapbooks *Touching Liliana* (Jumping Cholla Press 1998); *Mid-passage* (Nightshade Press 1998); and *My 47 Lives* (Palanquin Press 1999). At work on a methods text for ethnographic writing research and a textbook for writing poetry, she lives in Tallahassee with her daughter Morgan, son Tait, dog Lucy, cat Henna, and an as-yet-unnamed volunteer backyard armadillo.

YUET SIM D. CHIANG teaches courses in reading and composition and composition theory and practice at the University of California-Berkeley. Her research interests include teacher research, literacy, social constructions of identities, and the blurring boundaries of L1 and L2 English literacy. Please direct comments to her at chiang@uclink4.berkeley.edu.

ELLEN CUSHMAN, a lecturer in UC Berkeley's College Writing Programs, teaches both basic writing and a service-learning course. Her book, *The Struggle and the Tools: Oral and Literate Strategies in an Inner City Community*, explores the daily political striving and linguistic aptitudes area residents use as they negotiate with various public institutions. Winner of the 1996 Braddock Award and 1996 James Berlin Outstanding Dissertation Award, she also is co-editing the revised edition of *Perspectives on Literacy* with Eugene Kintgen, Barry Kroll, and Mike Rose. Cushman strives to research, teach and serve in ways that make university resources and opportunities available to traditionally under-served populations.

CHRISTINE FARRIS is Associate Professor of English and Director of Composition at Indiana University, where she teaches undergraduate and graduate courses in composition and cultural studies, literacy, and literature. While a poet-in-the-schools with Teachers and Writers Collaborative, her research adventures began serendipitously with an assistantship to Sylvia Scribner investigating the impact of creative writing programs on the literacies of NYC schoolchildren, and have continued with ethnographic forays into both composition and writing across the curriculum classrooms and programs. She is the author of *Subject to Change: New Composition Instructors' Theory and Practice* (Hampton 1996), as well as journal articles and book chapters on writing across the curriculum and the teaching of writing and women's literature.

CHRISTOPHER FERRY works at Clarion University of Pennsylvania. He teaches courses in writing, rhetorical theory, and critical pedagogy; these topics are his primary research interests.

NANCY MALONEY GRIMM, ANNE FRANCES WYSOCKI, and MARILYN M. COOPER are colleagues in the Humanities Department at Michigan Technological University, members of the Little Traverse Home Decorating Club, and members of the Academic Press Subsidiary Collective. Nancy is working on a manuscript on retheorizing writing centers; Anne is working on a manuscript on the visual aspects of texts; Marilyn is working on a manuscript on postmodern ethics in the writing class.

REBECCA MOORE HOWARD is Associate Professor of English and Director of Composition at Texas Christian University. She works in writing across the curriculum and writing program administration, but her scholarship focuses on print culture studies and stylistics. Her articles have appeared in the *Journal of Teaching Writing, WPA: Writing Program Administration, JAC: A Journal of Composition Theory, Computers and Composition,* and *College English*. She is author of the forthcoming *Standing in the Shadow of Giants: Plagiarisms, Authorships, Collaborators* (Ablex) and co-author of *The Bedford Guide to Teaching Writing in the Disciplines*.

BRIAN HUOT is an Associate Professor of English and Director of Composition at the University of Louisville. MICHAEL M. WILLIAMSON is a Professor of English at Indiana University of Pennsylvania. They both teach graduate and undergraduate courses in writing, its teaching and assessment. Their conversations on writing assessment have been evolving for over a decade now. Some of them have appeared in print, including "Rethinking Portfolios for Evaluating Writing: Issues of Assessment and Power" in *Situating Portfolios: Four Perspectives* and the edited collection *Validating Holistic Scoring for Writing Assessment: Theoretical and Empirical Foundations.* Both Michael and Brian are affiliated with *Assessing Writing,* the only journal devoted to writing assessment.

JANICE M. LAUER, Reece McGee Distinguished Professor of English at Purdue University, teaches in the graduate program in Rhetoric and Composition. In 1998, she received the CCCC Exemplar Award. For thirteen years she directed a national summer Rhetoric Seminar, has chaired the College Section of NCTE, and served on the executive committees of CCCC, the MLA Group on the History and Theory of Rhetoric, and the Rhetoric Society of America. Currently she coordinates a consortium of doctoral programs in Rhetoric and Composition. She has co-authored *Four Worlds of Writing and Composition Research: Empirical Designs;* and published on invention, persuasive writing, classical rhetoric, and composition studies as a discipline.

SUSAN PECK MACDONALD is currently Writing Director of the Humanities Core Course at the University of California, Irvine. Her book on writing in the disciplines, *Professional Academic Writing in the Humanities and Social Sciences* (Southern Illinois University Press 1994), received the CCCC Outstanding Book Award in 1996. She is also author of a book on Trollope, a co-authored book on the Victorian novel, and a rhetoric/reader co-authored with Charles Cooper (forthcoming, Bedford/St. Martins). She has previously taught at the University of California, San Diego, the University of Illinois, and Eastern Connecticut State University.

TERESE GUINSATAO MONBERG is a doctoral candidate in the Department of Language, Literature, and Communication at Rensselaer Polytechnic Insititute. In addition to teaching courses in composition and rhetoric, she has also worked extensively with Rensselaer's Writing Program in various administrative capacities. Terese is interested in the cultural and rhetorical connections among literacy, identity, and public participation. Her research focuses on the ways disciplinary and professional conventions highlight some perspectives while marginalizing or hiding others (including methodological issues in qualitative and quantitative research). Terese is currently completing her doctorate long-distance from Louisville, KY.

DEBORAH MUTNICK is Associate Professor of English at Long Island University-Brooklyn. She is the author of *Writing in an Alien World: Basic*

Writing and the Struggle for Equality in Higher Education, 1998 winner of the W. Ross Winterowd Award for the most outstanding book in composition theory. More recently, she has been researching and writing about autobiography, memoir, and the role of personal writing in composition studies. Her contribution to this volume was made possible by the Research Released Time Committee and the Trustees of Long Island University.

JOYCE MAGNOTTO NEFF is an Associate Professor of English and Director of Composition at Old Dominion University where she teaches courses in professional writing, the teaching of writing, and qualitative research methods. She reports on the first phase of her ongoing study of the teaching of writing via distance education in a forthcoming article in *RTE*. She is a writing consultant for the U.S. General Accounting Office and co-author of *Professional Writing in Context: Lessons from Teaching and Consulting in Wo lds of Work*. She has also published extensively on writing across the curriculum and on writing centers.

GAIL Y. OKAWA, Assistant Professor of English at Youngstown State University, is interested in the intersections among multicultural literacy, cultural rhetorics, sociolinguistics, and teaching, and explores the representation and use of autobiographical narrative in such studies. She has written chapters for such collections as *Race, Rhetoric, and Composition, Writing in Multicultural Settings, Ethnicity and the American Short Story*, and *Writing Centers in Context*. She is currently working on a study of mentoring among senior scholars of color and a book tentatively titled *Carving Our Own Faces: The Making of Language and Literacy Teachers of Color*.

SUSAN ROMANO is Assistant Professor of English at the University of Texas at San Antonio, where she currently serves as composition coordinator. She studies theories and histories of rhetoric and writing instruction, and her recent research examines early uses of electronic conferencing in writing courses. She has published articles on writing program administration and on gender, ethnicity, and theories of equity in electronic environments. Currently she is writing about Internet literacies in international environments. In 1993 she won the Ellen Nold award for best article in computers and compositions studies.

SHIRLEY K ROSE is Associate Professor of English at Purdue University, where she has recently completed a term as Director of Composition. She mentors graduate teaching assistants in the Introductory Writing Program and teaches graduate courses in Purdue's graduate program in rhetoric and composition, including a course in writing program administration. In addition to history and theory of writing program administration, her scholarly interests include gender and composition, citation studies, and the history of composition studies since the 1950's. Her publications include essays in *College English, College Composition and Communication*,

Rhetoric Review, and the *Journal of Teaching Writing.* Currently she is co-editing with Irwin Weiser a collection of essays on the writing program administrator as researcher.

RUTH RAY is associate professor of English at Wayne State University in Detroit, where she teaches writing, composition theory, and research methods. She has just finished a three-year fellowship under a grant from the Brookdale Foundation of New York to conduct interdisciplinary research on writing groups in senior centers and nursing homes. Her book on that project, *Writing a Life: Age, Gender, and Diversity in the Life Story,* is forthcoming. Her current research interests include writing and/as healing, service-learning through the computer classroom, and representations of age in writings by and about women.

DAVID SEITZ is an assistant professor of English at Wright State University in Dayton, Ohio where he teaches first year courses in writing, undergraduate courses in rhetorical theory and cultural studies, and graduate courses in composition studies, the politics of literacy, and ethnographic research. He currently plans to research rural and suburban working class students' responses to community service learning.

PETER VANDENBERG is assistant professor of English at DePaul University in Chicago, where he teaches graduate and undergraduate courses in rhetoric and composition. He is the editor of *Composition Studies/Freshman English News,* and co-editor of *Keywords in Composition Studies* (Boynton/Cook).

KATHLEEN BLAKE YANCEY is Associate Professor of English and Director of the UNC Charlotte Writing Project. She teaches undergraduate courses in writing and methods of teaching English and graduate courses in rhetorical theory, in tutoring writing, and in the discipline of rhetoric. Her publications include several edited collections (e.g., *Portfolios in the Writing Classroom,* and *Assessing Writing across the Curriculum*), the recent volume *Reflection in the Writing Classroom,* and numerous articles and book chapters. She also co-founded and edits the journal *Assessing Writing.*

JAMES ZEBROSKI is an associate professor of writing at Syracuse University. He is author of the book *Thinking Through Theory: Vygotskian Perspectives on the Teaching of Writing.* He has published over two dozen articles and essays in anthologies and journals on the social foundations of the composing processes. His current research includes work on the social formation of composition studies, the role of social class in and on composition, and the ways that cultural difference contributes to development.

INDEX